Doing Your
Masters Dissertation

SAGE Essential Study Skills

Essential *Study Skills* is a series of books designed to help students and newly qualified professionals to develop their skills, capabilities, attitudes and qualities so that they can apply them intelligently and in ways which will benefit them on their courses and careers. The series includes accessible and user-friendly guides to improving a range of essential life-long skills and abilities in a variety of areas, including:

♦ **writing essays and reports**

♦ **numeracy**

♦ **presenting information**

♦ **and communicating your ideas.**

Essential Study Skills will be an invaluable aid to all students on a range of higher education courses and to professionals who need to make presentations, write effective reports or search for relevant information.

Doing Your Masters Dissertation

Realizing your potential as a social scientist

Chris Hart

SAGE Publications
London ● Thousand Oaks ● New Delhi

First published 2005

Apart from any fair dealing for the purposes of research or
private study, or criticism or review, as permitted under
the Copyright, Designs and Patents Act, 1988, this publication
may be reproduced, stored or transmitted in any form,
or by any means, only with the prior permission in writing
of the publishers, or in the case of reprographic reproduction,
in accordance with the terms of licences issued by the
Copyright Licensing Agency. Enquiries concerning
reproduction outside those terms should be sent to the
publishers.

SAGE Publications Ltd
1 Oliver's Yard
55 City Road
London EC1Y 1SP

SAGE Publications Inc.
2455 Teller Road
Thousand Oaks, California 91320

SAGE Publications India Pvt Ltd
B-42, Panchsheel Enclave
Post Box 4109
New Delhi 110 017

British Library Cataloguing in Publication data

A catalogue record for this book is available
from the British Library

ISBN 0 7619 4216 5
ISBN 0 7619 4217 3 (pbk)

Library of Congress Control Number: 2004106562

Typeset by C&M Digitals (P) Ltd., Chennai, India
Printed and bound in Great Britain by TJ International Ltd, Padstow, Cornwall

Contents

List of figures and tables

Figures

Tables

Preface

There are many books on research spanning every conceivable methodological approach and tradition with many dedicated to particular disciplines. This is not yet another book on research methods. This book accompanies *Doing a Literature Search* (Hart, 2001) and *Doing a Literature Review* (Hart, 1998), forming three books essential for postgraduate research. It is a book on doing a dissertation at masters level aimed at masters students, though in parts it has much which will be of relevance to doctoral students. As such it tries not to be patronizing or simplistic. The overall aim is to overcome the 'bite size', skim across the top or thin learning approach that is now becoming more common (regrettably) in higher education. Materials and comments are included to engender higher level cognitive qualities of scholarship based on reflection, contemplation and critical thinking. It also aims to provide clarity, some of the essential 'nuts and bolts' and benchmarks in terms of:

♦ giving clear definitions on the nature and scope of the three main types of masters dissertation — the traditional, the work-based and the literature review dissertation;

♦ showing the criteria normally used to assess a masters dissertation, using them in different chapters to show how different sections need to be written in order to meet those criteria;

♦ providing numerous examples and illustrations on how to do the technical as well as intellectual aspects of constructing a dissertation;

♦ demonstrating the techniques that can be used to identify a topic and to formulate a clear research puzzle capable of resulting in a dissertation;

♦ showing how to write clear aims and objectives and formulate hypotheses;

♦ suggesting how to deal with ethical issues and sensitive situations, including working with a supervisor;

♦ providing robust and succinct guidance on how to write the many different sections which make up a dissertation; and

♦ providing robust referrals to other textbooks and Internet sources on data collection techniques, data analysis and writing.

Origins of this book

This book, like the others in the series, has its origins in my own experiences of doing a masters and doctorate and then going on to supervise others doing likewise. Learning how to do my own postgraduate research by trial and error was a good learning experience, especially when combined with the high standards set by my own supervisors. But it would have helped if there had been some sound guidance, in the form of some books and examples, to call on. Over the years I have applied the ideas of learning theory to reflect on my own experience and that of others to develop from them the principles of doing postgraduate research. Working in an institution where postgraduate research was just beginning meant that nothing could be taken for granted, that there were no organizational traditions to be followed and hence few limitations to experimentation. By looking at postgraduate research afresh, what others took for granted was looked at closely and scrutinized. The result has been to produce this book, which focuses in on the common concerns and needs of postgraduate students. Although I have tried to get as much in this book as physically possible, is not a book that will please everyone. It has not been written to do this. The chapters on methodology and examples chosen may cause some criticism, but the point to remember is that not everything in the social sciences can be included in this kind of book; that it is not a book on research methods, but on how to do a good masters dissertation, and in so doing become an informed researcher. For advice and instruction on methods there are many other excellent books and resources and at the end of each chapter suggestions are given for further reading. The purpose of this is to encourage wider reading, especially of primary sources, so that this book also acts as a reference point that the student can use to construct a reliable map for their research journey.

Acknowledgements

All academic enterprises involve many people and this book is no exception. It is the outcome of teaching and supervising many masters dissertations and doctorate theses on a wide range of topics over the past decade and more. It therefore owes much to those students who undertook their masters journey with me, some of whose work is represented in this book. Thanks go to these and my current masters students. It also must go to my doctorate students (Dr Sandra Foulds, Dr Jane Barford, David Kane, Judy Thompson, Mark Lum and Mo Bains) who have been subject to various incarnations of this book often in much longer versions than is printed here. Special thanks go to Denis Reardon for his comradeship over the years and his unstinting perseverance to maintain academic standards in the face of pressures to dumb down. Thanks must also go to the editorial team at Sage who saw the need for this and the other books in this series, in particular Karen Phillips, who has shown extreme levels of patience, and Michael Carmichael. Lynne Slocombe in particular gave constructive feedback on an incomplete and a rough first draft. Finally, sincere gratitude must go to Beverley, who once again put up with the demands of writing and the pressures on precious family time that such an enterprise demands, and although a little naff I dedicate this book to her and BB – a three-year-old who more than once pressed the delete key.

The author gratefully acknowledges permission to use material from: Sharon A. Cox, *Approaches to Assist the Formulation of Project Ideas*, School of Computing, University of Central England in Birmingham, 2001.

Chris Hart
Kingswinford, 2004

Part One

Essential Preparation for Your Dissertation

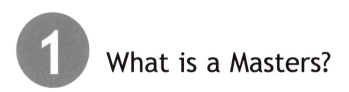

What is a Masters?

CHAPTER CONCEPTS

● THE MASTERS AS A LICENCE TO DO RESEARCH ● WHAT IS A MASTERS DISSERTATION? ● DISSERTATION OR THESIS? ● THE DISSERTATION AS PART OF A MASTERS COURSE ● CRITERIA USED TO ASSESS A DISSERTATION ● MARKING RANGES AND FAILURE ● CRITERIA AND THE EXAMINER ● DIFFERENT TYPES OF DISSERTATION ● HOW LONG DOES IT TAKE TO DO A MASTERS DISSERTATION? ● ARE YOU CAPABLE OF DOING A MASTERS DISSERTATION? ● A MASTERS IS NO MOUNTAIN ● WHERE TO DO YOUR MASTERS ● WHAT TO LOOK FOR ● LEARNING AND TEACHING STYLES ● COURSE SPECIFICATIONS ● SUMMARY OF THIS CHAPTER ● FURTHER READING

Increasingly more and more people are undertaking a masters level degree course (MA, MSc and MBA). The majority of these courses entail a dissertation of between 10,000 and 15,000 words. The dissertation is still seen as an essential element of the masters degree. In this chapter we look at what we mean by a masters dissertation, at the range of skills, capabilities, attitudes and qualities doing a masters will give you, at how a masters is normally assessed and at the different kinds of dissertation you can do. Our basic premise is that doing a masters dissertation is much more than a skills-based exercise. The purpose of this chapter is, therefore, to answer some basic but essential questions:

1   What is a masters dissertation?

2   What kind of document is a masters dissertation?

3   How long should a dissertation be?

4   What kinds of skills and capabilities will you need to do your dissertation?

Doing a masters dissertation should, we argue, allow you to experience a series of higher-level educational, intellectual and ethical issues which help you to grow as a person and a professional. We begin, therefore, by placing the masters in the conventional context of the Bachelors and Doctorate degrees.

The masters as a licence to do research

It was only in the late nineteenth century that the titles we know as the Bachelors, Masters and Doctorate became formal academic qualifications generally recognized around the world. Although they have their origins in the ancient universities when they were Church institutions, the range of modern higher degrees owes little to these origins. Table 1.1 shows the traditional roles of the main university degrees alongside a definition of current roles.

Although the scheme in Table 1.1 has its origins in the time when the Church controlled universities, and degrees, diplomas or licences to teach were awarded by the Church, the only remaining vestiges of this are the academic gowns used to signify different qualifications. In the 1400s the cleric masters wore black robes lined with lamb's wool or rabbit's fur (for warmth) that were trimmed with exotic fur, usually miniver, which also trimmed their hoods. A feature of their robes was colour. Medieval masters enjoyed a wide variety of colours for their robes to such excess that Oxford and Cambridge Universities under Henry VIII began prescribing academic dress as a matter for university control. The drab blackness of robes only became a feature during the seventeenth century when Puritanism dominated the universities and the Church. The range of colours we see today designating masters in different disciplines had its beginnings in the United States. From 1895 American universities and colleges opted to follow a definite system of colours and standards for academic gowns; for economics the colour is copper, for education light blue and for social work it is citron. British and European universities follow no such standards except that each university or awarding body has generally settled on using one colour to signify their institution.

The only other link to the ancient past is the nature of the masters as a licence to practice. In the modern sense this licence is an acknowledgement of research skills and abilities. In modern masters courses the dissertation is research oriented. It is intended to help the student acquire the necessary skills and capacities to undertake a substantial piece of coherent research. Taking this as our starting point, we will focus on the

TABLE 1.1   BACHELORS, MASTERS AND DOCTORATE RESEARCH

Degree	Traditional and current role	Research features
Bachelors	A measure of a general education in terms of developing the skills of critical evaluation but specializing in a topic, e.g. twentieth-century history.	Small-scale independent project usually related to a taught module and used as the 'honours' element of the degree.
Masters	Originally a licence to practice theology and now a measure of advanced knowledge of a topic.	An independent piece of research focusing on the selection and analysis of a topic, design of the research, its execution and presentation as a dissertation.
Doctorate	Originally a licence to practice as a teacher in a university and now signifies authority on the current knowledge of a subject with the ability to make a contribution to that knowledge.	An independent piece of research focusing beyond the selection and analysis of a topic, design of the research, its execution, demonstration of a high and consistent level of analysis, evaluation, and contemplation to make an original contribution to knowledge and presentation as a thesis.

masters dissertation as a piece of independent research to be successfully completed as part of a masters course.

What is a masters dissertation?

Within the context of the modern taught masters course, the dissertation is a significant and substantial learning activity. Its purpose is to give you the opportunity to demonstrate your 'mastery' of the skills of analysis, synthesis, evaluation, argumentation and data collection and handling by applying them to a specific topic. In addition there are other skills, such as writing, qualities, such as determination, and attitudes, such as honesty, which are necessary and we will come to these shortly. Taken together these abilities are expected to be acquired and applied to produce a coherent and reasoned piece of research.

The language used to define the dissertation tends to differ between various universities and awarding bodies. This language includes terms and phrases such as the following, but as you can see they are generally unhelpful:

♦ an extended treatment of a topic;

♦ research done for a masters degree; or

♦ a piece of empirical research and writing.

The following definition from Yale University states that the dissertation student attains:

> technical mastery of the field of specialization, is capable of doing independent scholarly work, and is able to formulate conclusions that will in some respect modify or enlarge what has been previously known. (Yale, 1975: 182)

Masters level research is, therefore, a display of your ability to identify a topic, justify that topic, write clear aims and objectives which are interrelated, search and review the relevant literature, design data collection tools, apply those tools, manage the data collection and make sense of it. This may also include making conclusions and recommendations. It is these abilities, listed in Table 1.2, which make the masters dissertation technically a substantial piece of work and significant both intellectually and personally (Appendix 1 provides an extended list of these).

DISSERTATION OR THESIS?

The statement from Yale (in the section above) is a definition of their doctorate (PhD) and not masters degree. This highlights a difference between many British and American universities. Most universities in North America call a PhD a dissertation and the masters a thesis, while most British universities call the PhD the thesis and the masters the dissertation. In this book we will use the word 'dissertation' for masters research and 'thesis' for doctorate research. This is because, when used in a research

TABLE 1.2   SKILLS, CAPABILITIES, ATTITUDES AND QUALITIES OF THE MASTERS

Standard expectations of the Masters			
Skills	Capabilities	Attitudes	
Brevity and succinctness	Synthetical thinking	Proactive	Integrity
Citation and attribution	Analytical thinking	Ethical	Objectivity
Copy-editing	Argument analysis	Trustworthiness	
Decision-making	Effective thinking	Responsible	Honesty
Defining and classifying	Problem definition	Persuasive	Self-confidence Adaptability
Document design	Managing projects	Self-awareness	
Drafting and editing	Self-management	Cultural awareness	Determination
Information finding	Graphical presentation	Reflective	Finisher
Meeting deadlines		practitioner	Self-discipline
Numeracy and statistics	Giving and receiving feedback	Anthropological Research orientation	Experimentation Self-evaluative
Record keeping	Concept application	Self-development	Sense of humour
Target setting	Theory application	Self-control	Storytelling
Time management	Data management	Inter-disciplinary	Consistency

Note: See Appendix 1 for an expanded version of this table

proposal or monograph, the word 'thesis' means theory maintained by an argument and as such refers to the dialectic nature of a piece of writing. While a masters has some elements of argumentation and discussion the reason for these is not the production of an original contribution to knowledge. The role of argument and theory in the masters is limited to justifying the topic, rationalizing the methodology and data collection techniques and discussing the findings in relation to the use of the methodology and literature. In the doctorate theory and argument are used more extensively to discuss and evaluate ideas, concepts and data in depth as well as breadth.

THE DISSERTATION AS PART OF A MASTERS COURSE

As part of a course the masters dissertation is often specified using aims and learning outcomes. Some typical learning opportunities (or education aims) may be:

♦ to provide a range of learning opportunities to allow students to acquire a sound understanding of the origins, nature and consequences of various methodological traditions;

♦ to enable students to appreciate the technical and intellectual aspects of research design and application including the management of a project; and

♦ to allow students to appreciate the diversity and opportunities of research in the discipline (for example, psychology, economics, literature and so on).

The research you do for your dissertation is a learning activity, the purpose of which is that you are expected to acquire masters ability to do capable and competent research. Hence, your dissertation is the physical evidence that you have acquired and been able to apply at an appropriate level and in an appropriate way your learning so as to be accredited as a competent researcher.

Your learning is often expressed by masters courses as learning outcomes. The following is a typical set of learning outcomes, based on those you can see in Table 1.2, for the dissertation element of a masters course:

1 To make connections between methodological assumptions, research design and soundness of findings.

2 To distinguish between the main types of research (for example, applied, strategic, evaluative and so on) and be able to select and justify appropriate type(s) for a given problem or topic.

3 To design and apply a range of tools for the collection of data, including the literature search.

4 To apply a range of techniques of analysis for the evaluation of argument and construction of argument to justify the research.

5 To use the literature as a corpus of knowledge to extract key theories, arguments, concepts and findings in ways which are critical and evaluative and provide a synthesis.

6 To appreciate the ethical issues in the application of research methodologies, data collection techniques and evaluation of the literature.

7 To analyse, arrange, tabulate and present findings in a way that is clear, coherent and systematic, including the construction of references and the bibliography.

These general learning aims and outcomes form the basis for the assessment of the dissertation and, in some cases, the research proposal and the dissertation as separate pieces of work. The usual method, however, is to use the research proposal as a tool to identify your research interest and give you a plan for your dissertation. To cover this practice we will look at criteria for assessing research proposals in a later chapter and focus here on the details of the criteria used to assess the dissertation.

Criteria used to assess a dissertation

The only evidence that you are of 'masters quality' is your dissertation. The educational aims and learning outcomes are normally assessed by employing hierarchical marking schemes that tend to go from the general to the particular. In general terms your dissertation should:

♦ focus on a specific problem or issue;

♦ relate the problem or issue to the relevant literature;

♦ have a reasoned research design;

♦ provide an analytical and critical approach to the literature and topic;

♦ maintain scholarly standards throughout; and

♦ use sound arguments with valid and reliable evidence.

TABLE 1.3 CRITERIA FOR A MASTERS DISSERTATION

Level	Aims and objectives	Literature review and citations	Topic rationale	Methodology and data collection	Argumentation and critical awareness	Presentation, structure and succinctness
100%	Extremely well-expressed aims and proper objectives, employing terms in a methodologically coherent way so that objectives are evidently capable of actualizing the aims.	Excellent review of the literature, clear arrangement and selection of key texts, thorough, consistent critical evaluation of main ideas, theories, arguments, approaches and findings synthesized and focused on the topic puzzle. Excellent citations demonstrating consistency, detail and accuracy.	Excellent use of argumentative structure, evidence and analysis to demonstrate thorough analysis of the topic to justify the research questions or hypothesis stated. Excellent use of the literature to provide authority and backing.	Excellent rationale for methodological approach including data collection tools. Highly appropriate and effective with a strong justification in terms of the definition of the topic and research questions set. Ample evidence of reading and learning from the methods literature. Overall research design is clear and systematic with validity and reliability clear.	Excellent use of argumentative analysis and argumentative structures to analyse and synthesize the literature, topic, methodology and data collected. Arguments are developed with evident clarity and logic in an unbiased and objective way. Extremely high standard of critical analysis and evaluation. Conclusions and/or recommendations directly linked to form the findings.	Excellent presentation throughout using clear and succinct expression, with sectioning and arrangement to form a coherent dissertation, use of figures and tables to present ideas and data. Figures and tables properly labelled. Highly effective use of language and scholarly conventions. Use of correct grammar.

(Continued)

TABLE 1.3 (CONTINUED)

Level	Aims and objectives	Literature review and citations	Topic rationale	Methodology and data collection	Argumentation and critical awareness	Presentation, structure and succinctness
69%	Clear aims and objectives but expression could be more succinct to employ terms so as to be logically coherent and focused or ensure that all objectives are linked to the aim and can actualize it or may not have enough objectives.	Good review of the key texts with clear arrangement, may lack consistency of critical evaluation or elements not fully synthe-sized or lacks thoroughness but is focused on the topic. Good citations may need more detail in some instances.	Good justifica-tion of the topic but may lack full use of argumen-tative structure and evidence to demonstrate a thorough topic analysis. Should have used more sources to provide authority and backing.	Highly appropriate methodological approach identified and data collection tools selected. Evidence of reading and learning from the literature. May lack strong justification or clarity in design or strong links with the definition of the research ques-tions. Some aware-ness of validity and reliability criteria.	Good use of argumentative structures and techniques of analysis. May lack consistency across chapters and within chapters or lack clarity and logic or contain some unsubstanti-ated statements or make conclusions and recommenda-tions not fully embedded in the results.	Good presentation with clear structure, might have benefited from better sectioning or use of figures and tables or better expression. Some sections not integrated into the whole. Grammar is good with few mistakes as is language use.

(Continued)

TABLE 1.3 (CONTINUED)

Level	Aims and objectives	Literature review and citations	Topic rationale	Methodology and data collection	Argumentation and critical awareness	Presentation, structure and succinctness
59% ←	Reasonable aims and objectives but may not fully use the correct terms or make a clear distinction between one or more of the objectives or have too many or too few objectives to meet the aims.	Adequate literature review identifying most of the key texts but lacks thoroughness or critical evaluative stance or clear arrangement and does not fully demonstrate ability to synthesize ideas. Acceptable citations but lacking detail, consistency or accuracy in some.	Relevant topic identified but lacks convincing argument to link analysis with research questions or hypothesis stated. Little use of sources to provide authority and backing.	Satisfactory methodological approach and data collection techniques identified but may lack clear justification between methodology and data collection tools or detail for the design or demonstrable relationship with the research questions set. Little evidence of reading and learning from the literature or need to have valid and reliable data.	Some attempt to employ argumentation but at a basic level not demonstrating a sound understanding of argumentative analysis or its need throughout the dissertation or containing too many unsubstantiated statements and assumptions. Weak conclusions and/or recommendations poorly expressed.	Basic use of structure but chapters mostly separate entities not integrated by the focus on the topic. Better sectioning needed along with more figures and tables, and consistent use of effective expression. Grammar has some common mistakes.
	Weighting 15%	Weighting 20%	Weighting 15%	Weighting 20%	Weighting 15%	Weighting 15%

It should also be coherent and not a series of separate and inadequately related elements. Before we look at how this can be done, Table 1.3 shows the main criteria used to make an assessment of a typical dissertation and although these have a small bias towards the traditional dissertation they are mostly relevant for other types of dissertation. When looking at these criteria remember that your institution will probably have a different way of formulating them and you should obtain these and discuss them with your supervisor.

MARKING RANGES AND FAILURE

As a piece of course work that is assessed and has a credit rating, the dissertation is normally marked out of 100. This marking may be in percentages from 0 to 100 per cent, or in alpha from A to F. Oddly, such work rarely attracts a mark of 0 or 100 even though the range is from 0 to 100. Our position is that if the mark range is 0 to 100, then the full range should be used. This means a dissertation that is deemed excellent by the markers should be awarded the full mark or very near to it. A mark of 70 per cent may be deemed to be excellent, but is in fact a 30 per cent failure. How can this be so when to gain the full mark of 100 per cent it requires a 30 per cent improvement? I believe that if a mark range is set at these limits, then they should be used and shown in the criteria used for specific masters degrees. Table 1.4 follows this through and shows the conventional mark range below 50 per cent. We have not included this as part of Table 1.3 because a mark of 40 per cent is equivalent to a 60 per cent failure mark.

CRITERIA AND THE EXAMINER

In some of the chapters that follow we will look more closely at different elements of the criteria in Table 1.3 and Table 1.4, to see what they mean in practice and how they can be adapted for assessing different kinds of dissertation. As you can see, the criteria are sets of interrelated expectations that your examiners are looking for from your dissertation. In Table 1.5 we have reformulated these as a series of questions examiners may use to show the relationships between the skills, capabilities, attitudes, qualities – the standards and technical requirements for a dissertation.

Table 1.5 also shows the reiterative nature of the criteria in terms that when combined they are used to assess both intellectual and technical abilities. Various criteria are

TABLE 1.4 50 TO 60 PER CENT ATTAINMENT

Level	Aims and objectives	Literature review and citations	Topic rationale	Methodology and data collection	Argumentation and critical awareness	Presentation, structure and succinctness
49%	Aims and objectives barely acceptable, should be better due to lack of clarity, wording, clear distinction between aims and objectives not evident, objectives not proper or consistent.	Barely acceptable review of the literature, not all key texts identified and reviewed, lacks appropriate depth and thoroughness, weak evaluation lacking critical elements, and clear focus on the topic. Poor citation of sources, lacking consistency, details and accuracy.	Generalized topic area identified possibly capable of research but lacks focus due to insufficient analysis. Weak argument with few or no sound links to the research questions or hypothesis. No significant use of sources.	Highly generalized identification and simplistic comparison of methodological choices and data collection tools. No evidence of reading and learning from the literature. Weak explanation of choices and research design with weak links to the nature of the topic. No attempt to address or demonstrate an understanding of validity and reliability.	Opinionated generalizations with no tangible evidence of sound argument. Highly descriptive and commonsensical using simplistic analysis. Analysis is superficial and conclusions and recommendations barely linked to findings. Considerable amount of bias and little recognition for substantiation of claims.	Sloppy presentation throughout with no evidence of concern for standards or a demonstration of scholarly conventions. Little or no use of figures and tables, under- or over-use of sectioning and no evidence of proofreading.
Less than 40%	You should not be left at this level if you listen and take advice from your supervisor.	You should not be left at this level if you listen and take advice from your supervisor.	You should not be left at this level if you listen and take advice from your supervisor.	You should not be left at this level if you listen and take advice from your supervisor.	You should not be left at this level if you listen and take advice from your supervisor.	You should not be left at this level if you listen and take advice from your supervisor.

TABLE 1.5   THE EXAMINER'S QUESTIONS

Criteria	Expectation as a question
Prior understanding	Has a demonstration been given of an understanding of a masters dissertation? Is this expressed through the soundness of the work, especially arguments, data collection and handling?
Perseverance and diligence	Have relevant databases for the literature search been identified? Have print as well as electronic sources been searched? Has the search been expanded and narrowed accordingly? Have clear and consistent records been made of the search? Is there an evaluation of the search?
Literature review	Have key concepts, ideas, theories, arguments and data been identified in the literature? Is the review comprehensive, covering both topic and methodological literatures? Have all necessary elements been categorized, compared and synthesized from the literature in a scholarly way? Are the citations clear, consistent and detailed? Has the literature been critically evaluated? Have all ideas and statements been fully attributed?
Coherence and thoroughness	Are the aims and objectives clearly stated and logically linked? Is the research design justified and capable of actualizing the aims and objectives? Does the justification amplify the aims and show use of argumentation and the literature? Have the data collection instruments been tested and evaluated? Are they a reliable and valid means to appropriate data? Is the data presented clearly and in full? Are anomalies in the data fully explained? Is the discussion of the data closely linked to the data? And are conclusions linked and related to the literature? Have clear links been made between the conclusions, data, literature and objectives?

(Continued)

TABLE 1.5 (CONTINUED)

Criteria	Expectation as a question
Justification and argumentation	Is clear justification (rationale) given for the project? Are definitions used properly? Is the issue, topic or problem clearly stated and justified, including the recognition of unstated assumptions? Are sound arguments used in the justification, evaluation of the literature and conclusions? Are different kinds of argumentation analysis used appropriately? Is the difference shown between informative and relational statements? Are the differences between inductive and deductive reasoning understood?
Scholarly standards	Have sources been correctly and fully cited and all proper attribution of ideas given? Is the bibliography as expected, containing all necessary seminal works? Is there sound use of research design to show understanding of internal and external validity, difference between description and explanation and different kinds of statements? Is this an ethical piece of research that conforms to the ethical standards of the university or profession? Are any moral statements justified and balanced with open discussion of alternative positions?
Methodological understanding	Are the origins, nature and consequences of different methodological traditions understood? Is sound justification given for the use of specific methodological assumptions? Is understanding shown of the relationships between methodology and data? Is there an overall research design incorporating methodological assumptions, data collection techniques and understanding of validity, reliability and limits on generalizability?

(Continued)

TABLE 1.5 (CONTINUED)

Criteria	Expectation as a question
Discussion, conclusions and recommendations	Is the discussion related to the review of the literature? Are statements and arguments clearly justified by the data or the analysis of arguments? Do conclusions follow from the evidence and argument presented? How do the conclusions relate to the aims and objectives set for the project? Are the recommendations properly arranged – recommendation, benefits, consequences and costs? Are they realistic, appropriate and based on the data or analysis?
Reflective practitioner	Are observations made which show ability to reflect and evaluate on what has been done? Is the evaluation related to the aims, objectives and management of the project? Are problems and gaps identified? Have areas for further research been suggested? Has the significance the research might have for practice been indicated (particularly relevant for vocational courses)?
Presentation	Is the dissertation well written in terms of proper grammar, including spelling and punctuation? Is the style and format that required by the university? Is the arrangement logical? Has editing been done to make it clear and coherent and of the right length? Are appendices appropriate? Is this dissertation as good as any other from a comparable university? Can this dissertation be released into the public domain for other researchers to use?

emphasized in different places in a dissertation but are, nevertheless, expected to be displayed throughout it. For example, argumentation is expected to be clear and succinct in the justification but have more depth in the review of the literature. However, this is not as complex as it may seem and we can see this by looking at different types of dissertation.

Different types of dissertation

Depending on the subject discipline and qualifications offered by your university, you will normally have the option of doing one of three types of dissertation: the traditional 'academic' dissertation; the 'literature review' dissertation; and the 'work-based' dissertation. This is a crude distinction and is in no way meant to indicate that one is somehow better than the other in terms of scholarship or practical value. All three types are equally valid if done properly as the same high standards are expected of all. There are no prescriptive criteria to determine which of the three you should do, but we do have some general advice that may be of help.

If you are studying for your masters on a part-time mode while working, then the work-based dissertation may be more suitable than the academic dissertation. This is because you will have some ready-made topics waiting for you in your place of work. If your employer is sponsoring your masters, then they may also expect you to do research that will have some benefit for the organization. In this case you are more likely to gain the necessary support from your organization to use them as your research topic. There are some problems with this and the main one is doing research on your employer and on a topic that is not too controversial. Work-based dissertations may result in findings and interpretations which your employer or someone in a senior position in your organization does not like or even see as criticism. Therefore the selection of a topic needs to be carefully considered.

The traditional dissertation may be more suited to students on a full-time mode masters course. This is because they will not only have a little more time than their part-time peers, but will have constant access to the library and other resources. It is also likely that they will be attending formal classes and therefore will not have opportunities to access an external organization. This does not mean, if you are a full-time student, that you cannot use an external organization for the basis of your research. There may be some advantages to using one, especially that you can take trips into the field knowing you can return to the relative political safety of your university.

In Chapter 5 we look more closely at the different types of dissertation, including the literature review dissertation. The following bullet points are, however, some of the features of the traditional and the work-based dissertations to help you think about which may be more suitable for you:

Traditional dissertation	Work-based dissertation
◆ Focused on a topic arrived at from using the literature.	◆ Focused on a specific work-based problem of significance to the sponsoring organization.
◆ Aimed at explanation, exploration or description of a puzzle.	◆ Aimed at drawing out options, recommendations and action lines.
◆ Grounded in the literature and based on key arguments and theories.	◆ Informed by the literature on 'best practice' in other organizations, industries and sectors.
◆ Provides relevant background information to justify the puzzle using argumentative structure and evidence from the literature.	◆ Provides relevant background information such as statistics, reports and evidence.
◆ Use of an appropriate methodological approach dependent on the definition of the topic and data needs.	◆ Use of an action-oriented methodological approach, usually action research.
◆ Use of relevant secondary sources including statistics for comparison.	◆ Use of secondary and primary data for comparison and validation of 'before and after' or for recommendations.
◆ Production of an academic dissertation normally in the format of a research dissertation.	◆ Production of a work-based dissertation normally in the format of a research report.

That there are different types of dissertation means it can be beneficial to look, before you chose which university, at the experience of different academic departments to see what preferences they have. Their preferences and experiences may be related to the kinds of learning and teaching styles they use, which may also have an influence on how comfortable you will feel doing your research (and masters) with them.

How long does it take to do a masters dissertation?

This may be a key question for you if you are doing a vocationally-oriented masters or, like most students, have limited resources and will find it more economic to do your dissertation in the shortest time possible. As a benchmark we can say from experience that the time required for planning, reading, collecting data, analysis, doing critical evaluative and comparative thought, drafting and writing, editing and polishing a 15,000-word dissertation is substantial. Figure 1.1 shows how we normally expect a student to use at least 600 hours to complete a dissertation. If your university requires a 20,000-word dissertation, then add on about another 125 hours. As a general rule of thumb, if we use word output as our measure, every 1,000 words needs about 25 hours. This is, of course, general because much depends on the nature of your topic, what kinds of data are required and, importantly, how you work and what time you can give to your research in a normal week.

The longer you take to complete your masters, including your dissertation, the more it will cost you financially. However, if you wanted to, you could take up to five years to do your masters. The general unforeseen events of life sometimes mean that you may have few choices and have to take this longer route to your goal. If this becomes the case for you the key point is *never give up* – if you have started it, finish it!

If you are a part-time student you will probably be used to working approximately 15 hours a week on your course. On the basis of this calculation it would take you about nine months to complete your dissertation if you continued at this level of output. You will, however, have semester breaks and university vacations when course work requirements may be lower, and these can be used to get on with your research. On this basis you will need to allow approximately 75 equivalent days of full-time work (eight hours a day) for your research. This is the ideal that in real life rarely happens. You are more likely to have concentrated periods of work when you move your dissertation on considerably and then have lean periods when it seems very little is being done. The main point is to keep thinking about your research and keep talking to your supervisor throughout, regardless of how much or how little you have managed to do.

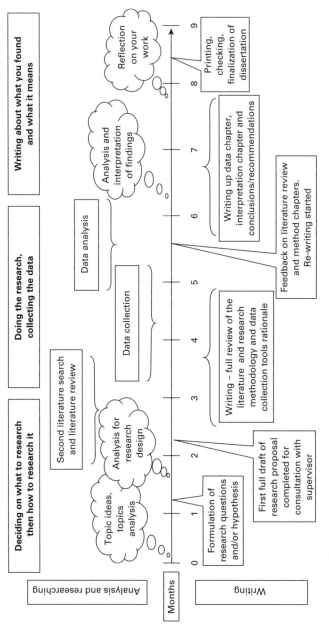

FIGURE1.1   TIMESCALE FOR A MASTERS DISSERTAION

The point about the supervisor is important and should not be missed. Whether you are full- or part-time, maintaining regular contact (telephone, in person, e-mail) – and by this we mean at least once every two weeks – is crucial. It does not matter if you have not been able to do much since last talking to them, but by knowing you are expected to stay in contact will act as a motivator to you when you need it most. Your supervisor will be able to help you maintain commitment to your research and will often be able to suggest what you can do to keep progressing your research when other things are not going according to plan.

You will have realized by now that doing a masters dissertation requires a substantial amount of commitment and dedication from you. Do not underestimate the transition from everyday life or from a taught course to an almost wholly self-motivated piece of work. You will face many pressures as other people, including your family and friends, will not fully understand what you are doing, the concentration required and the time you are taking from your relationships with them. Doing research can be a lonely experience. This may seem a little depressing, but we want you to be realistic about your progress whatever route you take. Your supervisors will appreciate what you are experiencing and will not want you to take longer than necessary to achieve your masters degree with a good dissertation. They will be as proud of you as your family and friends when you walk across the stage to collect your certificate and graduate as a master. If, however, the plan does not work out as expected, do not give yourself pressure or give up but take a realistic option by re-enrolling, paying a fee and completing your dissertation at a less stressful pace.

Are you capable of doing a masters dissertation?

When contemplating doing or just beginning a masters course with a dissertation a number of worries are often expressed by students. A common one is, 'I can't write 15,000 words!' It is highly probable that you can write 15,000: from experience of supervising many masters dissertations, it will most likely be the case that you will have the problem of getting your writing down to only 15,000 words. You only have 15,000 words to report on all the work you will do. Most students have this kind of fear when beginning their dissertation and although it is natural it is often unfounded.

A MASTERS IS NO MOUNTAIN

Doing a masters dissertation is a large undertaking but it is not an academic mountain. It is like walking ten kilometres when you have only ever walked one or two. In academic terms you may have only written essays and reports of, say, up to 3,000 words. Think back to your undergraduate days – how many assignments did you do and what was (approximately) the total word count? It will have been substantially more than 15,000 words. Therefore you have written a large amount of material; the only difference this time is that the dissertation will be one piece of work. It will, however, be made up of many different elements. Before looking at this we need to dispel some other common misconceptions.

Look at the following statements and think about which you agree with:

1 You need to be determined to do a masters dissertation.

2 You need to be *exceptionally* intelligent to do a masters dissertation.

3 You need to have commitment to doing research to do a masters dissertation.

4 You need to have a first class honours degree to do a masters dissertation.

5 You need to have a willingness to learn to do a masters dissertation.

Statements 2 and 4 are false and statements 1, 3 and 5 are some of the attitudes you do need to do a masters dissertation. For most people who successfully complete their dissertation a large degree of that success is their attitude and approach. A useful way to success to is to think of a dissertation as a series of tasks. If broken down into a logically sequenced set of tasks, such as searching the library catalogue, searching the Internet, beginning to compile the bibliography and so on, a dissertation looks less daunting and very manageable. Manmohan Bains, a student with Indian/Punjabi heritage, expressed this as the 'eating an elephant problem'. He asked, 'How do you eat an elephant?' And answered, 'One mouthful at a time.' Although an unusual way to put it, the point is clear. Do not be put off at the start, but if you break any large enterprise into smaller tasks you are more likely to achieve your goal.

In the chapters that follow we will show you how to divide a dissertation into tasks which are relatively straightforward to do. The result will be something that is greater than the sum of its parts, a masters dissertation you can be proud of.

Where to do your masters

This chapter finishes with some thoughts which may be useful when choosing where to do your masters research. If you are intending to use your masters to move into a different job, give you capital for promotion or begin a career in research, then the university department you choose may be a factor in your success. Different departments are often associated with different kinds of research – some will be oriented towards pure research and others applied research – and within these you will find specialisms which are often due to one or more members of staff. It pays to do a little research on where you would like (or can) do your masters before you begin. A note of caution would be, however, not to take too much notice of national league tables for universities because they are not always valid measures of actual quality. A more reliable means is to gather all the information published on your possible institutions and then contact them for details on staff, resources, research strategy and the culture of the department.

WHAT TO LOOK FOR

You will need to know what the research interests of the staff are, what they have published and how many successful masters students they have supervised. On resources ask them about what book-based and information communications technologies are in the department. How many computers do they have and of what specification? What other facilities do they have, such as printing, technician support and, importantly, student common rooms? Also inquire about the research collections in the library, including access to electronic sources and resources, especially the databases you will need.

If the department is serious about research, then expect it to have a detailed research strategy that provides information on the kinds of research it aims to undertake and support. Finally, because you will spend a substantial amount of your time working in the department, find out what its culture is like. By this I mean: is the place friendly, are first names used, is there an atmosphere of mutual support between staff and students, and are staff generally available for informal chats, do they have an 'open door' policy and is the departmental secretary friendly? You can find most of this out by visiting the department. Signs of a good department for research include such things as the state and content of notice boards informing students of what is going on, of research activities and seminars, visiting speakers and new books. Also look for a sense of humour. Do current students look happy? Ask them what it is like to do a masters in this department, focusing on the support they are receiving from their supervisors.

LEARNING AND TEACHING STYLES

Different academic departments (sometimes called 'Schools') tend to have different approaches to teaching and learning. This makes for diversity among universities and other institutions and allows for different kinds of research to be undertaken and, importantly, different views about the nature of research to be expressed. However, the teaching and learning preference of one department may not be the one suited to your own personal learning style. Honey and Mumford (1992) provide a detailed questionnaire to help you identify your learning style preference. The four main learning styles they describe are summarized in Table 1.6.

Even from this brief overview of the different styles you should be able to recognize features in some that you can associate with. It is not necessary to choose one rather than another. It is OK to associate with features from more than one of the styles. The purpose of introducing these is to help you to identify different learning styles used by different academic departments and, as we will see in Chapter 5, also help you to choose the type of dissertation most suited to your own learning style. You can begin to do the first of these – assessing the learning opportunities of different departments – when you visit the departments offering the masters courses you want to do. The kinds of questions to be addressed are listed below, and in part answers to these will be evident in the attitudes of staff, stated curriculum of the course and in the types of dissertations which have been done in a department.

1 Questions for activists

   ◆ What will I learn that I didn't know before?

   ◆ What specific and general research skills will I acquire?

   ◆ Will there be a variety of different activities or is the course based on lectures?

   ◆ Will it be OK to make mistakes and have some fun?

   ◆ Will I have tough problems and challenges?

2 Questions for reflectors

   ◆ Is enough time given over for reflection to assimilate ideas and think about issues?

♦ Are there sufficient facilities and opportunities to gather all relevant information about a topic?

♦ Will there be group discussions in which sharing of ideas and experiences happens?

♦ Do staff encourage listening to the views of others and give time for people to formulate considered responses?

♦ Is the teaching and tutoring based on pressure to respond?

TABLE 1.6   LEARNING STYLES

Learning style	Features
Activist	'What's new? I'm game for anything.' Activists learn best in situations where: • there are new experiences and problems to be solved; • they can engross themselves in the 'here and now'; and • there is a sense of competition and pressure.
Reflector	'I'd like time to think about this.' Reflectors learn best where: • they are encouraged to watch and think about activities and problems; • they have time to assimilate the facts and arguments before commenting; and • they have the opportunity to review what has happened.
Theorist	'How does this relate to that?' Theorists learn best where: • they have time to explore methodically ideas and theories; • they are in structured situations with clear objectives that nevertheless stretch their intellect; and • they can question basic methodological assumptions and the logic of arguments.
Pragmatist	'How can I apply this in practice?' Pragmatists learn best where: • they can see practical links between theory and a problem, especially in the workplace; • they have a chance to try out applications and evaluate their effectiveness; and • they can concentrate on practical issues facing real organizations and people.

3   Questions for theorists

♦ Will I encounter complex ideas and theories which will stretch my understanding and abilities?

♦ Do staff have a robust understanding of theoretical traditions in the social sciences?

♦ Does the curriculum have a clear structure and purpose both technically *and* intellectually?

♦ Shall I be with people of a similar calibre to myself?

4   Questions for pragmatists

♦ Will we be addressing real problems and actual issues rather than hypothetical ones?

♦ Will we be exposed to specialists and experts who have relevant and up-to-date experience?

♦ Is the curriculum clearly skills-based and practical?

♦ Will there be lots of useful tips and techniques?

COURSE SPECIFICATIONS

Additional pieces of documentary information you can request include the 'subject standards', course specification and module booklet. Most courses in higher education are required by the governing bodies to use the subject standards (benchmark statements) to specify their course. This includes providing statements on the aims and objectives of the course as a whole and on individual modules that are a part of the course, showing how the learning outcomes of each module contribute to the learning outcomes of the course as a whole. This course specification will give a good idea of what kind of educational philosophy, teaching and learning styles a department uses in the design and organization of its curriculum. It will show you to what degree they focus on a range of skills as a set of expectations which you should

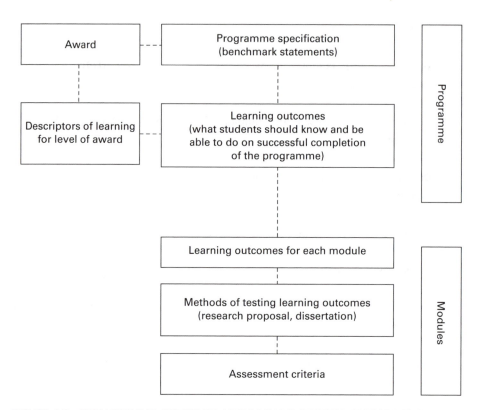

FIGURE 1.2   THE LEARNING OUTCOMES APPROACH TO MASTERS COURSE DESIGN

achieve at the end of the course. Your course tutor will probably explain to you the scheme of their masters course. Many follow a generic template represented in Figure 1.2. This is based on what is known as the learning outcomes approach to course design.

A well-thought-out and organized masters programme will have a clear coherence. This means there will be a clear set of statements describing the level for a masters qualification. Different universities have their own ways of stating award descriptors. These would normally include higher level cognitive and practical abilities of the type shown in Table 1.3 and Appendix 1, which are based on benchmark expectations for a knowledge manager. Each module on the course should then explain how specific learning outcomes will be acquired through doing that module and how they will be assessed, using what kind of criteria. Hence a module may state that a student will be able to give evidence of the application of knowledge. This may be expressed using verbs such as define, solve, manipulate, relate, use, assess and so on to state what, in the methods of assessment, will be tested. As a scheme the programme should be coherent, and by looking at the course documentation and at previous work done by students you should be able to make a sound evaluation of how well organized a particular masters course is.

Implicitly or explicitly the programme specification will also indicate the kind of person they expect to encourage both intellectually and professionally to succeed in their course. Table 1.3 indicates the kind of specification that I use when talking to new enrollers on masters courses. A more detailed one can be found in Appendix 1 that was developed for a masters in Knowledge Management for practitioners. Do not be put off by the length of the lists in each of the columns. Its purpose is to show you the range of skills, capabilities, attitudes and qualities that a good masters course, with research, will make available for you to exploit for your own personal development. Clearly, you will not have the time to acquire all of these and you will already be able to demonstrate many of them.

This is an important stage in beginning your masters and if you have a choice between universities then exercise it. You may find some interesting and significant differences between departments. In particular, it is not always the case that the department with the highest formal rating for research is necessarily the most supportive of research students or close enough to the job market to encourage useful topics. Look, therefore, beyond ratings to other indicators which suit your teaching and learning needs and choose a department that offers you the maximum learning opportunities to develop both professionally and as a person.

SUMMARY OF THIS CHAPTER

This initial chapter has attempted to provide you with an introduction to what a masters dissertation is about and has made the following main points:

◆ A masters dissertation is an exercise in research that demonstrates you are capable of doing research at masters level.

- ◆ A masters dissertation is a coherent piece of work and not a series of separate chapters.

- ◆ There are three main types of dissertation, the traditional, the work-based and the literature review dissertation, and the same high standards of scholarship are expected of all.

- ◆ A good dissertation demonstrates more than the acquisition of skills. It is testimony to the capability, attitude and qualities of the student to be accredited as a competent researcher.

- ◆ A dissertation is a major undertaking but it is not a mountain that only a few can climb; rather it is something many people are capable of achieving.

Further reading

Walliman, N. (2001) *Your Research Project: A Guide for the First-time Researcher*. London: Sage. Chapter 1 uses a range of quotes to indicate just what research is and what it is about.

Honey, P. and Mumford, A. (1992) *The Manual of Learning Styles*. Maidenhead: Peter Honey. Exactly what it says it is and includes exercises to assess your own preferences.

Learning gateway and learning styles. http://www.getting-on.co.uk/toolkit/learninggateway.html. One of many good Internet resources on learning styles.

Managing your transition to masters

CHAPTER CONCEPTS

● TRANSITION TO STUDY ● MANAGING THE TRANSITION AS A PROJECT ● GET TO KNOW THE STAFF ● MANAGE YOUR FAMILY AND FRIENDS ● SUGGESTIONS FOR ORGANIZING YOURSELF ● MANAGING YOUR TIME ● GET TO KNOW HOW TO USE YOUR TIME ● IMPLEMENT THE MAIN PRINCIPLES OF TIME MANAGEMENT ● MANAGING YOUR SPACE ● MANAGING THE LONELINESS AND ISOLATION OF RESEARCH ● NETWORKING ● LIFE ISSUES ● ESTABLISHING A DOCUMENT CONTROL SYSTEM ● CITING YOUR SOURCES AND CREATING BIBLIOGRAPHIES ● CITING REFERENCES AND ATTRIBUTION ● CREATING BIBLIOGRAPHIES ● USING THE COMPUTER ● KEEPING A RESEARCH DIARY AND A LEARNING LOG ● SUMMARY OF THIS CHAPTER ● FURTHER READING

Starting a new course at a new university can be a daunting prospect with so much to arrange and do and many unfamiliar people and places to get used to. Postgraduate study can be very different from what you have done before in level, intensity and the expectations your tutors will have of you. You will find that your status, as a masters student, will set you apart from the undergraduates – who will either look up to you or wonder why you have voluntarily signed up to do more study. Your status brings with it expectations that you will behave as a member of a scholarly research community and as such exhibit a mature attitude, bring a set of personal and professional qualities to your work and be part of a collegial group made up of your peers and the departmental staff. The basis of this chapter comes from long experience in a number of universities teaching many postgraduates. It tries to cover many of the most obvious points about being organized, but for whatever reasons are often the cause of problems for students. Some of the main questions for this chapter are:

1 How can you prepare for doing your masters research?

2 With so much to do, what are some of the ways to manage time and resources?

3 What kind of project management system will you need?

The intent therefore, while it may seem a little patronizing in parts and makes assumptions that students have families, is to look at how you might manage the transition to becoming a postgraduate, at how to become an active member of the research community, at life issues, and at how to set up a management system for the substantial amounts of information you will generate when doing your dissertation.

Transition to study

Moving from undergraduate to postgraduate study or from the workplace into the academic environment is like starting a new life. Many things, people, procedures and even finding your way around may, at first, be difficult. Added to this is the tendency for most masters courses to be intensive, even though they last for one to three years. For full-time students the norm is a 12-month course and for the part-time student 24 to 36 months. It is normal for the dissertation element of masters courses to begin, for full-time students, after the first semester, and for part-time students in the second half of year two. This means you may have about six to nine months to complete your dissertation on the full-time mode and between 24 to 36 on the part-time mode. It is essential, therefore, that you adapt quickly to your new environment and position and this means managing the transition to being a masters student in two to three weeks.

MANAGING THE TRANSITION AS A PROJECT

One way of approaching the transition is to see it as an opportunity to practise your project management skills and to exercise some of your personal qualities. You need to define the objectives for the transition period, and these will be:

♦ to become familiar with the geography of the university, especially the department;

♦ to become familiar with the procedures governing your course, especially the dissertation;

♦ to get to know who is who among the staff, how to contact them, what roles and responsibilities they have, especially the course director, and do not forget to find out who the departmental secretary is and where their office is; and

♦ to identify and check on important dates, especially for submission of course work.

It is seldom that any student has the time before their course to get to know the department. It is therefore important to gather as much information as you can on any initial visits, such as open days and interview days. As you are the 'customer' you have the right to make reasonable requests for all necessary information about the course you will be doing including staff lists, timetables and maps. It is now usual for most good universities to provide pre-start packs that contain most of the information you will need for your first couple of weeks. It is important to read your 'course handbook', as it is sometimes called, before you start – do not file it away, as it contains important information that tutors will expect you to know before you start your course.

GET TO KNOW THE STAFF

One of the key activities for you in the first week is to get to know the staff who are significant contributors to or administrators of your course. Normally there will be a time in the first week when you and your peers are introduced to the department, usually over some social function. Use this to go around and introduce yourself personally to each member of staff, talking to them about their speciality and about research they may be doing. This will be one of your first rounds of 'networking' in your new community.

Getting to know staff will help you in a number of ways, including:

♦ being able to ask questions without feeling awkward because they do not know you;

♦ going to see them about research ideas you have for your dissertation;

♦ borrowing materials for your research and reading; and

♦ seeking pastoral support for your learning and course work, especially when things are not going to plan and you feel you need to talk to someone.

Departments with an 'open culture' normally support what is called the open-door policy. This is when you do not need to make an appointment to see a member of staff

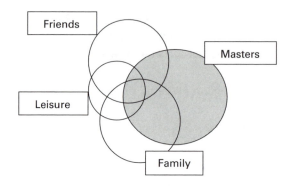

FIGURE 2.1   THE IMPORTANCE OF YOUR MASTERS IN YOUR LIFE

if it's a quick question. However, if you think you will need more than five minutes, make an appointment to guarantee the time with them. Access to staff is therefore important. So ensure you have the information on how to contact individual staff via telephone, e-mail, post and fax and also the departmental secretary. Use these methods to keep staff informed of your activities, especially if you are unable to attend a scheduled tutorial or class or you want to seek advice on a research idea. It helps staff if they have some idea of your research idea before you turn up to discuss it. E-mailing it to them in advance will allow them to think about it and to give you better feedback when you see them.

MANAGE YOUR FAMILY AND FRIENDS

Most people have a range of commitments outside university – family, friends and leisure activities, and, of course, paid work. Trying to keep up with all your usual activities simultaneously with doing your masters may not be possible and you may need to give up some things while you are studying. Try also to keep a balance between your study and other commitments, family, friends and social life generally.

Figure 2.1 shows the main spheres of most people's lives when they embark on doing a masters course. As you can see, the masters element is not only larger than the others but overlaps them. This is intended to show how doing a masters takes time away from the others to become the most dominant and demanding part of your life while you are on your course. There are two approaches you can take to this situation. One is to ignore all your family and friends and have no social life to focus exclusively on your masters work. Some people do this believing their masters research is their life. If this 'works' for you then this is fine, but do not be pressured by others into this form of existence. What we mean by this is that peer students will often exaggerate how much time they devote to their research, making it seem that you are spending too much time on other things. To suddenly drop all you have done before, the people you know and your leisure activities (hobbies and interests) to focus on your research can be unhealthy both mentally and physically and can therefore impact on the very thing – your masters research – that you sacrificed so much for. Any activity, including research, which largely excludes all others is excessive and can become compulsive behaviour, and when this happens you may need your family and friends to help you recover.

The second approach you may take, and the one we strongly recommend, is to see your research as a part of your life for now, as something that will be over in a relatively short period of time. This means, if you can, involving your family and friends in your ambitions, even if it is simply telling them about what you are doing, but not in too much detail as this will probably make you seem like a bore. By letting the significant people in your life know about your ambition they are more likely to believe they are a part of it and give the necessary support when you need it. This often ranges from taking the children to the park for a couple of hours while you work on some data analysis or taking you to the pub for some needed relief, to the ultimate help, which is proofreading something you have written. Never turn this kind of help away when it is offered because to do so may mean it is not offered again. As an aside, it can often be said that without the support of family and friends many students would not complete their masters – especially those doing it part-time. Husbands, wives and partners will often know your dissertation as well as you do and as such they deserve some form of qualification because it is they who have made sacrifices and taken on extra responsibilities so that you can do your masters. Having said this, do be prepared for the 'Educating Rita' situation. This is when people close to you, for whatever reason, resent what you are trying to achieve for yourself.

Suggestions for organizing yourself

It is important therefore to maintain your domestic life by finding ways to manage your time and the expectations others can reasonably have of your energies while you are doing your masters research. Whatever way you do this, it is usually tied to your particular personal circumstances, but I, from my own experience, suggest the following points – based on planning your activities and the expectations others may have of you – as suggestions you may wish to use.

♦ *Plan the year* When possible plan ahead. This means long- and short-term planning. Long term when you start your masters, draw up a timetable so you and your family know what commitments you will have and when. Things to include are deadlines for course work, times for attending university and, importantly, blocks of time you will need for work in the library or at home for study. Remember to build in to your schedule holiday time because you and your family and friends will need an occasional break from your masters research. If you go away from home for your holiday, say abroad; one thing we strongly advise against is taking work with you. Sitting on the beach reading a text book or, even worse, doing work on a lap-top computer, is very sad.

♦ *Plan weekly and for the next day*   On a weekly and daily basis make lists of what needs to be done. This means listing many of your normal routines and domestic tasks so as not to forget them, as this can easily be done when you are doing research. Do the same for your course-related tasks, listing what you need to do this week especially for major tasks coming up in a few weeks or a couple of months' time. This may include ordering books from the library to doing initial prepatory reading on a topic. As you achieve each task cross it off your list. There is a significant motivational boost to achieving even the simplest objectives so try to achieve some each day, especially the necessary ones.

♦ *Get organized*   Do not leave until tomorrow what you can do today. Get yourself into a routine based on preparing what you can before you need it. This includes preparing the night before the obvious things, such as clothes for college and food to take with you, to packing your case with the necessary books, pens and paper. Disorganization is no virtue to someone trying to manage an intensive course of study and a life.

♦ *Take for-me-days*   Occasionally, when you need some respite take what we call 'for-me-days'. These are days that are just for you and no one or anything else. The idea is if a day becomes available when other jobs can wait, take it for yourself and do whatever you want. Such days help you bring a sense of control and normality back to what may often seem like a hectic schedule.

♦ *Sleeping and eating*   Getting enough sleep and eating good foods are essential for body and mind. You cannot function at your optimum levels if you are tired or are lacking basic sustenance. For part-time masters students the one day and evening per week attendance can be extremely tiring. There is so much to cram into the day in between formal classes and tutorials that pacing yourself becomes an important part of your attitude for managing yourself. This may mean finding suitable places where you can take a 20–30 minute nap in the middle of the day. Short sleeps in the day and before an evening session can be very beneficial. They will rejuvenate your mental ability and ensure that you maximize your time in classes. This may also mean ensuring you get enough sleep the day before college, taking care with alcohol the night before as this will severely impair your concentration because it will make you tired the next day. Remember not to work too late into the evening as this may also make you over-tired the next day. From our experience it is often good to set a time when you do not work beyond, such as 9.30 p.m. Also before you finish for a session make brief notes on what you need to do next, so that when you pick up a piece of work the next day you do not spend time thinking about where you were and what you were doing, but have a clear set of tasks to get on with.

Although some of these suggestions may seem a little patronizing the intention is to help you maximize what you can get out of your time, as an investment you are making in yourself, doing a masters. They are the general philosophy I follow that works for me. You need to find out what works for you. Planning and organizing your time and yourself will help you to avoid drifting and wasting, what is to you, valuable time and limited energies.

MANAGING YOUR TIME

You probably know a substantial amount about managing your time and, like most of us, know of the frustrations of making the most of our time and thinking that we can find more if only we tried harder. Many of the anxieties we face in modern life are time-related, caused by us not having enough time to do everything we would like and sometimes need to do. You cannot find any more time than you already have. Time is a finite resource that cannot be saved, increased or bought. You can, however, make more effective and efficient use of the time you already have. If we take this as our starting point we can begin to look at how we may reorganize our activities and this means changing some of our behaviours and the claim others have on our time.

The starting point for using your time more effectively and efficiently is finding the motivation and self-discipline to alter some of your behaviours and radically change some habits. Breaking any habit is not easily done, but it is often our habits which contribute to some of our anxieties about time. Making some very basic alterations to

	Monday	Tuesday	Wednesday	Thursday	Friday	Saturday	Sunday
Morning	Domestic stuff	Study 2 hours	Free	Shopping	Domestic stuff	Shopping	Free
Afternoon	Work 1–4 p.m.	Work 1–4 p.m.	Work 1–4 p.m.	Work 1–4 p.m.	Work 1–4 p.m.	Study 2 hours	Free
Evening	Keep fit	Study 2 hours	Classes 1 hour	Classes 1 hour	Study 2 hours	Socializing	Free

FIGURE 2.2   RECORD OF TIME USE

habits and behaviours will give you a pay-off in terms of 'time-space' to do the things you need to do and will give you a sense that it is you who controls your time and not others. From my own experience I offer the following suggestions on how you may better manage the time that belongs to you.

Get to know how you use your time

You need to look carefully at how you use your time. This means making a record, over a week or two, of your time use so you can analyse your behaviours. A simple log in the form of a chart will give you the data you need. Figure 2.2 shows a typical time log that will show you how you are currently using your time, while Table 2.1 will help you to identify behaviours and factors you allow to eat into your time.

Looking at this weekly schedule we can see that this person has about 10 hours for study. But in reality this may not be the case, as they allow a range of distractions and other people to take some of this valuable time. Therefore this person needs to:

♦ see what they can take out of their weekly schedule;

♦ minimize some of the distractions; and

♦ minimize the claims others have on their time.

To implement some of these may not be popular with family and friends. But as we said earlier, if they support you then making small sacrifices in the claims they have on your time and even taking on some of your tasks and responsibilities are ways in which they can show their support. Figure 2.3 shows a revised weekly schedule and a

TABLE 2.1 ANALYSING DISTRACTIONS

Interruptions	No	Yes	Actions to minimize
Telephone – I always answer it and people often call me.		✓	Get an answer machine. Do not answer the phone during certain times of the day/night.
Prioritizing – I often try to do too many things at once, many of which are trivial tasks.		✓	Grade tasks into A tasks (urgent), B tasks (important), C tasks (not important). Do the A tasks in order and plan the B tasks. Leave the C tasks.
Visitors – people tend to call on me, at home, at work, unannounced and often only for a chat.		✓	Let people know when you are not available and if they still call on you strictly limit the time they take from you.
Deadlines – usually something comes up so I miss some.		✓	Plan as far ahead as possible for research tasks and all other important tasks. Establish time in your schedule to gather the information you need for tasks coming up in the medium term future.
Procrastination – is what I do best. I tend to put things off or find other things to do rather than what is important.		✓	Say no to distractions. Get into a routine of working certain times of the day. Set targets for each study session. Stop making excuses, you are responsible for yourself.

list of actions the person intends to take to minimize distractions and the claims others have on their time.

Implement the main principles of time management

It is from these simple data and analysis that anyone can begin to re-claim the time that rightfully belongs to them. This may seem a little harsh but your time is like your money – why give it away or waste it so freely except, of course, on those goals, activities and persons in your life which are important? Managing your time therefore has a number of implications which will affect people close to you, but also how you are

	Monday	Tuesday	Wednesday	Thursday	Friday	Saturday	Sunday
Morning	Domestic stuff	Study 3 hours	Study 3 hours	Shopping	Domestic stuff	Study 2 hours	Study 3 hours
Afternoon	Work 1–4 p.m.	Work 1–4 p.m.	Work 1–4 p.m.	Work 1–4 p.m.	Work 1–4 p.m.	Shopping	Free
Evening	Keep fit	Study 2 hours	Classes	Classes	Study 2 hours	Socializing	Free

30 minutes reading on the train

30 minutes reading on the train

FIGURE 2.3   REVISED WEEKLY SCHEDULE

seen and how you see yourself. Getting the balance between the different and competing elements of making life acceptable is what time management is about. Allocating and managing the time for these kinds of activities may, at times, be about managing the conflict between them and overcoming your want to do something other than what needs to be done. The following principles, shown in Table 2.2, may help you to manage such conflicts and at the same time change your time-using behaviours.

Implementing some of these suggestions and ones you think of may be a little painful at first. This is because we all miss things which we have become used to doing, but often when we reflect on these things we realize there was no real reason for doing them in the first place. You will have this time to do other, more important, things which will give you a better quality of life because you will be doing more real activities that are investments in your life and those around you.

MANAGING YOUR SPACE

A part of being organized is having a space of your own at home. Your research will generate a substantial amount of material which you need to have at hand to consult and the space to use. Articles, books, questionnaires, coding sheets, notes, card indexes, research diaries, literature search profiles, along with various stationery, take up space. We suggest that you make a space for a desk somewhere in your home. The key point is, get space for yourself to work in that is recognized as yours and which is not to be

TABLE 2.2 KEY PRINCIPLES OF TIME MANAGEMENT

Key principles	What they mean	Putting them into practice
• Do what is important.	Do not spend time on low-priority tasks and unnecessary activities.	• Prioritize your tasks. • Use daily and weekly task lists. • Say 'no', do not take on extra work or responsibilities. • Do not aim for perfection. • Stop doing some things like watching soaps on television.
• Direct your effort and energies.	20% of most effort results in 80% of activities.	• Get organized so as not to waste time looking for things. • Plan your time use in advanced, but do not think planning is doing. • Do important intellectual tasks when you are at your best in the day. • Do not procrastinate by doing pleasing jobs which have no value to your research. • Know what you are meant to be doing and do it. • Finish things and do not leave them. • Set deadlines and monitor them – even use a timer with an alarm. • Have a strict routine for domestic tasks and stick to it.
• Reduce time wastage.	Using too much time for some tasks takes time that could be used for your research.	• Set time limits for meetings with supervisors. • Remove distractions from your study space. • Minimize interruptions. • When you finish one job set up the next for your next study session. • Prepare in advance, e.g. food, clothes.

Source: Adapted from Cameron, 1997: ch. 5.

disturbed. When setting up your space the following are suggestions which might help you to stay organized:

♦ Keep your materials organized in ring-binders, magazine boxes and folders. You will be amazed at how much stuff in the form of notes, handouts, photocopies, assessed course work, floppy disks and the like you will generate. It will become increasingly important that you can find stuff when you need it. There are few things more annoying than not being able to find an article you know you have and wasting an hour or more looking for it.

♦ Get equipped with all the necessary pens and paper and keep these on or near your desk. Note taking, jotting ideas, drafting and doing diagrams use up lots of paper, so make sure you have enough and do not have to waste time going out to get more. Do not overdo the stationery by spending money on expensive pens and desk aids. Cheap pens, paper, paper clips, Post-it notes and ring-binders are all you really need and anything else will waste money you could be spending on books.

♦ If possible have your space clear of distractions. Keep photographs and the phone and any other unnecessary stuff away from your work-space. This also goes for the biscuit tin and kettle as it is easy to reach for snacks when things are not going as you want.

♦ It may be that you have a personal computer. This is good but even with major advances in technology they still take up a substantial amount of desk space. Try to keep enough space for writing and spreading out your articles, books and notes.

MANAGING THE LONELINESS AND ISOLATION OF RESEARCH

Doing masters research can be a lonely experience. This is because apart from your supervisor you will, most probably, be the only one really interested in your topic. Friends and family will, as a matter of course, show an interest but will in the main not want to know the details of how your research is progressing. When things do seem as if they could be going better, family and friends may help with encouragement but will not be able to do much more than this. Only you will know what needs to be done and how to do it and, of course, it is supposed to be your research done by you.

There is no way to avoid the loneliness of research, but you can share the feeling with others. Your peers will know what it feels like to be doing research and having only one other person to talk to who knows what it is you are doing. The following are, therefore, some simple suggestions about how to manage the loneliness and to feel as though you are not the only one to experience this when doing your research.

♦ **Establish peer support networks at the start of your masters course. These are small groups of people in your cohort who know the value of talking to one another in order to get the most out of the course you are all doing.**

♦ **Use the peer group network to identify the common issues and problems, and to discuss ideas and tactics to address these. Use Internet discussion facilities to set up a virtual group so that people unable to attend meetings can make contributions.**

♦ **Arrange regular meetings. Use these to focus on particular issues and problems that most of you seem to be experiencing. Think about inviting some of the doctorate researchers along to share their experiences and tactics for coping with doing research.**

♦ **Use the Internet discussion groups of previous cohorts to see what issues they identified and how they addressed them and use these as the basis for discussions among your peers.**

Finding someone else to talk to about your research who understands what it is like to do research can be a help in overcoming the occasional bout of intellectual loneliness. Some degree of isolation is, however, an essential part of the research experience. The times you have on your own to read and think are the times when you will be expanding your intellectual capacity to understand, assimilate and engage, at increasingly higher levels of sophistication, with theory and argument.

NETWORKING

A good graduate school will provide you with opportunities to network with staff and researchers from within and external to your university. You may already be a good 'networker', but if not do not be put off by your lack of experience. Use any opportunities which present themselves to practise your networking skills. As with the other skills and abilities associated with becoming a member of the research community, mixing with your peers is something you can learn to do.

When an opportunity presents itself, such as at a research seminar or conference, talk to someone known for their research. Do not worry if you see yourself as a little shy. Remember that they do not know you and will be only too pleased to talk to you about research. It is also the case that persons you see as being extroverts are not always necessarily good researchers. From my experience some of the most detailed and conscientious research has been done by individuals who would, by their own self-labelling, call themselves shy. Whether you see yourself as a 'theorist', 'pragmatist', 'activist' or 'reflector', face-to-face communication is an essential part of your remit as a masters student.

Life issues

The comments in this section may be construed as controversial. The issues discussed here are complex, not easy to present and will likely annoy some tutors and managers of educational institutions. In all walks of life people will encounter harassment or some form of discriminatory, sexist and exploitative behaviour (from staff as well as other students), and some students and staff may encounter racial or ethnic harassment. The comments that follow are from my postgraduates and illustrate some of the issues they have experienced. We make no claims for the generalizability of these, nor for any standing in research terms.

'I often feel very isolated from the everyday goings on in the Department, as an outsider, because their (male students and staff) conversations aren't usually about research...'

'I know I shouldn't but I always aim for perfection ... I believe my work has to be better than anyone else's for it to be taken seriously ... '

'Dr X is very critical and often dismissive of my work even though I know I work much harder and know far more than most of the men on our course.'

'Some of the staff seem to have one way of talking to the men on our course and another to the women. The men always seem to get praised for the slightest things and the women ignored ... I often feel quite low after certain tutorials, especially when I have done a lot of preparation that wasn't acknowledged.'

'You have to be careful with some of the male students. If you say something in a seminar group that they haven't thought of, they will often repackage it and pass it off as their own. One of them is very fond of saying, "Yes, I thought the same." '

'Dr Y seems to target individual women. He hangs around the notice boards, and often stops you in the corridor or gets in the lift with you … and in the coffee bar he is often with a female undergraduate. Basically his conversations are too personal … He has even asked A and B if they would like a lift home.'

'A couple of them just don't realize that we have to be away by 3.30 to pick up our children … and see us leaving and interpret this as a lack of commitment.'

I believe these comments have some relevance, in that even from the standpoint of a male supervisor, I have witnessed some behaviours by colleagues (male and female) and from students that I have personally believed to be discriminatory, sexist and exploitative. If you have a grievance ensure that you have copies of the relevant policies for your university that cover equal opportunities, grievance procedures and codes of conduct. If you believe you are being subjected to any form of unfair treatment I suggest you do the following:

♦ make contemporaneous notes on all the details;

♦ if possible get your peers to make statements detailing what they have witnessed regarding your case;

♦ consult the policies of the university to see what formal procedures you can use to pursue your grievance; and

♦ if you do not want to make a formal complaint, then you can inform the course director, head of the department or the dean of faculty to make them aware and request they take all the necessary actions to stop the situation. Remember to make notes on any meetings you have with staff, letting them know you are doing so in the meeting itself.

Of course, the majority of supervisors are highly experienced and will do all in their power to make your time productive and enjoyable. The above comments are merely precautionary.

Establishing a document control system

A masters dissertation will generate a lot of material which needs to be kept organized if you want to keep control of it and use it efficiently. You will need a system that works, and this does not mean a vague system based on filing everything on the floor. This is not to say that some floor space, if you can claim some, is not a good thing to have. Figure 2.4 gives an overview of the kinds and amount of materials you will need to manage when doing your dissertation.

Figure 2.4 does not really represent the substantial amount of stuff you will accumulate, but you will soon experience the reality of this as you get further into doing your dissertation. Therefore, before you get swamped with paper and computer files you cannot find because you forgot to make notes on them, think seriously

> Further information on the management of the literature search can be found in Chapter 6, 'Searching and reviewing the literature'.

about your project management system – how you organize your records and materials so that they can be managed. The suggestions which follow are from *Doing a Literature Search* (Hart, 2001) which, in essence, is all about information collection and management, and from Orna and Stevens (1995) about the general principles of managing information during a research project.

The following are the kinds of routine tasks you need to start doing as a part of your document control system:

♦ **Set up a physical filing system. Use a physical store to keep and index articles and copies of materials that you have made. You will collect many of these during your search. It is important to index and write an abstract for each of them and file them so that they can be retrieved when you need them.**

♦ **Set up files on your computer. Create and give consecutive file names to your bibliographies and working notes, and place these into directories on your computer. Put each chapter and parts of a chapter on separate memory devices to avoid over-writing and the loss of your data. Do not use an obscure software application but stick to common applications. Make a record in your search log of the names and content of your files and remember to delete files you do not need to avoid having multiple versions of a file on your computer and disks. Use easily recognizable file names, for example, 'ch1 introduction v1'.**

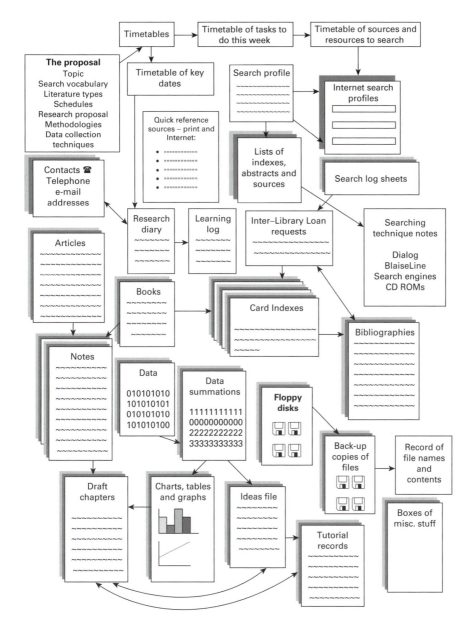

FIGURE 2.4   DIVERSE ELEMENTS FOR MANAGING A MASTERS DISSERTATION

♦ Make back-up files of your computer files at least once each week. Keep these in a safe place. As well as making copies of your files onto other memory devices you can send them via e-mail to a friend who has consented to store your copies on their machine. You can do this by incorporating the file-back-up task into your timetable of tasks to be done. All too often disks are lost or damaged and with a back-up you will avoid retracing work you have already done.

♦ Do printouts of your computer files as well as making copies of all your files after each time you work on one. Although this can be time-consuming, if by some chance a disaster does strike and you lose all your files, including the back-ups, at least you will have a hard copy to work from. Regular printouts will also give you material you can carry around with you to examine and analyse when you get the time.

CITING YOUR SOURCES AND CREATING BIBLIOGRAPHIES

As you identify relevant materials, such as articles, you need to record these in your bibliographies. It is important to take the citation details of every item you come across that you deem relevant to your research.

Citing references and attribution

You must keep full bibliographic details of items you find during your search. As you will probably have several sub-topics within your general topic, this means using your card index to construct several bibliographies in which some of the cards will be duplicates. Record the full bibliographic details of items that you have identified as relevant. The alternative is to try and remember the details, which is impossible, especially when you are likely to have 50 to 70 references for an undergraduate project and many more for a postgraduate dissertation or thesis. In *Doing a Literature Search*, Appendix 4, 'How to cite sources', you will find suggestions on how to cite references for a range of material including the Internet, but for further advice and updates see websites such as the following, which give links to the major sources on how to cite materials:

♦ *Librarian's Index to the Internet* (http://lii.org/).

♦ *The World Wide Web Virtual Library* (www.spaceless.com).

The full citation of other people's work is essential: this is known as 'attribution' – the scholarly standard of acknowledging where ideas in your own work have their origins. Not only is it unethical to use someone else's work without referencing it, but it can be an infringement of copyright to do so. Therefore make a record of the bibliographic details of work you consider relevant to your topic to ensure that you acknowledge the work of others that you use in your own research.

Creating bibliographies

There are various methods you can use to construct and maintain a bibliography. The manual method amounts to establishing a card index with each item being indexed on to one or more cards. The cards are then arranged in some logical order, say, alphabetically. However, given the massive amount of literature available, many researchers use electronic means to store, organize and retrieve citations. There are a number of ways a personal computer can be used to create a personal bibliography. In practice it is easier to record bibliographic items first on cards and then to transfer these to a personal computer. A simple card index for book materials might look like the example shown in Figure 2.5.

> **Tip:** you can print out the bibliographic details of articles and books from your searches of CD ROMS and stick them on to cards to save writing them out by hand.

A range of software for constructing bibliographies is widely available. Some people adapt word-processing packages, while others invest in dedicated software. Even the most simple of word-processing packages can provide a means to produce lists of items that can be regularly updated. The more sophisticated packages enable the researcher to print selections of records in a variety of formats for different document types. One of the most popular commercial bibliographical packages is *ProCite*, from CiteWise.com (a division of Cherwell Scientific).

The key advantages of electronic databases are:

♦ **you can extract bibliographical records in a variety of predetermined formats to suit different needs, for example, the different requirements of different journals;**

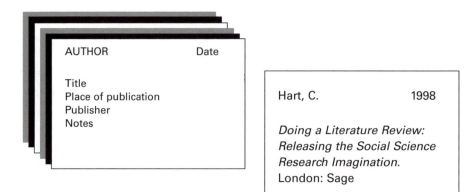

FIGURE 2.5   EXAMPLE OF A CARD INDEX

♦ you can search the bibliography using key words;

♦ you can automatically arrange the items according to different criteria, for example, date of publication, by author or by key word;

♦ you can check the spelling of author names and titles in your text;

♦ you can add notes to annotate the record;

♦ you can download data from CD ROM and online databases into the bibliography;

♦ you can make automatic changes to the typography to meet the needs of different journal styles;

♦ you can edit records easily and transfer them to other parts of the database; and

♦ you can copy all or part of the database to create a card index that you can carry with you when you need to check something, say in the library.

USING THE COMPUTER

It will be expected, by your university, that you have a computer that is capable of being used to produce a dissertation. This normally means that it will have the necessary capacity and software to enable you to produce text, figures, tables and graphs and that it is connected to the Internet. There will be computers you can use at your university; some will be for specialist searching of databases not available to the general public and some to enable you to do statistical analysis of data.

A computer is an essential tool that will help you to produce your dissertation. While we cannot give any guides to specification because these change so fast, I do recommend that prior to starting your masters course you obtain information on what computers and kinds (and versions) of common software they use. It will make such things as word-processing much easier if you use the same software package as used on the university's computers. This will ensure that you have compatibility and can get on with work when you are at university or at home.

KEEPING A RESEARCH DIARY AND A LEARNING LOG

It is very important to maintain a diary of your activities when doing your research. We are using the word diary in the sense of research as well as in the conventional sense of a calendar of dates. The main reasons for keeping a diary are:

♦ you can plan key dates in advance and agree deadlines;

♦ you will then be able to plan your work so as to meet your deadlines; and

♦ contacts, web addresses, details of books and so on can be noted in your diary and transferred to your other files at a later date.

Your diary is in effect a log of your research. It will become a record of what you did, when you did it, with what and what the outcomes were. It will become a reminder of what needs to be done and what things, such as inter-library loans, need to be followed up. Your diary is then a working document and a source of information for your dissertation. As a record of your activities your diary will provide you with the necessary details to help you evaluate your research, and this is usually included in the concluding chapter of your dissertation.

One method of keeping a research diary is to use it in two main ways. The first is as a plan of your activities, as you would use a conventional diary. The second is to use

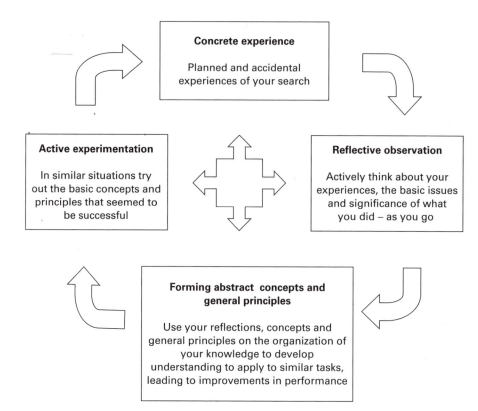

FIGURE 2.6   THE LEARNING CYCLE
Source: Adapted from Kolb et al., 1984.

it as a learning tool. This means that every time you think you have acquired new knowledge, a different viewpoint or skill, you make a note of what it is and how it was acquired. Figure 2.6 shows this as the learning cycle. This figure is derived from the work of Kolb, Rubin and MacIntyre (1984), who suggest that learning can be viewed as a circular process where experience is followed by attempts to make sense of that experience through reflection and contemplation. A part of this is conceptualizing the nature of the experience in more abstract terms in order to think about how its principles may be adapted and applied to other situations, often experimenting with them to see what happens. The whole process then begins again, going around as if circular. This approach can be used when things go right and when they go wrong. For example, when you have a block in thinking you can reflect on how it was overcome to think about its nature and possible causes. The irony here should not be missed. In practising this approach you may soon come to realize that perfection is not what is required and that it is a sign of your growing confidence the more you come to see and do only that which is required.

This approach to learning has links to the learning styles we introduced in Chapter 1. As an activist you will learn how to conceptualize, as a reflector you will learn to experiment, as a pragmatist you will learn to reflect and as a theorist you will learn look for experiences. The more you do the more resilient in attitude and behaviour you will become and this will show in the increasing levels of attainment you will be achieving. This will also show in your increasing resourcefulness in that you will learn and be able to apply an increasing number of techniques to learning. Finally, the more you learn and are able to achieve will be in part due to your increasing capacity to reflect on and about your experiences to such a degree that your analytical abilities will reach depths you never thought possible for yourself. This is the promise of masters research, but for now once you have begun the habit of *learning how to learn* you will soon experience, to greater degrees, the different learning styles. This will mean you will not only develop as a person, but you will be able to do many more things than you previously thought possible. In this way you will acquire, in addition to skills, a range of attitudes and qualities which are essential for the capable and confident masters graduate.

SUMMARY OF THIS CHAPTER

This chapter has attempted to provide guidance on how to manage the transition from work or undergraduate studies to doing a masters and has emphasized the following:

♦ It is important to establish a balance between your research and your 'real' life.

♦ You need to organize yourself and your materials for effective and efficient working.

♦ Time management is an absolute for most successful dissertations.

♦ Use your experiences as an opportunity to learn new ways of learning and working and by doing so you will become more resilient, resourceful and be able to reflect on how you learnt and so be able know how to learn more.

Further reading

Hart, C. (2001) *Doing a Literature Search: A Comprehensive Guide for the Social Sciences*. London: Sage. Chapter 3 'Search management' provides examples of search logs.

Silverman, D. (2000) *Doing Qualitative Research: A Practical Handbook*. London: Sage. Chapter 2 'The research experience' contains examples of research diaries kept by doctoral students.

3 Finding and formulating your topic

Your first rite of passage into the world of research is finding a topic for your dissertation. You can make the process difficult by ignoring the advice of your supervisors and this book or you can work through the tactics we suggest here and enjoy the challenge. The main problems some of our students seem to have in identifying potential topics are that they have misconceptions about what a masters research topic is. In this chapter we will look at some criteria to use when thinking about a topic, at sources for generating ideas for a topic and at ways to formulate your ideas into a topic capable of resulting in a masters dissertation. The stages and processes of this are shown in Figure 3.1. The main purpose of this chapter is to address the following kinds of questions:

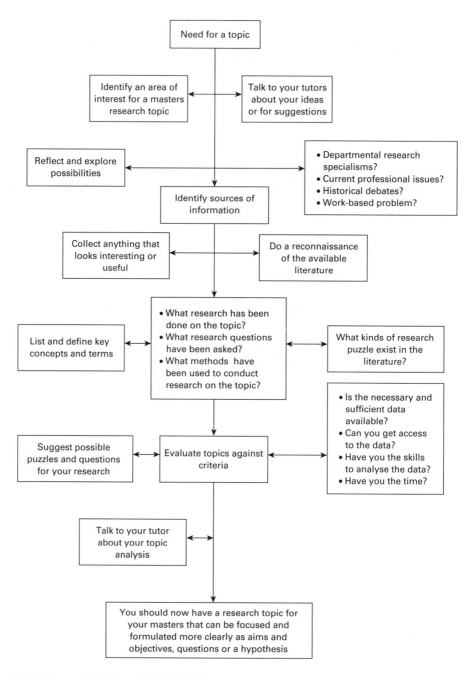

FIGURE 3.1   FINDING A PROPER TOPIC

1   What kinds of topic are suitable for masters level research?

2   What are research aims and objectives? How should they be written?

3   What is a hypothesis and proposition? Does all research need them?

4   How can a topic be justified?

We end the chapter by looking at defining your research topic in terms of how to formulate good research questions and hypotheses and aims and objectives, but for now we begin with some misconceptions about masters research itself.

Misconceptions about topics

There is the misconception that masters research should be something that makes a difference to the world, something that has an impact on our views or understanding and therefore, in some way, makes a contribution to the stock of scientifically acquired knowledge. There is nothing wrong with wanting to do research that has an impact for the good of human kind, that advances, in whatever way and to whatever degree, the stock of knowledge and ways of understanding the world around us. But at masters level these goals should not be paramount or be the criteria for topic selection.

The generally held belief that masters level research is about discovery, change and knowledge generation needs to be placed to one side. This belief about the nature of masters research is, however, quite understandable. It follows the general view that research is about discovery and bettering the conditions of human kind. This view often has the associations of the 'scientist' in the lab surrounded by expensive-looking equipment, working long hours on a 'problem', facing setbacks, fighting bureaucracy but eventually being triumphant against the odds. Historically there have been such people and their endeavours have been the subject of cinema and television. It may be that such representations are in part responsible for this view of research. The only aspect of reality from this that you may encounter is the problem with bureaucracy. The rest is largely myth.

For now it is important to understand that masters level research is not primarily about discovery or making an original contribution to knowledge, though it may do this. If it does, this should normally be a secondary consideration to the primary function of your dissertation. This function is to demonstrate your skills and abilities to do research at masters level. Your topic is, in the main, a vehicle for you to display your skills and abilities as a researcher and to demonstrate that you have the qualities and attitudes required to be a potential member of the broader research community and to be considered capable of being a research assistant or going on to do doctoral research. It is the same for the work-based dissertation, but in addition you also have to demonstrate the ability to be a practitioner and researcher and be able to manage the issues this involves. The topic you choose should therefore have the features necessary for you to exhibit the skills, capabilities, attitudes and qualities which are subject to assessment.

What is a topic?

Topics suitable for masters level research come in a variety of shapes and formats. Finding a topic is, however, essentially about formulating a set of questions or hypotheses that require research of some kind in order that answers can be provided or statements put to the test. The range and types of question that can be asked and the kinds of hypotheses which can be stated mean that there are an infinite number of topics. Added to this is the point that not all research topics require the collection of primary data. Some can be based on the existing literature and in such cases the literature becomes the data. What counts as data or evidence also varies, but is often closely related to the way the topic has been formulated and the preferences made for how it is to be researched. The common denominator for all research topics is that they are puzzles in need of investigation.

TOPICS AS PUZZLES

A puzzle is something requiring, if possible, a solution. I say 'if possible' because not all puzzles can be solved, and many of those which appear to have been solved can be subject to modification or different solutions by other research. By puzzle I mean something generally or specifically not known and therefore requiring sensible questions to be asked that are capable of solving the puzzle or a part of it. There are different kinds of puzzles and the main ones can be seen by using words in the research questions such as 'when', 'why', 'how', 'who' and 'what'. For example, the following are some simple puzzles capable of being refined to provide a focused set of questions:

♦ How are crime statistics related to crime?

♦ Why and how did Durkheim define suicide in the way he did?

♦ When and why did the romance novel become popular?

♦ What are the variables in television news selection?

♦ What are the key variables reproducing the cycle of deprivation?

We will shortly look at how to focus these general kinds of questions, but we will first look at the kinds of puzzles each exhibit. In Table 3.1, following Jennifer Mason's (1996) categorization of puzzles, we have identified five main types of intellectual puzzle which form the basis of research.

TABLE 3.1   DIFFERENT KINDS OF PUZZLE

Kinds of puzzle	Description	
Developmental puzzle	This is the *how much of Y exists or why did X develop?* Example: how and why did Durkheim define social order in the way he did? And what consequences have this had on the development of sociology?	Descriptive and illuminative research puzzles
Mechanical puzzle	This is the *how does X work?* Example: how are crime statistics compiled? And how is crime defined and how does this and the process of compiling the figures create the statistics for criminality?	
Correlational puzzle	This is the *what, if any, relationship is there between variable x and variable y?* You are attempting to identify if there is a relation-ship, association or no relationship between variables.	Correlational and explanatory research puzzles
Casual puzzle	This is the *why does (or strongly influences) x cause y?* Example: among the many events which occur daily, what variables influence the selection of stories for inclusion in the news? And what is seen (definitional work) by news selectors to count as newsworthy and why?	
Essence puzzle	This is the *why is X assumed?* Example: why is generality assumed to be the gaol of science? And what would the advantages be if this goal were put to one side to describe the essential features (essence) of phenomena rather than trying to explain them?	Ethnomethodological research puzzles

Source: Adapted from Mason, 1996.

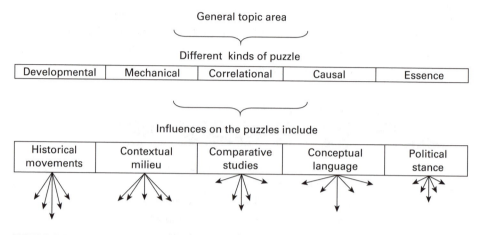

FIGURE 3.2   TOPIC PUZZLES AND INFLUENCES

We will look more closely at some real examples that illustrate the structure of these puzzles throughout this book. For now it is relevant to see how different kinds of puzzle give rise to many sub-puzzles due to the influence of history, context, comparison, concepts and political stance. In Figure 3.2 we can see the place of the different puzzles within the general scheme of a topic and I have attempted to indicate the different directions research may take as a result of these influences.

Figure 3.2 has been constructed from what Silverman (2000) suggests are the kinds of influences that can be used to sensitize you to various research issues. We have changed these a little and added 'conceptual language' and 'comparative studies' to his list, which are summarized in Table 3.2.

PUZZLES AS RIDDLES TO BE UNRIDDLED

One way of understanding puzzles is, according to Pertti Alasuutari (1995), to see them as riddles to be formulated and then to be unriddled – solved in some way. If we take this idea and synthesize it with Silverman's 'influences', then we have the basis for identifying a range of perspectives we may use when framing our topic. Hence, while I agree with Silverman, I would also recommend that these influences might be used to help you generate an understanding of a topic and then begin the processes of focusing in on a puzzle that has real researchability. Your focus may be on any one or a combination of the following:

TABLE 3.2   SENSITIVITIES INFLUENCING RESEARCH

Sensitivity	Amplification
Historical movements	The main elements of this are: (a) research is often closely related to intellectual movements and counter-movements of the time in which it was done, such as structural functionalism (1940s/50s), conflict structuralism (1960s/70s), symbolic interactionism (1960s), post-structuralism (1980s); and (b) the historical origins of research puzzles and developments in knowledge can usually be traced and their methodological assumptions identified as being, for example, foundationalist, positivist, anti-positivist.
Contextual milieu	The contextual elements which sometimes influence research are the social, economic, political, technological and legal variables deemed important at the time of the research. Within these are the policy movements which are receiving the most attention. These are often expressed in general phrases that imply a contrast or/and development from a previous state such as 'post-industrial society', 'information society' and 'knowledge economy'.
Comparative studies	'Poverty', 'mental illness', 'immigration' and 'sexuality' are categorizations used in many research studies, but have different uses based on different definitions, criteria and methodological approaches. From meta-theoretical studies to in-depth case studies, these kinds of categories result in different kinds of research depending on the purpose and preferences of the researcher. Hence, 'mental illness' is not a phenomenon able to be uniformly defined, but is dependent on context and historically-rooted definitions.
Conceptual language	Different perspectives in the social sciences, such as symbolic interactionism and post-modernism, have languages made up of concepts intended to describe and sensitize us to different kinds of social dynamics. Examples from the interactionist Erving Goffman include, 'stigmatization', 'presentation of the self', 'managing the self' and 'degradation ceremony'. This language is the discourse of the perspective and provides, like the discourse of other perspectives, a framework for understanding phenomena.
Political stance	A substantial amount of research is politically motivated and is aimed at revealing patterns of relationships such as 'inequality', 'discrimination', 'exploitation', and these are often seen as being a part of broader conceptual theories which attempt to explain 'inequality' as part of different forms of social organization, such as capitalism or patriarchy.

Source: Adapted from Silverman, 2000.

♦ the historical development and origins of a puzzle, revisiting the basic assumptions which were used and scrutinizing the data collected and interpretations made at the time, to identify alternative starting points and mis-interpretations of seminal works;

♦ the contextual milieu when the research on the puzzle was done, including cultural assumptions of the time, place and social group and on the use of various categorizations such 'political system' and contrasts categories used such as 'pre-industrial and industrial' and 'primitive and advanced', to identify the influences of cultural assumptions on classifications, research design and interpretations;

♦ comparative studies and findings from the same and different disciplines done at different times using different approaches, to compare and contrast in order to identify gaps and possibilities for the further development of a particular study;

♦ the concepts used to describe and categorize phenomena such as 'alienation', 'power' and 'control', analysing how these have been defined and operationalized in different studies, and how they have framed and restricted paradigmatic understanding of a topic, to identify other definitions and situations where they can be employed to understand social situations and dynamics; and

♦ the political and ethical biases in research to identify preconceived assumptions and their consequences, of the ways in which topics have been selected due to their usefulness in demonstrating the validity of assumptions, to critically evaluate such demonstrations and suggest alternative approaches which are less value-laden and biased.

Sensitivities can be useful to place into context a problem you are considering. They can help you to start the process of scrutinizing the literature by asking questions such as: How are these concepts related?; What definitions have been proposed for this phenomenon?; and What standpoint has this research been done from?

Basic advice on research topics

There are a number of points we can make at this stage to help you select an appropriate topic for your masters dissertation. The prerequisite to this advice is that whatever topic is finally chosen, it should be capable of resulting in a complete dissertation in the time you have available. This may seem obvious, but many good ideas for a topic cannot be done in the normal period of time expected for a masters dissertation. Most topics will take a lot longer to research than most people initially estimate. A good rule of thumb is to estimate how long the research will take you, triple that estimate and then consult with your tutor who, you will find, will add more time on to it. Research is very time-consuming. So how do you find a topic capable of being done in six to nine months for a full-time student and 12 to 16 months for the part-time student? The six kinds of advice we offer you are:

1 **The earlier you start the better.**

2 **Go from the general to the particular.**

3 **Avoid politicized topics.**

4 **Be careful with personal issues.**

5 **Find the line of least resistance between A and B.**

6 **Airing your topic.**

THE EARLIER YOU START THE BETTER

When is the best time to start thinking about and looking for a suitable topic? The answer is the earlier the better. The sooner you start to think about and investigate possible topics for research, the sooner you will decide on one and can begin to develop your research proposal. The earlier you select a topic, the more time you will have to do the research. This means you may be able to undertake research on a topic that requires slightly longer than another, or one you can investigate in a little more depth or use data collection techniques that are more sophisticated. As soon as you start your masters course, begin to think about and discuss with your tutors ideas for topics.

GO FROM THE GENERAL TO THE PARTICULAR

Think of the task of identifying a topic as a process of refinement. This will mean going from the general area in which you would like to do research to the particular aspect that you can do research in. The general area can be something like, 'moral panics', 'construction of statistics', 'analysis of advertisements', 'history of science', 'experience of immigration' or whatever. These phrases are broad categories that can often be used to tell others, when they ask, what your research is about. They are the higher-level abstract designators that can be used to look for specific research questions which may have the potential for a masters dissertation.

If there is an area you have an interest in, then consult with your tutor and ask if they have any suggestions for specific research in that area. At the same time do some visualization of what a topic might look like in terms of what else can be done in the area and can form the basis for your research. This may mean reading some secondary sources on the area to get an overview of what has been done, what kinds of assumptions have been made and where the general interest in the area came from. Figure 3.3 shows what we mean by this using the example of 'moral panic'.

In this example we can see how the phrase 'moral panic' can be used to investigate its origins, previous uses and how it may be used to generate an idea for a topic. In particular it shows how we can begin to think about the necessary issue of the availability of sufficient data.

AVOID POLITICIZED TOPICS

What is your motivation for doing the research? Your primary motivation should be to acquire and develop your research skills and capabilities alongside the necessary attitude of reflection that will help you to demonstrate your research qualities. You should avoid topics that you want to use to demonstrate a political argument or forward a moral cause. As with personal issues, politicized causes as research topics are inherently problematic. They take with them motivations that have little to do with the research and more to do with providing evidence for the cause.

If you intend to do such research, be clear on your reasons and how you will ensure the validity and reliability of your research. For example, we recently had a student who wanted to investigate what are called 'holocaust denialists' arguments' on the Internet. These are individuals and groups who deny that the extermination of 6 million Jews (and others including gypsies, Catholics, homosexuals and trade unionists) in Nazi concentration camps ever took place. This is a topic fraught with emotion, politics and prejudices and because of this is a difficult one to research clearly in an objective manner.

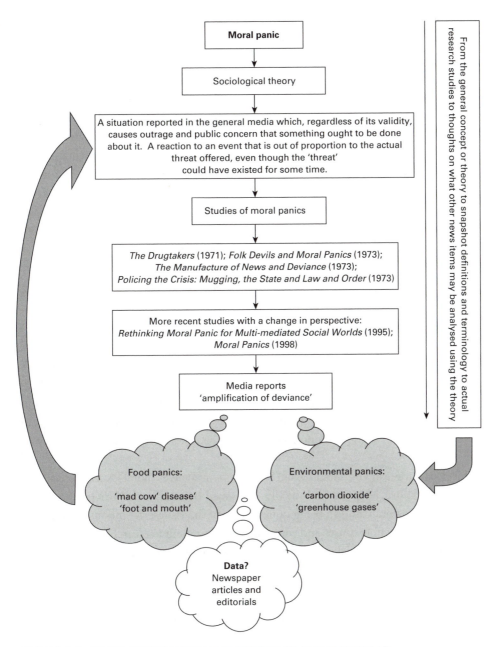

FIGURE 3.3   TOPIC ANALYSIS FROM THE GENERAL TO THE PARTICULAR

These problems were compounded by the student having a Jewish heritage and therefore the research committee of the university preferred her not to research the topic. However, because of the importance of the topic she was allowed to go ahead but under strict guidance from her supervisor, who insisted she took the denialist arguments seriously and took as her research puzzle the construction of their argument and compared these with the counter-arguments against the denialists to find out how something that had been historically documented and taken for granted could be challenged. Her dissertation became an investigation into argumentation and evidence, carefully analysing and describing the argumentative structures and use of evidence from opposing sides. She therefore looked carefully at the validity and relia-bility of historical evidence as a research puzzle and did not use any emotive language in her conclusions or allow her own (understandable) feelings to be expressed. This is the kind of topic that may be important to investigate but is very difficult to do in practice. You may wish to reflect on how you would have done such a project and what reasons you could give for going ahead despite the problems.

BE CAREFUL WITH PERSONAL ISSUES

If there is an issue you feel strongly about and have an 'axe to grind', do not choose this as your research topic. For example, euthanasia or abortion are topics which are embed-ded with substantial moral debates and from a research perspective will involve serious consideration of ethical issues. With such topics it would be difficult to start your research without a set of preconceived beliefs and attitudes toward the main issues.

This does not mean you should avoid research that involves moral issues. Topics such as poverty, abuse, adoption and the like are issued based. But this has not prevented many good research studies being done to clarify the issues, definitions or processes or to identify possible causes and consequences. Standpoint research – as it is called – is often the basis for social policy research and therefore has an important place in the social sciences.

FIND THE LINE OF LEAST RESISTANCE BETWEEN A AND B

If we take it that the objective of masters research is to produce a dissertation of sufficient quality to be deemed 'masters level' and that the means to this is doing research, then the less complex the research to be done the more likely it is that the dissertation will be done on time and to the required standard. This means selecting a topic that can not only answer 'yes' to the following questions, but provides the simplest of routes to 'yes':

◆ **Is the data available?**

◆ **Can you get access to the data?**

◆ **Have you the skills to analyse the data?**

Data for providing answers to your puzzle must be available. This means the data – whatever this is – must be 'out there' and be of the necessary kind. The sources of your data must be identifiable at the outset. You should be able to say what data is needed for your puzzle and why it is needed. Second, you need to be able to get access to the data. If you need responses from senior managers in the health services, what would make you believe they would be willing to fill in a questionnaire for you or even spend time allowing you to interview them? Third, do you know how you will manage and then analyse your data? Knowing that the kinds of data you need can be obtained is not enough; you also need to know how you will use this data to answer your research questions and/or test your hypothesis. If your statistical knowledge and skills are basic, quantitative data requiring analytical statistical techniques may not be a practical consideration.

If your time restricts opportunities to go into the field, you may consider doing a topic that suits your situation. This means looking for a puzzle in a topic area that can be done using desk-based research. This could be the analysis of a debate in the social sciences, the testing of criteria used to evaluate an Internet-based information source, the study of extracts of conversation or a media production. You will still need to search and review the literature, design instruments for the collection of your data and identify suitable techniques to analyse it. This is not a simpler strategy for doing your research, but one among the many alternatives open to you.

AIRING YOUR TOPIC

Each discipline in the social sciences seems to have its own preferences on what constitutes an appropriate way to do research and this often influences the kinds of topic expected from masters students. Be prepared for some degree of disciplinary and departmental opposition from some of your tutors. If you are studying in a department known for its quantitative research, then expect your tutors to express this when evaluating your research suggestions. But do not be afraid to put forward a topic and methodology that differs from the norm. Many interesting pieces of research, at all levels, were initially seen as deviations from the expected. If you follow this track, of pushing at the boundaries, then be prepared confidently to justify your topic using sound argument and evidence.

Sources for generating ideas

There are many sources you can use to begin generating ideas for your research. This process may even begin before you go to university to do your masters degree, and in Chapter 1 we made some observations about this that are also relevant here. Do not expect a sudden creative vision that leads to your research topic. Bright ideas for a topic are usually the outcome of research and reflection. Typical sources for initial ideas include the following:

♦ **Taught modules you are doing on your course. Have you covered a topic that interested you, which you would like to look at in more detail?**

♦ **Has a tutor mentioned a research study that you found interesting, even puzzling, that you feel needs questioning?**

♦ **If you are doing your masters as part of a professional qualification, look in the profession's journal to see what the current issues and concerns are and if these have a research possibility.**

♦ **At work, if your research is to be work-based, what are the main issues, development needs and management problems that require some research?**

♦ **Have you listened to a visiting speaker to your department who talked about a project that may have other possibilities?**

♦ **Are you interested in particular phenomena that you cannot find much about in the library?**

♦ **Have you observed a pattern of behaviour you found interesting or perplexing and would like to find out more about?**

♦ **What projects are staff working on; do these interest you?**

Analysing the possibilities of a topic

Once you have an idea for a topic and have discussed this with your tutor(s), you need to go to the library and investigate its possibilities. This means identifying sources of information, obtaining some literature and subjecting it to an initial scrutiny. The main stage in this part of the process is the initial search and review of the literature to identify research possibilities.

THE INITIAL SEARCH AND REVIEW OF THE LITERATURE

Use the library and not the Internet to plan an indicative search of the available literature. This is the literature that is in your library or available in electronic format – literature that can be obtained within a couple of days. In Chapter 6 we show you how to do a comprehensive search and review of the literature. If, however, you already have an advanced understanding of the topic area, then use the following books to ensure that you have the necessary skills for bringing your knowledge of the literature up to date:

♦ *Doing a Literature Search: A Comprehensive Guide for the Social Sciences* (Hart, 2001).

♦ *Doing a Literature Review: Releasing the Social Science Imagination* (Hart, 1998).

At this stage of your research you should be doing a reconnaissance of the library. Do not aim to define your main concepts or formulate clear research questions, but enjoy the freedom you have to explore the possibilities for your topic. This means looking to provide overviews that help you to have a basic understanding of two sets of questions. The first set is about the topic area itself and the second about the methods that have been used to do research into the topic area.

Topic questions

Once you begin to obtain some of the literature – books, articles and reports – subject it to a brief speed read. You are not looking to make copious notes on the details from individual books or articles, but to get an overview of the context of your topic. Look in your search for literature that provides initial answers to the following kinds of questions:

+ **What are the key texts and authors on the general topic area?**

+ **What concepts and theories have been used on the topic?**

+ **What is the history of the topic?**

+ **What kinds of arguments are there about the topic?**

Even a rudimentary understanding of the origins and context of the topic will enable you to start thinking about the possibilities for your own research. It will provide you with research themes and issues which have been developed and debated by researchers in the topic area. With this knowledge as your frame of reference you can begin the work of looking for a topic that has a research focus. This may mean developing a piece of research that has already been done or analysing contributions to a debate about the topic.

Methodology and data questions

By looking at the research elements of studies you obtain, you are aiming to understand how the studies were done and, if possible, what kinds of methodological approaches (that is, quantitative or qualitative) and assumptions were used. The kinds of questions you need to be asking are:

+ **Has anyone else done research on this topic?**

+ **If so, how?**

+ **What research questions did they ask?**

+ **Did they use an hypothesis?**

+ **What methodology and data collection tools did they use?**

+ **What did they find?**

Do not worry if you find that someone else has done research on a topic you have in mind to do. It is often possible to deconstruct existing research, to critique it and find ways of developing it in ways different from the original. The social sciences have many examples of this process. For example, sociological research into the phenomenon of suicide has its origins in the seminal study by Emile Durkheim, but many others have been done since, each exhibiting a different approach. Some of these can be seen in Figure 3.4, which indicates the range of different approaches that have been used from Durkheim's original positivistic approach to interpretivist, ethnomethodological and conversation analysis.

Validity and reliability questions

Although most research in the social sciences is valid and honest, some of it has dubious foundations. As with all forms of research, including that done in the physical sciences, there is a degree of unsubstantiated generalization, political and ethical bias and, on rare occasions, fraud. The two classic cases of the latter are the work of Cyril Burt on intelligence (Beloff, 1980) and the work of Bruno Bettelheim (1976) on the psychology of fairytales. Both exemplify how a person can reach the top of their profession, receive numerous accolades yet, as in the case of Burt, base his work on non-existent research, while Bettelheim gained fame by plagiarizing the work of another.

Do not assume that because a piece of research has been published or has attracted attention that it is valid and provides a solid foundation for your research. This does not mean you use extreme scepticism, but exercise moderate scepticism when you come across something that is taken for granted as *knowledge* or *fact*. Remember to ask your tutors about the research you find in the literature, especially about what they know of its origins and how it fits into the broader context.

WHERE YOU SHOULD NOW BE

Your reconnaissance of the literature in the library should have given you sufficient information, such as the names of authors, words and phrases used to describe the topic, and an understanding of the structure of knowledge on the topic. In Table 3.3 the essential information and knowledge that you will obtain from your initial search and review of the literature is summarized.

While Table 3.3 shows you the range and kind of information you will gather during an initial search of the literature, Figure 3.5 shows a simplified map of the main questions, concepts, methodological assumptions and methodological approaches for the

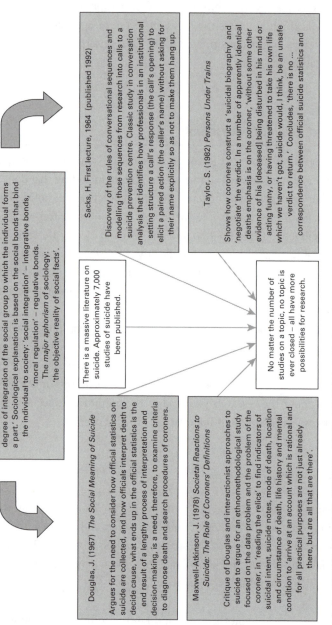

Seminal study

Durkheim (1897) *Suicide*

Statistical study presents 'social explanation': 'suicide varies ... with the degree of integration of the social group to which the individual forms a part.' Sociological explanation is based on the social bonds that bind the individual to society: 'social integration' – integrative bonds, 'moral regulation' – regulative bonds. The *major aphorism* of sociology: 'the objective reality of social facts'.

Douglas, J. (1967) *The Social Meaning of Suicide*

Argues for the need to consider how official statistics on suicide are collected, and how officials interpret death to decide cause, what ends up in the official statistics is the end result of a lengthy process of interpretation and decision-making, is a need, therefore, to examine criteria to diagnose death and search procedures of coroners.

Maxwell-Atkinson, J. (1978) *Societal Reactions to Suicide: The Role of Coroners' Definitions*

Critique of Douglas and interactionist approaches to suicide to argue for an ethnomethodological study focused on the data problem and the problem of the coroner, in 'reading the relics' to find indicators of suicidal intent, suicide notes, mode of death, location and circumstance of death, life history and mental condition to 'arrive at an account which is rational and for all practical purposes are not just already there, but are all that are there'.

There is a massive literature on suicide. Approximately 7,000 studies of suicide have been published.

Sacks, H. First lecture, 1964 (published 1992)

Discovery of the rules of conversational sequences and modelling those sequences from research into calls to a suicide prevention centre. Classic study in conversation analysis that identifies how professionals in an institutional setting structure a call's response (the call's opening) to elicit a paired action (the caller's name) without asking for their name explicitly so as not to make them hang up.

Taylor, S. (1982) *Persons Under Trains*

Shows how coroners construct a 'suicidal biography' and 'negotiate' the verdict. In a number of apparently identical deaths emphasis is on the coroner, 'without some other evidence of his [deceased] being disturbed in his mind or acting funny, or having threatened to take his own life which we haven't got, suicide would, I think, be an unsafe verdict to return.' Concludes, 'there is no ... correspondence between official suicide statistics and

No matter the number of studies on a topic, no topic is ever closed – all have more possibilities for research.

FIGURE 3.4 SOCIOLOGY AND SUICIDE: SAME GENERAL TOPIC, DIFFERENT WAYS OF RESEARCHING IT

TABLE 3.3 OUTCOMES FROM AN INITIAL SEARCH AND REVIEW OF THE LITERATURE

Outcomes	Questions
An initial bibliography of texts on the topic. A list of the key authors on the topic.	What are the key texts and authors on the general topic area?
A list of the main concepts used in works on the topic. A list of the main theories used by individual and groups of authors to account for the topic.	What concepts and theories have been used on the topic?
The origins and seminal works that gave rise to and initially defined the topic.	What is the history of the topic?
The historical development of the topic in terms of arguments and debates over theories, concepts and data. This includes the different perspectives, standpoints and approaches which have been taken to frame and understand the topic.	What kinds of arguments are there about the topic?
An understanding of how others have designed their research to investigate an aspect of the topic.	Has anyone else done research on this topic? If so, how?
A list of research questions which have been asked and an understanding of what has been considered important within the topic for research.	What research questions did they ask?
Identification of hypotheses which have been constructed and tested and how they were tested using what kinds of evidence.	Did they use an hypothesis? If so, what type?
An initial understanding of the methodological assumptions which were used and preferences for particular methodological approaches (quantitative or qualitative). An understanding of the main data collection tools commonly used.	What methodology and data collection tools did they use?
Lists of key findings from the main research studies. These can be used to make comparisons and identify gaps and need for further developments of particular studies.	What did they find?

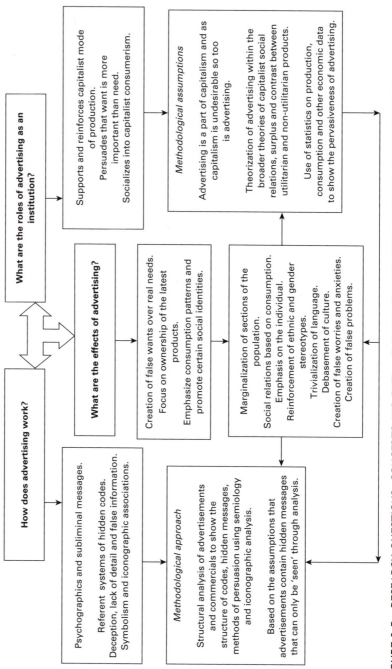

How does advertising work?

Psychographics and subliminal messages.

Referent systems of hidden codes.
Deception, lack of detail and false information.
Symbolism and iconographic associations.

Methodological approach

Structural analysis of advertisements
and commercials to show the
structure of codes, hidden messages,
methods of persuasion using semiology
and iconographic analysis.

Based on the assumptions that
advertisements contain hidden messages
that can only be 'seen' through analysis.

What are the effects of advertising?

Creation of false wants over real needs.
Focus on ownership of the latest
products.
Emphasize consumption patterns and
promote certain social identities.

Marginalization of sections of the
population.
Social relations based on consumption.
Emphasis on the individual.
Reinforcement of ethnic and gender
stereotypes.
Trivialization of language.
Debasement of culture.
Creation of false worries and anxieties.
Creation of false problems.

**What are the roles of advertising as an
institution?**

Supports and reinforces capitalist mode
of production.
Persuades that want is more
important than need.
Socializes into capitalist consumerism.

Methodological assumptions

Advertising is a part of capitalism and as
capitalism is undesirable so too
is advertising.

Theorization of advertising within the
broader theories of capitalist social
relations, surplus and contrast between
utilitarian and non-utilitarian products.

Use of statistics on production,
consumption and other economic data
to show the pervasiveness of advertising.

FIGURE 3.5   RESEARCH QUESTIONS, CONCEPTS AND DATA – THE EXAMPLE OF SOCIAL SCIENCE AND ADVERTISING

social science treatment of advertising. Figure 3.5 is intended to demonstrate how you can use diagrammatic representations of a topic to summarize key concerns, the research questions that have been asked and also to begin the task of identifying the methodological assumptions used for research into a topic.

USE REFERENCE AIDS

It can be useful to have at hand a selection of reference tools. These may be social science dictionaries and encyclopaedias which will help you to find quickly short summaries and definitions of key concepts and theories. Useful reference sources which you will normally find in most academic libraries include the following and are often quicker to use than electronic sources you find on the Internet:

♦ **The Blackwell Dictionary of Twentieth Century Social Thought (Outherwaite and Bottomore, 1993).**

♦ **The Social Science Encyclopaedia (Kuper and Kuper, 1999).**

Your lists of words, phrases and definitions will be of use when you need to search and review the literature in more depth. This will be when you have decided on your specific research problem and have written your research proposal.

Risking a poor choice of topic

We outlined some of the misconceptions about masters topics at the beginning of this chapter; here we want to draw your attention to some of the ways in which students in the past have made some basic mistakes when selecting their research topic. The following are some of the ways in which you can engender a high level of risk into your research with the probability that it will fail.

Risky behaviours	Implications
♦ **Choose a topic in a hurry**	♦ **With no or little analysis of the practicalities of researching a topic you may face far too many unanticipated problems to deal with in the time**

you have available. Topic analysis will identify most of the issues and problems you are likely to face in your research — this is why you need thoroughly to analyse your topic before you start.

◆ Select the method before the topic

◆ Methods of data collection and analysis should be appropriate to the topic and not the other way round. You may be good at statistics or talking to people, but these should not be the first criteria for selecting a suitable research puzzle. The puzzle should be clearly formulated before you select data collection methods, otherwise you will be introducing a bias into your research equivalent to selecting a topic because it fits in with your political view of the world.

◆ Procrastinate for months over different topic ideas

◆ Doing little by dallying over possible topics wastes the valuable time you would otherwise be using to get on with your research. If you cannot make a decision, then take direction from your supervisor and stick to the decision they recommend.

◆ Generalize about your topic

◆ Vague and generalized ideas will lead to vague and problematic research. The broader the research idea, the more work it will involve to manage. The narrower your topic puzzle, the more likely it is that you will be able to identify precisely what you will need to do to finish your research in the time available.

◆ Ignore the basic criteria

◆ If you do not know what kinds of data are needed, then you will not know if you can get access to them or how to analyse them. Ensuring that you know the answers to these questions is equivalent to knowing where you are going before you set out on your research journey.

◆ Do not talk to your supervisors	◆ Silence from you may mean you have done nothing and are embarrassed to tell your supervisor or that you need no guidance. In the first case your supervisor will not be embarrassed because they are there to guide you and help you through your research blocks. In the second case, how do you know you are doing your research in the ways expected if you are not seeking and receiving regular feedback?

Features of good topics

So far we have identified a number of features which, when combined, can result in a good topic for research and it may helpful to summarize these:

Criterion	Implications
◆ Data availability	◆ The data you need to provide answers or solutions to your research problem must be available to you in sufficient quantity and quality. This means there must not be too much or too little data and it must be available using reliable collection techniques. Good topics have actual (secondary) or potential (primary) data available.
◆ Access to the data	◆ The data you need may be available, but not to you or in the way you need it. It may be commercially or personally sensitive data or even expensive if it has to be purchased. Good topics have data available which you can access with few problems.
◆ Time available	◆ No amount of enthusiasm can create the time you need for a research project. A good topic is one that has been clearly delimited and can be done in the limited time you have available.

◆ Availability of resources	◆ Computing and software may be needed along with published materials, such as reports. If these are not readily available, then unnecessary risks will be encountered. Good topics tend to require few resources and those which are needed should be readily available.
◆ Capabilities and skills	◆ You may be impressed with a statistical technique or computer program, but if you do not have the necessary skills and understanding at the start of your project, then the time and energies needed to learn these may take too much away from the research itself for it to be successfully completed. Good topics are those that build and develop on capabilities, skills and knowledge that you already have.
◆ Symmetry of potential outcomes	◆ It can be uplifting to establish a link between variables and have a positive result from your research that shows a link and why one exists. It is equally valid to show that a link does not exist. Good topics have the capability of resulting in positive and negative results.

Using your supervisor

A key to the success of many dissertations is the supervisor. Use your supervisor as much as possible throughout your dissertation research. They have the experience of supervising many previous students and therefore have a knowledge you do not have. They will be able to help you formulate your ideas on a topic, direct you to reading and may even suggest a topic they know can be done. By exploring a topic with your tutor you will be more likely to develop a positive and constructive relationship. Remember that along with another internal and an external examiner your supervisor will assess your dissertation, so it is important to develop a good working relationship as early as possible.

As a basis for your initial discussions take with you an outline, on a sheet of A4, of your idea for your research. This does not have to be typed or neat. A handwritten and roughly sketched-out idea will normally be better than something you have spent time and effort making look good. At this stage neatness is a luxury that is not needed and is a waste of time. It is your ideas that count, so focus your efforts on these and be prepared to share them with as many of your tutors as possible. What you can expect from your tutors is feedback to steer your idea in a direction that leads to a researchable topic. Do not worry too much if you receive guidance that seems to be conflicting. Different tutors will naturally have their own ideas as to what kind of research your topic idea suggests; often this is based on their own research interests and methodological biases. If possible, ask for a list of the research interests of your tutors and a list of dissertations they have previously supervised. These will give you an idea of their research orientations and biases and the kinds of topics they tend to supervise.

Try not to be hesitant in sharing your idea for a topic with a tutor – remember that they are on your side and are there to guide you. Once you have broken the ice with a topic, set up a schedule of tutorials to explore your idea, giving yourself enough time between each to follow up on the guidance you have been given. Even if you find that you did not have enough time to do everything, or even anything between tutorials, still keep to the schedule using the tutorial for a general discussion about your topic. Whatever you do, do not fail to turn up for a tutorial because you have not done much as this may annoy your tutor who, quite understandably, having invested effort on your behalf doesn't want their time wasted. Failure to attend a session can also be embarrassing when you next see your tutor and can lead to avoidance tactics by both and in extreme cases breakdown of the supervisory/student relationship.

Focusing in on a potential research topic

If choosing possible topics is the first step in your research, then developing one into a set of research questions, propositions, possibly a hypothesis, with a clear statement of purpose and objectives are the next steps. By developing these you will be defining what your research will be about, why it is needed and what kind of research it will be. In this section we will look at the process and relationships between research questions and different types and purposes of research. Details of methodological approaches and traditions we leave until Chapter 7, but even at this stage your research questions will give strong indications of these and help you in designing an overall strategy for your investigation. But before this some corrections to pre-existing assumptions may be useful. Across the different disciplines of the social sciences there are some differences of opinion on what constitutes a properly formulated 'research' problem. In a guide to doing a dissertation the following statement is made:

> A second criterion is that the question should suggest a relationship to be examined. This is a particularly important characteristic, because the purpose of doing research is to advance science. Because science is the study of relationships between variables, no relationship, no science. No science, no thesis or dissertation. It is that simple. (Cone and Foster, 1999: 35)

This is a rather stark view of what constitutes a research problem and a dissertation. You may remember some of the comments made in Chapter 1 about the need for clarity of understanding in the social sciences. This statement clearly has no appreciation of this attitude. My position, after years of experience supervising dissertations, is that this is only one view among many of how to express a research problem and what can count as valid, meaningful and useful research and research for a dissertation. I therefore take issue with these kinds of views of research because they exclude the possibility of alternatives and by doing so are dogmatic. While this is not the place to engage in discussion of what may or may not constitute 'science', my view is that a more inclusive approach should be taken and for the sake of progress in understanding our world – human and physical – I will use the word 'research' when looking at the formulation of research problems for a dissertation.

DEVELOPING RESEARCH QUESTIONS

What you may have done so far is to identify some broad topic area and undertaken an analysis of it through a preliminary search and review of the literature. You should have eliminated from your list of possible topics those which were too risky or failed to meet adequately the criteria of access to data and time to do the research. With the topic or topics you are still considering it is time to choose one and run with it by developing an aspect of it into a puzzle for your research. One of the first steps in this is looking to see what questions can be stated which are puzzles needing research in order to be addressed. Note I say 'addressed' and not 'answered'. This is because your research may find that there is no answer, in any definitive sense, to a question, but it can give an advancement in understanding and clarification, which in themselves are worthwhile outcomes.

Research questions are questions you intend to employ systematic research to investigate; they are what is to be investigated. They should embody the purpose and type of research necessary to unravel the puzzle they set for investigation. Remembering the different types of puzzle – the developmental, mechanical correlational, causal and essence puzzle – your questions should have a focus on one of these. Typically a puzzle will have a series of questions such as: How well does this program work? How can we measure 'well'? What can we compare it to? How do users and providers assess 'well'? The focus here is on evaluating the performance of a programme, say in education, health care or in the community. This means that some form of evaluative research design will be required involving descriptive statistical data, possibly from a survey/questionnaire, along with qualitative data, possibly from interviews. General questions are OK as the starting point, but will usually need refining to make them more precise, clear and focused. Clough and Nutbrown (2002) suggest using what they call the 'Goldilocks test' and 'Russian doll principle'. The Goldilocks test looks to assess research questions in terms of how big they are. Big questions are usually too big to be answered. This is because they either lack precision, needing to be broken down into smaller, more manageable questions, or are too vague, needing precision to make the concepts measurable. For example, 'What is consciousness?' is, as a piece of primary research, a big question for a masters dissertation. But rephrased as 'How has consciousness been defined and those definitions operationalized in research?' may be possible, once clarified by undertaking a critical review of the literature. Questions need to be the right size in terms of allowing a research design to investigate the problems they pose. Hence the Russian doll principle; larger questions need smaller ones and these need to fit together into a logical set.

Your questions will now need to be developed by looking to see what specific objectives will be needed to actualize each question and how each concept is to be defined to identify its major variables. Figure 3.6 shows the main elements you will need to work on to construct a clear and coherent definition of your research topic. Once you have your research questions, which of these you work on next is in practice not important. You will find that alterations to one mean you revisit another in an iterative process of going around tweaking one then another.

DEFINING CONCEPTS

Concepts are words such as 'effectiveness', 'efficiency', 'performance', 'poverty', 'truth', 'impact' and 'community'. Due to the nature of language and the ways in which meanings are a product of a word's use, concepts cannot be assumed to have a universal definition. When used in a research question, the way in which they are to be used needs to be defined. The literature on the topic is usually a good source of

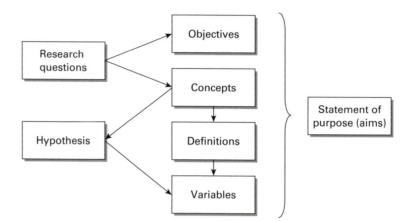

FIGURE 3.6 ELEMENTS IN DEFINING YOUR RESEARCH TOPIC

candidate definitions for this. Poverty, for example, can be defined in absolute (a person is in poverty because they have nothing) or relative terms (a person is in poverty because they lack what others take for granted) and even within these two general categories there are more specific definitions and arguments over whether such definitions are useful in measuring the concept. You can use the literature to examine and interrogate definitions used previously, categorizing these into what kind of definition they are. For example, you can look at definitions by example, by genus and differentia, by stipulation and operational analysis.

Whatever approach you use, remember that by defining your concepts you are entering into a research design that assumes it is possible to have a correspondence between words and things through the mediation of definition. We look at correspondence theory in much more detail in Chapter 7. But briefly, what this means is that you can measure the concept by defining variables assumed to correspond to the phenomenon. Poverty, for example, may be defined in terms of a range of indicators which state what a person does not possess (material things, social attributes, cultural capital and so on). The variables could then be defined in terms of such things as income level and value of assets, which would then be used to set a poverty line for the definition of poverty.

STATING THE AIMS AND PURPOSE OF YOUR RESEARCH

Another way of seeing the links between the different elements in defining your research project is shown in Figure 3.7. It provides an overview of where the problem statement (aims) fits into the process of research design (we look in more detail at research design in Chapter 10).

The process is, as we have indicated, not as clear-cut as shown in diagrams such as Figure 3.7. The process is largely iterative in that you will find yourself moving back and forth between writing aims and objectives, then recasting your problem statement and reading further into the literature on the methodological tradition and approach you have elected to base your research upon.

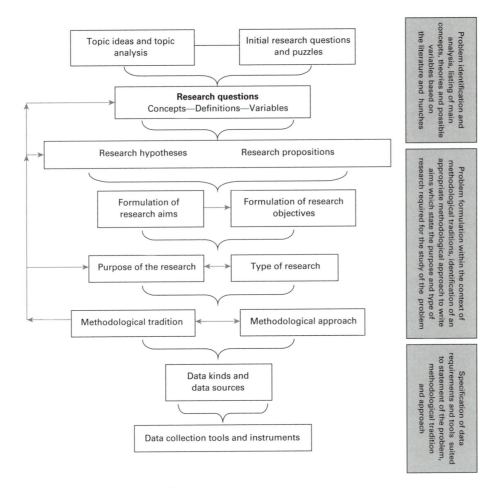

FIGURE 3.7   THE PLACE OF RESEARCH AIMS AND STATEMENTS IN RESEARCH DESIGN

Many researchers often experience some level of anxiety and frustration when writing the aims and objectives for a research proposal. This may be because there is no consensus as to what aims are, what objectives are and how they relate to each other. There is also the problem that different institutions have different ideas about what an aim is and what an objective is, sometimes using different words for the same thing, such as goal in place of aim. In this section we offer a guide to help you understand the nature of research aims and objectives that will help you to formulate good aims and clear objectives. We can begin by looking at the purpose of aims.

A research aim is one or more statements used to express the general *intent* (purpose) and indication of the *orientation* (methodological nature) you have decided on for your research project. Your aim should also include a gloss of the topic, for example, 'motivation', and a broad typification of your units of analysis, for example, 'masters students'. By 'intent' we mean the purpose (function) you are proposing for your research, for example, to evaluate, find a solution, identify something or bring about a change to a situation by your research. One way of thinking about this is to say, 'This research intends to [examine], [explore], [inquire into], [investigate] or [study] ... in order to [identify], [diagnose], [answer], [find out], or [understand] ...' some topic. By 'orientation' we mean the position you have elected to take regarding the nature of your research, for example, to base your research on a quantitative or qualitative description, analysis or experiment. It may be that you state the orientation of your research before your intent. For example, your aims may begin like the sample shown in Figure 3.8.

Although the aim shown in Figure 3.8 has the outcome to change the curriculum, this is not its primary intention. As a masters dissertation, the main intention is to demonstrate the ability to do research rather than effect change to a situation. Developing the curriculum to improve motivation is therefore a secondary consideration to recognizing that this is a proposal for a piece of formative evaluation that is focused on the questions, 'What do the students talk about as motivating them?' and 'How can we use this information to develop a curriculum that motivates?' Often such kinds of questions take the place of or complement a hypothesis.

If we look at the words and phrases which make up aims we can see that the intent and orientation of an aim are not mutually exclusive. In the example already introduced and shown again in Figure 3.9 we can see that there are a number of phrases

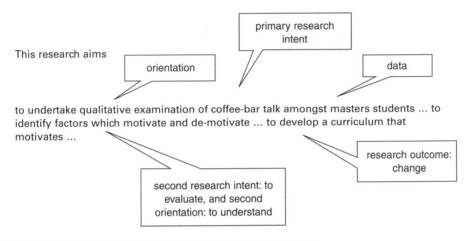

FIGURE 3.8   STRUCTURE OF STATEMENT OF RESEARCH AIMS

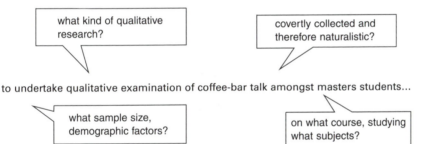

FIGURE 3.9   DELIBERATELY VAGUE PHRASES ALLOW FOR FURTHER EXPLANATION AT A
             LATER STAGE

which are intentionally vague because they can be explained in other parts of the proposal.

While the implicit references in an aim can be developed in other sections of the proposal, we can see in Table 3.4 the implications of using a specific word to indicate the orientation of the research. In the example the word 'examine' has been used and this implies that the research will be looking at coffee-bar conversations in detail to analyse them and identify from them talk about the elements of the course which motivate and de-motivate.

TABLE 3.4 VOCABULARY OF TYPES OF RESEARCH

Term	Amplification
Investigate	'to inquire into thoroughly' 'examine systematically' 'a process of finding out' 'search for evidence'
Enquire	'seek information by questioning' 'seeking answers' 'make an investigation'
Examine	'look at or actively observe' 'inspect carefully for detail' 'scrutinize'
Explore	'seek the unknown' 'diagnose a problem'
Explain	'discover cause and effect' 'identify independent and dependent variables'
Study	'carefully consider' 'critically think about' 'seek to understand' 'contemplate or reflect about'

Your research aims can sometimes be used to state the purpose of your research; to provide the purpose statement. Here is an example:

> The purpose of this study is to identify which demographic factors (age, sex, ethnicity) correlate with which social lifestyle factors (social networks, number of sexual partners, employment, education, residence) to determine risk factors in young adult injection drug users (IDUs) currently or recently in rehabilitation.

This is the kind of statement that can also be your aim and form the main part of your problem statement. Fully to be a problem statement you would need to state the known prevalence of the problem, why it is a problem, and for whom. This would be a very brief synopsis of research and data from the literature.

TABLE 3.5 USING RESEARCH TERMS TO DESIGN COHERENT RESEARCH

Using these ... →	Examine	Explore	Inquire	Investigate	Study
identify and gather data ... →	Data	Information	Facts	Answers	Principles
which is subjected to ... →	Scrutiny	Criticism	Contemplation	Comparison	Evaluation
and may result in ... →	Understanding	Relationships	Explanation		Knowledge
which can be used to ... →	Draw conclusions	Suggest solutions	Recommend actions	Make changes	Clarify debates

The words in Table 3.5 can be used in a number of ways depending on what you intend to do. You can use them singly or combine them. For example, you could state that your aim was to do an 'exploratory study', or 'critical study', or 'investigative inquiry'. You can also preface the orientation with a methodological one, such as 'quantitative examination'. There are many more words and phrases that can be used to formulate aims which embody the methodology of your research, including 'evaluate', 'identify', 'experiment', 'analyse', 'describe' and so on. As you can see from the matrix shown in Table 3.5, the vocabulary of research has different levels and dimensions. The point to remember is to ensure that whatever terms you use they should be logically related and used to formulate a coherent aim and set of objectives. We will now look at what we mean by aims being coherent.

We can see in Table 3.5 an example of how the different elements can be combined in different ways to achieve a desired outcome. There are two main points to note here. The first is that not all research has to result in a solution; understanding and the clarification of issues are as valid as any other outcomes for a research project. The second is that starting with a study of, say academic debate, then contemplating the nature and origins of that debate, then scrutinizing any data and arguments used in the debate, then subjecting data and argument to critical evaluation and reflection may result in a new (possibly) clearer understanding of the debate. The research will, however, have been coherent in that its elements were deliberately chosen from amongst alternatives and logically combined in such a way as to be fit for the purpose of the research. It is this vocabulary that can be used to formulate the aims of a research project. In your aims you are stating the choices you have made and which you are proposing will form the basis of your approach to researching your topic. The aims you write in the early stages of your research will, of course, be subject to change as you refine the purpose of your research and the methodological tradition and approach you want to use. Finally, there are other pieces of information you can also include in your research aims, such as scope, dates (for example, between 1815–1883), the title of a publication (for example, *Great Expectations*), name of a person (for example, Charles Dickens), reference to a theory or position (for example, atavism), and an analytical framework, such as case study or comparative study, a hypothesis and your main research question.

WRITING OBJECTIVES FOR YOUR RESEARCH

The objectives of a research project (a proposal for your research) are the tasks required to actualize adequately the main elements of the research questions. There is sometimes, as we have said, some variation over what some people call aims and objectives. Objectives tend to be defined as the tasks you will need to do, in the rough order, to complete your research. Most research projects will need a search and review of the literature, construction and testing of data collection instruments, analysis of the data and a research report. Taking these as the major parts usually required, one way of casting your objectives is to look at your research questions and identify what tasks need to be done in terms of the dissertation structure in order to answer them. This way may result in the following set of objectives:

1   To review the literature of public library use by students of basic adult education courses in order to identify which variables have been previously identified in terms of low-use patterns.

2   To interview a sample of students about their use and knowledge of what their local public library can provide related to their course and their patterns and reasons of use of the library service.

3   To survey a sample of adult education providers to find out what they know about what public libraries can provide for their students and what they know about their students' use of the library service.

4   To identify gaps in knowledge of what the public library can provide for students on basic adult education courses.

5   To make realistic recommendations on how libraries can make their resources known to providers and students of basic education courses and how they can mitigate some of the barriers to the use of those services for this group of people.

These objectives are from a study of public library use by students on basic adult education courses. They are numbered consecutively and give only the briefest of information on what will be done and what information will be the result. The main focus of the research question they are based on is why don't students on basic adult education courses make more use of the resources in public libraries to help themselves. Although the number of objectives do not always have to correspond to the same number of research questions, for both between five and seven are usually regarded as sufficient to express what you want to know and how you will go about finding out. The second main approach to objectives is to express them as outcomes; as products of different parts of your research. The following are from a study of information flow in the construction industry; an industry subject to many different statutory regulations and standards which are constantly changing. The example shows the main aims, problem statement and objectives.

The aims of this study are to identify the ways in which quantity surveyors in the UK construction industry obtain and use information and to evaluate the role of special libraries in supplying relevant information. The major problems facing quantity surveyors are the amount of information necessary in the form of regulations, standards and specifications, changes to the information and application to different kinds of construction. To investigate information flow it will be necessary to:

1   Detail the flow of information in terms of its supply and availability to its use by a sample of quantity surveyors.

2   Examine previous research on information flow in the construction industry, identifying its function and cases of failure.

3   Describe and evaluate the role of special construction libraries in the information chain.

4   Survey quantity surveyors on their knowledge and use of special libraries.

5   Compare the knowledge quantity surveyors have and their use of special libraries with other sources of information.

6   Suggest ways in which special construction libraries can be more effective in supplying information to quantity surveyors.

(Shoolberd, 2003: unpublished teaching notes)

After each objective it is legitimate practice to provide some explanation of what you are intending to achieve. This will help you to understand what will be involved in each objective and how they relate to each other and to your aims.

USING A HYPOTHESIS IN YOUR RESEARCH

Sometimes your research questions or the expectations of your supervisor may mean that you need to develop a hypothesis for your research. A hypothesis is an informed guess or hunch that a relationship may exist between two variables with one being the cause of the other. A hypothesis (H_1) is therefore a statement that asserts that a relationship exists between two or more variables, that x is caused by y, or that particular consequences (C) will follow if the hypothesis is valid, that *if* H_1 *then* C_1, C_2, C_3 and so on. For example, I know a little about motorcars and how they work and hence, sometimes, why they do not work. If I turn the key to start mine and nothing happens I can, on the basis of my existing knowledge, hypothesize a number of possible causes, but that the most likely is a flat battery. Stated as a hypothesis to be tested, this could be: cars with a flat battery will not start. As a consequence, if it is a flat battery then I also know that there will be a number of direct consequences, such as the radio will not work (and will have lost its memory of my favourite pre-set stations), the clock, being electric, will have stopped and the windows will not work. I could, if asked, provide more detail on why a flat battery causes the situation by taking the explanation to another level, say motorcar electrics. But I could not go much beyond this because I do not know enough about physics to talk about how a battery works at the level of atoms and electrons. There are, then, different levels of detail at which hypotheses can be used to give different possible explanations which have different levels of explanation. These differences are what Alan Garfinkel (1981) calls 'explanatory relativity'. This point is that a hypothesis should be appropriate to the level of detail required and that we remember it is not, as in our example talking about electrons, explaining the phenomenon but something about the consequences of the phenomenon. We are asking *why* will the motorcar not start, not *how* does a car battery work. The use of a hypothesis in research is more complex than in this example, but it illustrates the main principles of hypotheses such as:

♦ they are tentative propositions based on existing knowledge (even a theory) and its use to explain a situation;

♦ they are limited to the situation at hand, but the knowledge they are based on is general;

♦ the validity of the hypothesis in this situation is not known, but contains the details of what variables are to be investigated to test the validity of the hypothesis; and

♦ if found to be the cause from which the consequences have logically followed, this is the evidence for confirming the hypothesis.

Hypotheses therefore give direction to the investigation in terms of where to look, what to look at, what to test and as such have a deductive structure. This means that they can be expressed in terms of 'if', 'then'. Figure 3.10 shows the deductive structure along with the role of inductive inference.

In our motorcar example the hypothesis we used is called a *research hypothesis* because the problem it addresses is capable of being empirically investigated. Given the consequences, that electrical devices in the motorcar do not work, then our hypothesis is, on the basis of prior experiences, the most statistically probable. Hypotheses work well with physical events (or lack of) because they can be based on existing knowledge of the basic laws of physics. Sometimes, however, in physics, but more

> Analytical statistics, especially the Pearson-Product-moment correlation, plays a large part in the calculation of the data for hypothesis testing. For help with statistics, see Further Reading to this chapter.

often with human actions, events are the outcome of chance. The chance of 50 per cent of millionaires owning a Rolls Royce is 50 per cent may or may not be statistically correct. It is measurable and if found to be the case only tells us there is a 50/50 chance of millionaire y owing a Rolls Royce motorcar x. Similarly, if we say that there will be no difference between the reading habits of an equal sample of left-handed boys and left-hand girls aged 13 years, we are saying there is no relationship between reading

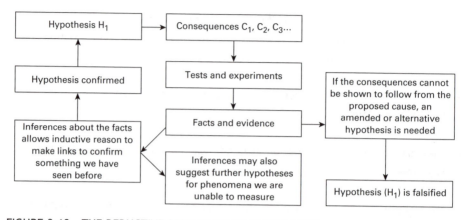

FIGURE 3.10   THE DEDUCTIVE STRUCTURE OF HYPOTHESES

habits and left-handedness. This type of statement is called the *null hypothesis* because it states there will be no difference statistically between the variables. We could measure the reading habits of the boys and girls and calculate the variance between the two sample groups, which would indicate (rather than strictly prove) whether the null hypothesis is acceptable or is to be rejected for an alternative research hypothesis. Note that we are using samples with the intent to generalize to a larger population and therefore need to know much more about sample selection techniques and the nature of generalization to use hypotheses. These are all parts of the research design which we will look at later in this book.

You should, as a mater of course, be thinking about samples and also about the elements of your hypothesis and research questions at this stage. This mainly involves looking to see how you can define your major concept (sometimes called constructs) and what indicators, variables and values you will use to operationalize it. For example, if you were looking at poverty and ill-health you may hypothesize that poverty is a major cause of poor health and mortality among low income families. Poverty, poor health and low income would all need careful consideration and recourse to the literature for definition, but for the sake of our example an initial design might look like the one shown in Table 3.6.

Outlines such as the one shown in Table 3.6 can be useful starting points for all types of research, not just those using a hypothesis. They help to clarify what kind of data will be needed in terms of their relevance, amount and detail and how they may be collected so as to be reliable and able to be compared.

TABLE 3.6 OPERATIONALIZING THE HYPOTHESIS

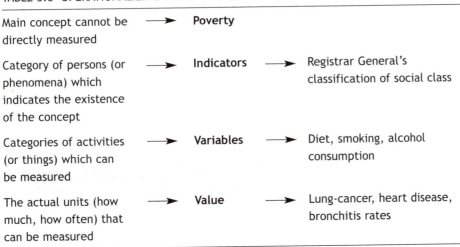

Main concept cannot be directly measured	➤	Poverty		
Category of persons (or phenomena) which indicates the existence of the concept	➤	Indicators	➤	Registrar General's classification of social class
Categories of activities (or things) which can be measured	➤	Variables	➤	Diet, smoking, alcohol consumption
The actual units (how much, how often) that can be measured	➤	Value	➤	Lung-cancer, heart disease, bronchitis rates

RESEARCH PROPOSITIONS

While hypotheses are usually associated with correlational and explanatory research, it is quite possible to use a form of hypothesis in other types of research and research approaches. For the sake of clarity and demarcation we will term these 'propositions' rather than hypotheses. A proposition is a phenomenon presented for consideration that wants to confirm or deny assumptions, methodology or methods used to define or apply the phenomenon. For example, we may propose that newly constructed university library buildings (say five) meet all the current building regulations but fail to meet the needs of students. We are proposing that there is a logical gap in the function of the building and could go on to propose why we believe this to be the case. Propositions are statements based on an argument which can be investigated through a similar research design to that shown in Table 3.6. Our example here may include definitions of a library, usage statistics of before (old library) and after (new library) to indicate usefulness as a concept, and questionnaire survey and interviews with users. This proposition could include the collection of a range of organizational statistics, quantitative responses and qualitative opinions. It would not result in any kind of strict correlation between the variables, but would fulfil the main purpose of raising a topic for critical discussion. My own research on the influences on library architecture uses such propositions combined with research questions (Hart, 1996). For example: What are the main conceptual influences on contemporary library design? How do these relate to the historic place and value of knowledge? How is the purpose of the library represented in its design? What role do librarians and users of libraries have in the design of libraries? Questions like these can form the basis of a propositional argument that has several related propositions, such as: contemporary library architecture represents information access rather than knowledge collection; they are designed using the concept of visibility, access and speed; the book is no longer valued because it is seen to represent elitism; hence the glass library building has replaced the stone one and computers have replaced books. This was investigated using images of recently built libraries.

SUMMARY OF THIS CHAPTER

This chapter has attempted to provide you with an overview of the initial stage of doing your masters dissertation. The focus has been on the general issues and techniques for finding a suitable topic for your research and how to define a topic in terms of questions which are research questions. These ways of defining a topic have only been touched on and you are advised to consult the literature, especially in the further readings to this chapter, and your tutors for detailed advice. But now that you know about defining a topic, some time needs to be given to considering methodological traditions and approaches before the research project is finally formulated into a definite design. These are issues that will be dealt with in Chapters 10 and 11. The key points made in this chapter include the following:

♦ The topic needs to be do-able in the time you have available. A do-able topic is one that has available data you can access and have the time to analyse.

♦ There are many different ways of framing a topic and most of these are as puzzles to be solved and the initial or indicative search and review of the literature is an important part of topic analysis.

♦ The earlier you start looking for a topic, the more time you will have to develop a clear puzzle and research design.

♦ Once you have some candidate topics, define them using research questions, hypotheses and propositions.

Further reading

Alasuutari, P. (1995) *Researching Culture: Qualitative Method and Cultural Studies*. London: Sage. Chapter 11 introduces the idea of research being about unriddling.

Blaxter, L., Hughes, C. and Tight, M. (1996) *How to Research*. Buckingham: Open University Press. A good starting point with some simple to do exercises on topics.

Booth, W.C., Colomb, G.G. and Williamson, J.M. (1995) *The Craft of Research*. Chicago: University of Chicago Press. Has a section in Chapter 3 on moving from topics to research questions.

Clarke, G.M. (1992) *A Basic Course in Statistics*. 3rd edn. London: Edward Arnold. A solid introduction to statistical techniques relevant to hypothesis testing.

Dalen, Van, D.B. (1979) *Understanding Educational Research: An Introduction*. New York: McGraw-Hill. A thorough introduction to hypotheses and related statistical techniques.

Dees, R. (1997) *Starting Research: An Introduction to Academic Research and Dissertation Writing*. New York: Pinter. See Chapter 3 on planning a focus for your research.

Kumar, R. (1999) *Research Methodology: A Step-by-Step Guide for Beginners*. London: Sage. Chapter 4 gives advice on formulating a research topic including using hypotheses and Chapter 5 on variables.

Lester, J.D. (1993) *Writing Research Papers: A Complete Guide*. New York: HarperCollins. Has advice in Chapter 1 on finding a topic.

Silverman, D. (2000) *Doing Qualitative Research: A Practical Handbook*. London: Sage. See Chapter 5 'Selecting a topic' for advice on strategies to overcome some of the most common errors when looking for a topic and at qualitative hypotheses.

Trochim, B. (2002) *Research Methods Knowledge Base*. Address: http://trochim.human.cornell.edu/ An Internet resource that includes a lot of advice on hypotheses, samples and statistics.

Walliman, N. (2001) *Your Research Project: A Step-by-Step Guide for the First-time Researcher*. London: Sage. Chapter 5 discusses hypotheses, research questions and propositions.

Imagining your dissertation

CHAPTER CONCEPTS

● STRUCTURE OF A TYPICAL DISSERTATION ● GENERIC DISSERTATION SKELETON ● UNITY IN A DISSERTATION ● THE PLOT OF A DISSERTATION ● ENVISIONING YOUR TOPIC AS A DISSERTATION ● ENVISIONING TECHNIQUES ● DIAGRAMMATIC REPRESENTATION ● YELLOW-STICKER PLOTTING ● USING ENVISIONING TO ANSWER KEY QUESTIONS ● WHEN TO START WRITING ● SUMMARY OF THIS CHAPTER ● FURTHER READING

The purpose of this chapter is to introduce the technique of *envisioning* that you can use to create an imaginary picture of your dissertation. This technique will help you to understand the structure of a typical dissertation and to identify the different parts of the intellectual and technical scaffolding you need to construct for a research proposal. The main questions we look at in this chapter are:

1   What are the chapters in a typical dissertation?

2   How can you imagine what chapters will be needed to tell the story of your research?

3   Why does a dissertation need to be more than the sum of its chapters? What is meant by saying a dissertation needs to be coherent?

The basic premise of this chapter is that if you can mentally envision what your dissertation may look like, then you can begin to think more systematically on what will need to be done to develop your research proposal and identify solutions to problems you foresee. We begin with an overview of the typical dissertation before looking at how to use envisioning techniques.

Structure of a typical dissertation

In Chapter 1 we learned that a dissertation is, in part, a piece of technical work. This means it involves doing a range of tasks such as designing a literature search, constructing bibliographies, designing data collection tools and writing. I recommended that the most efficient

> See Chapter 5 for the structures of different types of dissertation – the work-based and literature review dissertations.

way of thinking about and doing your dissertation is to break the whole down into its constitutive elements. But what does the whole look like? In this section we are going to look at some indicative and typical structures of masters dissertations.

GENERIC DISSERTATION SKELETON

You are expected to present your dissertation in a logical format that has unity and is systematic. In its simplest terms, a masters dissertation has the following seven sections:

1 Title

2 Abstract

3 Acknowledgements

4 Table of contents

5 Main text

6 Bibliography

7 Appendices.

Each of the main sections has a number of parts and these parts have their own role in the dissertation. If we expand the sections a little we can see what the broad content of each may be.

TABLE 4.1   PARTS OF A TYPICAL DISSERTATION

Parts	Contents
1 Title	A concise title to convey the topic and purpose of the research.
2 Abstract	A descriptive summary of the research.
3 Acknowledgements	Individuals and organizations who have helped you and copyright authorizations.
4 Table of contents	Full listing of the contents, figures and tables.
5 Main text	The chapters of the dissertation.
6 Bibliography	Works cited in the text arranged systematically using accepted standards for citations.
7 Appendices	Relevant supporting evidence, such as letters and exhibits.

Although it may not be evident in Table 4.1, the most important part of your dissertation is the main text. There are some typical chapters which are expected in the main text, but it is left to you to decide on how best to arrange them. Whatever arrangement of chapters and sections you use, it is essential to check with your supervisor that anything differing from the norm be approved first before you produce your dissertation. Table 4.2 gives an indication of the content of chapters to use as your starting point when envisioning the structure of your dissertation.

These chapters and arrangement are indicative and may differ depending on the approach to the topic. It is up to you, as the owner of your research, to decide on the most appropriate arrangement for the chapters in your dissertation. It is also up to you to decide the weighting in space and words to give to each chapter. Table 4.3 gives an indication of typical lengths for chapters based on the seven-chapter arrangement we have used.

In some kinds of dissertation, such as one based on an analysis of the literature, the dissertation will be a series of literature review chapters. Therefore this is not a fixed format, but one to be used to orient your understanding to the necessity for structure in a dissertation and for that structure to maintain a focus on the main themes of the research.

TABLE 4.2 CHAPTERS IN A DISSERTATION

Chapter	Title	Contents
Chapter 1	Introduction	The general introduction to the research and the topic. This chapter is a re-working of the research proposal and should include the aims and objectives, hypothesis and/or research questions, the scope of the research, justification and definition of technical terms. Also included is whatever background information is necessary for the reader to understand the context of the topic. Depending on the complexity of the arguments the background may be presented as a separate chapter. All works referred to in the text should be cited systematically and in detail at the end of the chapter using the numeric method.
Chapter 2	Literature review	A state-of-the-art search and review of the literature on the topic. This should use an appropriate structure and should focus on the ideas, issues, arguments and findings in the literature and not on single items or authors unless there is good reason for doing so. All works referred to in the text should be cited systematically and in detail at the end of the chapter using the numeric method.
Chapter 3	Methodology	This chapter is for a description and justification of the methodological assumptions, data collection tools, sampling and techniques of analysis used in the research. All works referred to in the text should be cited systematically and in detail at the end of the chapter using the numeric method.
Chapter 4	Findings/Results	This chapter is for the findings or results of the research and is intended to be descriptive. If the findings are based on a quantitative questionnaire, then they will consist of tables showing the responses. This chapter should not include any in-depth discussion or manipulation of the data, it is for the presentation of your data. All works referred to in the text should be cited systematically and in detail at the end of the chapter using the numeric method.

(Continued)

TABLE 4.2 (CONTINUED)

Chapter	Title	Contents
Chapter 5	Analysis	The findings are subject to whatever techniques of analysis are appropriate for the data. This may be statistical analysis showing degrees of correlation between variables or other techniques such as semiological or conversation analysis. All works referred to in the text should be cited systematically and in detail at the end of the chapter using the numeric method.
Chapter 6	Discussion	Focusing on the questions and/or hypothesis set, this chapter contains a discussion of the degree to which the research has answered the questions or tested the hypothesis. The implications for the use of the concepts or theory can be discussed in terms of the literature. The implications for practitioners, either in a profession or research, can be highlighted. The discussion should also relate the findings to the literature in terms of showing what the research has contributed to the literature on the topic and what the literature can do in helping to show the meaning of the research. All works referred to in the text should be cited systematically and in detail at the end of the chapter using the numeric method.
Chapter 7	Conclusions/ Recommendations	This chapter brings together the work done and what has been found. It is more than a summary of the contents of the dissertation. It should show the contribution, including the methodological assumption and data collection tools used, that the research has made to the literature and include an evaluation of the research in terms of the degree to which the aims and objectives were achieved – this is part of doing 'reflective practice'. Ideas for further research should also be included. If the work has implications for practice, then also include suggestions stating the recommended action, its benefits and costs. All works referred to in the text should be cited systematically and in detail at the end of the chapter using the numeric method.

TABLE 4.3 WORD COUNTS FOR DIFFERENT CHAPTERS

Introduction	Literature review	Methodology	Findings/ Results	Analysis	Discussion	Conclusions/ Recommendations	Total
1,000	3,500	3,500	1,500	2,000	2,000	1,500	15,000 words

Unity in a dissertation

Earlier I introduced the suggestion that a dissertation should have unity. One way of thinking about what this means is to look at the structure of dissertations to see how the contents are interrelated. In Table 4.4 (story structures) and Figure 4.1 (narrative logic) we have attempted to show how the different parts of a typical dissertation are connected. In Chapter 5 we will look more closely at the structure of dissertations, but in the two illustrations here you can see how the first chapter is usually a summary of the main issues and arguments present in the literature, provides a rationale for the project and sets down the aims and objectives to be fulfilled. In a similar way the concluding chapter brings together what has been done by providing an evaluation of the degree to which the aims have been fulfilled and how the findings have filled a gap in our knowledge and made a contribution to the literature. The dissertation therefore has a beginning, middle and end and each section and all the parts should be focused on providing information and discussion relevant only to the topic.

THE PLOT OF A DISSERTATION

Without intending to be patronizing, from what I have presented you can now see that a dissertation has typical sections and parts. In its simplest form it is a story of why and what (a telling and showing) you did, what you found and what the meaning is of what you did and found. Table 4.4 shows the narrative structure of a dissertation.

The narrative structure shown in Table 4.4 is a simplified version of the narrative structure we often see presented in a dissertation. The story in a dissertation is usually a little more intricate than we have indicated here. As with any good story, you will have different connections and relationships at different levels and varying degrees of detail in different parts of the dissertation. A useful analogy, but by no means the only one, for seeing the dissertation as a plot is to think of it in terms of the detective novel.

TABLE 4.4   THE STORY STRUCTURE OF A DISSERTATION

	Story parts	Dissertation parts
Beginning	There was once this problem or issue ...	The rationale for the topic in the introduction and used in the research proposal.
	which some researchers or profession believed was important ...	The literature review.
Middle	that I thought might be a suitable topic ...	The proposal for the research including the aims and objectives.
	so, what I did was ...	The methodology and data collection tools.
End	and found that ...	The results and findings.
	which means we now know this.	The conclusions and recommendations.

As a simple analogy the narrative logic of typical detective novels ('who done it') can give us an insight into the structure, and to some degree the methodological approach, of many dissertations. With the exception of ethnomethodology and conversation analysis most structuralist approaches, especially those based on semiology, can usefully be understood as having an approach similar to the detective novel. The puzzle to be solved may seem simple, but is not because what appears to be the solution is not the case. Surface appearances, the manifest clues or empirical observations are many and do not have any definite structure and therefore seem to lack relationships between them. The complexity in the twists and moves in the detective novel are the result of the imagination of the author, which is similar in academic analysis. The structuralist analysis looks for the complexity of relationships among the simplicity of the manifest appearances, aiming to discover multiple relationships rather than simple one-to-one relationships. As the analysis progresses so the puzzle deepens, becoming more complex than initially thought but, as in the end of a detective novel, the story unfolds as all the disparate parts are shown to have a pattern and the conclusion becomes the solution to the puzzle.

Seeing the dissertation as a story has a number of useful advantages. In particular it can help you to think about your topic as a story, what you intend to do, how you will do it and that you will need to have an ending, the conclusion (see Figure 4.1). In Chapter 5 (Tables 5.4 to 5.8) you can see some contents pages from dissertations. There are two main things to note from these. The first is that the contents pages

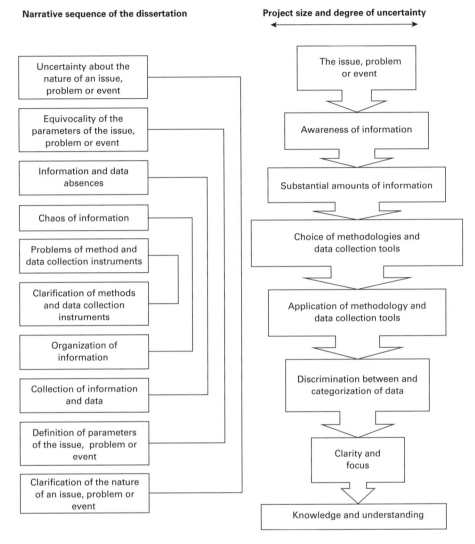

FIGURE 4.1   THE NARRATIVE SEQUENCE OF A DISSERTATION AND RESOLUTION OF UNCERTAINTIES

differ in the degree of detail and have minor differences in the structure. The second is that all have used a narrative arrangement to tell the story of their research from how it began, the introduction, to what needed to be done, the rationale, to how it was done, the methodology, what was found, the findings, to what it means and how it relates to the original aim, the conclusions. It is this interrelated sequencing that gives a dissertation its unity as a themed story.

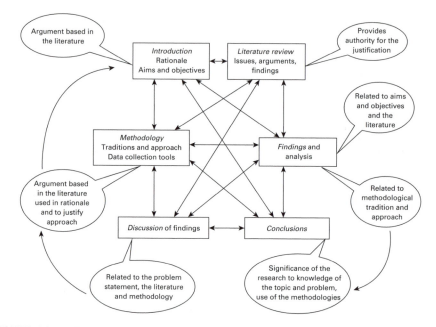

FIGURE 4.2   INTERRELATEDNESS OF CHAPTERS IN A DISSERTATION

The key to unity is to keep focused on the main topic and the issues which you identified in the literature. Your dissertation should not be a collection of free-standing or loosely related chapters. Each chapter should be purposeful and form a unified whole. Figure 4.2 shows some of the main connections between the main parts of a dissertation in terms of a dissertation being more than the sum of its parts.

From the very beginning of your research, during the stage when you are playing with ideas for a topic, push your thinking to see the whole and then conceptualize the main parts of that whole. By doing this you will habituate yourself into a mode of thinking that is much more conceptual and strategic. It will enable you to designate the necessary parts for building the intellectual and technical scaffolding and to give some rough content for the substance of your research proposal.

Envisioning your topic as a dissertation

You may, at this stage of your thinking, have an idea for a topic. It does not matter if this idea lacks specifics and that you are unclear on what kinds of research questions or hypothesis you will use. Being at the ideas stage affords an ideal opportunity to engage in some creative and analytic thinking using the techniques of envisioning. This consists of using your visual imagination to 'see' the strategic possibilities of your topic ideas. Envisioning means to think about, imagine and idealize about your topic as if it were a dissertation. The basic premise of envisioning is the question: If this idea were a dissertation, what would this dissertation look like? You are trying to imagine your idea as an object and that object is your completed dissertation.

ENVISIONING TECHNIQUES

The two main activities that are often useful in envisioning a possible dissertation are:

♦ **diagrammatic representation; and**

♦ **yellow sticker (Post-it notes) plotting.**

Diagrammatic representation

Using a series of simple diagrams you can begin to build up a picture of your topic using knowledge and information already gleaned from your indicative review of the literature. Try to draw:

♦ **the main theory and related concepts of research which have already been done on your topic. Figures 4.3 and 4.4 show the kind of diagram we have in mind. These diagrams have been done using a wordprocessor in order to assist with the printing process of this book. Normally I would use only a pen and paper.**

♦ **more diagrams to show the relationships between the theories and concepts and the research questions which have been asked and the kinds of data used in previous studies. Figure 4.5 shows how you can extend the initial diagram to show the kinds of relations between concepts, variables and data.**

With these descriptions of the current situation you are now in a position to begin to visualize (and diagnose) possible ways in which you could do research within the topic. This is not as difficult as it may seem. It is like the gardener or the house buyer. The gardener looks at an unkempt piece of land, overgrown with weeds and 'sees' in their imagination what it could look like. Similarly the house buyer looks at the

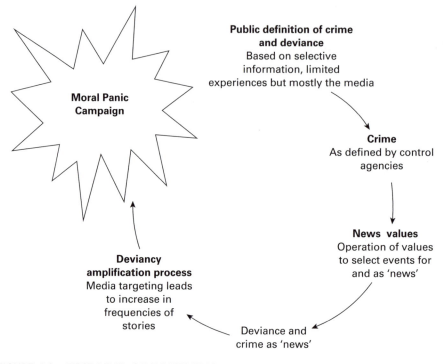

FIGURE 4.3   FIRST LEVEL OF ENVISIONING

derelict building and 'sees' a smart modern home. Both know what their possible garden or house could look like because they have seen other gardens and houses. You have seen, in outline, what a masters dissertation looks like and therefore have this same capability to use what you have seen to visualize what could be. The second diagram, shown in Figure 4.4, needs to incorporate your critical thinking about what research has already been done on the topic and to ask questions which may have a strong possibility for research. In this case we have shown how the model of moral panics can be used to generate questions about 'science' panics – panics that have scientific research available from the biochemistry fields. How, we may ask, can science be a matter for interpretation and how can 'facts' be used to construct definitions and understandings of a problem? There are a whole basket full of questions here about the nature of science, but placing these to one side our possible research topic may be one that looks at the presentation of data across different newspapers to ask; Is there a difference in reporting, if so, what and how? We may even suggest an initial hypothesis based on the statement that social panics share the same essential reporting features as science panics.

What relationships exist between news reporting of events and the actual facts and public and government reaction to events reported?

Cohen (1980), _Folk devils and moral panics_

Argues: media don't report reality but are a part of the process that actively constructs meaning and understanding. Agents of social control, e.g., police, amplify deviance by their focus on and definitions of some behaviours rather than others as needing their attention.

Cases of 'mods' and 'rockers' 50s and 60s

Therefore the media has an ideological role in constructing what is to be seen as 'real' or 'important' despite the actual frequency of a behaviour or its threat to the general public. The police react to media definitions in order to be seen to be doing something and thereby become part of the process of amplifying deviance and this itself becomes reportable, as further evidence of the deviance, and so on.

Definitions of social problems

Social control

Definitions of social reality – some people have more power than others to define what is and is not a social problem – and are in a position to have their definitions seen as more authorative, legitimate and trustworthy than others.

Conspiracy theories? Fowler (1991), Hall (1982) – 'the ideological power of the media is not attributable to the individual but the institutional processes of the media – ideology is a "function" of the discourse and of the logic of social processes, rather than an inertia of the agent.'

What is the language of moral panics?
How is rhetoric used?

McRobbie – revisited moral panic theory – argues: the process model of moral panics needs to be updated to take account of the ways in which it is now in widespread use – people, including the media, know about the dynamics of moral panics, as do pressure groups and use it to define social issues and problems.

Social reality is how it is communicated in language and is always partial. Therefore we have competing representations of reality as definitions constructed by different groups. Even within the media there are competing groups.

At this stage you can see the generation of topic ideas and a new focus on communication, science and moral panics.

Looking at communication, some key questions

Environment

Health issues

How are facts used in reporting an issue?
How is information presented in a media representation/ definition of an issue?

BSE, foot and mouth, global warming, landfill, salmonella eggs, mobile phones, cancers

FIGURE 4.4   SECOND LEVEL OF ENVISIONING

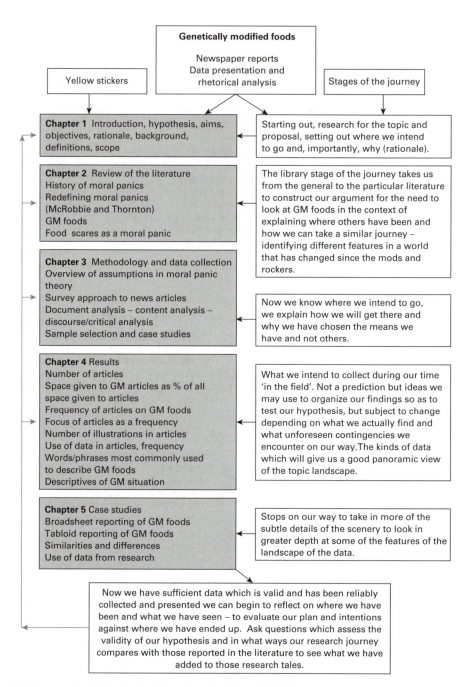

FIGURE 4.5   TAKING AN IMAGINARY RESEARCH JOURNEY

What you will achieve by expressing your understanding on paper in these ways is a mental as well as a physical representation of the current boundaries of research on your topic. By plotting boundaries you will also have begun the process of mapping out the structure of existing research and knowledge on your topic which will provide you with:

♦ the necessary starting point for constructing a case (justification);

♦ materials and structure for your literature review of the topic; and

♦ materials for your exposition of methods used to research the topic.

Yellow-sticker plotting

Using a pen and Post-it notes (yellow stickers, Post-it notes or similar stickers) you can begin to construct, using your imagination, the essential sections and parts of a typical dissertation. In doing this you are taking an imaginary journey into your possible future to a time when you have completed your research and written your dissertation. On this imaginary journey you can describe what you see and tell yourself a story about it. Figure 4.5 is an imaginary map of an imaginary journey of an imaginary dissertation on moral panics. In our map we have visualized a rough sequence of events using the sections and parts of a typical dissertation. It shows us what an imaginary dissertation on moral panics may look like if it were real. The purpose of this is to encourage you to see the whole and work out what parts and tasks will be needed to make the dissertation. In this way you will be more likely to relate the parts to the whole by seeing the purpose of each part.

By plotting out our possible journey we have again used what we already know about doing research and about dissertations. We can see how Figure 4.5 shows where we might start from and where we are aiming to go. These kinds of diagram can help to give us our sense of purpose and direction and help us to anticipate problems which we might meet on the way. You may also have realized that these activities are not esoteric but can be of measurable help in a number of ways including:

♦ enabling you to begin the process of envisioning your research proposal;

♦ beginning the task of narrowing down the scope of your idea;

♦ habituating you to imagine possibilities and problems before you begin; and

♦ showing you a possible focus for your research.

This activity will also provide you with some tangible evidence of your thinking and analysis of your ideas that you can use in tutorials with your supervisor.

USING ENVISIONING TO ANSWER KEY QUESTIONS

Envisioning your dissertation can help you to think about the important questions – what kind of data will you need, is it available to you and how can you analyse it. In our example in Figure 4.5 the data will be newspaper items – articles, illustrations, cartoons and editorials – and these are available on CD ROM and from the British Library as well as many central public libraries. So the data is available and you can get access to it. But remember to keep in mind how many newspapers are published daily, including the weekend specials, and how much data this may result in. You will therefore need to think about your sample, to look carefully at how to select a sample of newspapers over a given period of time to use as your case studies. Fortunately newspaper indexes on CD ROM make calculating frequencies much quicker than if you had to look and measure each newspaper in turn. You will, however, need to look at a large number to calculate such measures as space given as a percentage of the total space given for all items (excluding classified advertisements). As this will be very time-consuming you will also need to look at the logistics of what is possible and this will take you back to the definition of your scope and sample.

In Table 4.5 we have outlined some examples of possible research topics presented in a way that shows how, once you have generated some ideas for a topic, you can identify (in broad terms):

♦ what kinds of puzzle you may formulate;

♦ how you can amplify the ideas;

TABLE 4.5   ADDRESSING KEY DATA REQUIREMENTS FOR YOUR TOPIC

Idea for a topic	Type of puzzles possible	Amplification	Data requirements	Potential problems
The vision of the world brain	Developmental Mechanical Correlational Causal	H.G. Wells had a vision of the world brain – a library of all human knowledge. How was this vision developed? How has it influenced the structure of electronic communications, especially the Internet? What relation exists between the spread of the Internet and growth of digital libraries? Where can this vision be seen, e.g. film, books?	Primary writings of H.G. Wells. Interpretations of Wells's writings. Lists of films, books and television programmes using the vision. Statistics on the growth of the Internet, digital libraries.	The writings of H.G. Wells are generally available in the public domain, as are secondary interpretations. Would you have the time to read what is a substantial corpus of literature that includes much context-setting reading? Data on the growth of the Internet and directories listing films. It would be a relatively easy matter to extract relevant information from these. But what would you do with it?
Witchcraft and sorcery in children's literature	Developmental Mechanical Correlational	Witchcraft, the occult and sorcery have become (or always were?) popular as the basis for fiction. What are the origins of such in children's literature? How has the genre developed?	Primary writings in the genre. Secondary interpretations and taxonomies of the differences in the genre. Lists of examples of relevant cinema films.	For some people this may be a sensitive topic. The occult attracts some serious opposition even when expressed in children's books such as the *Harry Potter* series. The data is generally available, but will take time to read and analyse.

(Continued)

TABLE 4.5 (CONTINUED)

Idea for a topic	Type of puzzles possible	Amplification	Data requirements	Potential problems
		What are the typical narrative structures? What relationships exist between different media (books and cinema) and growth of interest?	Sales figures for books and audience figures for the cinema.	Film directories will provide film titles, but are the originals available for viewing? Sales and audience figures are published, but have you the statistical ability to do correlation?
Staff development and organiza- tional change	Developmental Mechanical	Many organizations face intense pressures both internally and externally to maintain relevancy and competitiveness. How can organizations change to fit with their environment? What role can staff develop- ment have in bringing about planned change? In what ways is staff develop- ment used strategically? Is there evidence to indicate it can be an effective factor for organizational change?	Questionnaire survey and interviewing. Environmental audits. Case studies of a sample of organizations. Secondary literature for examples of good practice.	The changing social, political, economic, legal and technological environment are problems for many organizations. The data is available via questionnaires, interviewing and internal organizational strategic analysis, which means sponsorship will be important to gain access. A high degree of interpersonal skills will be needed to get the confidence of staff and senior managers. An understanding of organizational change, strategy and environmental audits will also be needed.

(Continued)

TABLE 4.5 (CONTINUED)

Idea for a topic	Type of puzzles possible	Amplification	Data requirements	Potential problems
Using communications technology to communicate across a geographically dispersed organization	Developmental Mechanical	Information communications technologies (ICT) make it possible for people geographically dispersed to share information. How can ICT such as Lotus Notes be used to meet the information needs of organizational personnel? What kinds of information is suited to ICT? What are the cultural barriers to using ICT?	Questionnaire survey and interviewing. Information needs audit. Case study of a specific information-intensive organization. Secondary literature for examples of good practice.	A specific organization would be needed to enable an in-depth investigation and analysis of the situation. Access to key people in the organization would be crucial. Technical knowledge of how ICT (e.g. Lotus Notes) works would be required, along with case examples of its use in other organizations. Statistical ability to process and analyse questionnaire data would also be needed.

♦ how you can begin thinking about the necessary data which will be needed; and

♦ what problems you may have with the data.

You should now be able to appreciate that there are many technical issues you can extract from the yellow-sticker exercise which will help you to plan ahead to make your research journey less problematic and more likely to succeed. It will also indicate to you what kind of attitude and qualities will be needed in the process of doing your research, such as being proactive, having a research orientation, being adaptable, having self-discipline and finishing things you start.

When to start writing

You do not start writing until you have collected all the data, starting with chapter one and finishing with the concluding chapter. You start writing your dissertation when you first put down on paper your initial ideas for a topic. From the very beginning accept that what you first write will be edited and re-worked many times before it is of sufficient quality to be included as part of your draft dissertation. This may seem a little laborious at the beginning, but the process of drafting, writing, editing, proofing and rewriting will soon become routine and even a pleasure. This is because writing is a technical art form based on developing your abilities and as such you are creating something that has never been created before. Figure 4.6 shows the early stages in the research process when you will start to write. Jottings of ideas for your topic to the formulation of your research proposal are all parts of the writing process and some of this material will eventually end up in your dissertation. In the process of creating, you express a little of yourself and develop your skills and attitudes until writing becomes an habitual activity, so much so that you may have some difficulties in editing your dissertation down to 15,000 words!

The main thing at this stage is to start writing. Do not, as we have said, try to get things perfect. Try not to be tempted by the possibilities of word processing and doing diagrams on a computer. Whatever you write at this stage is a draft, therefore see it as an expression of ideas and work in progress. As such your drafts will

> Remember to establish a system for record keeping, storing your work and naming computer files. See Chapter 2 for advice on managing your project.

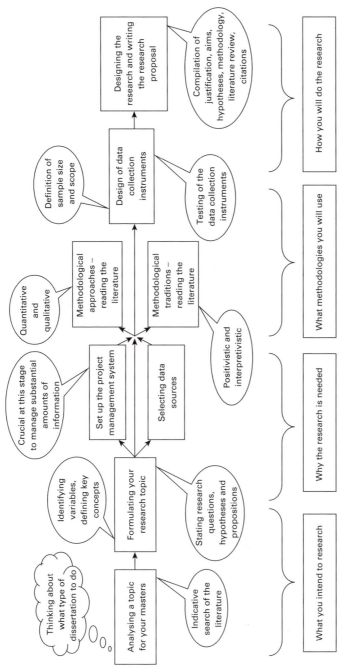

FIGURE 4.6   FROM TOPIC IDEA TO PROPOSAL

be incomplete and will have gaps where the contents will be indicated with a note to yourself. Also treat your drafts as problem-solving tools, as work in progress that needs problems of structure and expression to be solved. In a later chapter there will be more on the writing process, but at this stage in your academic career take time to enjoy the freedom of being able to express your work in a draft and take risks by trying out ideas on your tutors. At the end of the process it is not the drafts which will appear in your dissertation, but many of the notions on how to express and structure your ideas.

SUMMARY OF THIS CHAPTER

This chapter has attempted to introduce an essential part of the masters research process — envisioning — and has emphasized the following.

♦ It is expected that a dissertation follows a conventional structure and this structure can be understood as a plot.

♦ A dissertation is not a series of separate parts, but should be a coherent and interrelated set of parts focused on a main topic.

♦ Envisioning techniques will help you to 'see' a possible dissertation as a whole and allow you to think about contingencies and how to deal with them.

♦ Envisioning will help you to construct diagrams that can be an essential aid to understanding and expressing your ideas.

Further reading

Alasuutari, P. (1995) *Researching Culture: Qualitative Method and Cultural Studies*. London: Sage. Chapter 7 discusses narrativity and the structure of the story as a whole.

Coffey, A. and Atkinson, P. (1996) *Making Sense of Qualitative Data: Complementary Research Strategies.* London: Sage. Chapter 3 is a sound and interesting introduction to narrative and story structures in qualitative writing.

Moore, N. (2000) *How to do Research: The Complete Guide to Designing and Managing Research Projects.* 3rd edn. London: Library Association. A good example of the journey analogy to describe the research process.

Golden-Biddle, K. and Locke, K.D. (1997) *Composing Qualitative Research.* London: Sage. Focuses on the story as a structure for writing research.

5 Choosing which type of dissertation to do

CHAPTER CONCEPTS

● DIFFERENT TYPES OF DISSERTATION ● THE TRADITIONAL DISSERTATION ● DIFFERENT KINDS OF TRADITIONAL DISSERTATIONS ● THE STAGES OF A WORK-BASED DISSERTATION ● KEY CHALLENGES OF THE TRADITIONAL DISSERTATION ● THE WORK-BASED DISSERTATION ● ACTION LEARNING AND THE WORK-BASED DISSERTATION ● THE STAGES OF A WORK-BASED DISSERTATION ● KEY CHALLENGES OF THE WORK-BASED DISSERTATION ● THE WORK-BASED DISSERTATION AS A RESEARCH REPORT ● SELF-EVALUATION IN THE RESEARCH REPORT ● THE LITERATURE REVIEW DISSERTATION ● THE STAGES OF LITERATURE REVIEW DISSERTATIONS ● LITERATURE REVIEW AND DECISION-MAKING (EVIDENCE-BASED REVIEWS) ● EVIDENCE-BASED REVIEWS ● CHALLENGES OF EVIDENCE-BASED REVIEWS ● LITERATURE REVIEW AS ANALYTICAL THERAPY ● THEORETICAL ANALYSIS DEFINITIONAL CLARITY ● CHALLENGES OF THERAPEUTIC-BASED REVIEWS ● LITERATURE REVIEW AS HISTORICAL ANALYSIS ● SUMMARY OF THIS CHAPTER ● FURTHER READING

There are different types of research and therefore different types of dissertation. Depending on your topic and how you have framed your research questions and who is sponsoring your studies, there are at least three main types of masters dissertation you can choose from. It may not be the case that the university department you have chosen can support all three but has expertise in one or two. Which type you do is a matter for you to think about, but before you decide look at the features of all of them. In this chapter we look at the features of the different types of dissertation building on the characterizations given in Chapter 1. The purpose of this chapter is to outline the different types of dissertation you can do by answering the following questions:

TABLE 5.1   DIFFERENT TYPES OF DISSERTATION

Type of dissertation	Brief description
Traditional dissertation	Usually based on primary data collection to test a hypothesis, proposition or fulfil a research aim. Can include evaluation studies and analysis of secondary data sources.
Work-based dissertation	Usually based on the identification of an issue that has demonstrable significance to an organization and which is investigated with the aim of making recommendations to implement change.
Literature review dissertation	Use of a topic and/or methodological literature to explore an issue or argument or origins of an idea, or provide evidence for decision-making.

1   **What are the different types of dissertation?**

2   **What kinds of topic and research are suited to which type of dissertation?**

3   **What do the different types of dissertation 'look like'?**

4   **How do you choose which type of dissertation to do?**

As far as possible the descriptions of the different types follow a similar format. The advantage of this is that you will be able to make comparisons between the types and also see the ways in which different elements from each may be combined to form a hybrid dissertation.

Different types of dissertation

There are three general types of dissertation at masters level which you can chose to do and these are shown in Table 5.1.

This three-type division is arbitrary in that in practice you can combine elements from all three or of two. For example, the work-based and the traditional dissertation both include a literature review, while some literature-based dissertations can be highly focused on a workplace issue. We are going to look at these three main types of dissertation, but remember these are only suggestions to get you thinking about what

TABLE 5.2   DEVELOPMENTAL APPROACH TO THE DISSERTATION IN MANAGEMENT STUDIES

General level	Requirements
Certificate project	Review of the related literature to identify the issues which may need to be addressed when considering a problem, development or opportunity in an organization.
Diploma project	A detailed review of the topic and methodological literatures to identify good and bad practices when applications of key concepts, techniques and methods have been used in other work-based situations.
Masters dissertation	The application of the main concepts, techniques and methods to a clearly defined issue that is of significance to an organization. It provides an evaluation of the research design and its application as a reflective practice and makes recommendations for lines of actions to address the issue and may implement those recommendations and provide an evaluation of effectiveness.

type of dissertation you may like to do. They are not prescriptive or the only types you can do, but indicate the range available from which you can select ideas.

You may also have noted from your own enquiries that some subject disciplines have a preference for a particular type of research and this is reflected in the dissertations their students produce. For example, management studies tend to prefer action research and the work-based dissertation, sociology the theoretical approach and the literature-based dissertation and psychology prefers hypothesis testing and the traditional dissertation. Do not feel obliged to follow these kinds of preferences, but do the type of research and dissertation suited to your research problem. In some cases you may also find that a department makes a distinction between what kinds of research activity counts as masters level. Check therefore with your supervisor on these matters before you start work on your research. Table 5.2 shows the kind of hierarchical distinctions sometimes found in management courses and generally reflects a developmental approach to producing a dissertation.

The logic of the management approach shown in Table 5.2 is that as a student you undertake work that prepares you for the next stage in your research. Even so, it is now being increasingly recognized that the literature review is much more than a prerequisite for the other two levels. The literature is now regarded as an important repository of

TABLE 5.3   DIFFERENT TYPES OF RESEARCH AND MASTERS DISSERTATIONS

Kind of research	Description
Descriptive survey	Dissertations based on the collection of primary data using tools such as questionnaires and interviewing. Often as the basis for testing hypothesis, propositions, measuring attitudes or describing patterns of behaviours and quantities.
Evaluation research	Dissertations based on developing criteria by which a product or service can be evaluated for such qualities as effectiveness, comprehensiveness, accuracy and validity.
Critical research	Dissertations based on identifying a collection of materials and subjecting it to analysis such as semiological analysis or content analysis, textual, discourse or citation analysis.
Comparative research	Dissertations based on making comparisons between products, services, critical incidents, before and after and occasionally between different countries and cultures.
Correlational research	Dissertations based on measuring the degree to which a relationship exists between two sets of variables using standard analytical statistics.

knowledge and practice. Its use requires advanced abilities for analysis and synthesis and can therefore be the basis of a masters level dissertation in its own right.

The traditional dissertation

Use of the term 'traditional' as a category is a little misleading, for all the types described in this chapter have become conventional formats for masters dissertations over the past two decades. Traditional as a type does, however, allow us to make some distinctions and draw attention to masters research based on the application of generic data analysis techniques such as semiology, content analysis, discourse analysis, conversation analysis, correlational analysis and the like.

DIFFERENT KINDS OF TRADITIONAL DISSERTATIONS

There is a wide range of approaches that can be included in the category of the traditional dissertation, especially the various approaches to research shown in Table 5.3. A point to note about these is that they tend to be small-scale research projects and therefore do not usually have large samples, evaluate major social programmes, undertake major international comparisons or employ large sets of variables for analysis.

The different kinds of research shown in Table 5.3 encompass the kinds of puzzles which were discussed in Chapter 1. Descriptive research can be the basis of correlational, causal, mechanical and developmental puzzles by providing both qualitative and qualitative data. In a similar way each type of dissertation can be influenced by the particular historical, contextual, conceptual and political stance taken. Hence when we talk about data we can mean a range of things including responses to a questionnaire or from interviewing, short extracts of conversation, Internet web pages, and all manner of archives such as cartoons and illustrations, football fanzines, popular women's magazines and posters. You can see some of these points in the two examples of traditional dissertations we have included: Table 5.4 illustrates the use of a questionnaire to measure the attitudes of public librarians to popular romantic fiction, while Table 5.5 shows the use of content analysis to research popular women's magazines.

THE STAGES OF A TRADITIONAL DISSERTATION

The traditional dissertation, like all other dissertations, has a number of stages which are typical and include:

- ◆ *Stage 1* Indicative search and review of the literature is undertaken to formulate a research problem, provide evidence of the problem, clarify any major concepts and provide definitions. The aims, research questions and specific objectives for the research are written and its purpose formulated with limitations set. The necessary data is then evaluated for access and manageability.

- ◆ *Stage 2* Comprehensive review of the literature is undertaken to show the origins of the topic and the problem, to help you become familiar with the main arguments and studies, to map the knowledge on the topic and show the relevance of your problem within the context of the literature.

- ◆ *Stage 3* Construction of the design for the research and rationalizing the choice of techniques is done and discussion of general methodological and ethical issues constructed. Next the methods are applied to collect the data and present it in appropriate formats.

- ◆ *Stage 4* Analysis and interpretation of the data with reference to the problem and the literature is undertaken to show how the findings address the research problem and relate to the existing body of knowledge. From this conclusions are made about the study in terms of what the findings may mean for understanding the topic.

TABLE 5.4   EXAMPLE OF A QUESTIONNAIRE-BASED TRADITIONAL DISSERTATION

Contents list of the dissertation	Comments
Introduction Setting the scene Aims and objectives Scope Propositions Benefits and justification Background	Introduction sets the context by providing statistics on the millions of romance books sold in the UK each year and showing that they are the most popular items borrowed from public libraries. From this the proposition is that professional librarians have a bias against romance books and that this is a form of cultural censorship. This proposition is based on an indicative review of the literature and therefore requires testing.

Literature review
Introduction
Definitions of popular
   romantic fiction
Origins of popular romantic fiction
The appeal of popular
   romantic fiction
Popular romantic fiction
   and the public library
Romance borrowing in the UK
Librarians' attitudes and
   opposition to stocking
   romances – professional ethics
	The literature review develops the themes and proposition made in the introductory chapter. Definitions of the genre are looked at to see in what ways different authors have framed the subject. The appeal of the genre is looked at from an historical perspective to show how widespread it is and includes such authors as Jane Austen and Shakespeare. Secondary statistical data is presented to show the industry of the romance. Finally, the literature about librarians' attitudes is reviewed and it is found to show a general bias against contemporary romantic fiction and its readers.

Methodology
Introduction – Value neutrality –
   Literature review – Attitudinal
   measurement techniques –
   Survey method – Sampling
   and sample – Self-completed
   questionnaire – Piloting and
   distribution of the questionnaire –
   Final version of the self-completed
   questionnaire – Rationale of the
   questions – Interview – Rejected
   methods – Data analysis
Interviews with publishers of romance
	The methodology begins with a series of statements based on the traditional literature, about the nature of the place and the role of values in research. This is because it is the value judgement of the librarians being questioned, therefore the values of the researcher are also deemed important, which are about serving the needs of readers rather than making assumptions about them. Questionnaires and interviews are selected and explained in relation to other possible methods.

Findings Introduction Personal reading habits and preferences of librarians	The responses from the questionnaire survey are presented in tabulated form based on the responses for each question. Thus, question one responses are labelled

(Continued)

TABLE 5.4 (CONTINUED)

Contents list of the dissertation	Comments
Personal opinions of librarians towards popular romantic fiction – Overall opinions – Romantic fiction as a product How fiction is chosen for the library – Concepts of professionalism – Romantic fiction and the public library – Selection procedures and user satisfaction – Professional opinions of romantic fiction	'Table 1', with the question being restated as findings. No attempt is made to provide an interpretation. The focus is on the presentation of the results in ways which are clear and systematic.
Analysis and discussion of findings Analysis of the responses Personal opinions of romantic fiction – Mills & Boon The appeal of romantic fiction – Acquisition policies – Romantic fiction and financial constraints – The selection process – Guidance used when selecting romantic fiction – Reluctance to stock romantic fiction – Ambivalence towards romantic fiction – Romantic fiction and the library – Romance and the reading habit – Justification for stocking romantic fiction Conclusions	The responses are analysed using a combination of techniques to measure attitudes, such as the Lickert scale and aggregation of responses. The qualitative aspects of the questionnaire where respondents have provided explanations are used to identify common practices and attitudes, and differences in attitudes and practices. The analysis and discussion stays close to the format of the questionnaire to avoid straying from the data and making unsubstantiated claims about the practices of the librarians. The findings from the survey are related to the findings of the literature review. There is a high degree of similarity in that a widespread bias against popular romantic fiction amongst professional librarians is found.
Conclusions and recommendations Attitudes of librarians Understanding the appeal of romantic fiction Acquisition procedures and collection development Recommendations – Librarian attitudes – Treatment of romantic fiction – Practitioner ethics Further research and discussion	The conclusions are related to the practice of stock selection in terms of the professional attitude to provide quality literature for the learning benefit of library users. Recourse to the professional role of the librarian is, however, found to be a secondary rationalization used to justify bias, but due to the high demand for popular romantic fiction does not prevent the librarians stocking increasing amounts of newly published romances. Recommendations are made based on developing an appreciation of reader needs and the nature of the genre.
Appendices Pilot questionnaire Final version of the questionnaire Interview schedule Follow-up interview schedule	The appendices provide full versions of the data collection tools.

Source: Adapted from Smullen, 1999 ('Survey of librarians' attitudes to popular romance books').

TABLE 5.5   EXAMPLE OF A DESK-BASED TRADITIONAL DISSERTATION

Contents list of the dissertation	Comments
Introduction Setting the scene Propositions Aims and objectives Benefits and justification	The introduction sets the context for the research in that information in the form of verifiable research is not normally associated with popular women's magazines. The proposition is that women's magazines disseminate a substantial and measurable amount of health information and that, contrary to popular belief, this is an effective and non-ideological method to do so.
Background information A brief history of the magazine industry in the UK The current magazine marketplace – Characteristics of the market for women's magazines – The future of the marketplace for women's magazines – Summary of the current marketplace Influences on the development of women's magazines Ideology and women's magazines	The topic is first set in the context of the women's magazine market. This is done to demonstrate the size of the market for publishers and the extent of the readership of the magazines. Women's magazines are shown to have a long history and a range of diverse titles. The market for the magazines is shown to be highly segmented, with different groups of titles being aimed at women in different socio-economic groups and life-style categories. The common approach to women's magazines as ideological publications is introduced and is looked at in more detail in the next chapter. This chapter therefore shows the women's magazine market to be substantial and not something that can be explained only in relation to ideological frames of reference.
Review of the literature Dominant ideology theory Feminist stylistics Portrayal of women in women's magazines: changes over time Magazine advertising Health information in women's magazines	The argument of the preceding chapter is continued to allow a movement from conventional social science approaches to women's magazines to a focus on the information content and, in particular, the health information in the magazines. The conventional approaches are represented by an examination of the usefulness of the 'dominant ideology thesis', as an approach, and 'feminist stylistics' as a technique of analysis, to the identification and measurement of health information. Both are found to be unhelpful for this particular task, but useful for understanding the changing portrayal of women.

(Continued)

TABLE 5.5 (CONTINUED)

Contents list of the dissertation	Comments
Methodology Primary data sources Content analysis Obtaining the sources: problems and issues Selection of data categories	The focus on information, it is argued, requires a technique of analysis based on measurement of quantity and categorization of types. The kinds of data – a sample of women's magazines from about 1900 to the present day – are identified. Content analysis is identified as the most appropriate technique to measure the quantities, frequencies and changes to the health topics covered by the magazines. Problems in obtaining sufficient magazines are discussed, as it was assumed publishers would have back copies when in fact they didn't. A range of different collections were located, however, which were able to provide access to a sufficient number of titles over a sufficient time period.
Results Volumes of health information – Total magazine length – Volume of health information – Number of items of health information – Length of health information items – Topics of health information – Health topic categories – Analysis of specific diseases and conditions – Comparison with mortality and morbidity statistics – Main subjects of items of health information – Practical health – Presentation of health information – Format of health information – Style of health information	The measurements of quantity are presented in tables, while the frequency of topics is presented in the form of frequency lists. The main aim is to present the findings in ways which are simple and clear. This is made difficult, however, by combining the analysis and discussion of the findings within this chapter. What we get is a two-part chapter, with the first part made up of numeric tables and lists and the second part made up of a discussion of the amounts of health reporting and what is reported. Within this there is recourse to the literature on information in popular magazines and to secondary statistics on health, including mortality and morbidity data. No definite relationship is found to exist between mortality, morbidity and health reporting in women's magazines. The range of health topics is found to be wide and modes of presentation to be simple yet informative, being largely based on medical research.

(Continued)

TABLE 5.5   (CONTINUED)

Contents list of the dissertation	Comments

Conclusions
Volume of health information –
  Health topics – Main subject
  of health items – Practical
  health – Format of health
  items – Style of health items –
  Evaluation of the proposition
Further research
	The main proposition is revisited and briefly discussed in terms of the amount, frequency and range of health topics in popular women's magazines. The contrast between this and other studies of women's magazines is emphasized and a claim is made for the information role of women's magazines. Further research on information analysis is suggested on the basis of its scarcity in the literature in relation to popular commercial publications such as magazines.

Appendices Births and deaths of magazines Top women's weekly magazines Readership profiles of women's magazines Data collection form	Appendices provide information and data on women's magazines, showing the high number of titles that have existed, and giving circulation and readership figures. This data is referred to in the main body of text as evidence of the substantial market coverage their popular women's magazines have and therefore potential as providers of information rather than ideology. The form used to collect the data is also included.

Source: Adapted from Oliver, 1998 ('Health information in women's magazines').

KEY CHALLENGES OF THE TRADITIONAL DISSERTATION

The main features of the traditional dissertation are also present, to a large degree, in the work-based dissertation. The identification and definition of a research problem, search and review of the literature and design of research are common features of both types. Both include a search and review of the literature on the topic and the methodology which gives them an overlap with the literature review dissertation. The main challenges of the traditional dissertation are as follows, but depending on the topic its scope may be extended to include some from the other two types:

♦ **A topic needs to be identified in a very limited timeframe which is capable of being researched, therefore finding a focus and making the process as simple as possible demands concentration.**

- There are many different elements including literature searching and reviewing, research design, data collection and analysis, which may include advanced statistics. Thus there is a wide range of skills to be acquired.

- Within the design and approach to a topic there are often many issues to be faced such as honesty, integrity and trust, which do not have a section in the dissertation. These qualities need to be thought about and made manifest in the doing of the research itself.

- The limitation of 15–20,000 words places severe constraints on how much of the work can be included in your dissertation. Therefore you need to learn to write in a way that is concise, clear and systematic and to be self-critical of your writing so as to be able to edit it for clarity and conciseness.

- The technical aspects of the research, such as data summation and statistical analysis, can take up a large amount of time and effort, leaving little time for interpretation of the data and reaching conclusions on what it means. Extra effort is therefore often needed near the end of the research period to ensure that interpretations have the necessary breadth and depth required and that the conclusions are based soundly on the data.

The work-based dissertation

A work-based dissertation is about contextualizing learning by extending it into the workplace. The rationale behind this is to optimize the return, for the student and their organization, on the investment in the masters course. It is usual to find that courses which prefer work-based dissertations are based on what is called 'action learning theory'.

ACTION LEARNING AND THE WORK-BASED DISSERTATION

The main aim of the work-based dissertation is that its findings and subsequent recommendations must be 'actionable'. This means whatever recommendations are made they must, at least, be capable of being implemented. It is sometimes required that the recommendations have been implemented and evaluated and this reported in the dissertation as a part of the research. The dissertation then contains a section discussing the implementation of the actions along with implications and outcomes of those actions. Initiating change through the problem definition and the research itself is seen, therefore, as a major deliverable of work-based action research.

THE STAGES OF A WORK-BASED DISSERTATION

The process of the work-based dissertation has three typical stages:

♦ *Stage 1*   An exploration and analysis of the literature to establish a framework for the study which includes critical evaluation of any prior findings on a similar situation, definitions of similar problems, and meta-evaluation of methods and findings from previous studies. This is used to recommend a research design in which the data and evidence can be collected in ways that are valid and meaningful.

♦ *Stage 2*   Within the context established by the analysis of the literature and what has been identified as 'good' and 'bad' practice, the data collected is analysed and interpreted in relation to the specific organizational problem. The key aim is to draw out the options, make clear and justifiable selections from these and construct sensible recommendations for lines of actions to be implemented.

♦ *Stage 3*   The actions recommended are, if possible, implemented and evaluated. The researcher-as-practitioner (organizational player) is expected to demonstrate a range of attitudes and qualities which have assisted them in collecting data and to implement lines of actions. Within this stage it is common for the researcher to reflect on their learning experiences and produce a brief evaluation of what has been learnt.

Table 5.6 and Table 5.7 show examples of work-based dissertations. In the first example you should be able to see the different elements common to this type of dissertation. It also shows the combination of an action approach to learning with standard methods such as the questionnaire and interview. The different stages can be seen in the content of the different chapters. What cannot be seen are the attitudes and qualities you would need for this kind of research which are necessary for managing the sensitivities of colleagues who may see you as interfering in their work or even questioning their competency.

TABLE 5.6   EXAMPLE OF A WORK-BASED DISSERTATION

Contents list of the dissertation	Comments
Introduction Organizational background issue definition Aims and objectives Scope of the research Benefits and justification	Introduction to the organizational issues of information sharing and information access in an information-intensive occupation. The aims are to assist the practitioners to self-analyse their information-seeking practices and to find more ways of using the available tools such as Lotus Notes.
Background information The probation service in the West Midlands Workloads and organization Service management Communication structures	The changing nature of regulations and policies and on-going operational informational needs are identified. The argument is made that with increasing workloads a more effective and efficient information system would increase productivity and the value of practitioners' knowledge.

Review of the literature
Introduction
What works and modernization of the probation service
Information needs studies
Information technology –
  NPSISS – Probation officers and information technology –
  Lotus Notes
Conclusions
	The literature is reviewed to identify previous strategies and tactics in the modernization of the probation service. Elements of good and bad practice are identified and related to the current information needs of practitioners. Secondary sources based on prior research of probation workers' training needs and skills at using information technology are employed to show levels and scope of current usage.

Methodology Literature on the action learning approach – Focus groups – Implementation issue – Literature review on surveys, questionnaires and interviewing – Usage statistics of Lotus Notes use – Questionnaire survey – Interviews – Research ethics	Methodology is not strictly an action approach, but is based on the responses of probation workers to questionnaires and follow-up interviews. The aim is to obtain primary data linked to individuals and small groups on their usage patterns and awareness of Lotus Notes in relation to their common information needs. The general and specific ethics of information sharing among the probation workers are discussed, which shows awareness of the information sensitivity and regulations that govern such services.

(Continued)

TABLE 5.6 (CONTINUED)

Contents list of the dissertation	Comments
Results Introduction Results from the questionnaires – Sources of information – Other useful information – Lotus Notes – Ease of use – Technical issues – Training – Lotus Notes development – Usage statistics – Information requirements – Summary of main findings – Results from the interviews	The findings are linked to individuals and small groups. Probation workers encouraged to reflect on their common information needs and to identify common sources available through Lotus Notes, which they were under-utilizing. Therefore the methodology is about awareness raising. The results of interviews using the questionnaire survey results as stimulus materials are presented using the major issues, which emerged from the secondary sources, interviews and questionnaires. The focus is on information needs, sources of information and use of the sources.

Analysis of findings
Sources of information – other
   useful information – Lotus
   Notes – Ease of use – Technical
   issues – Training – Lotus Notes
   development – Usage statistics
Conclusions
	The patterns of use and awareness identified are analysed in relation to levels of skill and awareness in using Lotus Notes. Skills and knowledge gaps are identified and related to the information needs of the probation workers, along with the need to improve various technical and access issues. Some of the findings from the questionnaire and secondary usage – age, usage, computer literacy – statistics are subject to statistical significance tests.

Discussion and evaluation
The information needs of
   probation practitioners in the
   West Midlands
Sources of information most
   commonly consulted –
   Information needs currently
   provided by Lotus Notes – Lotus
   notes databases – Staff use and
   access to Lotus Notes databases –
   Barriers to use – Patterns of use
Conclusions
	The discussion summarized the main findings, to provide an evaluation of the current and potential future use of Lotus Notes and a common information resource for probation workers. Common usage patterns are identified and ranked and related to variables such as age, gender and information-seeking knowledge. Various barriers to use are identified and translated into potential lines of action which are proposed as solutions to overcoming them.

(Continued)

TABLE 5.6   (CONTINUED)

Contents list of the dissertation	Comments
Conclusions and recommendation Improving information provision Enhancing staff use of Lotus Notes Reflection on the research	The findings are briefly related to the issues identified in the Introduction and shown to be in common within the West Midlands Probation Service. Lines of action are recommended which would make information seeking by the workers more efficient and effective (timely and relevant). Finally, what has been learnt whilst doing the research is outlined in a section on self-reflection.
Appendices Organizational management chart Examples of databases used Questionnaire Interview schedule Questionnaire significance tests	Appendices provide information on the organization, information databases relevant to the probation workers, along with the data collection tools and the calculations for the significance tests.

Source: Adapted from Sawbridge, 2001 ('Information needs of probation staff using Lotus Notes').

KEY CHALLENGES OF THE WORK-BASED DISSERTATION

There are a number of problems which those opting for a work-based dissertation often face, including identifying a real organizational problem or issue, getting agreement from the organization to study the problem, and managing relations with colleagues, subordinates and senior management, especially when implementing lines of action. Hence the need for good 'people skills', which include attributes such as honesty, openness, self-confidence, trustworthiness and objectivity.

In terms of selecting and rationalizing an organizational issue you will find that organizational issues tend to have four possibilities:

1   Doing research on an issue you know well in a familiar situation – the familiar task and familiar situation.

2   Doing research on an issue you know little about in an organization you know well – the unfamiliar task in a familiar organization.

3 Doing research on an issue you know in a situation you do not know very well — the familiar task in an unfamiliar organization.

4 Doing research on an issue you know little about in a situation new to you — the unfamiliar task in an unfamiliar situation.

Each of these possibilities share, to a lesser or greater degree, the following features which present a series of challenges:

♦ The work-based dissertation is a limited piece of research aimed at making a difference to a specific issue in an organization when viewed from 'before' and 'after'. It therefore needs to have clearly defined parameters.

♦ The nature of the issue facing the organization needs to be clearly defined and justified with robust evidence and sometimes obtaining sufficient quantitative evidence can be difficult, especially with 'human'-related issues.

♦ Data and evidence are broad-ranging, encompassing information from secondary sources (company documents, industrial statistics) and primary sources (interviews, questionnaires, observations). A good working knowledge of many data capture methods is therefore needed, with some requiring good technical abilities such as statistics, communication and people skills.

♦ Based in the 'now' and near future the research can be seen as having a value in organizational terms, though this may not be long term, and therefore care needs to be taken not to select an issue that will correct itself before the research is completed.

♦ The research may give the researcher a higher level of visibility in their organization than previously and this may lead to conflicts with colleagues. There will be the need for conflict resolution strategies to be ready when and if needed.

♦ As the researcher you are responsible for your research, especially for the careful and thoughtful implementation of any recommendations. The impact on the organization beyond the local setting may have to be taken into account and these may outweigh the benefits.

♦ The dissertation tends to have the structure of a report but must contain the following three main kinds of evidence. Ensuring these are at an appropriate level can be difficult within the format of a formal report:

(a) evidence of appropriate arrangement – a statement of the topic as an organizational issue, review of relevant literature including industry statistics and organizational documents to contextualize the issue, a review of methodological approaches applied in similar situations, justification for the methodology employed and clear presentation of findings including related evidence from secondary sources, succinct discussion of findings and emerging implications, identification of options for action, selection and justification of recommendations and proposed implementation plan, implementation (if appropriate) and its evaluation, conclusions, including identification of key deliverables, self-reflection on learning and identification of further research which could be undertaken;

(b) evidence of personal and project learning outcomes – clear statements to show continuous development of the ways in which skills, capabilities, attitudes and qualities have been applied through the process of doing the research; and

(c) evidence of critical thinking – in the review and use of the literature and analysis of the findings, critical evaluation and interpretation must be demonstrated in a number of sections, including justification of the topic, identification of a research gap, comparison of findings with those in the literature and evaluation of alternative lines of possible action.

These challenges and kinds of evidence are the main features of the work-based dissertation. Although they make the work-based dissertation distinct from the other types, it is nevertheless expected that all three types exhibit the same high standards of scholarship. In the second example of a work-based dissertation, shown in Table 5.7, some of what we mean by evidence can be seen. It shows an international comparison aimed at taking the best practice of one country and making recommendations of how and where it can be applied in another country. International or cross-cultural comparisons are very difficult to do. One of the main problems is that as a researcher you will need to be competent in the languages of both countries and very familiar with the two kinds of organizations being compared.

TABLE 5.7   EXAMPLE OF A WORK-BASED COMPARATIVE DISSERTATION

Contents list of the dissertation	Comments
Introduction Setting the scene Aims and objectives Benefits and justification	Introduction identifies some of the major strategic and organizational problems in Romanian academic libraries with brief comparisons to academic libraries in the UK. The aims are to identify possible ways forward for Romanian academic libraries in terms of a national strategy.
Background information Structure of academic libraries in Romania Current state of development of academic libraries in Romania Problems in academic libraries in Romania	The organizational issue is a management problem related to the need for strategic thinking. This is developed using specific examples based on secondary sources including statistics. A series of initial claims are made which are substantiated with data and further backing. Note the assumption that UK academic libraries can be used as a benchmark for the evaluation of Romanian academic libraries.
Review of the literature Literature on Western/UK academic libraries – Information and communications technologies – Academic library marketing – Academic library management Literature on Eastern/Romanian academic libraries – Information and communications technologies – Academic library marketing – Academic library management Conclusions	The comparative basis of the study is explained and the relevant literatures on British and Romanian academic libraries identified. The comparative literatures are looked at in turn using categories identified in an initial or indicative review of the literature done for the research proposal. In the case of both literatures some incursions are made into the broader literatures, especially secondary sources, to bring in examples of practice and approach in the main areas selected for attention. Out of the reviews major approaches and concepts are identified which researchers and practitioners have found to be useful. The findings of the literature review are summarized and their usefulness in terms of understanding the issues related back to the initial statement of the problem.

(Continued)

TABLE 5.7   (CONTINUED)

Contents list of the dissertation	Comments
Methodology Methodological overview – Identifying and reviewing the available literature – Establishing the current state of developments in Romanian academic libraries – Carrying out a Delphi exercise The literature – Delphi Technique – The panel – Questionnaires vs. interviews – Questionnaire design Conclusions	The techniques for collecting and analysing data on the issues are focused on the Delphi Technique. The justification for this is developed by looking at the nature of the problems to show that the Delphi Technique is the most suitable in these circumstances. The methodological literature on the origins and development of the technique are reviewed in terms of its methodological standing for producing reliable and valid data and what data collection tools are best suited when it is applied. Discussion of questionnaires and interviews are used to demonstrate a sound understanding of these methods and this is further shown in the discussion on the design of a questionnaire.
Implementation Response rates Round 1 Round 2	The results of the application of the Delphi Technique are presented along with data on the response rates. No attempt is made to interpret the responses. The proper use of the technique is demonstrated in the way in which the results are presented – as a series of applications within two rounds.
Results Priority areas of change in your library: targets Major ways forward: how to achieve targets General strategy	The responses from senior stakeholders in UK and Romanian academic libraries have provided three general categories of concern. Each of these is described with detailed references to the responses to show what the major views of the respondents are and how these overlap.
Discussion and analysis The current state of developments in Romanian academic libraries – General library environment – Information and communications technology – Personnel – Library marketing and management	The understandings and concerns of the respondents, having inductively provided three major categories, are used to discuss the areas of concern found in the literature. We now have six categories for discussion, which are all focused on the major aim of identifying ways forward for Romanian academic libraries.

(Continued)

TABLE 5.7 (CONTINUED)

Contents list of the dissertation	Comments
Priority area of change in your library: Targets – general library environment – Information and communications technology – Personnel – Library marketing and management	Note how the initial findings from the literature have been further refined because of the incorporation of the findings from the respondents – further sub-categories have been included, such as 'personnel'.
Major ways forward: How to achieve targets – General library environment – Information and communications technology – Personnel – Library marketing and management	The discussion is systematic, looking at each area in turn. This helps to maintain the focus on the initial aim and to demonstrate good practice when interpreting the significance and meaning of the data. It also shows how the findings from the literature review can be fully incorporated into the discussion to obtain a much broader and deeper understanding of the issues than would be had if only one source had been used.
General strategy – General library environment – Information and communications technology – personnel – Library marketing and management	
Conclusions	
Conclusions and recommendations for change	The major categories which were an outcome of the data collected are employed to frame a series of detailed recommendations which are proposed as actionable.
Priority areas of change in your library: Targets	
Major ways forward: How to achieve targets	
General strategy	
Recommendations	

Source: Adapted from Deaconescu, 2000 ('Change in Romanian academic libraries').

THE WORK-BASED DISSERTATION AS A RESEARCH REPORT

It is normal for the work-based dissertation to be presented in the format of a formal report. A formal report has been defined as:

> A formal statement of the results of an investigation, or of any matter on which definite information is required, made by some person or body instructed or required to do so. (*Shorter Oxford English Dictionary*)

You can see, in the examples accompanying this section, the arrangement some researchers have used to present their research. But in a work-based dissertation it is more than the results which are included. The term 'results' when applied to the work-based dissertation means the results of the work you did to produce the dissertation. This includes the results of your considerations when constructing your research design, the results of your search and review of the literature, the results of defining and justifying your research problem and the results of your data collection. Results in this context has a much broader meaning than is normally assumed for a formal research report. You may, however, place your major findings and recommendations at the beginning of your report in an 'executive summary' to allow the reader to see what you found before moving on to read about how you made these findings. In the work-based dissertation the main sections of the report consist largely of description and explanation of how and why you did what you did. It is this which will enable you to provide sound evidence for your arguments and it is the only way in which you will be able to make the case for the reasonableness (that is, validity) of your findings and recommendations. More is said about the difference between research reports and others ways of presenting your research in Chapter 12, 'Writing your dissertation'.

SELF-EVALUATION IN THE RESEARCH REPORT

The work-based dissertation is not a research report in the strict or conventional use of the format. This is because it must include a discussion of issues not normally contained in a conventional research report. One of these is the self-evaluation of the research, which is not done in a single section but in various locations throughout the dissertation. The main point to note about 'reflective practice', as self-evaluation is sometimes called, is it is about addressing a range of issues, which we can state as a series of questions, such as the following:

♦ **The research questions**: How and why were the research questions stated in the way they were, and how, if one was used, do they relate to the hypothesis? Were the questions capable of being researched, if so, to what degree? How would you change them with hindsight? What assumptions did you make at the start of your research and how have these changed now you have finished the research – for example, were they justified, and did they influence your interpretations?

♦ **The search and review of the literature**: How effective was your search for relevant literature? What terminology did you use and why? What problems did you encounter with the literature and how did you solve them? How did you limit your search and what impact did this have on your understanding of the issue?

♦ *The procedures employed*: Were the procedures you selected for the research appropriate when used in the field? What problems did you encounter and how did you deal with them? What skills, attitudes and qualities did you need to apply the research design and collect reliable and valid data? Were there any technical and personal problems with the research, if so, what, and what was the impact of these on the findings?

♦ *The conclusions and recommendations*: Are all the recommendations fully supported by the data collected in the research? What influence did your own cultural or organizational position have on how you framed your conclusions and recommendations? What kinds of implications can you draw from the conclusions in terms of the literature, the issues you investigated and your own learning development?

You may also include those persons who were a part of it – your colleagues and managers – by asking them to make an evaluation of your research. In this way you will get relevant feedback on such matters as how far you have strayed from the main issue, how you have retained a sense of reality and achievability in your recommendations and, importantly, how you have managed their understandings of your intentions.

The literature review dissertation

In the early 1990s tremendous advances were made in providing indexes and abstracts in electronic formats, such as CD ROM and on-line. All of the major databases that indexed the publications in the social sciences have become available in electronic formats and many have now retrospectively indexed the article literature going back into the 1960s. Added to this is the ease by which we can now search these databases, making a search of the literature a far less time-consuming task than previously. Some of the outcomes have been the formulation of different kinds of search and literature review. In this section we will look at the three main kinds of literature review that can be used as the basis of a masters dissertation: the *review for decision-making*; the *review for analytical therapy*; and the *review for examining the history of ideas*.

THE STAGES OF LITERATURE REVIEW DISSERTATIONS

The processes involved in undertaking a literature-based masters dissertation differ in the details from a work-based dissertation, but have some generic stages which are outlined below:

♦ *Stage 1*   Definition of the problem and research questions are set. It is argued that the relevant literature will be able to provide answers to, or better under-standing of these when examined in the context of the problem. The literature is therefore identified as the main source of data for the research.

♦ *Stage 2*   Careful design of the literature search strategy is undertaken to identify the necessary sources and resources which will be comprehensively searched. This incudes clear definition of the criteria and procedures for evaluating the relevance of the literature for inclusion and exclusion from the research.

♦ *Stage 3*   Critical analysis of the literature is undertaken to identify appropriate contributions to the topic problem. This consists of identifying the different ways in which the problem has been defined and approached, deconstructing the main arguments, evaluating them against the criteria set, and, if based on 'findings', assessing these on an individual and aggregate level.

♦ *Stage 4*   The elements of the analysis are synthesized into relevant categories, which are justified by being based in the literature and used to express complemen-tary and opposing, alongside highly relevant and confused views on the problem, to show with more clarity knowledge of the problem, its origins and development or how the literature can provide a basis of recommendations for lines of action.

LITERATURE REVIEW AND DECISION-MAKING (EVIDENCE-BASED REVIEWS)

The use of findings from the research-based literature has been developed into a major form of literature reviewing by policy studies and health informatics. This is despite the literature review not being recognized as a legitimate research activity in the UK until 1995, when the Research Assessment Exercise allowed them to be included in submissions. The evidenced-based approach is based on the assumption that all avail-able verified and reliable evidence should be used to inform decision-making. In the case of health practice there are three main ways in which this translates into practice where evidence is used to:

♦ improve the choices patients have of services and treatments;

♦ make measurable improvements in clinical practice; and

♦ improve the management of health service provision.

While some of the problems of evidence-based literature reviewing are beyond the scope of this book (because they are about bio-medical applications), the approach does have value for areas within the social sciences such as social policy, information studies and management studies. The examples we include show this value and indicate how some of the practices of this form of reviewing can be used in all literature reviews.

EVIDENCE-BASED REVIEWS

Within the remit of evaluation studies questions about which programme, treatment or approach works best has been developed into a major international research programme in the medical fields (Gray, 2001), including social and behavioural psychology (Smith and Glass, 1977). The basis of the evidenced-based review is to identify in a systematic way relevant studies on a condition and its treatment, subject the studies to a through evaluation and aggregate the findings from controlled experimental mega-trails (involving 20,000 subjects in the control and non-control groups). The purpose is to collect evidence that is reliable and valid and that can be used to enhance the effectiveness and efficiency of decision-making. The emphasis on the usefulness of the research literature began in 1972 when Archie Cochrane, a British epidemiologist, argued that there was widespread ignorance among health care professionals of the findings from an immense research literature (Cochrane, 1989). Cochrane showed that the results of a systematic review of randomized control trials (RCT) on a course of corticosteroid given to women prone to premature childbirth could reduce the risks to babies dying of immaturity. Two decades later more trials had been completed and these were aggregated with the earlier results, showing a stronger relationship between the effectiveness of the treatment and survival of the immature babies. As a result of Cochrane's work, an international collaboration of expert reviewers has developed and established the Cochrane Collaboration and Cochrane Centre. The outcome of these is several databases of meta-analysis published as a part of the Cochrane Library.

Meta-analysis is not confined to the medical fields but is a part of most disciplines. The difference between the Cochrane Reviews and others is often a matter of the type of research included in the review. Cochrane Reviews mostly include the results of experimental trials (published and unpublished) while other reviews, usually based on meta-analysis, include findings from other types of research. An example of meta-analysis in social psychology can be seen in Smith and Glass (1977). In this study, done before the general availability of electronic databases, the aim was to evaluate the effectiveness of therapies practised by psychotherapists. Some 375 original studies were analysed, which included approximately 50,000 subjects. Applying a range of standard statistical techniques for all the studies, at least one effect size was calculated, resulting in 833 calculated effects. For each study the dependent variable was the effectiveness of a treatment related to a range of independent variables (level and type of treatment). Smith and Glass (1977) concluded from their meta-analysis that psycho-therapies do make improvements to subjects. Importantly they provide a note of caution about which therapies work 'best'. Those showing a greater measure of effec-tiveness, they point out, may be due to other variables not able to be controlled (con-founding variables), such as the most effective treatments being used to treat the less complicated conditions. The more complicated the condition, the less effective the treatment, therefore the ranking of therapies cannot be taken as representing the real effectiveness of therapies.

CHALLENGES OF EVIDENCE-BASED REVIEWS

The main challenges of the evidence-based dissertation are focused around the issues of reliability of the data in the literature and the need for a high level of technical proficiency in the biological sciences and statistical techniques. We can list these in the following way:

♦ the language of the article and monograph literature is usually that of the biological and chemical sciences in relation to the practice of medicine and therefore requires a competent level of experience with these;

♦ most of the sources report that findings of trials use statistical techniques, there-fore a sound and proficient understanding of these techniques is needed along with experience of medical trials, product testing and experimentation;

♦ many sources have an evident bias towards the positive rather than the negative, therefore an understanding of this practice and how to recognize and balance it is required;

♦ the disciplines on which the literature is based are intimately connected to commercial research, which, for commercial reasons, is highly secretive and therefore not everything is reported in the literature;

♦ the ways in which the literature is indexed and abstracted varies between services and therefore requires an understanding of the vocabulary of bio-medical indexing, and for abstracts to be persuasive rather than descriptive and evaluative; and

♦ as the purpose of the literature is to inform decision-making, a thorough knowledge of the different techniques of decision-making is needed.

The systematic review is, I would argue, an essential part of all research and can form the basis of a dissertation in any discipline on any topic. When used to inform or even implement courses of action to make changes to a situation, the standards of the review must be thorough and fully accountable, displaying a sound knowledge of the different types of research, especially the differences between experimental and non-experimental studies.

LITERATURE REVIEW AS ANALYTICAL THERAPY

When one goes back into the history of masters research in the UK we see that the majority of dissertations are 'thesis' type analysis and discussions of the major theorists and theories. These are often critiques of an existing approach such as functionalism, chronologically based interpretations of a theory such as Marxism, or overtly value-driven arguments such as feminist critiques. Many of these dissertations tend to exhibit sound argument and a good understanding of the philosophy of the social sciences. These kinds of dissertation may now be in the minority, but are nevertheless still very relevant because they can provide a deep understanding of the foundations and origins of the social sciences. They are an excellent vehicle if you are looking to expand substantially your understanding of the theoretical, methodological and philosophical aspects of the social sciences and your abilities to undertake advanced critical evaluation and thinking. The two we will look at in this category are those that seek to clarify the ways in which assumptions and procedures have been used in order to take us out of misunderstandings, and those that seek to analyse the meaning and use of words and phrases.

Before we look at these it is important to note that these types of dissertations are not to be classed as theory-driven or esoteric, but can, as the example in Table 5.8 shows, be based on contemporary organizational issues, like a work-based dissertation. The main difference is that, unlike the work-based dissertation, the review-based dissertation often

TABLE 5.8 EXAMPLE OF A LITERATURE REVIEW DISSERTATION

Contents list of the dissertation	Comments
Introduction Executive summary Aims and objectives Scope Overview of methodology	Introductory chapter to justify the topic and define the nature of the problem selected, explaining why a review of the literature is needed. The aims set out the investigative analytical approach while the objectives identify the major milestones necessary to achieve the aims. The scope sets the limits or parameters for the problem and in so doing the limits for the search and use of the literature.
Background and context Definitions – knowledge – knowledge management	As a relatively new development in the literature, KM (knowledge management) nevertheless has a large and growing literature. The student therefore shows the range of differing definitions of the main elements of the KM movement – knowledge and management. Both are extremely difficult to define and this is shown.
Organizations implementing KM New Employment Trends in British Petroleum 3M Royal Mail Consulting Dow Chemical and Scandial Link Hewlett-Packard Consulting	If companies such as those selected have implemented or are in the process of implementing KM in their organizations, then what is it they are implementing? How do they define or characterize KM? This links the different definitions in the academic literature to the different working understandings of practitioners at a company level. It provides for two comparative sets of definitions, those in the literature and those of the companies.

Core features of KM
    implementation
Reasons for implementing KM
Core competencies – Audits –
    Information technologies –
    Culture
	Examination of the elements assembled to implement KM in different organizations are looked at using four categories – two related to skills and competencies, one to information communications technologies and, finally, one to organizational culture.

(Continued)

TABLE 5.8 (CONTINUED)

Contents list of the dissertation	Comments
	From these are extracted the features used to implement KM and therefore what are taken to be the main elements which may be the common features for the construction of a definition.
Theoretical aspects of KM Data, information, knowledge and wisdom Process of knowledge creation – Tacit knowledge and explicit knowledge – Different purposes of organizational knowledge – Intellectual capital Conclusions about knowledge	Different definitions are found to be linked to different understandings and use of the vocabulary in the KM literature and to conceptualizations of what KM is about and how it can be explained. Definitions used are linked to different understandings of how organizational knowledge is created, how it can be described and what its purposes are. In addition, the assumptions about the competitive advantages of knowledge are looked at under the heading 'intellectual capital' and this is related to the purposes of knowledge and different types of knowledge.
Methodological approaches to implementing KM Best practice transfer – Intellectual capital – Learning organization Innovation – Agile organization Information technology – Business process re-engineering – Total quality management – Core competencies – Information management Ten methodological approaches to implementing KM	Different definitions and different ways of implementing KM are looked at in terms of the broader but highly related management literature on organizations, such as the 'learning organization' and 'agile organization' – characterizations and recommendations in the literature about what kinds of organizational structures and cultures will be required in the near future for competitive relevance. These characterizations are examined and shown to be related to conceptualizations and recommendations in the literature specific to KM and preceding KM. Hence the origins of KM are shown in terms of a developmental process to the understanding of organizational dynamics and, in part, strategic direction. In total, ten methodological approaches to KM are identified from a combined analysis of the literature and the mini case studies of organizations.

(Continued)

TABLE 5.8 (CONTINUED)

Contents list of the dissertation	Comments
Results Table 1 Authors citing various methodological approaches to implementing KM – Table 4 Organizations practising various methodological approaches to implementing KM – Figure 1 Structured conceptual pathway (SCP) depicting the intellectual capital approach to KM – Figure 2 Structured conceptual pathway depicting the learning approach to KM – Figure 3 Structured conceptual pathway depicting the innovative approach to implementing KM	The results are not statistical but summative in that what has been identified in the literature and in practice can be categorized into one or more methodological approach to KM. Using a series of figures and tables, authors are classified as promoting a particular methodological approach and this is followed by a similar classification for the organizations. What we now have is the use of a typology into which authors and organizations can be placed depending on their preferred methodological approach to defining, characterizing or implementing KM. From the different methodological approaches the three most common are schematized and described as 'conceptual pathways' to depict the main elements in the processes used within the main methodological approach, e.g. 'learning organizational' approach.
Discussion of results *Findings from the tables* KM and BPR (Business Process Research) – KM and TQM – KM and core competencies – KM and information management and technologies – KM and intellectual capital – KM and the learning organization – KM and innovation KM and the agile organization – Three approaches to KM *Structured conceptual pathways* Elements of SCPs Components of the SCPs One approach to KM	The construction of the typologies came out of the analysis of the literature and the ways in which different companies are implementing KM. This is then used as the basis for examining the relationships of KM to a range of management and organization concerns, looked at earlier in the dissertation, such as total quality management (TQM). This analysis also revisits some of the main approaches to the understanding of organizations, such as 'the learning organization' and to characterizations of organizations, such as 'the agile organization'. From this application and subsequent analysis of the typologies, a series of common points of reference are identified which are used to suggest that there are three main approaches to KM. These are represented in diagrams showing the main methodologies, elements and processes.

(Continued)

TABLE 5.8 (CONTINUED)

Contents list of the dissertation	Comments
	From these it is shown that a comprehensive definition is not possible or desirable, but that KM can be characterized in terms of the ways in which an author or organization has elected to take in approaches to the essential elements of KM. These different ways are the conceptual pathways. Importantly, the three conceptual pathways are then shown to be based on common objectives and outcomes and can therefore be synthesized into one main approach to KM. This is posited as the definition of KM.
Conclusions Reflections on the research Reflections on the literature encountered in the research	Where the analysis has been, how it got to where it ended up, and what its significance is are briefly discussed in terms of the aims and objectives set for the research. The nature and features of the literature are also discussed to highlight common and interesting elements, along with problems and difficulties encountered.
Bibliographies	Comprehensive bibliographies are provided to show the scope of the literature.

Source: King, 1999 ('What is knowledge management? A critical analysis of the literature').

results in understandings that have a long shelf-life in terms of personal understanding and the long-term contribution the review-based dissertation can make to the literature. I have called these types of dissertation 'therapeutic' because they can bring awareness, understanding and clarity to a problem, in that we can see its cause and the means to eradicate it.

Theoretical analysis

There is a range of ways in which you can do a theory-based dissertation, including examining the following:

♦ **development of a major or minor theory through an examination of seminal studies;**

♦ **the implications of the theory to a particular issue or problem;**

+ the methodological origins of theory or approach; and

+ a clarification of methodological puzzles raised by a study.

All of these will involve a thorough review of the literature and a commitment to acquiring a sound understanding of the methodologies of the social sciences. What this means is that if you are interested in, for example, the application of postmodernist ideas to public spaces, then you will also need to encompass in your work other approaches to show the origins of postmodernism. In these kinds of studies you are dealing with ideas, arguments, concepts and the ways in which they have been applied. For example, if you were interested in the dramaturgical approach of Erving Goffman you would review his major works and those of other pre-symbolic interactionists such as George Herbert Mead and Charles Cooley. Your aim might be to examine the development and use of Goffman's major concepts to characterize his model of interaction or to compare and contrast his work with that of another, such as Harold Garfinkel.

A prerequisite for this kind of study is the ability to read sociologically (Anderson et al., 1985). This means looking at the work of any theorist as exhibited in the exercise and application of reasoning about an issue. In the case of Goffman we may choose to see his writings as a project in which he is systematically exploring and developing his analytical framework. It may involve taking his books and articles in chronological order to see how he develops his ideas through his use of examples. This would lead us to an examination of his starting point and his methodological assumptions, to see how he develops them using certain kinds of reasoning and argument. Our systematic reading of Goffman's work would lead us, if we have been careful and open to his ideas, to an understanding of some very sophisticated reasoning in sociology, which is quite at odds with the way Goffman writes. His articles and books are often written in a style that seems casual and not scholarly. Hence if we were to show the complexities and sophistication of his reasoning, then we would be showing that contrary to some popular beliefs about his work Goffman was a major social theorist.

Definitional clarity

There are many words and phrases used throughout the social sciences which are in common usage, but which are difficult to define, characterize or understand. The relationship between how something has been defined and how applied may be hard to understand. In the work-based dissertation you will have noticed that the identification of concepts is important. In identifying the main concepts relevant to an issue you also need to be able to unpack the ways in which the concept has been put together so that you can evaluate its usefulness in application and operationalization. There are many classic studies in the social sciences which have done this, including those which have looked at community, alienation, power, bureaucracy and so on.

> See 'Defining' in *Doing a Literature Review* (Hart, 1998) for more on definitions and concepts applied to the concept of community and suicide.

Table 5.8 shows an example of an investigation to bring clarity to the phrase 'knowledge management'. Each of these words is difficult in itself to define, but even more difficult when they are combined. As categories for the designation of commonly used words, knowledge and management have come to be used throughout the management and organizational literatures. There is now a substantial body of literature across the social sciences about knowledge management. Taking as a starting point the observations and arguments of Gilbert Ryle (1949), we can see in Table 5.8 an attempt to describe the different ways in which different authors have used the phrase 'knowledge management'. This detailed description of use makes visible for analysis the kinds of assumptions different authors are using to construct their understandings, including recommendations, for their preferred position on the meaning and implications of knowledge management. The analysis therefore is able to evaluate the degree to which groups of authors share common assumptions as well as the degree to which they have thought carefully about their use of categories and concepts. In total, some ten methodological approaches to understanding knowledge management are identified in the literature. These are then related to the ways in which a range of actual organizations are or have implemented a knowledge-management strategy. Comparing different conceptualizations of knowledge management with different ways in which different companies have implemented a knowledge-management strategy shows that there is no general agreement as to what knowledge management is. However, further analysis of the language of the organizations and the literature enables the vocabulary of knowledge management to be mapped in a series of typological diagrams. These maps are offered as representations which show the methodological history of definitions and understandings of knowledge management and importantly where problems resulting from equivocal definition originate. These diagrams are called 'conceptual pathways' because they map the conceptual paths the methodological approaches have taken. By doing this it is possible to see where confusions have arisen and also where common points of comparison and similarity can be identified.

CHALLENGES OF THERAPEUTIC-BASED REVIEWS

Therapeutic dissertations are based largely on a search and review of the literature. Some of the challenges we raised for the evidence-based reviews are also applicable here, but we have some which are specific to the therapeutic dissertation including:

♦ the literature can be wide-ranging, covering many subject disciplines across the social sciences and therefore a good grounding in the main methodological and philosophical traditions will be needed;

♦ the literature, because it is multi-disciplinary, will exhibit many different styles of writing and argumentation, and so you will need to be flexible and open to these differences;

♦ some of the literature will take you into the major social theories and since these can have extensive literatures of their own which can be both technical and abstract, you need to be able to absorb ideas and arguments quickly;

♦ with extensive literatures you may not be able to complete your review within the normal time allocated for the dissertation, and so you may have to consider taking longer or preparing your research in advance of the dissertation period;

♦ the amounts of information generated by the search and review can be substantial, requiring not only a good document management system, but also that you be capable of cognitively synthesizing a broad range of ideas, concepts, arguments and theories;

♦ you may find yourself challenging some of the long-held assumptions in the social sciences or some major theories and theorists, and therefore you need to be aware of the responsibilities and consequences of your analysis, which means paying close attention to scholarly standards in your work; and

♦ questioning and challenging assumptions in the literature is not an easy thing to do, nor is placing to one side long-held assumptions you may have about what constitutes research — both require a degree of bravery and willingness to 'play' with ideas.

These are some of the challenges and if you are already familiar with the methodological literature of the social sciences you may have noticed the implicit bias towards the work of authors such as Ludwig Wittgenstein, Gilbert Ryle and Peter Winch. This is because this kind of thinking, approach and analysis provides powerful routes into many of the methodological arguments common in the social sciences, to unravel some of the most puzzling debates and to clarify common mistakes of reasoning.

LITERATURE REVIEW AS HISTORICAL ANALYSIS

Another approach to using the literature is to look at a theorist or social movement or group which has been forgotten or largely dismissed. The aim here would be to show the relevance of the theorist at the time of their major writing and possibly for current social science. For example, the work of Albion Small and Robert Park were until recently assigned to the not-so-interesting section of sociological history. But in the 1980s their work was revisited by people such as Martin Bulmer (1984) and his *The Chicago School of Sociology* was shown to have been a major influence on the development of a number of research themes including community studies, the understanding of immigration and settlement, and ethnography. A variant on this theme is to employ visual data within the review to construct arguments about how the data may be seen to exhibit key theories in the literature (Bauer and Gaskell, 2000).

This may include the study of citations. A citation is the bibliographical details of a publication. Each time an article is published in a recognized journal its full citation details are recorded, along with the list of citations the author of the article has referred to. In

> See *Doing a Literature Search* (Hart, 2001), Chapter 9, and *Doing a Literature Review* (Hart, 1998), pp. 167–70, for examples of citation analysis

this way the citation indexes for the social sciences has built up an incredible database, recording who has cited whom in their publications. The main citation indexes for the social sciences are the Social Science Citation Index (SSCI) and the Arts and Humanities Citation Index (A&HCI). It is therefore possible to plot historically the origins of an idea, theory, development or argument. You do so by searching the citation indexes.

SUMMARY OF THIS CHAPTER

In this chapter different types of dissertation have been described. The key points that have been made in this chapter are:

♦ There are different types of dissertation and all, if done properly, are legitimate contributions to masters level research.

♦ Each type of dissertation contains common elements such as a justifiable research design and grounding in an existing research literature.

♦ The types of dissertation described in this chapter are suggestions as to what is possible. Your own dissertation will be unique, embodying your particular topic and research design.

Further reading

Anderson, R.J., Hughes, J.A. and Sharrock, W.W. (1985) *The Sociology Game: An Introduction to Sociological Reasoning*. London: Longman. See Chapter 7, 'Reading sociologically: Goffman as an example'; this provides a good example of the elements required for reviewing a theorist's work.

Gray, M.J.A. (2001) *Evidence-based Health Care: How to Make Health Policy and Management Decisions*. London: Churchill Livingstone. A comprehensive introduction to evidence-based decision-making based on literature reviewing.

Hart, C. (1998) *Doing a Literature Review: Releasing the Social Science Imagination*. London: Sage. Companion to this book. See Chapter 5, 'Organizing and expressing ideas' for more on defining, comparing, and the work of Ryle and Wittgenstein.

Hart, C. (2001) *Doing a Literature Search: A Comprehensive Guide for the Social Sciences*. London: Sage.

Hughes, J. and Sharrock, W. (1997) *The Philosophy of the Social Sciences*. 3rd edn. London: Longman. Clear and concise introduction, includes excellent overviews of the work of Peter Winch who translated the philosophy of Wittgenstein for use in the social sciences; especially useful for understanding the nature of 'therapeutic research'.

Searching and reviewing the literature

The search and review of the literature is a critical evaluation, analysis and synthesis of existing knowledge relevant to your own research problem. It is critical in that you are required to evaluate what you read. It is an analysis in that you are required to extract different kinds of information from what you read. It is a synthesis in that you are required to show the relationships that exist between different studies and show how these relate to your own research. You are aiming to assess critically what definitions of the topic/problem have been offered and how they have been used and to evaluate the methodological approaches employed and to identify gaps in empirical work and assumptions used. A literature review is not therefore a summary, synopsis or series of annotations or a description of other people's work. A good literature review: exhibits technical competencies in searching for and selecting items; has clarity of expression in writing and arrangement of materials; undertakes argumentation analysis in the evaluation of existing work; and is used to structure the reasons for your proposed research and to show where your research, once completed, relates to existing knowledge. The key questions looked at in this chapter are:

1 What will a search and review of the literature contribute to a dissertation?

2 What is the literature and how do you find relevant publications?

3 How can you analyse the literature?

4 How can the literature be used to justify your topic?

5 What is a literature review and how do you write one?

Students often say that searching the literature is one of the most enjoyable parts of doing research, but that reviewing what they find is one of most difficult. This chapter will help you to do both of these necessary tasks in ways which give you the opportunity to develop the ability to become competent and efficient literature searchers and reviewers of different types of literature. This chapter is divided into two main parts – searching the literature and reviewing the literature. The focus throughout is on enabling you to plan and execute an indicative and comprehensive search for literature on your topic and on possible methodological approaches for your research.

What is the literature?

The literature for most masters research projects is made up of various published and non-published items including books, statistics and reports. Table 6.1 lists the main items which make up the literature. Note from this range of publications the inclusion of such things as conference papers and patents. It you intend to do a state-of-the art search, then the latest thinking on a topic or method is usually to be found in the conference literature.

If your project is work-based, possibly looking at something like research and development, then the patents and trademark literature may be relevant. Different types of dissertation, topic and methodology therefore demand different kinds of literature to be searched. For these reasons you need to plan your search before you begin. Your main source of help in planning for an effective and efficient search is:

♦ *Doing a Literature Search: A Comprehensive Guide for the Social Sciences* (Hart, 2001).

TABLE 6.1   THE LITERATURE

monographs	legal publications	statistics	textbooks
anthologies	trade literature	patents and trademarks	articles and editorials
edited works	conference papers	official publications	theses

Below is a summary of the key points you will find in *Doing a Literature Search*. Also remember to consult your librarian for advice on new developments in electronic databases.

WHY SEARCH AND REVIEW THE LITERATURE?

There are many good reasons for searching the literature on your topic. In the early stages of your research, when you are thinking about what topic to research, an indicative search and review will be absolutely necessary to identify what has already been done and what may need doing to fill a gap in our knowledge. The main reasons for searching and reviewing can be expressed as a series of questions you will need to answer about your 'topic'. These can be divided into three broad groups: the first contains questions about the basic features of your topic; the second is about the nature and extent of the knowledge on your potential topic; and the third is about mining the methodological details from the literature.

Basic questions to ask are:

1   What research and theory is there on my topic?

2   What are the key sources (books, articles, reports) on my topic?

3   Who are the main theorists and researchers in this area?

4   What is the language of my topic and how is it used?

5   What is the history, chronological development, of the topic or problem?

Intermediate questions to ask are:

6   How has the topic or problem been defined?

7   What are the different frames of reference for researching and discussing the topic?

8 How has theory been related to practice or to empirical research?

9 What methodological assumptions and approaches have been used?

10 What key concepts, variables or factors have been identified?

11 What are the agreements and disagreements between theorists on my topic?

12 What gaps in knowledge, theory or application of a methodology are there in my topic area?

Once you begin to formulate some answers to this group of questions, you have begun your review of the literature. As you gather a better understanding of your topic you will be able to interrogate your sources to find answers to the following questions:

13 What inconsistencies, shortcomings or contradictions are there in our knowledge of the topic?

14 What evidence is lacking, inconclusive or too limited?

15 What alternative approaches are there for understanding the topic which have not been used?

Your interrogation will enable you to state what research, theory and approaches have been unsatisfactory and, importantly, explain where there is a need for new research, theorizing or approach on the topic. A good search and review of the literature will provide you with:

♦ a state-of-the-art understanding of your topic;

♦ a means of mapping out the theoretical and methodological structure of the current knowledge on the topic;

♦ an analysis which enables you to compare and contrast approaches to the topic and to construct a new synthesis; and

♦ evidence for constructing a reasoned argument for your particular definition of and approach to the topic.

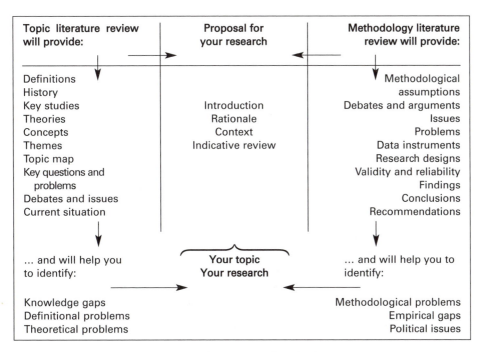

Topic literature review will provide:	Proposal for your research	Methodology literature review will provide:
Definitions History Key studies Theories Concepts Themes Topic map Key questions and problems Debates and issues Current situation	Introduction Rationale Context Indicative review	Methodological assumptions Debates and arguments Issues Problems Data instruments Research designs Validity and reliability Findings Conclusions Recommendations
... and will help you to identify:	Your topic Your research	... and will help you to identify:
Knowledge gaps Definitional problems Theoretical problems		Methodological problems Empirical gaps Political issues

FIGURE 6.1   THE LITERATURE AND YOUR RESEARCH TOPIC

Given that a literature review will furnish you with the necessary topic and subject knowledge and means of justifying your approach to the topic, we can say a review is an absolute foundation for all research. Figure 6.1 provides an overview of how your search and review can contribute to your research.

It is not only at the beginning of your research, however, that you will need your review. The literature is a resource to be used and referred to, as we show below, throughout the dissertation. Now we know the reasons for reviewing the literature we can look at how to find the literature.

Searching for relevant literature

A literature search can be systematic and precise or it can be random and chaotic. At masters level you are expected to be able to demonstrate the ability and capacity to undertake a systematic and precise search for relevant literature and to be able to manage the large amounts of information you will find. To help us in this the science of librarianship has, over the past 150 years, developed some useful ways of organizing the knowledge of all subjects. Your academic and public libraries are manifestations of a highly organized system of schemes and tools which collect, categorize and make accessible human knowledge. By knowledge we refer to most of what has been written in

Remember that you will need a system for managing the information you generate from your search. See Chapter 2 for some suggestions on this.

various media (paper and electronic), statistical data, dictionaries and encyclopaedias and all manner of 'texts' including ephemera. Your starting point for designing a search for literature relevant to your topic is with what are called guides to the literature.

GUIDES TO THE LITERATURE

Across the social and natural sciences and arts and humanities there are guides which list what tools can be used to search the literature. The main tools are indexes and abstracts. When an item is published, say an article in a journal, its details (called bibliographical details) are recorded in an index for the topic to which it belongs. So an article in the *British Journal of Sociology* will be indexed in *Sociological Abstracts*. Guides to the literature will tell you which indexes and abstracts are relevant to your topic and methodology. Useful guides include:

♦ *Manual of On-line Search Strategies* (Armstrong and Large, 2001)

♦ *A Guide to Finding Quality Information on the Internet: Selection and Evaluation* (Cooke, 2001)

♦ Your supervisor – she or he will know the literature and should be able to guide your efforts.

These and other guides will help you to find indexes and abstracts for planning a literature search. Many of these tools are reference sources such as encyclopaedias and dictionaries and these can be very useful in helping you to understand the vocabulary of your topic.

PLANNING YOUR SEARCH

It is certainly worth the time and effort getting to know how knowledge is organized. As a masters level researcher this is an expectation and what you learn will be skills

TABLE 6.2   INITIAL PREPARATION FOR A GENERIC LITERATURE SEARCH

Task	What to consult and use
1 Define the topic Write down the main topic and what disciplines you think will have had some-thing to say about it.	Consult the dictionaries and encyclopaedias in the *quick reference section* to develop a list of key words that can be used to search the library catalogue, abstracts and indexes.
2 Think about the limits of your topic Limit your search by placing parameters around the timeframe (dates), language(s), place and population.	Use materials from the encyclopaedias and dictionaries to define the scope of your topic and to write a working title. Adapt the '*Literature search profile*' to write down the criteria for your search – what to include and what to exclude.
3 Identify the main reference tools for your discipline Identify the main indexes and abstracts and any other reference materials that cover the disciplines for your topic.	Use *guides to the literature* from the quick reference section of the library to identify relevant indexes and abstracts and reference sources, including Internet gateways. Check which reference tools the library holds that you can use.
4 Think about the housekeeping Design a means of recording what you find and cross-referencing materials.	Use ring binders to store notes and index cards to record citations.
5 Plan the sources to be searched and start your search List the sources you intend to search in the order in which you intend to search them.	Use your notes to construct a list of abstracts, indexes and other reference sources to be searched.

and knowledge you can transfer into everyday life when you need to know something. A typical search has five main elements and these are described in Table 6.2. A good point to remember when planning your search is to make it cross-disciplinary.

Cross-disciplinarity means that even if your topic is in, say, psychology, you should search indexes and abstracts in other subject areas, such as sociology. This will give you a broader base from which to select relevant items and offer different perspectives on your topic which you may wish to incorporate into your study. In many masters courses evidence of cross-disciplinary knowledge is an expectation.

FINDING TOO MUCH OR TOO LITTLE AND IDENTIFYING CORE TEXTS

With many searches of the literature you will merely 'round up the usual suspects' which are recognized as the core texts. This is not a problem in itself, but many research students often face a number of related problems when searching. These include:

◆ **Finding too much: this problem is common and occurs when you use search terms which are too general and when you have not planned your search in sufficient detail. The way to overcome this is to think very carefully about the terms and phrases** you will use for your search and the relationships between them. Use dictionaries and encyclopaedias to construct a list of terms, phrases and synonyms.

> See *Doing a Literature Search* (Hart, 2001), Chapter 10, for guidance on developing a vocabulary for your search.

◆ **Not finding enough: this problem is often the result of being too specific in what terms you use for your search. Every topic has a literature that can be searched. It is usually a matter of looking to find out where in the structure of the literature your topic has been classified. Your college librarian will be able to help you with this and show you how books have been classified and what vocabulary is used by the different journal indexing services.**

Another method is to look at the references (or bibliography) of items you obtain on your topic. The items others have cited can lead you to other items which in turn have citations. As you analyse the references of more items on your topic, you will soon see what are the most commonly cited sources. These often form part

> A text can be said to be core if it has made a landmark contribution to defining, researching or/and understanding a problem, topic or/and phenomenon.

of the core literature of a topic or discipline and will give you a resource to construct more detail using precise terms and phrases for systematic searching of the indexes including citation indexes.

Citation indexes record the citations an author has given in their article. Therefore when you know the bibliographic details of an article on your topic you can enter this into a citation index and locate it. Once found you can look at the citations and get the citation index to search for who else has used the article you are looking at as its citations. The main citation indexes are supplied on the *ISI Web of Science* by the Institute for Scientific Information (www.isinet.com/). Searching the citation indexes will help you to identify those items which are the main sources in the literature for the general and particular aspects of your topic.

LOOKING FOR ALTERNATIVE LITERATURE ON YOUR TOPIC

Your search skills and common sense should lead you to the main items on your topic. What it may not do is take you beyond the usual suspects. What we mean by this is that most topics within a particular subject field have a literature that has common citations. Being able to identify this literature involves exhibiting a set of technical skills which are standard expectations of the masters student. There is, however, an issue here concerning the expectations. Most topics have a literature that is cited by interested parties who expect to see the same or similar literature cited by others. In finding what is already known about your topic you are finding what is sometimes accepted as the 'knowledge' by those recognized as the knowledgeable on your topic. To some degree the major refereed journals publish the articles of those recognized as the knowledgeable and therefore frame and give boundaries to the topic and this can often be seen in the structure of the literature. Hence there is, on occasion, literature which is outside the major journals and is rarely cited in the most commonly cited articles and books. A classic example in the social sciences is the literature from ethnomethodologists (Garfinkel, 2002: 121–35). When one looks at studies of work and organizations we often find a standard literature *about* organizations that does not include many references to studies *of* work. Figure 6.2 gives an indication of the phenomena by providing two lists of literatures: one you would normally find (taken from a very popular sociological textbook, Haralambos et al., 2000), and the other you may not.

While the conventional literature about organizations looks at concepts such as 'power' and 'hierarchy' and makes comparisons between ideal forms of bureaucracy, the alternative literature does not. It focuses on looking to see just how what people do in organizations can be described so as to show how they do what they do. The detail of what people do in everyday work to achieve a sense of 'just what something is, means, should be done' concerns those pursuing the alternative social science.

Conventional literature *about*	Alternative literature *of*
The Affluent Worker: Industrial Attitudes and Behaviour. (1968) Goldthorpe, J.H., Lockwood, D., Bechhofer, F. and Platt, J. Cambridge: Cambridge University Press.	*New Technology and Practical Police Work: The Social Context of Technical Innovation.* (1992) Ackroyd, S., Harper, R., Hughes, J., Shapiro D. and Soothill, K. Buckingham: Open University Press.
Working for Ford. (1973) Benyon, H. Harmondsworth: Allen Lane.	'Utterances and operations in air traffic control', Anderson, R., Sharrock, W. and Watson, R. (1989) *Langage et Travail*: 221–34.
Workers' Attitudes and Technology. (1974) Wedderburn, D. and Crompton, C. Cambridge: Cambridge University Press.	'The work of a (scientific) demonstration: respecifying Newton's and Goethe's theories of prismatic color', Bjelic, D. and Lynch, M. (1992). In Watson, G. and Seiler, R.M. (eds.). *Text in Context: Contributions to Ethnomethodology.* London: Sage: 52–78.
The Dynamics of Bureaucracy. (1963) Blua, P. Chicago, IL: University of Chicago Press.	
Modern Organizations. (1964) Etzioni, A. Englewood Cliffs, NJ: Prentice-Hall.	'The mundane work of writing and reading computer programs', Button, G, and Sharrock, W. (1995). In ten Have, P. and Psathas, G. (eds.). *Situated Order: Studies in the Social Organization of Talk and Embodied Activities.* Washington, DC: University Press of America: 231–58.
'Influence and authority among physicians in an outpatient clinic', Goss, M.E.W. (1969). In Etzoni, A. (ed.). *A Sociological Reader on Complex Organizations.* 2nd edn. New York: Holt, Rinehart & Winston.	
Patterns of Industrial Bureaucracy. (1954) Gouldner, A. Glencoe: The Free Press.	'The work of a discovering science construed with materials from the optically discovered pulsar', Garfinkel, H., Lynch, M. and Livingston, E. (1981) *Philosophy of the Social Sciences.* 11: 131–58.
Industrial Labour: Class Struggle at Work and Monopoly Capitalism. (1977) Friedman, A. London: Macmillan.	'Technical work and critical enquiry: investigation in a scientific laboratory', Lynch, M. (1982) *Social Studies of Science* 12: 499–533.
The Sociology of Work: An Introduction. (1991) Grint, K. Cambridge: Polity Press.	*Plans and Situated Action: The Problem of Human Machine Communication.* Suchman, L. (1987) Cambridge: Cambridge University Press.

FIGURE 6.2 LITERATURE 'ABOUT' AND LITERATURE 'OF' WORK
(*Note*: For the purpose of clarity, the style of citation is different from those recommended.)

In many areas of social studies you will be able to find this kind of dual literature. This does not mean one is the right literature and the other wrong; it is simply that there are alternative ways of approaching a topic for research, understanding and interpreting events. As approaches, these literatures have a particular way of 'doing' understanding based on different starting points for defining the topic. Seeking out this kind of literature can be a little more difficult than searching and finding the conventional literature. A good starting point is the following source:

♦ **The International Institute for Ethnomethodology and Conversation Analysis (IIEMCA http://www.iiemca.org/).**

Ethics of using the literature

If you use another person's work – text, diagrams, tables, data, pictures – without their permission or fail to give proper acknowledgement (attribution) to key ideas, phrases and words or change the arrangement of words in an extract you use, then you will certainly be breaking ethical standards of authorship and may be liable under the laws governing copyright. Here is some basic advice on avoiding becoming a plagiarist, how to cite your sources and what copyright means.

AVOIDING BECOMING A PLAGIARIST

In order to avoid the stigma and shame of being labelled 'plagiarist', here are some simple and easy-to-follow guidelines:

♦ Make notes on where you found the main ideas, words, phrases and other materials you intend to use so that you can include in your dissertation citations which attribute the origins of those ideas, words, phrases. This shows you have a clear understanding of ethical standards, that you have done your literature search and have been able to incorporate materials. It will also protect you from claims that your ideas cannot be traced and therefore from doubts about the quality of your work.

♦ Use a consistent style to cite the sources of your ideas, words and phrases. The two main styles or methods are the Harvard System and the Vancouver Method. Check to see if your institution has a preferred style. The basic principle of both methods is that you can attribute a source in-line and at the end of a line. Below are examples of the use of each as methods of citing sources in your writing (note that some recommend different ways of constructing the citation based on these two methods).

An example of the Harvard System:

> Research on fathering has expanded in scope and breadth over the last several decades (e.g. Berman and Pedersen, 1987a; Pedersen, 1987). Nonetheless, investigations of and conceptualizations about men's behaviors in and attitudes toward families are still sparse compared to studies of mothering and family processes, more generally. Indeed, relatively little is known about what residential fathers actually do, how their activities vary, and what the variability means (Harris and Morgan, 1991: 541; Lamb and Oppenheim, 1989; Radin, 1994, 1988). Arguably, even less is known about the parental involvement of formerly married fathers who do not reside with their children: 'the parenting alliance has received modest empirical attention in both intact and divorced families' (Gable et al., 1992: 285).
>
> (Arendell, 2003)

Each of the references cited in the text would normally be listed as full citations at the end of the chapter or end of the dissertation in alpha order (A–Z).

For more information on using the Harvard System see:

♦ **Holland, M. (1996). *Harvard System* (online). Poole: Bournemouth University. Available from: http://www.bournemouth.ac.uk/service-depts/lis/LIS_Pub/ harvardsyst.html (accessed 1 December 2003).**

An example of the Vancouver Method:

> Jhally's conclusions are short and confident. He believes that his 'empirical' procedure has shown advertisements to be 'structured along some definite lines, particularly audience codes' (102). He claims to have uncovered not only two gender codes (103) but their sub-codes (104). Primetime television, according to Jhally, employs the codes of emotion, love, sensuality, pleasure … [it] is dominated by 'magic' codes, affecting products more directly than rational codes (105).
>
> (Hart, 1993)

Each number refers to a reference that can be found at the end of the chapter or end of the dissertation. Here is the list based on the extract above:

> 102 Jhally, S. (1987) *Codes of Advertising: Fetishism and the Political Economy of Meaning in the Consumer Society*. Co-published by St. Martin's Press, New York, and Frances Pinter, London: 171

103 ibid: 131–139
104 ibid: 170
105 ibid: 171

For more information on using the Vancouver Method, see:

♦ **Rudjer Bolsover Institute Library, Zagreb at http://nippur.irb.hr/eng/vrl/ citations.html**

♦ **http://www.lib.monash.edu.au/vl/cite/citeprvr.htm**

♦ **http://www.le.ac.uk/library/teach/irsm/irsm71.html**

Give full bibliographic details of the items you use in your dissertation. This is normally done at the end of each chapter or at the end of the dissertation. These are your references. Include a reference to everything you have used to produce your dissertation and do not include any source that has not made a contribution. Bolstering or padding the reference list with items you have not read or used is a violation of academic integrity and amounts to falsification of sources. In Table 6.3 you will see some basic advice on the style that may be used to cite your sources.

CITATION STYLE

Correcting inaccurate citations is one of the most common copy-editing jobs for many dissertation students. This is normally a time-consuming and laborious task that can be largely avoided by paying close attention to getting the details of your citations consistent from the start. There are numerous guides to citation practice and you will find that most of them give different recommendations on how citations should be done. Before you start your project check out what style is acceptable, or even recommended, by your university. In this section we will look at some of the unusual items in the literature that you may have to cite. For more comprehensive guidance, see:

♦ **Modern Language Association (MLA): http://cctc.commnet.edu/mla/practical_ guide.html**

♦ **International Standards Organization ISO 690-2 — information and bibliographic references: www.nlc-bnc.ca/iso/tc46sc9/standard/690-2ehtm**

TABLE 6.3   CITATION STYLES

Type	Example and notes
Books	Hart, C. (1998) *Doing a Literature Review: Releasing the Social Science Research Imagination*. London: Sage.
	Sub-titles must be included and should be separated from the main title by a colon, as shown above.
Articles	Hart, C., Shoolbred, M., Butcher, D. and Kane, D. (1999) 'The bibliographic structure of fan information', *Collection Building*, 18 (2): 81–90.
	Do not use 'et al.' but include all the authors. Some do not have quotation marks at the beginning and end of the article title.
Chapters in books	Francis, D. and Hart, C. (1997) 'Narrative intelligibility and membership categorization in a television commercial'. In Hester, S. and Eglin, P. (eds). *Culture in Action: Studies in Membership Categorization and Analysis*. Washington, DC: University Press of America.
	Some place the 'ed.' or 'eds' in brackets, e.g. (eds). Include as much information as possible, e.g. DC as there are a number of Washingtons.
Thesis	Hart, C. (1993) 'The social production of an advertisement'. PhD thesis, Manchester Metropolitan University/J. Walter Thompson Ltd. DoRs: Dr D.W. Francis (Manchester Metropolitan University) and Dr W.W. Sharrock (Victoria University of Manchester).
	Give as many details as possible as theses are difficult to locate and obtain. Also try to include the Directors of the Research (DoRs) and their institutions.
Internet articles based on a print source	Vanden Bos, G., Knapp, S., and Doe, J. (2001) 'Role of reference elements in the selection of resources by psychology undergraduates'. (Electronic version). *Journal of Bibliographic Research*, 5: 117–23.
	Use the full 'and' rather than the '&'. The article title is not capitalized, but the title of the journal is. No need to use 'pp.' for pages.
Article in an electronic journal	Fredrickson, B.L. (2002) 'Cultivating positive emotions to optimise health and well-being'. *Prevention & Treatment*, 3, article 0001a, from: http://journals.apa.org/prevention/volume3/pre0030001a.html (accessed 7 March, 2000).
	The '&' is in the title of the journal. Give the full Internet address and the date you accessed it.
Document from a private Internet site	Dingwall, R. 'Oration for Harold Garfinkel', from: http://www.pscw.uva.nl/emca/oration.html (accessed 5 September, 2002).
	Some of these sites do not have an obvious author or data of publication so give all detail possible.

Source: adapted from Sage Publications, *Guidelines for Authors and Editors* and APA Online www.apastyle.org/.

Table 6.3 includes the most common and some of the most difficult items to cite.

COPYRIGHT AND INTELLECTUAL PROPERTY

Copyrights along with trademarks and patents are ways of protecting what people create. Patents and trademarks ensure that the originator of a machine or process owns the rights of that machine or process. Patents require formal registration; copyrights do not, but are nevertheless governed by laws. Copyrights simply mean you have rights to what you write and this includes diagrams, tables, software and pictures; it also includes material you find on the Internet. To use another person's work without their permission is an infringement of copyright law and you could be liable for payment of damages. It is therefore important to understand copyright. The problem with this is that the laws, regulations and practices of copyright are subject to continual change. For this reason check out the latest position by consulting one or more of the major information science gateways, such as BUBL (http://bubl.ac.uk). What follows is a brief guide to the present position.

Duration of copyright: Within the EU, author's life +70 years; non-EU, author's life +50 years.

Moral rights: Under UK law authors have moral rights to their work, which includes the right to be identified and not have their work degraded in any way, for example, distorted.

Fair dealing/use: Very little case law on this. It refers to the use of small parts of a publication in ways that do not affect its market potential or value, its meaning or quality in the case of picture reproduction. In the UK the Society of Authors and the Publishers Association have published guidelines in an attempt to quantify what may be considered fair use so that publications can be used without formal permission but must be fully acknowledged:

♦ **single extract (prose): up to 400 words;**

♦ **series of extracts from the same work (prose): up to 800 words, of which no one extract shall exceed 300 words.**

There are far more complicated guidelines for the use of poetry, music and lyrics and for use of these you are recommended to consult direct with the owner before you use them. The good news is that for most academic work, especially for dissertations, most authors and organizations are quite willing to give permission for you to use their materials.

Reviewing the literature you find

Now that you know a little about designing and implementing a search for relevant literature, we will look at what you do with what you have found. This section outlines some of the methods and techniques you can use depending on what kind of dissertation and research you are doing. It also tries to take into account the situation in which you are studying – full-time, part-time or distance learning. For more information on reviewing the literature, see:

♦ *Doing a Literature Review: Releasing the Social Science Research Imagination* **(Hart, 1998).**

USING THE LITERATURE TO FORMULATE YOUR TOPIC AND WRITE AN INDICATIVE REVIEW

One of the requirements before you begin your research is to research and write a proposal. In a later chapter we will look in more detail at the research proposal. Our concern here is with using the literature to formulate your topic in order to produce an *indicative literature review* for inclusion in your proposal. An indicative review is normally three to six pages and covers only the basic items, usually about six. There are various ways in which you can produce an indicative review and the four we will look at, adapted from Cox (2002) and summarized in Table 6.4, were developed for students with different kinds of research dissertation.

For information on different types of literature review, see Chapter 5, where evidence-based reviews, theoretical reviews and historical reviews are discussed.

Domain mapping

Mapping out a domain with which you are familiar, even a specialist in, involves using a series of subject domain maps (mind maps) to identify potential areas for research.

TABLE 6.4   METHODS OF ANALYSIS FOR PRODUCING AN INDICATIVE REVIEW

Method of analysis	Useful for students who are:
Domain mapping	subject specialist
Problem analysis	industry specialist
Structured themed review	distance learners
Context shaping	specialist in new field

There are five stages in producing a domain map:

♦ *Stage 1*   Prepare mind maps of the subject area using the course documentation (the lecture list, readings and so on).

♦ *Stage 2*   Identify in the mind map those areas in which you have strengths and knowledge. These are your areas of interest.

♦ *Stage 3*   Prepare a mind map for each area of interest using key texts from the literature.

♦ *Stage 4*   Review and evaluate each mind map and eliminate those which have the highest risk, that is, ones requiring more knowledge and skills than you currently possess or which have 'data' problems. Identify the domain that has the lowest risk factor and conduct a search and review of literature in this field.

♦ *Stage 5*   Using the literature produce a detailed mind map of the selected domain, identifying issues, problems and opportunities for research.

You may include some author citations in your domain map, but not all the details of the studies from which the main and sub-categories have been taken. It is more economical to focus on the main concepts and positions and add the detail to the main review of the literature.

Problem analysis

Identifying a problem in a workplace situation can be done using the problem analysis technique. It is useful when one is a specialist and is looking to undertake a work-based dissertation. There are three basic stages in using problem analysis to define your research problem:

♦ *Stage 1* Identify from the current periodicals and trade literature concerns in your industry or organizational type. If required, assess these in terms of your own organization.

♦ *Stage 2* Undertake a search and review of available literature to find out the origins of the concern, what is being done, what has been done, what critiques have been made of what has been done, what evidence there is to support the concern and what opportunities there are for research into the concern.

♦ *Stage 3* Identify from your review an area for research or analysis and state what this is. Using the literature justify your aim in relation to a set of achievable objectives for a research project. Identify which elements of your course materials you will draw upon and how your research may contribute to the literature in general and understanding of the concern.

Note that the way in which problem analysis is presented here a distinction is being made between research undertaken in the workplace and research undertaken for the industry. The latter is being emphasized as a way of avoiding problems in the workplace, such as change of management, role or employment.

Structured themed review

When studying at a distance you are largely responsible for your own learning and this includes formulating a workable proposal for your research. Using a structured approach to identifying a theme for a topic can be one way in which you can systematically work through a relatively small body of literature to identify a potential topic. Typically, the literature you look at would be part of the reading for your course. You are therefore looking to find a topic from within the syllabus of the taught elements of your masters. Table 6.5 provides an example of the stages of doing a structured themed review over a five-week period (Cox (2002) does this over a 14-week period).

The weekly schedule can be an effective means of setting yourself deadlines for achieving a modest amount of work. You also know that you can 'bounce' ideas off your tutor, who can be expected to be a specialist in the field of the curriculum you are analysing.

TABLE 6.5   DOING A STRUCTURED THEMED REVIEW IN FIVE WEEKS

Week	Activities and deadlines	Example from Cox (2002)
1	Review the course syllabuses and identify potential topic areas for research. Select two or three themes and identify at least two academic papers on these to see how they have been framed.	Identify potential project themes within the workplace. Internet design. Customer relationship management. E-business strategy.
2	Review potential themes in terms of possibilities for research, including access to data and/or materials, skills for analysing the data and timeframes. Select the least risky theme for development.	Identify at least two academic papers relevant to each project theme. • *Internet design* Wen, H.J., Chen, H.-G. and Hwang, H.-G. (2001) 'E-commerce web site design: strategies and models', *Information Management and Computer Security*, 9 (1): 5–12. Vescovi, T. (2000) 'Internet communication: the Italian SME case', *Corporate Communications*, 5 (2): 107–12. • *Knowledge management (customer relationship management)* Beijerse, R. (1999) 'Questions in knowledge management: defining and conceptualising a phenomenon', *Journal of Knowledge Management*, 3 (2): 94–110. Logan, D. and Caldwell, F. (2000) 'Knowledge mapping: five dimensions to consider', *Gartner Report: DF-11-3834*, 20 July 2000. • *E-business strategy* Rozwell, C. and Berg, T. (1999) 'How to devise a practical, effective e-business strategy', *Gartner R-09-4033*, 27 September 1999.

(Continued)

TABLE 6.5 (CONTINUED)

Week	Activities and deadlines	Example from Cox (2002)
		Marchewka, J.T. and Towell, E.R. (2000) 'A comparison of structure and strategy in electronic commerce', *Information Technology and People*, 13 (2): 137–49.
3	Develop the selected theme into a broad research aim. Identify key sources in the literature to be consulted, use a selection of those sources to frame your justification for the topic of your research. State the aim of your research along with a set of clear objectives which will actualize the aim.	• Framework for Managing Knowledge in XYZ Ltd. • Approach to Formulating E-Business Strategy.
4	Assess different approaches to research and select, according to your aim, the most appropriate approach. Justify this in terms of a short comparative argument for your approach, using the literature to support you choice.	Identify key publications that may be used during the project. • Framework for Managing Knowledge in XYZ Ltd: *Journal of Knowledge Management Information Technology and People Corporate Communications* • Approach to Formulating E-Business Strategy: *Journal of Strategic Management E-Business Review*

(Continued)

TABLE 6.5   (CONTINUED)

Week	Activities and deadlines	Example from Cox (2002)
5	Construct a realistic timetable for conducting your research, identifying possible contingencies and ways in which these will be accommodated.	Specify the aim(s) and objectives. *Aim*: Develop a strategy for managing knowledge to improve customer relations in financial services. *Objectives*: • Identify critical success factors in customer relations. • Define problems in managing customer relations. • Identify components of knowledge management. • Assess benefits of knowledge management to customer relations. • Develop a framework for knowledge management in customer relations. • Develop a strategy for managing knowledge in customer relations.

Context shaping

Students converting from one subject area to another using a masters as the means often find context shaping a useful tool to identify research topics based on their prior experience and knowledge. The basic principle to the approach is to take an area with which you are familiar and analyse it to see how it can be used in a new area. The process usually involves a five-stage process of gradually refining, through exploration, what it is you already know to guide you into a new field:

♦ *Stage 1*   Prepare a mind map of the skills, knowledge, qualities and interests you already have along with your career goals.

♦ *Stage 2*   Identify potential areas for research based on your self-analysis. Using the literature from your course, identify themes which fit with your existing profile. Map out some of the themes to identify potential opportunities for research.

♦ *Stage 3*   Using the same literature, define the scope of the different themes. Assess each theme for suitability in terms of how much you can use what you already have to take advantage of a research opportunity and what you would need to acquire in terms of new skills and knowledge. Select a theme that meets your needs based on your existing skills.

♦ *Stage 4*   Map out the theme selected and identify potential primary and secondary research opportunities. Draft out general aims of intent for the research you have identified and assess what will need to be done (tasks) and what skills/knowledge you will need to acquire.

♦ *Stage 5*   Using the literature, construct a justification for your research that includes reference to your existing knowledge and skills and what is required to supplement these to complete the research. State what the main aim is and write out the objectives for achieving the aim.

The main outcome of these and other techniques of using the literature is to enable you to produce an indicative review of the literature which demonstrates that you understand the topic and can justify your research.

EXTRACTING INFORMATION FROM YOUR SOURCES

Once you have begun to obtain some relevant items, you need to start reading them with a purpose. This means analysing them to extract the kinds of information, argument, concepts, definitions, approaches, findings and conclusions relevant to your own topic or problem. In *Doing a Literature Review* (Hart, 1998) I gave advice on reading to review and suggested that you use a range of tools and methods to record systematically your findings from the literature. In this section these have been adapted to show you a method of assessing different aspects of your literature and how to use it to construct a review. The scheme, shown in Table 6.6, illustrates the different kinds of information that you will be expected to extract from your literature. Some of the categories may not be relevant to your needs, but it is nevertheless good for you to be aware of them in order to say why they are not relevant to your research. The scheme in Table 6.6 is based on making a critical evaluation of six aspects of a study.

The principle on which Table 6.6 is based is 'interrogation': as the knowledge base, the literature is subject to different levels of interrogation based on a series of questions. The questions to ask are a matter for you to decide, but they should be relevant to

TABLE 6.6   A SCHEME FOR THE SYSTEMATIC ASSESSMENT OF A LITERATURE

Areas for assessment	Amplification
Assessing the questions or hypotheses	What are the hypotheses or questions of the research? How well have these been expressed? Do they show any biases in the way they are expressed and have been tested? What variables or factors has the research identified for comparison or framing the problem? Are these adequate? What others could have been used and why?
Assessing the context of justification	How has context been defined or implied? What influence has this had on framing the hypothesis or problem? Have alternative ways of framing the context been given or rejected? If not, what alternatives could you envision? Is the nature of the literature fully understood? Is this selective? How has it been used to formulate the context? Is the context based on a closed- or open-research design? What difference would an alternative make to the aims of the research and findings?
Assessing the methodology	Have the main methodological assumptions of the research tradition and approach been critically discussed? If not, what kinds of assumptions have been made about knowledge? In the design of the research, what is seen as valid data and why and how has this been obtained? Is the design coherent and a systematic application of the methodology?
Assessing awareness of alternatives	Are alternative methodological traditions and approaches acknowledged? What limitations are recognized to the methodology used? Has alternative data been identified? If not, what kinds of data can you find and what does this mean for the research? Is the data, whether statistical or textual, coherent and adequately presented? Are there alternative ways it could have been presented? If so, how might these have influenced what significance could be made of it?

(Continued)

TABLE 6.6 (CONTINUED)

Areas for assessment	Amplification
Assessing the findings or results	Are the reported findings or results consistent in terms of collection methods and any statistical methods used? What inconsistencies are identified and how are these explained? If a hypothesis was used, how has any significance been achieved? How are findings related to other studies? Are there any indications of selective presentation?
Assessing the conclusions and recommendations	What weight is given to the findings/results? What level of generalization is being used? Is this justified by the data and research design? Is the conclusion based only on the results, as it should be? Or are other factors, including values, introduced that are not in the data? Is there a sense of critical evaluation of the findings or is the conclusion presented as self-evident? Are recommendations (where given) clear, consistent and properly formulated? Do they cite what findings they are based on? What other conclusions can you draw from the data?

your topic and the purposes of your research. An important aspect of this is to ask questions which combine information extraction with justification. This means once you have the who, what, when and how, look to ask 'Why?', 'Based on what, with what consequences?' and 'What if?' Chapter 8 looks in more detail at the consequences of different research strategies.

USING GRIDS TO ORGANIZE YOUR ANALYSIS

It is necessary to have some means of organizing the information you extract from your literature. There are a number of ways of doing this, including 'spider diagrams' and tables which show the main themes in the literature. Table 6.7 shows a tabular approach in which the literature on supporting management learning in the workplace has been themed. Table 6.7 shows parts from two themes in the literature on action learning presented in tables by Teare (1999).

WRITING AN INTEGRATED REVIEW OF LITERATURE ON YOUR TOPIC

The result of your hard work, your reading, analysis and note taking, is the production of a literature review that is relevant to your topic or problem and the methodology you intend to use in your research. The kind of review you write will, of course, depend on the type of dissertation you are doing and the purpose of your research.

Both quantitative and qualitative aspects, including findings, are capable of integration into a review. With each kind of study and data there are, however, some points worth noting about integration. With quantitative data you will usually be attempting to integrate descriptive and analytical statistics such as means and modes along with correlations and significance. You will therefore need to have competence in using and applying statistical techniques. This may involve doing one or more of the following with the literature:

♦ *Showing the chronology of the topic or problem*: Tables and matrixes should portray the results of previous studies in chronological order. This will help you to show and describe the development of the problem and different ways in which concepts, variables, methods and techniques were applied.

♦ *Summarizing results of studies*: With studies conducted using the same method and techniques on sample populations exhibiting similar characteristics, you can

TABLE 6.7   USING TABLES TO ORGANIZE YOUR INFORMATION

Theme 1: Managerial learning and work		Theme 4: Work-based action learning	
Author/study date	Focus and sub-theme	Author/study date	Focus and sub-theme
Shenhar and Renier (1996)	Modular approach to defining managerial work and roles so managers can self-assess complexities of own jobs and identify development needs.	Harrison (1996)	Critical examination of the concept of action learning (AL). Argues AL offers potential to develop strategic awareness in turbulent times.
Margerison and McCann (1996b)	Advocates self-profiling in eight areas of work so managers can work more effectively with others.	Chan (1994)	Relates action learner's experience of action research (AR) to discuss how AL and AR can deliver a balance of knowledge and action relevant to management.
Oshagbemi (1995)	Discusses the nature of the reality of management work and how managers spend their time.	Reeves (1996)	Compares two companies' use of action learning, one for individual staff, the other where a problem-solving ethos pervades corporate life.
Margerison and McCann (1996a)	Profiles key communication skills and relates them to different approaches to problem solving and describes a self-assessment resource for personal and team development.	Howell (1994)	Case study of the International Management Centres. Shows that graduate managers can operationalize AL and AR to bring about organizational, professional and personal developments.

Source: Adapted from Teare, 1999.

aggregate the results using secondary statistical techniques. The technique involves producing a meta-analysis of data from existing studies. The techniques of meta-analysis have been developed since the 1970s and are now relatively sophisticated. Care should be taken with this and good advice and guidance can be found in:

- *Synthesizing Research* (Cooper, 1998)
- *Evidence-based Health Care* (Gray, 2001)
- *Conducting Research Literature Reviews* (Fink, 1998)

♦ *Portraying results of studies*: Results from individual studies on the 'same' topic or problem can be presented in tables and matrices to summarize the key findings and characteristics of each study. The point is not to describe each study in turn, but to systematically identify similarities and differences among the studies. A methodological approach to using tables and matrices can be found in:

- *Evaluating Social Science Research* (Black, 1993)

♦ *Critiquing studies*: The purpose of summarizing the literature is to provide an organized set of materials for critical evaluation. Look to evaluate the appropriateness of the research design, sampling techniques, measuring instruments, presentation of the data, statistical tests done and inferences made. Both Black (1993) and Gray (2001) provide detailed discussions on evaluating the quality of quantitative research.

♦ *Synthesizing critiques of studies*: The aim of most quantitative studies is to generalize on the basis of the use of representative samples. Using formal statistical techniques of analysis, especially multiple regression, meta-analysis can produce meta-generalizations (on 30 or more studies) and at the same time identify weaknesses in existing research and areas where there are issues about the quality of data. A good source of advice on synthesizing quantitative research is:

- *The Handbook of Research Synthesis* (Cooper and Hedges, 1994)

In Example A below you can see a textual summary of research about the correlation of violence on television and violent behaviour. We have selected this one because it is typical of many to be found on the Internet in that it exhibits typical failings of non-refereed publications. Read this for yourself before looking at what we have to say about it.

Example A: Impact of televised violence: correlational studies

Extract from the literature review

The weight of evidence from correlational studies is fairly consistent: viewing and/or preference for violent television is related to aggressive attitudes, values and behaviors. This result was true for the studies conducted when television was new, and the measures of children's aggression were teachers' ratings. It is still true for more recent studies when the measures of aggressiveness have become more sophisticated. To choose several studies as examples: Robinson and Bachman (1972) found a relationship between the number of hours of television viewed and adolescent self-reports of involvement in aggressive or antisocial behavior. Atkin, Greenberg, Korzenny, and McDermott (1979) used a different measure of aggressive behavior. They gave nine- to thirteen-year-old boys and girls situations such as the following. Suppose that you are riding your bicycle down the street and some other child comes up and pushes you off your bicycle. What would you do? The response options included physical or verbal aggression along with options to reduce or avoid conflict.

Comments

This is clearly a review of quantitative research from a behavioural frame of reference. One would expect the data from the studies to be made available in the review.

What is the basis for this selection? There is very little detail of the studies, for example, methodology, data collection instruments. Only studies confirming the correlation are mentioned. No mention of the particular television programme(s) viewed.

Example A: Impact of televised violence: correlational studies

Extract from the literature review

Comments

These investigators found that physical or verbal aggressive responses were selected by 45 per cent of heavy-television-violence viewers compared to only 21 per cent of the light-violence viewers. In a further study, Sheehan (1983) followed two groups of Australian children, first- and third-graders, for a three-year period. He found that for the older group, now third through fifth grade, both the overall amount of violence viewing and the intensity of viewing were signifi-cantly related to the child's level of aggressive behavior as rated by their classmates. Finally, in a study focused on adults, Phillips (1983) investigated the effects of the portrayal of suicides in television soap operas on the suicide rate in the United States using death records compiled by the National Center for Health Statistics. He found, over a six-year period, that whenever a major soap opera person-ality committed suicide on television, within three days there was a signifi-cant increase in the number of female suicides across the nation.

This section of the review is biased towards the view that there is a correlation between watching violence on television and people being violent.

(Adapted from Murrey, 2003)

While Example A shows a selective summative integration of correlational studies on the topic, when using the data from such studies there are some basic points of good practice it fails to follow. The studies selected are presented in a chronology, which is good practice, but the review is too selective given the substantial literature on this topic. Little attention is given to contextual factors, making for differences between the studies, or to technical matters such as sample size, research design or statistical techniques used to analyse the data. No data, as such, is presented. The use of words like 'true' tend to be employed by those who have preconceived beliefs about something. In this case the selective use of studies and the rhetorical writing style indicate that a preconceived position is being substantiated by the studies mentioned. Studies included are described in vague terms with no results being portrayed systematically. There is no attempt to make any evaluation of the studies; they are accepted at face value.

The synthesis of qualitative studies is a little more difficult than the synthesis of quantitative studies. The main reason for this difficulty is the different purposes of qualitative research. Qualitative studies are not normally aiming to make statistically based generalizations through the application of formal comparable techniques. This is not to say that qualitative research cannot produce generalizations, for clearly many do. The kinds of studies reflected here are those based on participant and non-participant observation, unstructured interviewing and use of non-statistical data sources for analysis. With care it is possible to analyse qualitative studies on the same topic and draw out similarities and differences based on the use of concepts and approaches. Due to the difficulties of synthesizing qualitative studies, there are not many sources on how to do it; the following are some of the most useful:

> See *Doing a Literature Review* (Hart, 1998: 67–71) for an example of a good review of qualitative community research.

♦ *Meta-ethnography* (Noblit and Hare, 1998)

♦ *The Qualitative Dissertation* (Piantanida and Garman, 1999)

Using the following set of headings we can organize our analysis and notes to provide the necessary materials for an evaluative integration of qualitative studies:

♦ *Show the chronology of the topic or problem*: Trace the chronology of studies and draw out of them the different ways in which the topic or problem was defined, how concepts were used and what methodological assumptions were employed.

- *Categorize the aspects of studies*: From the individual studies similarities in use of concepts, assumptions, data, perspective and standpoints can be extracted and grouped into categories. Diagrams can be very useful for portraying the categories and you will find many throughout this book and in *Doing a Literature Review* (Hart, 1998).

- *Summarize results from studies*: A combination of tables and text can be used to summarize the key features and characteristics of the studies to highlight commonly used assumptions, arguments, conclusions and recommendations.

- *Critique the studies*: Critically evaluate and appraise what you find by examining the level of generalization offered, claims for validity and rigour, the influence of ethical and political standpoints, the implications and logical consequences of conclusions and/or recommendations of studies.

- *Synthesize the evaluation of studies*: From the critical evaluation you can identify a set of conclusions and recommendations which identify the issues that need to be addressed in future studies and which concepts, approaches and assumptions may be useful.

While Example A shows the use of some findings from a literature, there are many other uses of the literature at the beginning and throughout a dissertation. Example B shows the use of the literature in health care research to examine the definitions of the problem.

The literature review and your research

By now you will have realized that a search and review of the literature is an essential part of all research. Figure 6.3 shows how the literature can be used throughout a dissertation, in the rationale for your research, methodology, discussion of what you find and making inferences and conclusions. The latter you can relate back to previous research to show how your research makes a contribution to knowledge on the topic or problem.

THE ASSESSMENT ELEMENTS OF THE LITERATURE REVIEW

One way of approaching the 'contribution question' is to look at the ways in which your search and review is assessed. Table 6.8 and Table 6.9 outline some of the generic

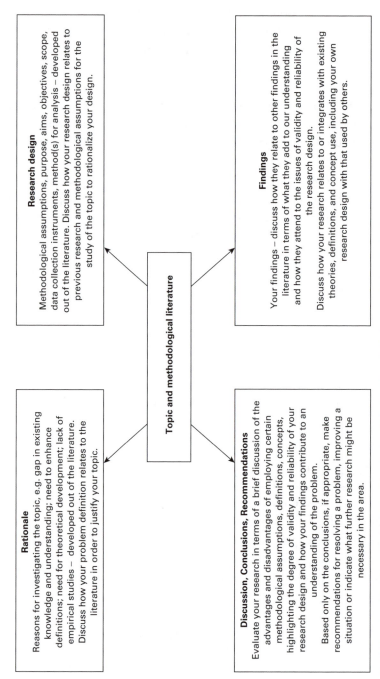

Research design

Methodological assumptions, purpose, aims, objectives, scope, data collection instruments, method(s) for analysis – developed out of the literature. Discuss how your research design relates to previous research and methodological assumptions for the study of the topic to rationalize your design.

Findings

Your findings – discuss how they relate to other findings in the literature in terms of what they add to our understanding and how they attend to the issues of validity and reliability of the research design.

Discuss how your research relates to or integrates with existing theories, definitions, and concept use, including your own research design with that used by others.

Topic and methodological literature

Rationale

Reasons for investigating the topic, e.g. gap in existing knowledge and understanding; need to enhance definitions; need for theoretical development; lack of empirical studies – developed out of the literature. Discuss how your problem definition relates to the literature in order to justify your topic.

Discussion, Conclusions, Recommendations

Evaluate your research in terms of a brief discussion of the advantages and disadvantages of employing certain methodological assumptions, definitions, concepts, highlighting the degree of validity and reliability of your research design and how your findings contribute to an understanding of the problem.

Based only on the conclusions, if appropriate, make recommendations for resolving a problem, improving a situation or indicate what further research might be necessary in the area.

FIGURE 6.3   RELATIONSHIPS BETWEEN THE LITERATURE AND THE PROJECT ELEMENTS

Example B: A review of definitions

Extract	Comments
Hider et al. (1998b, p22, L1), and Hobbs in an editorial opinion (1995, L9) highlight the problem of defining and counting emergency admissions. Government reviews (NSW Health Council 2000; The Scottish Office 1998) echo this concern:	The literature is largely made up of reports from government bodies.
'The range of opinion offered to account for emergency pressures suggests a lack of coherent information regarding all aspects of emergency care. Major uncertainties remain, responses have been uncoordinated, and few of the many initiatives undertaken have been properly evaluated or costed against their objectives'. (Scottish Office 1998, para 210.) It is increasingly important that the levels and types of emergency admissions are properly defined and monitored, not least to enable evaluation of the impact of any action arising from the work of the Task Force, as well as to enable fair comparisons between hospitals' performance. A better understanding of the route of presentation and admission is also required, particularly in light of a growing perception in	The use of italics is not necessary. Quotations of more than three lines should be indented.

Example B: A review of definitions

Extract

Comments

Melbourne that Emergency
Departments are being used by frus-
trated referring clinicians and
patients as a way to circumvent
waits for surgery or diagnostic procedures. Hider et al. (1998b) report
on a study conducted by the New
Zealand Ministry of Health which
found that while GPs were the
largest source of referral (51%), EDs
themselves accounted for 43%
(p25). They also report that there is
little evidence of large-scale abuse
of the emergency admission category in either New Zealand or the
UK (p65). They conclude that the
rise in acute medical admissions
cannot be attributed to longer waiting lists for elective procedures.
Conclusion: Clearer definitions of
the various categories of emergency
and urgent admissions, and better
data are required, to support
ongoing efforts to manage hospitals
in which emergency admissions
predominate.

It is acceptable to use 'et al.' for multi-
author publications, but include all authors
in the reference.

The implications of the literature are
provided in a conclusion that points to
what further work needs to be done.

(Adapted from Dwyer and Jackson, 2001: 12)

criteria often employed to assess the quality and contribution a review makes to a dissertation. Table 6.8 provides an overview of the technical and intellectual aspects expected of the literature review. Note the emphasis on citations, identifying key texts

TABLE 6.8   GENERIC ASSESSMENT CRITERIA FOR THE LITERATURE REVIEW

Literature review and citations	Grade
Excellent review of the literature, clear arrangement and selection of key texts, thorough, consistent critical evaluation of main ideas, theories, arguments, approaches and findings synthesized and focused on the topic puzzle. Excellent citations demonstrating consistency, detail and accuracy.	Excellent
Good review of the key texts with clear arrangement, may lack consistency of critical evaluation *or* elements not fully synthesized *or* lacks thoroughness, but is focused on the topic. Good citations but may need more detail in some instances.	Good
Adequate literature review identifying most of the key texts, but lacks thoroughness *or* critical evaluative stance *or* clear arrangement and does not fully demonstrate ability to synthesize ideas. Acceptable citations but lacking detail, consistency or accuracy in some.	Adequate

and argumentation. You might want to take these criteria and apply them to some of the extracts we have included in this chapter to gain some experience of applying, rather than meeting, formative criteria.

In Table 6.9 the criteria of argumentation are outlined. The purpose of this is to show that a literature review involves analysis and con-struction of an argument. The literature on a topic is analysed and evaluated and from this a case is made for further research into the topic.

> See Chapter 4 of *Doing a Literature Review* (Hart, 1998) and Further Reading to this chapter for advice on argumentation analysis.

It is therefore important to understand and be competent in analysing the soundness of argument and to be able to construct a sound argument.

THE RESEARCH IMAGINATION AND REVIEWING

In part the search for relevant literature is a series of technical tasks. Being able to demonstrate, through application, the skills of doing an efficient and effective literature search is important because it is an essential prerequisite of research. But there is often a marked difference between those reviews based only on the application of technical

TABLE 6.9 ARGUMENTATION ASSESSMENT CRITERIA FOR THE LITERATURE REVIEW

Argumentation and critical awareness	Grade
Excellent use of analysis and structures of argumentation to analyse and synthesize the literature, topic, methodology and data collected. Arguments are developed with evident clarity and logic in an unbiased and objective way. Extremely high standard of critical analysis and evaluation. Conclusions and/or recommendations directly linked to and from the findings.	Excellent
Good use of argumentation structures and techniques of analysis. May lack consistency across chapters and within chapters *or* clarity and logic *or* contain some unsubstantiated statements *or* make conclusions and recommendations not fully embedded in the results.	Good
Some attempt to employ argumentation, but at a basic level not demonstrating a sound understanding of argumentation analysis *or* its need throughout the dissertation *or* containing too many unsubstantiated statements and assumptions. Weak conclusions *and/or* recommendations poorly expressed.	Adequate

criteria and those based on an imaginative use of technical ability. This difference was noted by C. Wright-Mills, who said:

> The [research] imagination ... consists of the capacity to shift from one per-spective to another, and in the process to build up an adequate view of a total society and its components. It is this imagination ... that sets off the social scientist from the mere technician. (1978: 232, orig. 1959)

By having a research imagination we mean using and developing practices and attitudes which take you beyond the 'usual suspects' in the literature. Going beyond the usual means actively seeking citations that are not usually found in reference lists or have not been fully discussed in an article or book. Once you have identified some minority citations, seek out the details others have overlooked or left to one side, then follow such trails to see if they amount to anything new or different. You often find that some of these citations lead to whole new literatures not represented in mainstream textbooks and articles in the key journals. They may also provide an added list of terms and phrases for your search vocabulary that can help you search the indexes for more of the 'marginalized' literature. Another effective technique is to take a walk around the library, serendipitously browsing, to see what is in books and journals you would not normally look at. You will find ideas and theories with which you may not be familiar that will often give you different views on what you have already read. Taking a broader view is an essential attribute for all researchers. To do this you will need to take or develop an 'open attitude' to ideas and theories you are not familiar with and this includes exercising such attitudes and qualities as being proactive, positive, discrete, reflective, anthropological, inter-disciplinary, adaptable, sociological and willing to play, through experimentation, with ideas. Dismissing work because it seems too difficult to understand or having prejudicial prejudgements about an approach are signs that you need to develop a more open attitude or are intellectually too lazy to question the parochial restrictions of a perspective you find comfortable.

SUMMARY OF THIS CHAPTER

The purpose of this chapter has been to provide an overview of an important part of the research process — the search and review of the literature. The main points which have been made include:

♦ A search and review of the literature is essential for all research projects because it provides the basis for defining, framing and designing your research topic or problem.

♦ A literature review is an analysis and synthesis of ideas, arguments, concepts, definitions and theories from the literature.

♦ A literature search requires a creative attitude in order to maximize searching skills.

♦ There are many literatures, not just one, and so a search should encompass as much as possible in the time available.

Further reading

Fisher, A. (1993) *The Logic of Real Arguments*. Cambridge: Cambridge University Press. A clear introduction to understanding argumentation.

Gash, S. (2000) *Effective Literature Searching for Research*. 2nd edn. Aldershot: Gower. A generic introduction for most subjects.

Hart, C. (2001) *Doing a Literature Search: A Comprehensive Guide for the Social Sciences*. London: Sage. A comprehensive introduction to planning and searching the literature.

Hart, C. (1998) *Doing a Literature Review: Releasing the Social Science Research Imagination*. London: Sage. A systematic and pedagogical approach to a difficult task.

Part Two

Research Design and Methodology

Methodological assumptions and beliefs

This chapter will help you to think about some of the methodological assumptions which can be used to inform and shape your research. The next chapter will look at some of the consequences of using certain methodological approaches to design and implement a research strategy.

All research has a starting point and this normally consists of thinking about and then formulating a topic. A part of this process, especially when you begin to look at designing your research and reading the literature, is consideration of methodological issues – that is, the assumptions you choose to make, or in some cases take for granted as those that are normally used, as the basis for doing research. For example, if you have a belief that facts are important and only that which can be observed and measured can count as data, that objectivity is possible, that there is a universal reality, that something is either true or false and there is no role for cultural values, then you may have a preference for a *positivist* approach to research. Alternatively, you may have different preferences in research. If you believe that the role of research in the social sciences is to interpret and understand as well as to explain; that truth and falsity are relative concepts; and that the subjective nature of human behaviour – with its complex, different social values being the defining properties of social life that create different realities – then you have a preference for an *interpretivist* approach to research. Given the complexity of the philosophy of social research, this chapter will attempt to answer the following questions:

1 **What are methodological assumptions? Why are they important in social research?**

2 **What kinds of assumptions have theorists made about the nature of social reality?**

3 **How can knowing the history of social theory help us to understand methodological debates?**

4 **In what ways are different methodological assumptions different ways of describing social structures?**

From the standpoint of most people contemplating their masters research, when they encounter the philosophies of research the common reaction is one of bewilderment. The methodological literature of the social sciences is substantial, full of complex and advanced level arguments and seems to lack any clear purpose for research itself. As we aim to show, it is essential that you at least become familiar with the terrain of this literature; getting to know the basic vocabulary of names given to the different positions and approaches, to the theorists and to the basic assumptions being employed.

One of the most difficult tasks facing anyone doing advanced research for the first time is coming to terms with what seems to be a bewildering range of different philosophical arguments on what constitutes science, knowledge and truth. Clearly these words have something to do with research, but questions about just what and how have generated a substantial literature, which is often referred to as the philosophy of science or philosophy of research. What this literature has to say is complex, and just what it is that philosophical debate has to do with doing research is rarely discussed. This chapter will not even try to summarize all of the major positions constituting the philosophy of research; rather, it will present some of the assumptions about research and debates about these assumptions. This will highlight the nature of the major positions and arguments in this literature so that you can become more aware of, and adept at understanding the nature of argument and how there are alternative possibilities for determining what constitutes knowledge, truth and science.

Using and understanding this chapter

If you are new to social science research and writings (the literature) you may find that reference books such as the following will help you to understand and appreciate the scope of methodological assumptions, approaches and issues:

♦ *The Blackwell Dictionary of Twentieth Century Social Thought* (Outherwaite and Bottomore, 1993)

♦ *The Oxford Companion to the Mind* (Gregory and Zangwill, 1998)

You will find it useful to have such reference books at hand while reading this chapter. There are also several recommended further readings accompanying this chapter that are written in a style which make methodology accessible to the novice. In places through-out this chapter these are used to direct you to specific readings which give more in-depth expositions of the more complicated ideas and arguments. This is not a chapter on how to do methodology, but about methodological positions and arguments. It is based on a number of basic contrasts including those between the positivists and interpretivists, real-ists and idealists, externalists and internalists. The purpose of making these contrasts is to show the argumentation of methodological debates.

The idea of a science of society

The idea of a science of society can be found in the writings of eighteenth- and nineteenth-century thinkers such as Saint-Simon (1760–1825), Auguste Comte (1798–1857) and Herbert Spencer (1820–1903). Many of their writings are still widely available today in academic, public and virtual libraries. In their separate works they show a common belief that a science of society is possible and desirable. A scientific understanding of society would uncover the *laws* of the social society in much the same way as the *naturalist* approach

> Key theories and analogies associated with this period include: utilitarian liberalism, evolutional theory, organic analogy, social dynamics, social statics and social statistics.

had begun to uncover the laws of nature (evolution). This would be based on the collection of facts and this *empiricist* data, rather than theories, myths or belief, could be used to determine the truth about social reality, dismissing myth, superstition and religion as the basis for explanation. Reason would replace earlier forms of non-scientific explanation and be used to accumulate more and more knowledge about how society works and therefore how changes could be made to it for the betterment and improvement of humanity. This new positive philosophy, called *positivism* by Comte, would enable humans to exercise their reason to forward the evolution of society towards higher and more refined levels of civilization.

The reforming influence of the early social philosophers can be seen throughout the history of the social sciences and especially social policy up to the present day. The most striking example for most people in the UK was the slum clearance and construction of 'communities in the sky' (tower blocks) in the 1950s and 1960s. The aim to improve, make something better and eradicate some social problem is a feature of much research done throughout such disciplines as sociology, psychology and economics. The social survey movement, for example, used the principles of positivism to collect substantial amounts of statistical data on the variables of poverty. The following are some of the classic examples for which details are readily available in libraries and via the Internet:

♦ *London Labour and the London Poor* (Mayhew, 1851)

♦ *In Darkest England and the Way Out*, (Booth, W., 1890)

♦ *Life and Labour of the People in London* (Booth, C.,1889)

♦ *Poverty: A Study of Town Life* (Rowntree, 1901)

CHARACTERIZING POSITIVISM AND SCIENCE

The frame of reference for the early social survey movement and for others who have followed their aims is the belief that positivism in its principles and its methods can be used to study society. Before characterizing positivism and science we need to point out that saying what science is and how scientists do it is highly debatable and that there are complex and subtle variations within positivism. Therefore what is offered here is a characterization intended to help you approach such debates so that you understand them and can use them to make reasoned choices for your own methodology.

POSITIVISM AS A SCIENCE

The idea that knowledge of the world, of what is true and is not true, is possible is a bedrock assumption of the positivist position. This includes the aspirational claim that knowledge that is objective, universal, true and cumulative is possible. The general assumption is that commonsense, everyday knowledge and understanding is flawed because it is not systematic, sceptical and free from values and is therefore not objective, is particular, is based on how the world appears to us and does not accumulate in terms of building a total unified picture of the inter-connectedness of things. As we will see, some or all of these claims are open to serious challenge. Table 7.1 attempts to summarize many of the assumptions and consequent arguments of the positivist tradition. In constructing Table 7.1 a deliberate bias has been employed to skew it towards the positivist conceptions for a social science rather than a positivist view for the natural sciences.

SCIENTIFIC ATTITUDE

The early positivists had an attitude to the study of society that to a large part underpins much of what we take for granted today about how research ought to be done. Robson claims there are three major parts both to the scientific attitude and also to what is called, the 'research attitude'. 'Research', Robson claims, 'is carried out *systematically, sceptically* and *ethically*':

systematically means giving serious thought to what you are doing, and how and why you are doing it; in particular, being explicit about the nature of the observations that are made, the circumstances in which they are made and the role you take in making them;

sceptically means subjecting your ideas to possible disconfirmation, and also subjecting your conclusions to scrutiny (by yourself initially, then by others);

ethically means that you follow a code of conduct for the research which ensures that the interests and concerns of those taking part in, or possibly affected by, the research are safeguarded. (2002: 18)

Robson holds to the view that through the application of this attitude, even though it may be more difficult to implement than to state, most researchers should be able to produce 'something worthwhile' (2002: 19). The assumption that research should have a practical value is explicit in this position, but as you will see by the end of this chapter, research requires an understanding of the methodological arguments and choices which need to be made and this in itself is a valuable outcome of any research.

TABLE 7.1   CHARITABLE SUMMARY OF EARLY POSITIVIST ASSUMPTIONS AND ARGUMENTS

Assumptions	Arguments
Realism	There is only one real world not dependent on how people think it is. Science attempts to uncover laws which are hidden from everyday perceptions and are beyond common sense, which may give unsuspected explanations of familiar things and reveal relationships and objects beyond the range of the normal senses.
Demarcation	Science is different from common sense and other forms of knowledge, such as theology and speculation. Non-scientific views of the world are beyond the boundaries of testability and verification and therefore cannot be proved either true or false. This does not mean that such forms of knowing are valueless, for they may assist the imagination and conjecture.
Foundations	Observation and experimentation provide the foundations for testing and generating hypotheses and theories. It is not, however, a simple matter of collecting 'facts' (directionalist empiricism), but of systematically studying differences and similarities between things and identifying relationships between them.
Cumulativeness	Scientific knowledge is built on what is already known to be true through testing theory against observation. Scientific knowledge is therefore cumulative, but is always open to test as successive facts and truths are discovered.
Subject matter	Each science studies a realm of distinct facts about one part of reality and aims to describe the quantities, qualities, properties and relationships of and between phenomena.
Many methods	Science has many methods including description, classification, observation, generalization, comparison, experimentation – all aimed at subjecting theories to tests against the facts they seek to explain.

(Continued)

TABLE 7.1 (CONTINUED)

Assumptions	Arguments
Laws	Scientific knowledge produces empirical generalizations (descriptive statements of regularities), theories (hypothetical explanations) and hypotheses (carefully stated conjectures that include the conditions for their verification or falsification).
Explanation and prediction	Testability provides the basis for reliable prediction, action and control. Pure and applied aspects of any science cannot be divided from each other because to understand and to control something are necessarily connected.
Ethics and morals	The application of scientific methods (means) should be free of prejudices and aimed at the acquisition of knowledge for the betterment of the social, cultural, intellectual and physical environment of human kind (ends).
Qualities of scientists	An open mind and humility before the facts is required along with rigorous care with data, integrity and honesty about the conditions of testing, and a readiness to change explanations when faced with disconfirming evidence.

Source: Adapted from Fletcher, 1971.

THE TERRAIN OF THE POSITIVIST VIEW OF SCIENCE

From the brief discussions above you already know something of the nature of positivism, a major methodological tradition. In this and the next section the major twentieth-century positivist theorists and their arguments will be looked at more closely. It is, as will be seen later in this chapter, important to get to grips with the terrain of this literature because you will need to know what the origins and consequences are of the methodological approach you have taken, and this includes the criticisms which may be made of your research based on your methodological assumptions. To begin with, Figure 7.1 attempts to provide an overview of the main assumptions along with the names of key positivists. It uses a loose chronology of positivism to show the development of positions, often in contradiction to each other.

Using Figure 7.1 as a reference point (and guide for your further reading) the main assumptions and arguments in the development of positivism in the twentieth century

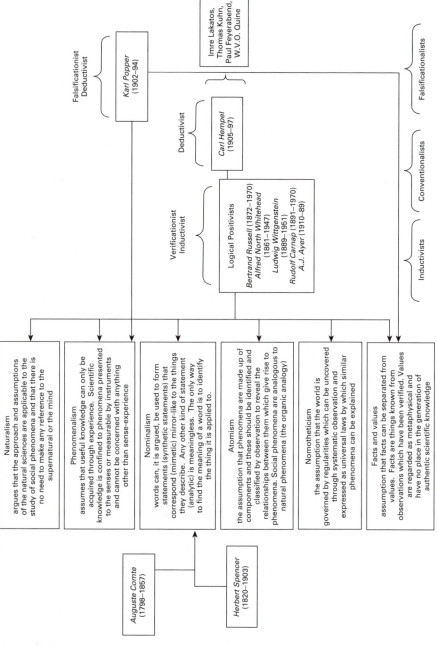

FIGURE 7.1   POSITIVISTS AND THEIR ASSUMPTIONS IN THE NINETEENTH AND TWENTIETH CENTURIES

can be outlined. A point to note is that while many theorists have been labelled as positivist, some may disagree with this. Among those who accepted the label there were disagreements and differences on the specifics of what constituted science.

THE VIENNA CIRCLE

The main reference for understanding positivism and its influence on the social sciences is the Vienna Circle, which introduced itself to the world in 1929 with a manifesto entitled *The Scientific World-view: The Vienna Circle (Wissenschaftliche Weltauffassung. Der Wiener Kreis)*. The Vienna Circle was a European philosophical movement led by Ernst Mach, Mauritz Schlick and Rudolf Carnap, and was to include many of the philosophers who influenced the social sciences such as Ludvig Wittgenstein, Karl Popper, Alfred Whitehead, Bertrand Russell, Alfred Ayer and Carl Hempel. Although there is no generally accepted way of providing a brief characterization of what the Vienna Circle was about, a quote from the British philosopher David Hume, on whose work the positivists had built some of their own arguments, captures the essence of the attitude of the Vienna Circle:

> When we run over libraries, persuaded of these principles, what havoc must we make? If we take in our hand any volume; of divinity or school of metaphysics, for instance; let us ask, Does it contain any abstract reasoning concerning quantity or number? No. Does it contain any experimental reasoning concerning matter of fact and existence? No. Commit it then to the flames: for it can contain nothing but sophistry and illusion. (Hume, 1910)

The positivism of the Vienna Circle centred on the elimination, from science and scientific knowledge, of metaphysics (values, notions, ideas, conjectures). The principal instrument that was identified as making this possible was the development of a logical analysis and application of language to provide objective descriptions of a verifiable world. The principle of verification would provide theories developed from observations with the means of confirming or disconfirming the power of the theory to predict and explain similar things. The spread of the movement was rapid. This was mostly due to a series of congresses (meetings) held throughout Europe and America during the 1930s, the publication of many journals and books and the emigration of key members to America, fleeing the Nazis. Whether we like it or not, the influence of the *logical positivists*, as the Vienna Circle came to be known as, was widespread and our debates in the social sciences today are largely a dialogue with the heritage of positivism.

The overall aim of the Vienna Circle was to correct what they perceived as faults in earlier understandings and formulations of a positivist science. We can sum up their arguments in the following series of points:

♦ in the natural sciences the detailed accumulation of facts has resulted in major measurable advances to human knowledge and control of the natural environment;

♦ the assumptions and methods of the natural sciences have uncovered regularities in nature that we were previously unaware of, for example, evolution;

♦ the assumptions, attitudes and procedures of the natural sciences can be applied to the study of the social world and its problems;

♦ to do this all traces of speculative ideas and values should and can be removed from the procedures involved in the production of scientific knowledge;

♦ only when this is done can we have an objective science and objective knowledge;

♦ this can be done by separating facts from values;

♦ we can begin from the natural science knowledge that the world is made up of atomic facts — there is only one world and this world is made up of physical things (physicalism);

♦ this world can be described using carefully constructed statements that correspond (mimetic approach) to these facts;

♦ only statements that can be demonstrated to be true through testing against observational data can be accepted (synthetic statements); all other statements are meaningless in scientific terms;

♦ there is, therefore, a neutral observational language that all sciences can use to describe their particular aspect of the world, and so there is a unity to science given in a universal descriptive language;

♦ from the systematic repeated observation of phenomena hypotheses can be developed to go beyond what has not been directly observed to infer dependent relationships, and therefore cause, and so give rise to theories and explanations;

- correlations between data can be tested (variable analysis) and from these explanatory theories developed which are to be tested against observations in controlled conditions to verify the power of the theory to predict and explain the behaviour of similar things;

- where a theory cannot yet be established as a general law of explanation, regularities repeatedly observed between specified variables of a phenomenon can be used to construct a model of the phenomenon to provide the means of calculating the probability of the occurrence of that phenomenon under certain conditions;

- the same data will be collected by any competent scientist in their field of study, therefore replication of observations is possible and a way of providing verification; and

- the competent scientist brings no values to work and uses methods to collect data which have no effect on the data; both scientist and methods are therefore unobtrusive.

This summary of points includes arguments from Carnap, Wittgenstein, Schlick, Whitehead, Russell, Ayer and many others. However, it does not do justice to the complexities and sophistication of the arguments made by the individuals involved in the movement. You are recommended to refer to the suggested readings (especially Smith, 1998 and Hughes and Sharrock, 1997) to look for yourself at longer explications of positivism and at some of the primary sources which are available through most academic libraries and Internet sources.

FROM VERIFICATIONISM TO FALSIFICATIONISM

Karl Popper (1902–94) found it difficult to hold most of the assumptions of logical positivism (see Table 7.1 for an outline of these). His particular criticisms were made on two fronts: on the criteria which demarcated science from non-science and on the growth of knowledge.

> Epistemology: the study of, and debates about, ways in which we know things and have knowledge – often distinguished from *ontology*, the study of reality. Epistemologist are often divided into either empiricists (e.g. Locke, Berkeley, Hume) or rationalists (Plato, Descartes, Leibniz).

In terms of demarcation, the logical positivists held the view that *inductive empiricism* was the method of science which produced descriptions of the things in the world. Descriptions were verified by observing instances of a phenomenon and falsified if a disconfirming observation was made. There was then an *asymmetry* in inductive empiricism; disconfirming cases were not sought but confirming ones were. It is impossible to conclusively verify a statement by reference to experience. There was always the possibility, however, of a disconfirming case and this made inductivism a probabilistic exercise where a single case could threaten the theory. Therefore, no matter the weight of confirming observations, one falsifying one would suffice to challenge the whole theory. It is therefore not possible to have an accumulation of reliable knowledge because the method is too fragile to support that certainty in one's knowledge. Popper substitutes inductivism with deductivism and verificationism with *falsifiability*. We will look at his deductivism in a moment. The basis of Popper's falsifiability theory originated in his admiration for the theories of Einstein. He noted that Einstein had proposed a very risky theory that, at the time, was highly improbable. Einstein had also shown within his theory the conditions by which it could be disproven rather than confirmed. Comparing other theories Popper notes that ones such as psychoanalysis could not be falsified, not even in principle. This led him to state that the demarcation between a scientific and a non-scientific theory is the criterion of falsifiability. To be a scientific theory, a theory must have in principle a conceivable way of being falsified. The longer the theory is not falsified is testament to its robustness and power to explain and predict.

On the second front Popper challenges the logical positivists' view that observations and descriptions corresponded with real things and were based on pure observation free from theory and values. For Popper our understandings and hypotheses about the world do not arise only from observation. Theories, he argues, arise in many different ways and often initially take the form of hunches and guesses. The origin of a hypothesis is of no consequence – whether from a dream, the imagination or fancy – the point is they are aimed at solving problems. Science for Popper starts from attempting to understand and then solve

The hypothetico-deductive model can be seen in many studies in the social sciences including:

- Durkheim's (1897) *Suicide*
- Barker's (1988) *The Making of a Moonie*
- Goldthorpe et al. (1968–69) *The Affluent Worker Studies*
- Oakley's (1974) *The Sociology of Housework*
- Young and Willmott's (1973) *The Symmetrical Family*.

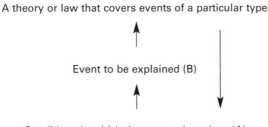

A theory or law that covers events of a particular type

Event to be explained (B)

Conditions in which the event takes place (A)

FIGURE 7.2   THE HYPOTHETICO-DEDUCTIVE MODEL OF EXPLANATION

some problem and not from some disinterested observation. The problems we recognize are often the outcome of our personal biography and therefore are not value-free. The growth of human knowledge proceeds from our formulation of problems and attempts to solve them. Popper suggests that problem solving is essentially a mental activity: that we use our imaginations to reason (conjecture) about the nature of the world around us and in so doing challenge existing theories. This sets him apart from most of the logical positivists who held a *empiricist epistemology*; that knowledge comes from observation. Popper's *rationalist epistemology* holds that knowledge comes from deductive reasoning about hypotheses. The process is what Popper called the *hypothetico-deductive model* (or scheme). The hypothetico-deductive model holds that explanations have three parts: (i) general; (ii) a more specific thing or event to be explained; and (iii) the conditions under which the general can explain the particular. Figure 7.2 shows how an explanation of an event can be deduced from a general theory or law within the conditions set for the explanation.

The hypothetico-deductive model expressed the law in terms of 'whenever A, then B'. From the law a hypothesis can be deduced to explain an event. This can then be tested against the relevant facts to see if the predicted features of the event do exist or happen according to the law. The truth or falsity of a hypothesis could then be checked by observation.

CLOSED SYSTEM ANALYSIS

In the social sciences, especially those fields concerned to provide explanations of behaviour through correlational and experimental studies, the positivist approach can be characterized as 'closed systems analysis'. This approach has the methodological aim of isolating the key variable(s) that cause the behaviour. This is done by constructing a strict boundary made up of definitions of concepts, their operationalization and measurement. This boundary is constructed to purge the research field of any extraneous variables from the situation which must, according to the protocols of the method, be subject to full control. Hence the behaviour under study is also isolated in controlled conditions to ensure that it is not contaminated by unknown variables. This means that the intrinsic predispositions of individuals who do other than comply with the method are, by the design and imposition of the method, excluded from all measurements. While this approach has been generally successful for the experimental fields of the natural sciences, it is not always applicable or desirable for obtaining faithful portrayals of human understanding and interpretation. Some of the debates among social scientists are therefore cast in terms of quantitative versus qualitative because it has been common to find statistical techniques used when attempting to apply a closed-systems approach to explain human behaviour. However, this is to simplify the argument because it often fails to take into account the broader methodological positions and logic of employing an approach that is either largely numbers based or one that is not. Hence the need for Popper's critical stance in all research, in order to avoid slavish acquiescence to method because it is assumed to be more 'scientific' than alternative ways of finding answers to our research questions.

Although Popper's work is much criticized, he gives us a critical stance towards theories and research. He insists that critical reasoning is an essential part of science and should be used to interrogate all existing theories. This comes from his argument that all knowledge is provisional, conjectural and hypothetical. Critical interrogation is to be used to eliminate weak theories: those which have inconsistencies; have confused the empirical and logical elements; have little empirical content and predictive power; or for which empirical applications cannot be derived from the conclusions. Popper's advice is that we challenge the boundaries of our theories no matter how sacred they may be in our disciplines. Only in this way, he argues, will we be able to discriminate between good and bad theories and progress, through trial and error, in our knowledge. Before moving on it may be worth noting that this text has in effect told a story. Much of what follows, and which can be read in the literature of the philosophy of research, are narrative accounts of who said what and interpretations of what they meant. It is mostly

> *Rationalism* stresses the role played by reason in preference to that of the senses in the acquisition of knowledge. *Rationalists* maintain the possibility of a priori knowledge – that a 'truth' can be established independently of any sensory observation.

about trying to make some acceptable sense about what this stuff means and what its relevance may be for us doing research. To this end, namely understanding, we turn now to what are called epistemological problems, that is, where our knowledge of whatever we take to be real comes from.

Differences over the nature of knowledge

This textual characterization has so far made no comparisons between positivistic approaches and other approaches to research methodology. This section will highlight the basis of the arguments that have been made to expand on some of the main differences between the various positions regarding knowledge. This procedure, by its very nature, will be selective and because of this the ways in which the differences will be presented are not the same as those you will find in many other books on research. This section begins with the familiar, by typifying those who prefer a positivist closed-system approach as 'externalists' and those who find the positivist approach too restraining or logically a problem as 'internalists'. It then goes on to look at the argumentation of the debates between those who hold a correspondence theory and those a congruence theory of knowledge.

EXTERNALISTS AND INTERNALISTS

Following Hilary Putman's (1981) discussion we can begin with a simple comparison between those who hold an externalist position and those who hold an internalist position regarding knowledge. For the externalist there is a real world existing independently of the ways in which we think of it. Finding out how the world really is gives science its main purpose: to discover, through the systematic collection of data, experimentation, comparison and testing of theories, how the world really works. The ways in which we often think things are is not always the case. Science uses a different form of attitude from that used in everyday life to uncover the 'real' nature of reality and to correct our mistaken, incorrect or partial views of reality. Whatever exists has a basis in physical or material reality. Therefore all things, including what we often term the 'mental' and 'cultural', are describable by reference to a physical reality.

In nature things belong to classes and are generally ordered hierarchically within and among the classes. Science aims to identify what individual things belong to what classes of things and to find the relationships between and among the different classes. Although each science has its own realm of interest, using a universal descriptive language, it is possible to have descriptions that correspond to the structures which exist in nature and which provide a unified description of reality.

The internalist hold that the only way of knowing what is in the world is to use a frame of reference to describe things. Internalists do not doubt the 'reality' of reality, but do not see how it is possible to have a description of reality that has no reference to a framework in which the description can be made sense of. Although this may seem a little odd, here is an example, provided by Anderson et al., which encapsulates what it means for a description to require a frame of reference:

> Consider the task of describing a woodyard and its contents. We can talk of pieces of wood, perhaps, but of what kind? There is teak, mahogany, oak, plywood, hardwood, pine, etc. and, if the person making the description knows their woods, then it is likely that such descriptions will be right. But there is another way we could proceed. We could describe the woodyard as consisting of tongue and groove boards, window frames, doors, wall panelling, and so on. This description, too, can be perfectly sound and correct. (1985: 36)

From the internalist standpoint we can only make sense of the world by using descriptions that have a frame of reference suitable for our purposes. Internalists look to collect empirical data like the externalists, but any description, interpretation or conjecture about the data is generated from within, rather than being external to, a theory. Our theories about the nature of the world are necessary for us to assess the relevance of what we observe, and not the other way around.

CORRESPONDENCE AND CONGRUENCE THEORIES:
THE DEBATE BETWEEN TALCOTT PARSONS AND ALFRED SCHUTZ

The issue most theorists in the social sciences have attempted to address is the problem of how best to conceive of what constitutes social reality and how it can be studied. To focus on this issue we will look at a debate between two of the key social theorists of the last century, Talcott Parsons (1902–79) and Alfred Schutz (1899–1959). During the 1940s, Parsons and Schutz corresponded with one another over how the social sciences could (and should) conceive the characteristics of social activities (their letters are reproduced in Grathoff, 1978). In other words, they discussed the question 'What must social reality be like in order for it to be able to be described?' In terms of our everyday common sense this kind of question may seem odd, but as will be explained later it is crucial to all social research. This is because if you do not have a formulation of what it is you are studying, then how can you study it? In their letters there is a clear difference of assumptions about what characteristics can be studied. Their two positions are termed the 'correspondence theory' and the 'congruence theory' respectively. The debate between Parsons and Schutz is a complex one and in places makes implicit assumptions about larger debates in philosophy. Their arguments will therefore be presented as a sequence of points which I believe encapsulates the essence of the two *logics* for the assumptions they hold about how best to conceive of what constitutes social reality and how it can be studied.

Talcott Parsons: his contribution and argument

The work of Parsons amounts to a substantial collection, over many decades, of systematic reasoning about the nature of social reality and the subject matter for sociology. Although no longer 'in vogue', Parsons's theory of social action has rarely been matched for its depth and breadth by those who seek to criticize it and it is for this reason that, whatever you may have read about Parsons, his work deserves serious consideration. Parsons's assumptions go like this:

◆ the social world can be divided into those elements which are rational and structured and those which are unique, random and non-rational;

◆ the properties of rational actions are capable of being scientifically described;

◆ science is the systematic investigation of reality based on doubt, scepticism and value neutrality;

◆ commonsense descriptions of social reality, unlike scientific ones, fail to distinguish from the flux of appearances and cannot penetrate everyday reality to uncover the orderly structures of which individual actions are a part;

◆ social science does not therefore begin with common sense or with individual actions, but with abstraction by theoretically reconstructing the observable elements into phenomena of orderly relationships — abstractions which are more than the sum of the parts — for example, institutions, systems, wholes, power, control, bureaucracy and so on;

♦ social science should produce abstract descriptions of the intensively complex reality hidden from everyday perception and superficial descriptions;

♦ scientific sociological descriptions should be based on a view of social reality that is ordered and has logical relationships;

♦ human reasoning is a part of rational reality and can therefore be used to formulate abstract descriptions of the rationality of the larger social wholes of which it is a part; and

♦ social reality, although infinite and changing, is that which is ordered and has a logic describable by means of human reason (Kantian position).

Alfred Schutz: his contribution and argument

Of those social theorists to have engaged seriously with the methodological debates in the social sciences, and in particular with the work of Parsons, Schutz and Garfinkel stand out. Interestingly, Garfinkel's own work owes as much to Parsons as it does to that of Schutz. Schutz, however, had a radically different approach from Parsons to characterizing the nature of social reality and the subject matter for sociology. Schutz's phenomenological assumptions go like this:

♦ phenomenology rejects the distinction between how things appear to us and how they may really be; perception does not stand as an inferior version of 'reality', but it is itself a part of (constitutive) reality;

♦ things (phenomena) are real to the extent and ways in which they are experienced and acted upon; however, if two persons perceive the same thing in different ways, then for each the thing is different;

♦ this does not mean our descriptions of the world are relative, without any agreed point of reference;

♦ rather, a distinction needs to be made between the attitude most of us hold in everyday life (a natural attitude), in which our experiences have an objective character that we take for granted (do not systematically doubt), and an attitude we can take to describe those experiences;

♦ everyday activities are a form of rationality and are different from the 'rationality' of science. Science differs from the natural attitude in terms of means and ends: organized knowledge is an end for science, while in the natural attitude it is a means for achieving particular purposes. The person in everyday life is only interested in the state of their knowledge in so far as it can be used to realize their plans and intentions;

♦ knowledge in everyday life is not chaotic, random or disorganized, but only appears that way if viewed from an idealized model of rationality as proposed by science. People organize what they experience by using what they already know about how to organize experiences. Social reality for most people, including scientists, is particular in that it is the product of particular problems and needs in a specific time and place;

♦ in applying the recipes we have for organizing our experiences into types, we do not follow rules of rational thought, as science might, but employ the general techniques and frames of reference we know about and which have worked in the past; in so doing we add to our stocks of knowledge about how to understand. Hence there can be differences between stocks of knowledge and therefore differences between how one person or group understands a situation and how another does. Social reality is experienced by us as 'objective', but in a multitude of ways at different times;

♦ phenomenology aims to study the natural attitude as a reality based on experience;

♦ to do so it must not assume there is an underlying reality of a hidden 'logic' that structures an individual's experiences (to be penetrated by analysis), but that the natural attitude can be studied as a phenomenon in its own right;

♦ phenomenology is an empirical programme that aims to empirically investigate all forms of activity in everyday life, from teaching a class of six-year-olds, to conducting an experiment in a laboratory, to experiencing bereavement; and

♦ the topics for phenomenology are everything in the social world and the task is to describe what it is that makes one experience this experience and not something else (its essence).

Parsons and Schutz looked at the characteristics of social reality very differently from each other and in ways which are largely irreconcilable. An illustration of their differences is their respective use of the term 'actor'. Both employ 'actor' in their writing, but they have very different understandings of what they mean by the term. For Parsons the actor was the agent exhibiting features according to a predetermined theoretical standpoint to the phenomenon. For Schutz the actor refers to a person experiencing some commonly occupied social situation. Parsons's conception, because it removes the person and their understandings, is often termed the 'objective' conception of the actor. This conception of abstractedness is frequently seen in research reports and journal articles when the researcher and their subjects are referred to in the third person. Schutz's conception, because it focuses on experience, is often termed the 'subjective' conception of the actor. It consequently has a vocabulary, different from that of Parsons, which looks to describe the ways in which experiences are assembled into a recognizable order. The difference between the two at this level is therefore one of different frames of reference.

Knowledge as situated rather than universal

The Parsons–Schutz debate has highlighted some of the main differences in the social sciences. This is expressed in various dichotomies including the 'objective–subjective', 'positivist–phenomenological' and 'positivist–interpretivistic'. Note that it is definitely not a 'quantitative–qualitative' comparison, which is a commonly mistaken assumption. This section will look at some of the main attempts to clarify and characterize the process of scientific development and at how this can help us to understand just what it means to do positivistic research or interpretive research. The section begins with what is possibly the most influential book for the current philosophy of science, *The Structure of Scientific Revolutions* (1962/1970) by Thomas Kuhn.

SCIENTIFIC PARADIGMS

Kuhn (1922–96) was a graduate of theoretical physics who looked at the history of science in order to give introductory lectures to humanities undergraduates. As a newcomer to the humanities, and in particular to the history of science, Kuhn soon had a view of the development of science that contrasted with those commonly accepted. His research led him to look seriously and critically at many long established assumptions and in particular those of the positivists and falsificationists, especially Popper. Popper's view of science was one that included the following main claims:

1 Falsificationism was the logic that drove scientific knowledge forward.

2 Scientific knowledge was evolutionary, progressing through a process of trial and error underpinned by the logic of criticism.

3 Knowledge and truth accumulate, not as universals but in terms of degrees (verisimilitude).

4 There is no such thing as social science because what passes for social science is not falsifiable. Added to this, social science in following the goal of positivist reformation of society will lead to uniformity, thereby negating the open criticism and plurality of argument which is the basis of epistemological evolutionism.

Kuhn's studies of the history of science revealed something different from that described and advocated by Popper. Looking at such developments as Aristotle's *Physics* and Newton's physics, he found that rather than both being at different positions on a continuum, neither were within the same spectrum (Crotty, 1998: 34). Most of the time scientists work on specific problems employing a common view of what science is and how it is to be done (Kuhn, 1977: 188–234). Their framework is what Kuhn terms 'a paradigm'. A paradigm is a way of looking at and understanding the world and is made up of a cluster of values, views, opinions and understandings on what criteria gives worth to something. New scientists are socialized into the general paradigm and most come to accept and work within it. A small number, however, challenge some of the basic assumptions or premises of the normal paradigm and occasionally change the theories of the paradigm to such a degree that the new theory is incommensurable with the old one. A new paradigm provides a new way of seeing old problems and brings into view new problems; it also largely replaces the old paradigm. Science therefore comes to work within the new paradigm, leaving the old one behind as a historic relic.

Kuhn is not saying that scientific progress does not take place, but does argue that progress cannot be measured as if on a linear continuum. Each development is judged, he maintains, by applying rational criteria accepted at that time for that particular 'science'. For Kuhn critical rational thought is a part of the institution of science in much the same way as it was for Popper. This is not the only point of similarity between the two. Popper and Kuhn also share a degree of agreement over the place of non-rational sources for the generation of ideas and breakthroughs in understanding, over the need to be able to test conjectures, and in recognizing that diversity and differences between scientists are good for critical debate. With so many similarities, what is it that Kuhn did and what is its relevance to research?

One way of approaching this question is to see Kuhn as taking an element in Popper's work which acknowledges the use of sociological analysis. Kuhn takes this and follows it through to see where it may lead. Popper's assumptions and recommendations are used by Kuhn on Popper's own work; Kuhn can be seen as applying Popper's own standards to Popper's notions about science. This is not an unusual thing to do, but Kuhn does it in such a subtle way that if you do not know Popper well much of Kuhn's analysis and argument can be lost or easily misinterpreted. In one respect Kuhn's work makes visible many of the sociological features of Popper's work. These include: the place and role Popper gave to values in the research process, as being a source of some of the most interesting and risky conjectures; the function of words, which Popper saw as doing more than providing names for things (nominalism); and a blurring of the demarcation between science and non-science, in that methodological procedures of the different sciences each aim to provide descriptions, rather than a unified account, of reality. Popper is therefore left as a key figure in science by Kuhn, for he opened up for investigation science as a multiplicity of context dependent activities. This may not be a reading everyone agrees with, but it does give a way of understanding the relevance of succeeding debates about science found in the writing of theorists such as Lakatos and Feyerabend (more on these below). It asks us to see science in broader historical terms as something individuals chose to do and which is now associated with established institutions. Kuhn's portrayal of science is of humans pursuing their interests prudently, with an attachment to why they are doing what they are doing, and doing it in ways which incorporate the highest degrees of validity and reliability possible within the techniques they can apply. The practice of research is, it may be argued, similar to the way Kuhn portrays science; that it is value-laden, focused on solving puzzles, does not always result in generalizations and is not unified, but nevertheless involves reasoning.

LAKATOS, FEYERABEND, PUTNAM AND HACKING

Even if the history of science is not a continuum, the debates about it do exhibit an interconnectedness. They share a common concern to characterize either how science represents the world or aims to intervene to makes changes to it. The names used in the sub-heading are representative of contributions to the science debate and what I will do next is summarize elements of contributions which are relevant to contemplating research methodology.

Imre Lakatos (1922–74) and Paul Feyerabend (1924–94) were close associates and for a period had a great deal in common regarding the ideas and arguments of Popper and Kuhn. Lakatos critically appraised Popper's position and attempted to realign some of Kuhn's insights on the development of scientific knowledge to show that knowledge was cumulative because it was a rational activity. He focused on the criteria for demarcating science from other forms of knowing. He examined inductivism, conventionalism and falsificationalism and found each in their turn unacceptable as demarcation criteria. Like Popper, he dismissed induction and conventionalism for not acknowledging the accumulation of knowledge as a gradual and real process. However, with falsificationism he argued there was some hope. Popper's falsificationism, he thought, had been largely misunderstood and had been applied in a dogmatic fashion. Popper's suggestion that a hypothesis, even if empirically refuted, could still be useful attracted the attention of Lakatos. He looked to Kuhn to see how scientists working in particular research programmes held on to theories which had either been refuted or were incapable of falsification. He argued that the disciplinary and institutionalized existence of science created research programmes (a rough substitute for Kuhn's paradigm). Theories such as Marxism, relativity, gravity and psychoanalysis were, in Lakatos's terms, research programmes which had a *core* set of assumptions and propositions on which individual scientists and theorists had built their careers. Such propositions and assumptions were not, therefore, to be easily given up even in the face of the severest criticism. Each research programme has, argues Lakatos, puzzles its adherents approve of and believe lie within its remit and those it sees as outside of or not possible to address within its parameters. Programmes of research are substantial enough to protect ideas which would be unacceptable in other programmes and have the ability to adapt and re-invent aspects of them to remain progressive. Programmes which do not do this but merely repair old ideas are not progressive and are liable to decline.

Scientists working within research programmes are therefore often actively trying to make sense of the ideas around their core propositions in ways that Lakatos and Popper would term as rationalist epistemology rather than empiricist epistemology. This position strongly implies that there are social, psychological and historical considerations to be taken into account when looking at science and knowledge and that they can be invoked to show how knowledge has progressed because of rational thought. This is largely where Paul Feyerabend made his major entrance into the debate.

As a student of Popper, close friend of Lakatos, admirer of Wittgenstein's work, nearly the production assistant to Bertolt Brecht, and involved with quantum physics, Feyerabend was professionally and socially at the centre of the debates about science. Starting out with arguments for a realist position for science as opposed to logical positivism, his early work was very similar to Popper's falsificationist rationalist epistemology, conventionalism and rejection of empiricism. Feyerabend ended up being seen as a radical *relativist* who, from the 1960s onwards, argued that science has the capability to contribute to a free and open society but that the science advocated by logical positivism could lead to a monolithic, closed and totalitarian society. Feyerabend's position was that science as a form of life and knowledge is no better or worse than any other form of life and knowing. Alternative medicine, voodoo, oracles and religion (Feyerabend, 1993: 36) are all different, not comparable and are, to use Feyerabend's term, *incommensurable* (a term also employed by Kuhn). Western science is for Feyerabend a dogma that exercises an imperialistic domination over how we view other ways of knowing. Science is given its privileged position because, argues Feyerabend, it has succeeded in getting accepted myths about itself; that it is objective, unified and progressive. Feyerabend sees the nature and history of science as an ideology, having been written so as to appear to be a unified, systematic, continuous evolution of knowledge. He is therefore not against research but against 'scientism', the belief that science is supreme in method and knowledge to all other forms of knowing. He attempts to show that scientists held in high regard, such as Galileo and Copernicus, were not objective and disinterested collectors of facts and tellers of truths. Feyerabend portrays them as self-interested, self-propagandists who were not impeded by the facts not fitting their theories. Feyerabend uses the case of Copernicus to show that science is far from systematic, to claim it is ad hoc, accidental and often a political activity (1993: 157). These views may be seen as challenging the ways in which what people do are reported and how they actually do what they do. He uses his cases to argue that it is not rationalist empiricist argument that decides the usefulness of a theory, but that the personality, politics and general social milieu are more of an influence than anything else. Hence, Feyerabend was labelled an 'irrationalist' 'relativist' and accepts for himself the role of outlining an anarchistic methodology (1993: 13).

Feyerabend's solution to the problem is to recommend the *principle of proliferation*. This principle contains the recommendation that we challenge the concepts and theories with which we are familiar by using *counter induction* (1993: 53). This means using hypotheses which contradict established theories to highlight the historically rooted assumptions we employ in our theories. This links to Feyerabend's conventionalism; the view that theories and concepts (frames of reference) are historically conditioned (1993: 51) and that the point of science and politics is to push at the boundaries of these in whatever ways our creativity can construct. In this way Feyerabend advocated *methodological pluralism* and *relativism* as the rational rules for science (1993; Caldwell, 1994).

Hilary Putnam (1975), whose work we met when we introduced his distinction between internalists and externalists (Putnam, 1978), has made some significant contributions to the debate. Putnam agrees with many empiricists that science, as an approach to applying a range of methods, produces reliable knowledge. But unlike the rationalist empiricists, he advocates that researchers look to describe the very *essence* of the phenomena they are investigating. By essence he means the very things (substances and relationships) that make a thing what it is and not something else. Putnam is mainly referring to physical objects, as can be found on the periodic table. Just what makes gold what it is and not lead? When we look to see what makes a thing (or behaviour) what it is, Putnam argues, it does not matter too much what we call it, for the stuff that it is made of and its relationship to other things will not change if we change its name. This position has a number of other implications. One is that there can be continuity between the theories of different paradigms, for the theory may change but the substance, in itself, does not. Second, there is here a recommendation to look at a thing closely, to see the detail of what it is. Ian Hacking's (1981 and 1983) work also recommends we should look to see how scientists have intervened in the world in order to be able to collect data, make measurements and conduct experiments. From this we will be able to see the range of ways in which research is and can be done and look at the range of ontologies researchers use to anchor their epistemologies. In this way the internal consistency of a theory becomes the standard by which research done within that theory can be judged as adequate or not. There can then be, according to Hacking and Putnam, many theoretical frames of reference and many different and possibly competing conceptions of how different aspects of the world are organized. There is no need to aim for a correspondence between descriptions and reality, but to produce, through our research methods and techniques, systematic descriptions and accounts of what we find. Diversity and difference become embodied within this conception of research, and notions about the unification of science, universal laws and the like are unnecessary. Things are the way they become because of how they were observed and thus become exhibits or artefacts of the investigation.

Relativism and values in research

From the summaries so far, the philosophers of science seem to not only eschew inductivism, but many also share a concern to express their values and to say that our theories of the world are contingent on the cultural context and time in which they were produced. What we have, then, are the issues of how we can deal with the problems of the possibility of *relativism* – that there are truths but no universal truth, and what role *values and ethics* should or can play in research.

RELATIVISM OR RELEVANCE?

What we have said so far may imply that we are moving towards a relativist view of knowledge; that there are competing views on what reality is and all are acceptable within certain conditions. This debate is intimately involved in many discussions about the role of values in research, but for the sake of a little clarity we have made an analytical distinction between the two. This distinction is based on the use of language to describe things in the world rather than to argue for how people ought to behave. This is because most of the debates about relativism are about how we make connections between the words we use to name/describe what we want to name and describe (for the reasons we have). The key figures involved, usually used as reference points in the literature, for this debate include Peter Winch (*The Idea of a Social Science*, 1958/1990), Thomas Kuhn (*The Structure of Scientific Revolutions*, 1970) and Karl Popper (*Objective Knowledge*, 1972).

From the above outline of Kuhn's ideas, it appears that reality can only be described from within a frame of reference and that there are many frames of reference which can be used to describe the same thing. Hence, if there are different ways of describing reality, then this is an argument for saying that there are different ways of describing reality and not that we cannot know about reality. Winch (1958), like Kuhn, does not attempt to provide any argument about the respective truths of science or claim that all versions of reality are equal. His major concern is to translate the work of Wittgenstein (1958) on using language for use in the social sciences. His main point is to provide conceptual clarity to the ways in which social science has and can use language to understand (rather than explain or compare) other cultures. In his critical examination of studies of other cultures, in particular that of Evans-Pritchard's study of the belief in witchcraft and oracles among the Azande people (Evans-Pritchard, 1965), Winch shows that a mistake has been made in attempting to find a reason for what are believed to be incorrect beliefs. Evans-Pritchard approached the Azande's beliefs as a puzzle for scientific explanation; of how another culture could believe and organize much of their collective behaviour around witchcraft and oracles. As if in need of correction or explanation as to its point, Azande behaviour was not taken as a part of a larger and more complex mode of cultural existence. Evans-Pritchard, by focusing too much, largely separated beliefs from the social organization of Azande society. Popper (1972) also holds with the argument that there are different frameworks for understanding the world and that it is the differences between them which make for useful discussion rather than incommensurability. The frameworks he identifies are: that for describing the *physical world*; that for *states of consciousness*; and that of external *objective knowledge*. The latter includes theoretical systems and logic, which he claims exist independently of the individual – as a part of the logic developed and uncovered by the human mind over millennia. That logic includes critical engagement with theories about how the world can be best described and it is this that is objective knowledge because it is a product we inherit through our socialization into the activities of science.

The claims that all alternatives to positivism and the conventional view of science necessitate a relativist position are largely unfounded. Anderson et al. (1985: 36) argue that with the woodyard (in the example given above), as with anything, we can have multiple descriptions of the same 'thing' and each can be as correct as the others. Some social scientists would see this as an argument for relativism; as there cannot be one definitive description of social reality, we are left with the problem of competing descriptions and an associated barrier to accumulating knowledge. In its extreme form it is known as 'the anything goes' position, but as we will see in the next section this is a naïve reaction that displays a thin understanding of the nature of social reality. This is because we can and do have different descriptions of the same thing. Different in terms of the point of view being taken by the one doing the description and using a particular frame of reference to make their description relevant.

In the frames of reference in the woodyard example earlier in this chapter there are two schemes of classification: ways of describing types of wood and ways of describing wood products. The purpose of the description strongly influences which classification scheme is selected as the frame of reference to be used. Different classification schemes are designed to bring out different features of the thing being described. It is normal to have different rather than competing descriptions of the same thing. Asking which is correct is senseless, for it ignores an essential characteristic of social life, which is the human capacity, on the one hand, to generate, establish and develop highly complex and sophisticated ways of classifying things and events they find in their world, and, on the other, to express them using only a few terms.

VALUE CHOICES

One of the assumptions of the logical positivists was that science, as a process, could divorce itself from the ethical commitments and value relevances of the individual and community for the sake of scientific knowledge. Values and ethics would impact on the product of the process and result, possibly, in a biased view or description of the phenomenon under investigation. Despite attempting to use science to make positive improvements to 'society', ethical and value neutrality was seen as an essential prerequisite for reliable knowledge. Emile Durkheim, for instance, in his *Rules of Sociological Method* (1895/1982), says that two key rules of science are firstly that scientists must focus only on the data and not bring to it assumptions or preconceptions, and secondly that we must only pay attention to the external properties of a phenomenon (1982: 69–72). Durkheim may be characterized, along with others such as Talcott Parsons and Robert K. Merton, as belonging to the naturalist position regarding the role of values in research. This position holds that social science ought to be based on social facts (for example, rates of suicide) and these be treated as things which exist. This followed the positivist conception of science and its procedures. But alongside the development of positivism as exhibited in the work of Comte and Spencer was an alternative that, like that of the positivists, can be traced back into Greek philosophy. The *interpretivists*, as they are collectively labelled, held that there was a difference between the natural and social worlds and that different approaches and in some cases assumptions should be used for the study of each. From the late 1600s, French and German scholars offered up this alternative to the positivist and materialist conception of a science of society. Battista Vico (1660–1744), Jean-Jacques Rousseau (1712–78), Georg W.F. Hegel (1770–1831), Karl Marx (1818–83), Friedrich D.E. Scheiermacher (1768–1834), William Dilthey (1833–1911), Heinrich Rickert (1863–1936) and

Max Weber (1864–1920) are the main protagonists in the dispute over methods for the study of human culture and history (the '*Methodenstreit*'). Their positions, although they had some significant differences, centred on the meaning and interpretation of culture and in particular the interpretation of textual materials, and consequently of the culture and history of humanity. For these thinkers positivism failed to recognize, let alone acknowledge, that culture and history were the products of the creativity possessed and expressed by humans which was beyond the laws of nature and reduction to biology and materialism. Hence the dualism between mind and body (the material) in much of their arguments, along with a distinction between the objective and subjective. Humans were essentially subjective in their world, which was based in interpretation and meaning; we live, to paraphrase Weber, in webs of signification which we, our contemporaries and forerunners have created (Geertz, 1973: 3). This position gives rise to the role of value choices and ethical commitments in social research.

Max Weber is often used as the main reference for the debates over values and ethics in research. His position, though not a simple one to understand, may be characterized as having its origins in his assertion that social reality is infinitely complex and that any description of it will necessarily be selective and partial. Being a part of that which we study as social investigators, we bring to our investigations preconceived notions, beliefs and values about what is important and how best to study it. In an attempt to bring some clarity to the matter, Weber makes a number of recommendations about how problems are chosen because of their relevance to us and how the methods we use can be free of values. First, he believes that our own place within our culture at a particular time in human society is an influence on the problems we choose for investigation. Our own value relevance influences our choice of topic and the way in which we define that topic. The interests, passions and politics of a researcher may be the genesis for their research and at the same time provide the frame of reference for describing their problem. However, Weber argues that when investigating a problem an attitude of value-freedom should be adapted so as to avoid, as far as possible, bias in data collection, categorization and interpretation. This means the researcher taking a position that is distanced from the topic they are investigating. At the same time Weber believed it was the responsibility of the researcher to set out the evidence for whatever they were talking about for others to judge the adequacy of the interpretation offered.

The selection of a problem using issues one is familiar with is something akin to Popper's claim that it matters little where a problem originated. This view is not, however, shared by all in the research community. It is common to see objections being made to research proposals because they are based on an issue or problem close to the researcher. Our position is that some of the best problems in applied and evaluative research are due to the fact that they have been suggested because of a personal involvement with a problem and that this is the case in both the social and natural sciences. Value freedom, however, raises a number of much more complex issues. Many researchers seriously question whether detachment is a realistic possibility given the value relevance that often leads to the selection of a topic in the first place (Gouldner, 1975; Bell and Newby, 1977; Eckhard and Ermann, 1977; Rosaldo, 1989; Parkin, 2003: Stanley and Wise, 1993). Parkin (2003), for instance, claims that the lack of moralization in a theory does not make it objective or value free. Similarly, Becker (1967), in his famous article 'Whose side are we on?', accuses much of sociology and implicitly psychology of ignoring that research, especially positivistic research, epistemologically favours some form of social control. Research assists either practically or ideologically in providing legitimation for the beliefs of the powerful to enact various forms of control over the 'underdogs'. Following some of, though not all, the arguments of Stanley and Wise (1993) we can say from experience that one's own self and sense of purpose is always a part of the research one does and that good research is often the outcome of a tenacious and motivated person who has some experience of the problem they are investigating.

Is a natural observational science of human action still possible?

The complexity of human behaviour is not something easily overlooked and because of this numerous attempts have been made to capture this complexity by developing highly sophisticated methodological positions and measuring instruments. Positivism, verificationism, falsificationism and hypothetico-deductivism, along with attempts to reduce human behaviour to biology or psychology, are only some of the attempts to deal with the problems of complexity and diversity of human behaviours.

In this section the work of Harvey Sacks is introduced. The reason for this is to show you that there is an alternative strategy to analysing social phenomena. In the early 1960s and into the 1970s the American sociologist Harvey Sacks looked closely at the conventional paradigm in the social sciences in respect of developing a sociology that was a stable natural observational discipline, that is, a scientific discipline. His approach, developed alongside that of Harold Garfinkel, is radically different from all others. In order to understand and appreciate it, a good place to start is with his critique of the assumption of correspondence.

THE PROBLEM OF LITERAL DESCRIPTION

A core assumption of the conventionalist approach in the social sciences, exemplified by Parsons, is the assumption of correspondence. This assumption holds the view that it is possible, and logical, for some kinds of descriptions to be accurate and correct literal reflections of things as they are, rather than as they appear, in the world. The correspondence theory therefore aims to answer the questions of what exactly 'this thing' is and what is really going on here. There are many examples in the library in the social science literature of attempts to take specific phenomena and apply just these questions; among them are studies of poverty, criminality, educational under-achievement, gender relations and so on. The theory further holds that it is only through analysis of the seemingly chaotic appearances can the real reality of a phenomenon be determined and described.

For Garfinkel and Sacks the goal of literal description is misguided and if dropped can, they demonstrated, lead to a distinctive alternative for the social sciences. In a series of exercises he gave to students, Garfinkel demonstrated the practical impossibility of pro-ducing a literal description of even the most routine event – a conversation. Students were asked to report on a mundane conversation they had recently had with someone (Garfinkel, 1967b: 24–34). On the right-hand side of a sheet of paper they were asked to write down what was said and on the left-hand side what the conversation was about. No matter how much the students explained what the conversation was about, Garfinkel could find more questions to ask for further clarification. The more elabora-tion that was provided, the greater the opportunity to ask more questions on clarifica-tion. As a phenomenon the conversation was understandable, but once described became something else in which the possibility of literal description became more difficult. Sacks also identified this problem when he made the following observation:

> How is the scientific requirement of literal description to be achieved in the face of the fact … that a description of even a particular 'concrete object' can never be complete? That is, how is a description to be warranted when, how-ever long or intensive it may be, it may nonetheless, be indefinitely extended?

> We call this the 'etcetera problem' ... to any description of a concrete object (or event, or course of action ...), however long, the researcher must add an etcetera clause to permit the description to be brought to a close. (1963: 10)

If we accept the possibility of correspondence, then to meet this we would need to have complete descriptions of things and events. As Sacks and Garfinkel show, this is impossible: all we can have are incomplete descriptions. This does not mean our descriptions are flawed, but that we recognize the opportunities afforded if we drop the goal of literal description. This is a point both Schutz (Grathoff, 1978), in his correspondence with Parsons, and Anderson et al. (1985), in their example of the woodyard, were making. This opportunity involves looking to see what an alternative – the congruence theory – may offer. This would involve taking the things we experience as real, but not different from the way in which we experience them. This does not mean we take experiences at face value and never express doubt or investigate them, but that we treat them as things which cannot be divorced from what it is we understand within our frame of reference. The methods we routinely use to apply our knowledge are, according to Garfinkel (1967), indistinguishable from the things our methods and knowledge are being used to understand and describe; there is congruence between *how* we accomplish understanding and the categorization of *what* is going on and *what* something is.

SACKS AND THE POSSIBILITY OF A PRIMITIVE OBSERVATIONAL SCIENCE

During his relatively short lifetime (he died aged only 40), Sacks published very little but left behind a substantial amount of lecture material he had prepared for his classes. Fortunately, many of his lectures were recorded onto tape and have been transcribed (Sacks, 1992). In his lectures Sacks attempted to deal systematically with his project to see if human interaction and action could be studied in such ways that the analysis and data could be reproducible. What Sacks is arguing for is making sociology a stable natural observational discipline. His reasons for setting this grand aim were in part as a provocation to the kinds of social science then taken for granted, such as structuralism, semiology, cognitive psychology and behavioural psychology (Schegloff, 1992: xxxi). What he means by 'stable' is a discipline that can provide analysis *and* findings *and* data which are all reproducible for anyone to inspect, assess and make their own analysis. This is based on the observation that very few studies include the full data and specify in detail how the analysis of the data was done. Most studies, whether based on hypothesis testing or ethnographic observations, ask the reader to 'take on trust' the data because it cannot, usually due to the amount, normally be included in an article or monograph. Schegloff, in his introduction to Sacks's lectures, explains what is meant by reproducibility:

> Contributions to science … are composed of two essential parts. One is the account of the findings. The other is the account of the scientists' actions by which the findings were obtained. What discriminates science from other epistemic undertakings is the claim that its findings are reproducible, and that reproducibility is itself grounded in the claim that the results were arrived at by courses of action reproducible by anyone in principle. Other investigators can, by engaging in the same actions, arrive at the same findings.
>
> Sacks argued that both of these parts of contributions to science are 'science', and not just the findings. For it is reproduction of the actions reproducing the results which make the findings 'scientific', and the description of those courses of action which make their reproducibility possible. If the results are scientific, the descriptions of the actions for reproducing them must also be science. (1992: xxxi)

The kind of social science Sacks thought about and pursued in his work is, however, very different from what was then (1960s–70s) and is still largely taken to be social science. His starting point, like that of Garfinkel, was with investigating what a non-ironic and non-correspondence theory of reality could look like. Figure 7.3 is an attempt to provide an overview of Sacks's position in relation to conventional social science.

Sacks states his position, and epistemological difference, in relation to conventional social science by saying, 'the problem is that, … each major treatise that has set up scientific fields starts out by saying that what people know and use is wrong' (quoted in Watson, 1994: 173–4). In contrast, what he wants is a sociology that does not use concepts such as 'false-consciousness', 'ideological', 'hidden codes' or distinctions between appearance and reality, the *etic* standpoint (Pike, 1967: 37), to account for behaviour. Such an approach, he notes, negates the details of what people actually do and how they do what they do, in their social interaction which accomplishes the sense of that interaction and reproduces social order. He says that what he wants to do 'is see if we can look at the enforceable and usable procedures for whatever knowledge persons happen to have' (quoted in Watson, 1994: 173). This means looking at social interaction from within, from the standpoint of an *emic* reality (Goodwin, 1984: 243–4), to see what

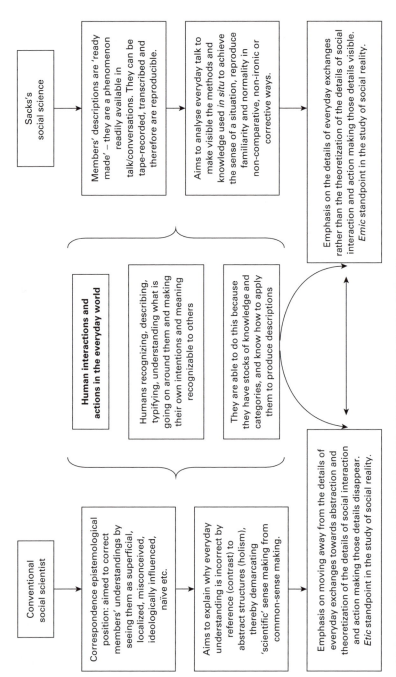

FIGURE 7.3   SACKS'S POSITION IN RELATION TO CONVENTIONAL SOCIAL SCIENCE

kinds of infrastructure participants use to accomplish that interaction for what it is, that is, recognizable-reportable. Sacks is therefore rejecting 'scientism'; that is, the tendency in conventional social science to attribute meanings to behaviour by using labels such as 'primitive mentality', 'superstition' and 'dysfunctional' through the use of grand theorizing, hypothesis testing and the operationalization of concepts by elaborate measuring instruments and subsequent statistical formulae.

His focus is on, then, the grossly observable, readily available mechanisms of social interaction. The most common and pervasive feature of social life is conversation, talk between persons in the pursuit of their everyday purposes. Whatever a researcher may come across in a scene, including conversations, news interviews, telephone calls, talk over emergency radio frequencies, are the kinds of data which are the stuff of social interaction and as such are recordable and preservable for analysis.

THE MECHANICS OF SOCIAL INTERACTION

The following is a typical extract (from the 1964–65 lectures) used by Sacks to analyse the apparatus of social interaction:

A: This is Mr Smith, may I help you?

B: I can't hear you.

A: This is Mr *Smith*.

B: Smith.

(Sacks, 1992: 3)

This extract is from a telephone call to a suicide prevention centre. It illustrates the simplicity of the data and complexity of the phenomenon Sacks attempted to address. From recordings of calls to the centre Sacks noticed that most callers resisted giving their name and that this was a recurrent phenomenon. Callers used responses such as 'I can't hear you' as common (methodical) ways of avoiding giving their name. Similarly Mr Smith does not, at first, ask directly for the caller's name, but uses a commonly used opening to an exchange that would normally elicit the other's name. Sacks is drawing our attention to the mechanics or apparatus of how we do social interaction and the analysis of social interactions (Schegloff, 1992: xxi). In this and other cases he is showing that exchanges occur in *units* and these have typical *sequences*.

How participants produce the sense they do in their exchanges and what they accomplish can be observed in the sequences of their exchanges. Hence sequences could be analysed as phenomena in their own right; as the basis of how members accomplish the sense of the world they are currently engaged with.

It is important to note that we are not talking here about doing analysis of narrative or discourse or saying what most members already know. Sacks is taking us to a level of analysis that gives us an unusual way of applying demarcation criteria. This can be seen, first, in his vision of what kind of analysis he is attempting to achieve: he likens this to the machinery of culture. By 'machinery' Sacks is referring to our socialization into a culture that gives us the knowledge of applying an apparatus to generate the recognizable sense/intention of our actions. The second way in which this can be seen is in his analysis of the story 'The baby cried, the mummy picked it up.' This was a description produced by a young child. Figure 7.4 attempts to show how Sacks analyses this simple, everyday story in a way that makes visible the apparatus of how the activity of describing is done and done recognizably.

Although Figure 7.4 has had to leave out much of the detail of Sacks's analysis of the child's story, it shows what makes his analysis a *sociological finding* and not merely a reformulation of any member's description. Sacks shows how there is an intimate and unavoidable relationship between the understandings and knowledge of the investigator and that of persons in everyday life. Observations such as the mummy in the story is 'heard' as the mother of the baby and the baby cried before its mother picked it up are reformulations of what anyone could say about this story. There is nothing scientific in this because it produces nothing about the phenomenon we did not already know. Sacks, however, produces findings about the ordering of interpretive procedures (Schegloff, 1992: xxxvii) which make visible the apparatus employed to generate the recognizable sense of the story and this apparatus was not known about prior to Sacks's analysis: it is therefore a finding. It is also a finding based on his research question about how 'know-how' is used by members engaged in social exchanges in ways that make them self-explicating, self-describing commentaries on themselves. Psathas (1995) summarizes the distinctiveness of Sacks's position when he outlines the basic assumptions of conversation analysis.

Conversation analysis studies the order/organization/orderliness of social action, particularly those actions that are located in everyday interaction, in discursive practices, in the sayings/tellings/doings of members of society.

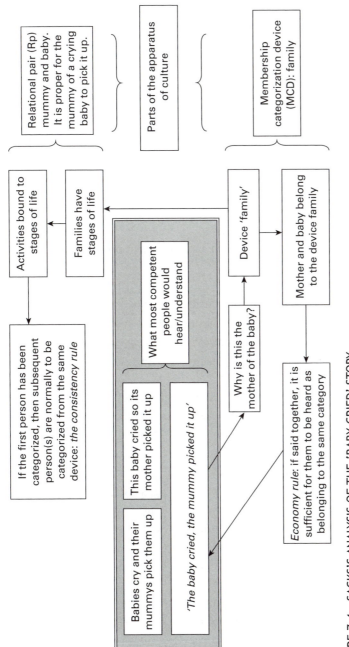

Relational pair (Rp) mummy and baby. It is proper for the mummy of a crying baby to pick it up.

Parts of the apparatus of culture

Membership categorization device (MCD): family

Activities bound to stages of life

Families have stages of life

Device 'family'

Mother and baby belong to the device family

If the first person has been categorized, then subsequent person(s) are normally to be categorized from the same device: *the consistency rule*

What most competent people would hear/understand

This baby cried so its mother picked it up

Babies cry and their mummys pick them up

Why is this the mother of the baby?

The baby cried, the mummy picked it up'

Economy rule: if said together, it is sufficient for them to be heard as belonging to the same category

FIGURE 7.4   SACKS'S ANALYSIS OF THE 'BABY CRIED' STORY

Its basic assumptions are:

1 Order is a produced orderliness.

2 Order is produced by the parties in situ; that is, it is situated and occasioned.

3 The parties orient to that order themselves; that is, this order is not an analyst's conception, not the result of the use of some preformed or preformulated theoretical conceptions concerning what action should/must/ought to be, or based on generalizing or summarizing statements about what action generally/frequently/often is.

4 Order is repeatable and recurrent.

5 The discovery, description, and analysis of that produced orderliness is the task of the analyst.

6 Issues of how frequently, how widely, or how often particular phenomena occur are to be set aside in the interests of discovering, describing, and analysing the *structures*, the *machinery*, the *organized practices*, the *formal procedures*, the ways in which order is produced.

7 Structures of social action, once discerned, can be described and analysed in formal, that is, structural, organizational, logical, atopically, contentless, consistent, and abstract, terms. (1995: 3)

Although the methods of analysis Sacks left in his lectures and few published articles have not entered mainstream social science, they have inspired a substantial amount of detailed empirical analysis by those who have understood the logic of his project. Among his main achievements were the ways he side-stepped any need to employ neo-Kantian epistemology of correspondence that constructs a description to correct those produced by members. He sees

Neo-Kantian: in the context used here, to refer to Heinrich Rickert's contention of there being an irreconcilable difference between the natural and the social sciences, means social reality was too complex to be known by other than simple categories and was incapable of generalization from the particular.

as tragic (Watson, 1994: 176–7) that the work of Durkheim has been held as the model for social science. For Sacks, Durkheim's definition and operationalization of the concept of 'suicide' ignores the commonsense category 'suicide'. He argues that if the commonsense category is ignored, then what Durkheim constructs for his analytic-theoretical purposes is a characterization for theoretization: it solves the problem of theorizing *about* the phenomenon. Sacks's position is diametrically opposed to this position. His insistence on the need to understand the everyday use of any category to make visible the interpretive procedures *of* the phenomenon is an essential starting point for the description of social order. Sacks's position is therefore irreconcilable with that of the constructive analysis of Durkheim because, in the same way Durkheim's analysis makes everyday understandings disappear, so Sacks's analysis makes Durkheim's analysis disappear. We therefore have two main approaches to doing social analysis, each of which are not easily characterized, simplified or synthesized.

SUMMARY OF THIS CHAPTER

In this chapter we have introduced some of the main, though by no means all, theorists who have contributed to the debates about the ontological and epistemological status of knowing and knowledge. The space has been used to get across some of the points of reference in the story of methodological choices. The language used is at times a little dense and cannot always be used to definitively categorize someone as this rather than that. You may have noticed, especially if you have looked at other books on research (for example, Anderson et al., 1997), what is often called 'the interpretative approach to research'. There is no section labelled 'interpretivist' in this chapter. The reasons for this are that the exposition of the debate between Parsons and Schutz served to introduce many of the key features of the interpretivist approach. Their correspondence highlights the kinds of fundamental differences which exist, and will continue to exist, among social scientists. Interestingly, when you read the journals of the natural sciences, those dedicated to biology or chemistry, you see few references to ontology and epistemology. You see debate over interpretation and method, but no great worries about observations being dependent on theories. The key points that have been made include:

- The histories of the philosophy of science usually have very little to do with research, but they can show us how to understand and develop abilities in argumentation and logical reasoning.

- Individual theorists such as Popper and Feyerabend show us that there are often ethical and political aspects to recommendations about the nature of science and that these are usually allied to the promotion of democracy.

- Challenge, where possible, the boundaries and *core assumptions* of whatever discipline you work in. In this way you will become more aware of the strengths, weaknesses and opportunities for your discipline and will enhance your abilities to understand other disciplines and their core assumptions.

- Textbooks are not normally a reliable source for getting to know what something is because they are only representative stories which sometimes attempt to make systematic that which is fragmented and occasional. There is no substitute for going and looking at the behaviour of those people you are interested in (or even living as they do), if you want to experience the *essence* of their existence. Hence you cannot know what research is until you do some yourself.

Further reading

Crotty, M. (1998) *The Foundations of Social Research: Meaning and Perspective in the Research Process*. London: Sage. Brings a degree of clarity to the complex relationships between epistemology, ontology, theory, methodology and methods.

Hughes, J. and Sharrock, W. (1997) *The Philosophy of Social Research*. 3rd edn. Harlow: Addison Wesley Longman. A sound companion to Smith (1998) (see below), providing a thorough overview of the complexities of the relationship between philosophy and social research.

Ryan, A. (1970) *The Philosophy of the Social Sciences*. London: Macmillan. Still one of the most sophisticated introductions to the problems and issues facing the social sciences.

Slife, B.D. and Williams, R.N. (1995) *What's Behind the Research: Discovering Hidden Assumptions in the Behavioral Sciences*. Thousand Oaks, CA: Sage. A systematic exposition of many much-used yet not stated assumptions in psychology.

Smith, M. (1998) *Social Science in Question*. London: Open University/Sage. One of the most comprehensive introductions to the methodological issues for social scientists and researchers. With many diagrams and illustrations to show the consequence of different approaches.

8 Methodological choices and consequences

A key question about methodological traditions that is often asked by research students is, 'What does it matter which approach we use?' In normal masters research it does not matter which research tradition you have a preference for. But you must be able to demonstrate in your discussions of the research literature that you understand the terrain of the philosophical traditions, what the consequences can be of using those traditions as a starting point for your research and argue convincingly for your preferences. In this chapter we will look at some of the consequences of research done in different methodological traditions. We are going to look at five cases of research and, with each, describe the research and highlight some of its consequences and issues. There is space only for five, if we are to look seriously at them; you can, no doubt use the library and find many more pieces of research and theorists to examine for yourself. We cannot look at every aspect, but pull out from these cases some of the main consequences and issues of doing research. The purpose of this chapter is, then, to think about the nature of research as an activity that embodies the aims of the researcher and in so doing their values, biography and their ontological and epistemological assumptions – as *their* strategy for their research. Following on from the previous chapter, this chapter looks at the following questions:

1 How do researchers use methodological assumptions to design a research strategy and project?

2 How do methodological assumptions have consequences?

3 When used as the starting point for research, what kinds of issues do certain methodological assumptions raise for consideration?

The theorists and their work reported on in this chapter represent some of the main methodological alternatives in the social sciences and are intended to show the complexity of the choices available to you. The first two theorists (Goddard and Lombroso) show the use of an early *positivist* and *realist* set of methodological assumptions within a closed systems approach. They show the use of an externalist approach to producing categorizations in the role of predicting behaviours. The study of the third theorist (Lévi-Strauss) also shows application of a realist set of methodological assumptions, but a much more sophisticated one than the others. It shows the basic assumptions on which many 'structuralist' approaches are based and how analysis of cultural artefacts has been used to 'uncover' hidden mechanisms of the mind. The fourth theorist (Goffman) shows the use of an *idealist* (or specifically a version of neo-Kantian) set of methodological assumptions. It shows how behaviour can be observed from the standpoint of the *naturalist* and co-existing interpretations of a behaviour produced. The final theorist (Garfinkel) shows how the issues surrounding the comparisons between *internalist* and *externalist*, *realist* and *idealist* can be side-stepped to produce detailed analysis of how people continually produce the objective sense of their world.

It is not being recommended that you follow any of these approaches, but use them to develop your understanding of how methodological assumptions are used to create a research strategy. Although some of these examples may, at first, seem a little difficult, bear with them. By doing so you will soon expand your ability to think methodologically and better navigate your way through whatever methodological literature your own research will use.

Studies of feeble-mindedness

Henry H. Goddard (1866–1957), the American psychologist, is best known for his work on the inheritability of intelligence. Influenced by Mendelian genetics, his interest was in 'morons' – defined by Goddard as 'high grade defectives' – and he believed that 'feeble-mindedness' was the result of a single recessive gene. Morons, according to Goddard, lacked self-control, making them susceptible to sexual immorality and vulnerable to other individuals who might exploit them for use in criminal activity (Goddard, 1912: 54–6).

In 1906, Goddard began research as the director of research of the 'Vineland Training School, New Jersey, for feeble-minded boys and girls'. Applying the Binet–Simon measuring scale (Binet was the originator of the IQ test), he sent research assistants into the homes of families identified as feeble-minded to learn what they could about the history of the family through questioning (1912: vii). Of the 300 families studied, the Kallikak family remains the most famous. The name 'Kallikak' is a pseudonym created by Goddard from the Greek words Kallos (beauty) and Kakos (bad). The two-part name was meant to indicate that the Kallikak family was divided into two strains, one 'good' and one 'bad', both of which originated from a common progenitor, Martin Kallikak, senior. Goddard published his research in journal articles and books, the most famous being *The Kallikak Family: A Study in the Heredity of Feeble-mindedness* (1912) and *Feeble-Mindedness: Its Causes and Consequences* (1914).

GODDARD'S STUDY OF THE KALLIKAK FAMILY

Goddard's study of the Kallikak family was largely based on a genealogy of the two parts of the family: the 'bad' or feeble-minded, and the 'good' or normal. The starting point was with Martin Kallikak, senior. When he was a young soldier, he had a liaison with an 'unnamed, feeble-minded tavern girl'. Martin Kallikak, junior, was the result and he displayed the Kakos (bad) strain and it was from him that the feeble-mindedness of the Kallikak family descended. Martin Kallikak, senior, later married a Quaker woman from a so-called good family and from this the Kallos (beauty) line descended. The basic influence of this can be seen in Figure 8.1, part of the family tree drawn by Goddard. On the side of Martin Kallikak, junior, Goddard identified 'generations' of 'mental defectives' who were characterized by (in Goddard's words) illegitimacy, prostitution, alcoholism, epilepsy and lechery. Figure 8.1 also shows that the other side of the family exhibited opposite traits. Goddard argued that the differences between the two branches of the family were due to the different genetic input from Martin Kallikak, senior's two partners – the women (1912: 105–6).

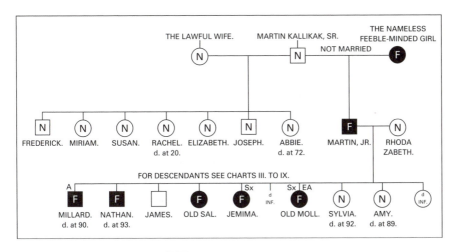

FIGURE 8.1   KALLIKAK FAMILY TREE.
Source: Goddard, 1912: Chart II, p. 37.

The genealogical chart shown in Figure 8.1 is based on 24 family trees (Goddard, 1912: 37) with N = normal, F = feeble-minded, A = alcoholic, Sx = sexually immoral and EA = epileptic alcoholic, with circles being females and squares males.

GODDARD'S RECOMMENDATIONS

On the basis of his study Goddard made a number of recommendations about what could and should be done about feeble-minded persons. The following extract, although long, illustrates very well his argument for his recommendations.

Chapter V   What is to be done?

No one interested in the progress of civilization can contemplate the facts presented in the previous chapters without having the question arise, Why isn't something done about this? It will be more to the point if we put the question, Why do *we* not *do* something about it? We are thus face to face with the problem in a practical way and we ask ourselves the next question, What *can* we do? For the low-grade idiot, the loathsome unfortunate that may be seen in our institutions, some have proposed the lethal chamber. But humanity is steadily tending away from the possibility of that method, and there is no probability that it will ever be practiced. But in view of such conditions as are shown in the defective side of the Kallikak family, we begin to realize that the idiot is not our greatest problem. He is indeed loathsome; he is somewhat difficult to take care of; nevertheless, he lives his life and is done. He does not continue the race with a line of children like himself. Because of his very low-grade condition, he never becomes a parent. It is the moron type that makes for us our great problem. And when we face the question, 'What is to be done with them – with such people as make up a large proportion of the bad side of the Kallikak family?' we realize that we have a huge problem.

The career of Martin Kallikak Sr. is a powerful sermon against sowing wild oats ... Even the people of his generation, however much they may have known about the circumstances, could not have begun to realize the evil that had been done. Undoubtedly, it was only looked upon as a sin because it was a violation of the moral law. The real sin of peopling the world with a race of defective degenerates who would probably commit his sin a thousand times over, was doubtless not perceived or realized. It is only after the lapse of six generations that we are able to look back, count up and see the havoc that was wrought by that one thoughtless act. Now that the facts are known, let the lesson be learned; let the sermons be preached; let it be impressed upon our young men of good family that they dare not step aside for even a moment. Let all possible use be made of these facts, and something will be accomplished ... Had Martin Kallikak remained in the paths of virtue, there still remained the nameless feeble-minded girl, and there were other people, other young men, perhaps not of as good a family as Martin, perhaps feeble-minded like herself, capable of the same act and without Martin's respectability, so that the race would have come down even worse if possible than it was, because of having a worse father.

When we conclude that had the nameless girl been segregated in an institution, this defective family would not have existed, we of course do not mean that one single act of precaution, in that case, would have solved the problem, but we mean that all such cases, male and female, must be taken care of, before their propagation will cease. The instant we grasp this thought, we realize that we are facing a problem that presents two great difficulties; in the first place the difficulty of knowing who are the feeble-minded people; and, secondly, the difficulty of taking care of them when they are known.

A large proportion of those who are considered feeble-minded in this study are persons who would not be recognized as such by the untrained observer. They are not the imbeciles nor idiots who plainly show in their countenances the extent of their mental defect. They are people whom the community has tolerated and helped to support, at the same time that it has deplored their vices and their inefficiency. They are people who have won the pity rather than the blame of their neighbours, but no one has seemed to suspect the real cause of their delinquencies, which careful psychological tests have now determined to be feeble-mindedness. The second difficulty is that of caring for this large army of people. At the lowest estimates of the number needing care, we in the United States are at present caring for approximately one tenth of the estimated number of our mental defectives. Yet many of our States think that they are now being over-taxed for the care of these people, so that it is with great difficulty that legislatures can be induced to appropriate money enough to care for those already in institutions. It is impossible to entertain the thought of caring for ten times as many. Some other methods must be devised for dealing with the difficulty.

Before considering any other method, the writer would insist that segregation and colonization is not by any means as hopeless a plan as it may seem to those who look only at the immediate increase in the tax rate. If such colonies were provided in sufficient number to take care of all the distinctly feeble-minded cases in the community, they would very largely take the place of our present almshouses and prisons, and they would greatly decrease the number in our insane hospitals. Such colonies would save an annual loss in property and life, due to the action of these irresponsible people, sufficient to nearly, or quite, offset the expense of the new plant. Besides, if these feeble-minded children were early selected and carefully trained, they would become more or less self-supporting in their institutions, so that the expense of their maintenance would be greatly reduced.

The other method proposed of solving the problem is to take away from these people the power of procreation. In recent years surgeons have discovered another method which has many advantages. This is also sometimes incorrectly referred to as asexualization. It is more properly spoken of as sterilization … The operation itself is almost as simple in males as having a tooth pulled. In females it is not much more serious … Objection is urged that we do not know the consequences of this action upon the physical, mental, and moral nature of the individual … A more serious objection to this last method comes from a consideration of the social consequences. What will be the effect upon the community in the spread of debauchery and disease through having within it a group of people who are thus free to gratify their instincts without fear of consequences in the form of children? The indications are that here also the evil consequences are more imaginary than real, since the feeble-minded seldom exercise restraint in any case.

Taking this family as a whole, we have the following figures: there were 41 matings where both parents were feeble-minded. They had 222 feeble-minded children, with two others that were considered normal. These two are apparent exceptions to the law that two feeble-minded parents do not have anything but feeble-minded children. We may account for these two exceptions in one of several ways. Either there is a mistake in calling them normal or a mistake in calling the parents feeble-minded; or else there was illegitimacy somewhere and these two children did not have the same father as the others of the family. Or we may turn to the Mendelian law and we discover that according to that law there might be in rare instances such a combination of circumstances that a normal child might be born from two parents that function as feeble-minded. For practical purposes it is, of course, pretty clear that it is safe to assume that two feeble-minded parents will never have anything but feeble-minded children.

From all of this the one caution follows. At best, sterilization is not likely to be a final solution of this problem. We may, and indeed I believe must, use it as a help, as something that will contribute toward the solution, until we can get segregation thoroughly established. But in using it, we must realize that the first necessity is the careful study of the whole subject, to the end that we may know more both about the laws of inheritance and the ultimate effect of the operation. (1912: Internet edition)

Goddard, as the director of an institution for the training of persons categorized as 'feeble-minded, was in an ideal position to undertake extensive research over a number of years. Yet what dominates his published studies is an argument he returns to again and again. The key points of this argument are: feeble-minded people were 'multiplying at twice the rate of the general population' (1912: 71); thus producing 'more feeble-minded children with which to clog the wheels of human progress' (1912: 78); unable to control themselves, feeble-minded people were the principal cause of many social problems, including crime and illegitimacy; and as no amount of education or training could change a feeble-minded person into a normal one, rehabilitation is not an option. Within this argument there is the claim that doing nothing will cost taxpayers more in the long term than doing something in the short term. The logical conclusions Goddard arrives at are based on his argument, which he states in the following way:

The Kallikak family presents a natural experiment in heredity. A young man of good family becomes through two different women the ancestor of two lines of descendants – the one characterized by thoroughly good, respectable, normal citizenship, with almost no exceptions; the other being equally characterized by mental defect in every generation. This defect was transmitted through the father in the first generation. In later generations, more defect was brought in from other families through marriage. In the last generation it was transmitted through the mother, so that we have here all combinations of transmission, which again proves the truly hereditary character of the defect. We find on the good side of the family prominent people in all walks of life and nearly all of the 496 descendants owners of land or proprietors. On the bad side we find paupers, criminals, prostitutes, drunkards, and examples of all forms of social pest with which modern society is burdened.

From this we conclude that feeble-mindedness is largely responsible for these social sores. Feeble-mindedness is hereditary and transmitted as surely as any other character. We cannot successfully cope with these conditions until we recognize feeble-mindedness and its hereditary nature, recognize it early, and take care of it.

In considering the question of care, segregation through colonization seems in the present state of our knowledge to be the ideal and perfectly satisfactory method. Sterilization may be accepted as a makeshift, as a help to solve this problem because the conditions have become so intolerable. But this must at present be regarded only as a makeshift and temporary, for before it can be extensively practiced, a great deal must be learned about the effects of the operation and about the laws of human inheritance. (Goddard, 1912: Internet edition)

CONSEQUENCES OF THE KALLIKAK FAMILY STUDY

Goddard's books were very popular until the mid-1930s, due partly to the presentation of the genealogies and detailed case studies. As a landmark the Kallikak study in heredity was influential, leading to compulsory sterilization laws being passed in 30 US states by 1941. Contributing to this popularity was the large number of immigrants from Europe. In 1913 Goddard was invited to Ellis Island to give advice and help in detecting morons among the newly arrived immigrants from Europe. In his 'Mental tests and the immigrant' (1917) he asserted that most of the Ellis Island immigrants were mentally deficient. He stated that 83 per cent of the Jews, 80 per cent of the Hungarians, 79 per cent of the Italians and 87 per cent of the Russians tested were feeble-minded. Goddard's work influenced the US Immigration Restriction Act, passed in 1924 (which remained until 1965).

The original German edition of *The Kallikak Family: A Study in the Heredity of Feeble-Mindedness* (*Die Familie Kallikak*) was printed in 1914 and reprinted in 1933, shortly after the Nazis came to power. Goddard's research was used to justify state-sponsored 'ethnic cleansing', even though he never intended such use or had any connections with Nazism. In 1938 and 1939 he tried to use his name to help the daughter of a Jewish colleague escape from Austria (Zenderland, 1998: 333–5). Even though Goddard made several public declarations stating he had reversed many of his opinions about feeble-minded persons (Goddard, 1927: 41–6), psychology textbooks as late as 1961 (Garrett and Bonner) still provided summaries of Goddard's earlier recommendations and praised his research for the ways in which it gave support for the eugenicist movement.

> Francis Galton (1822–1911) coined the word 'eugenics' (1883), meaning 'good birth'. A cousin of Darwin, he believed a better breed of humans was possible by allowing only 'higher order' humans to reproduce.

THE ISSUES

Goddard's general argument and assumptions are not particular to him; these kinds of views and opinions, along with the language and categorizations, were in common usage in the late nineteenth and into the first half of the twentieth centuries. Words and phrases such as 'feeble-mindedness', 'idiocy', 'retard', 'savage', 'stupid', 'cretinism', 'degenerate' and others are not acceptable now for everyday use or as scientific descriptions. This is not only because of the stigmatizing connotations these words have as labels, but as concepts they are extremely difficult to operationalize. Goddard's procedure was based largely on maintaining that a trained observer could recognize the manifestations of feeble-mindedness; these included poverty, drunkenness, prostitution and other forms of 'immorality'. The context, that is, the social environment of such behaviours (placing to one side all definitions of them as unacceptable for now), is not seriously acknowledged by Goddard. The economics of poverty, of its causes in economic systems, of typical reactions to it, are sidelined. Prostitution, the need to earn a living in a welfareless society, the largely middle-class customers for fee-based sex, are similarly not acknowledged. The reason for this is that Goddard's explanatory frame of reference is hereditary; he firmly believed in nature over nurture as the main causal determinant of human behaviour. His idea of demonstrating this using the genealogy of the Kallikak family can generally be said to be innovative for the time. This was one of the first longitudinal studies conducted and did, to some degree, conform to notions about what the correlational comparative method might consist of. He had an extensive data set, a large number of living subjects, a set of variables and a theory. The main issue with his results is that he used the genetic frame of reference, to the exclusion of all others, for his observations, measurements and interpretations. His work on testing the intelligence (whatever this may be taken to be) of newly arrived immigrants to the United States excluded consideration of the context for the tests. These were peoples from many parts of the world, many of whom could not speak English, and who were probably disoriented, as is common with immigrants. A long sea voyage, followed by official processing by persons in police and medical uniforms, was not conducive to the 'objectivity' Goddard claimed for his tests. This illustrates the issues of employing a closed system of research that relies on a priori assumptions.

Criminal types

Cesare Lombroso (1835–1909), the Italian criminologist, is widely known for his studies which attempt to explain criminal behavior by designating criminals as 'types', relating different types to physical features of the individual. Lombroso assumed, following Darwin, that careful, disciplined observation and detailed measurement of criminals would enable a classification of criminal types to be constructed to aid in the identification of criminals before they committed a crime.

Lombroso studied at the universities of Padua, Vienna and Paris (1862–76), and became professor of psychiatry, forensic medicine and hygiene at the University of Pavia. From 1896 he was professor of psychiatry and criminal anthropology (1906) at the University of Turin. He was also the director of a mental asylum in Pesaro, Italy. His published work, *L'uomo delinquente* (*The Criminal Man*) (1912) and *Le Crime, Causes et Remedies* (1899), had a significant influence on criminology in Europe and America. *L'uomo delinquente* was the most popular of his publications and grew from 200 pages in the first edition to over 3,000 in its fifth. By the 1880s he had acquired the status of the leading expert in the theories of criminal physiology and was often called to perform as expert witness – to assess the criminality of the accused based on their physical features – at criminal trials.

LOMBROSO'S RESEARCH AND THEORY

Lombroso's research was based on an examination that measured the physical characteristics of 400 Italian prisoners. Using mechanical and electrical equipment Lombroso measured and recorded details of the prisoners' skull shapes (using the craniograph), handwriting, tattoos, ears, mouths, noses, arms, eyes, physical strength (using the dynamometer), walking, and the like. Photographs were taken of prisoners and, according to their physical features and the nature of their conviction, classified into criminal types. How the measurements were done is recorded in detail along with advice on how to do an examination in *Criminal Man* (1912: 219–57). The following list summarizes some of the main physical features which distinguish the criminal type:

♦ **arms: excessive length compared with stature;**

♦ **eyes: hard expression, shifty glance, dropping eyelids, eyes too close together;**

♦ **eyebrows: bushy in murderers and violators of women;**

♦ **ears: large size in relation to head, standing out from the face (like a chimpanzee);**

♦ **nose: frequently twisted, up-turned or in thieves, flat and in murderers, like the beak of a bird of prey;**

♦ **mouth: general bony elevation, in violators of women, fleshy protruding lips and swindlers, thin straight lips;**

♦ **skull: adhesions, thickening of the meninges, especially on the left-hand side and differences in brain cells;**

♦ **tattooing: extensive body tattooing is indicative of vices; and**

♦ **handwriting: shaky, zigzag letters, closeness of letters and words, dashing strokes indicate differences between normal, criminal and lunatic.**

Many of the physical features associated with violators of women and thieving are likened to features found in dogs and apes and 'Negroes' (1912: 10–24). It is interesting to know how Lombroso claims to have discovered the relationship between physicality and criminality. While involved in a post-mortem on a criminal who died in the insane asylum in Pavia, Lombroso says he noticed an abnormality common to apes and this:

... was not merely an idea but a revelation. At the sight of that skull, I seemed to see all of a sudden, lighted up as a vast plain under a flaming sky the problem of the nature of the criminal atavistic being who reproduces in his person the ferocious instincts of primitive humanity and inferior animals. (Sawyer, 1972: 63)

Lombroso's insight led him, presumably, to his research topic and the subjects he measured. In *Criminal Man* he makes a series of statements which encapsulate his major theory:

The criminal is an atavistic being, a relic of a vanished race. This is by no means an uncommon occurrence in nature. Atavism, the reversion to a former state, is the first feeble indication of the reaction opposed by nature to the perturbing causes which seek to alter her delicate mechanism. Under certain unfavourable conditions, cold or poor soil, the common oak will develop characteristics of the oak of the Quaternary period. The dog left to run wild in the forest will in few generations revert to the type of his original wolf-like progenitor, and the cultivated garden roses when neglected show a tendency to reassume the form of the original dog-rose. Under special conditions produced by alcohol, chloroform, heat, or injuries, ants, dogs, and pigeons become irritable and savage like their wild ancestors.

This tendency to alter under special conditions is common to human beings, in whom hunger, syphilis, trauma, and, still more frequently, morbid conditions inherited from insane, criminal, or diseased progenitors, or the abuse of nerve poisons, such as alcohol, tobacco, or morphine, cause various alterations, of which criminality – that is, a return to the characteristics peculiar to primitive savages ...

The aetiology of crime, therefore, mingles with that of all kinds of degeneration: rickets, deafness, monstrosity, hairiness, and certain cretinism, of which crime is only a variation ... Heredity is the principal organic cause of criminal tendencies. It may be divided into two classes: indirect heredity from a genetically degenerate family with frequent cases of insanity, deafness, syphilis, epilepsy, and alcoholism among its members; direct heredity from criminal parentage. (Lombroso, 1912: 135–7)

CONSEQUENCES OF LOMBROSO'S THEORIES

The practical implication of Lombroso's findings was that criminal types could be identified before they committed any crime. Even if a cure was not possible, prevention was. Although Lombroso discusses the alternative penalties for convicted criminals, his main position was that as biology is the determining factor in most criminality, criminals should not be held responsible for their actions. He argues therefore that society should not punish those who are driven by biology and who cannot make distinctions between what is morally right and wrong. Punishment should only be administered to those criminals who violate the rules of society by choice and who could, knowing the punishment, be deterred. The atavistic criminal was to be seen as a degenerate and not considered fully human or civilized, even if they looked so. Criminals could seem normal to ordinary people, but the trained criminal physiologist could detect them: the professional analyst was therefore to be accorded a privileged position as one who could detect what others could not.

In many criminal trials Lombroso was called as an expert witness. In the case of a French woman being tried for murder, Lombroso was sent her picture. In his opinion she was abnormal due her round, small skull, flat forehead and virile expression on her face. He classified her as an hysterical epileptic with cretin features, susceptible to commit crime when under the influence of alcohol. Other doctors in the case had concluded that her 'victims' had died of natural causes. The court therefore made attempts to think of ways in which she could have made this seem to be the case because she was a criminal type and therefore must be guilty (*The Times*, 1908: 7).

THE ISSUES

Lombroso's research attempts to confirm the existence of biological determinism by invoking a theory he relates to Darwin's ideas of evolution. *The Origin of Species* had and continues to have an extraordinary impact on the ways in which we understand the world, especially how we account for the diversity of what we can see. Lombroso's work is one among many from this period which attempted to uncover the laws of human behaviour, but began with the preconceived notion that there existed different categories of behaviour, some of which were unacceptable. His work is based on assumptions about what is acceptable and what is not acceptable; it is, therefore, based on a moral standpoint. Although not clearly defined, the differences between criminality and deviance are not thought to be important, nor is there any acknowledgement of the cultural and temporal relativity of behaviour. Abnormal behaviour which he regards as deviant or criminal is pathological by default and is correspondingly a social problem. Classification of the elements by which pathology can be observed is the method he employed to produce a catalogue for the prediction and explanation of deviant types. Classification of human behaviour, as with everything else, is a common activity across the natural and social sciences and is predicated, to a large degree, on commonsensical ways in which we generalize an object, event or behaviour in everyday life by using an abstraction into which to place them.

Applying the procedures of detailed measurement gave Lombroso the method for confirming what were already commonly held assumptions about deviance and criminality: that some groups of people displayed atavistic features which showed them to be less developed in terms of the social and intellectual development of persons such as Lombroso and 'society'. Applying positivistic ideas to produce a scientific catalogue of atavistic features may have been done to ensure that those categorized as criminal or deviant were seen not to be responsible for their own behaviour and therefore any punishment should fit the person and not the crime. In its time, and for several decades later, this was generally the understanding and rationale for such research; it was about providing the means for social reform in the form of benevolent intervention. This may mean the segregation of criminals from 'normal' society in colonies because for some, whose atavistic development was too chronic, there could be no reformation of their behaviour. The method and these assumptions found a believing audience, especially among the social reformers, from across the political spectrum, including some from the Fabian Society. The method gave legitimacy to classifying persons, assessing them according to their features and predicting what could and could not be done on their behalf. This was early social work that had the aim of ridding society of an illness, sharing many of the same methods of measurement as research into poverty and educability. Those subject to its help were, as a matter of course, denied any voice, for they were being 'helped' for something that was not their fault, but for which the science of criminology had a solution.

The universality of mind

Claude Lévi-Strauss (1908–), the French anthropologist, is widely known for his work on the structural analysis of culture, especially kinship and myths. Influenced by structural linguistics, Lévi-Strauss argued that Western cultures are neither superior nor unique and that the human mind is everywhere essentially the same. It is this universality of the mind, he attempted to demonstrate, through his analysis of myths, what makes human beings essentially the same. Any culture can be seen as a system of communication that can be reduced into its constituent elements and the structural relationships between those elements identified, thereby allowing structures to be uncovered and the principles of their operation described.

Lévi-Strauss undertook a substantial amount of fieldwork studying the indigenous peoples of South and North America. Educated in philosophy and law at the University of Paris (1927–32), Lévi-Strauss taught sociology at São Paulo University, Brazil (1934–37) and at the New School of Social Research, New York (1941–45). In 1948 he was appointed professor at the Institute d'Ethnologie, University of Paris, and after 1959 was Director of Studies at the Collège de France. From a prodigious output his most popular and notable writings include: *Tristes Topiques* (1955, tr. 1992), *The Elementary Structures of Kinship* (1949, tr. 1969), *The Savage Mind* (1962, tr. 1966), *Structural Anthropology* (1958, tr. 1963) and *The Raw and the Cooked* (1964, tr. 1990).

STRUCTURAL STUDY OF CULTURES

The work of Lévi-Strauss is a systematic and detailed attempt to demonstrate, through the formal analysis of anthropological exhibits (myths, kinship, art), that the human mind is everywhere the same. He argues that Nature has an order, even though it may not be directly observable, and as the human Mind is a part of Nature, it too must share some of the properties of order found in Nature. Lévi-Strauss's work has an overriding concern with the 'structure' of the human mind: a structure that is a quality rather than an empirically observable object. The structure of the mind is like, he argues, a set of mathematical equations which can tell us many things about, for example, the strength, weight, trajectory, endurance and the like of constructions even before they have been created. The mind, like mathematical equations, does not have empirical existence but can be used to model the structural relationships between the elements of most things actual or capable of being conceived. The basis for this is the ways in which humans constantly look to order through categorization the things they encounter through their senses. All input into the brain is, according to Lévi-Strauss, subjected to arrangement into categories which are present in Nature:

> Starting from an ethnographic experience, I have always aimed at drawing up an inventory of mental patterns, to reduce apparently arbitrary data to some

kind of order, and to a level at which a kind of necessity becomes apparent, underlying delusions of Liberty.

Mythology has no obvious practical function: ... it is not directly linked with any kind of reality, which is endowed with a higher degree of objectivity than its own and whose injunctions it might therefore transmit to minds that seemed perfectly free to indulge their creative spontaneity. And so, if it were possible to prove in this instance, too, that the apparent arbitrariness of the mind, its supposedly spontaneous flow of inspiration, and its seemingly uncontrolled inventiveness imply the existence of laws operating at a deeper level, we would inevitably be forced to conclude that when the mind is left to communicate with itself and no longer has to come to terms with objects, it is in a sense reduced to imitating itself as object; and that since the laws governing its operations are not fundamentally different from those it exhibits in its other functions, it shows itself to be the nature of a thing among things ... since it is enough to establish the conviction that if the human mind appears determined even in the realm of mythology, *a fortiori* it must also be determined in all its spheres of activity.

In allowing myself to be guided by the search for the constraining structures of the mind, I am proceeding in the manner of Kantian philosophy, although along different lines leading to different conclusions. The ethnologist ... instead of assuming a universal form of human understanding ... prefers to study empirically collective forms of understanding, whose properties have been solidified, as it were, and are revealed to him in countless concrete representational systems ... he chooses those that seemed to him to be the most markedly divergent, in the hope that the methodological rules he will have to evolve in order to translate these systems in terms of his own system and vice versa, will reveal a pattern of basic and universal laws ... my ambition being to discover the conditions in which systems of truths become mutually convertible and therefore simultaneously acceptable to several different subjects, the pattern of those conditions takes on the character of an autonomous object, independent of any subject.

I believe that mythology, more than anything else, makes it possible to illustrate such objectified thought and to provide empirical proof of its reality ... it is the same with myths as with language: the individual who conscientiously applied phonological and grammatical laws in his speech, supposing he possessed the necessary knowledge and virtuosity to do so, would nevertheless lose the thread of his ideas almost immediately. In the same way the practice and the use of mythological thought demand that its properties remain hidden: otherwise the subject would find himself in the position of the mythologist who cannot believe in myths because it is his task to take them to pieces ... [and] claims to show, not how men think in myths, but how myths operate in men's minds without their being aware of the fact. (1970: 10–12)

Consequently, humankind, who created culture, divides everything around them into groups or classes (Leach, 1970: 21). When they construct the artificial things of culture, they actually try to imitate Nature: 'the products of our culture are segmented and ordered in the same way as we suppose the products of Nature to be segmented and ordered' (Leach, 1970: 21). Lévi-Strauss believes that by studying these classifications and the way humans use them, much can be learnt about the human brain and the way 'it' thinks. Humans are able to communicate through signs and language, due to the structural characteristics of the human mind. Through binary discriminations the mind divides things into sub-classes, then divides each of these further into an X and non-X, and so on, thereby creating a system of 'relations' and forming an algebraic matrix. The brain also operates in a similar way when it uses non-verbal elements of culture to form a 'sign' language. Combined, these two processes form the ultimate relational system, or a human culture. Thus, the human brain can think on a multi-dimensional level – metaphorically and metonymically at the same time. Lévi-Strauss believes this mental process extends to all means of communication, including myth.

THE STRUCTURE OF MYTH

If, according to Lévi-Strauss, the structure of human minds is universal, so the structures of cultural items that come from it, such as myths, are universal too. Hence he has a methodological starting point:

In order to understand what a myth really is, must we choose between platitude and sophism? Some claim that human societies merely express, through their mythology, fundamental feelings common to the whole of mankind, such as love, hate, or revenge or that they try to provide some kind of explanations for phenomenon which they cannot otherwise understand – astronomical, meteorological, and the like. But why should these societies do it in such elaborate and devious ways, when all of them are also acquainted with empirical explanations? ... Mythology confronts the student with a situation which at first sight appears contradictory. On the one hand it would seem that in the course of a myth anything is likely to happen. There is no logic, no continuity. Any characteristic can be attributed to any subject; every conceivable relation can be found. With myth, everything becomes possible. But on the other hand, this apparent arbitrariness is belied by the astounding similarity between myths collected in widely different regions. Therefore the problem: if the content of a myth is contingent, how do we explain the fact that myths throughout the world are so similar? (1963: 207–8)

His analysis and interpretation of myths is a sustained and detailed attempt to demonstrate that they are not just stories with meaningless sequences of events. Like cooking, they are cultural creations which distinguish culture from nature, but also mediate the oppositions felt by humans. They have a logical structure and are usually concerned with deep intellectual problems of the human mind (Cuff et al., 1998: 211). These problems are circumstances in life that constantly trouble humans and to which no 'satisfactory, stable solutions' can be found. Myths attempt to resolve this unstable logical position by confronting contradictions and making it seem that logical differences can be overcome. This is done through an intellectual 'trick'. The real message of the myth is concealed in a code, and the structure of the message creates a sense of well-being in the intellectual structure of the brain. The mind feels the contradiction is somehow resolved, even though it knows this is not really the case. The outcome of myths is to make the problem easier to live with, and hence they are a form of 'collective self-delusion' (Cuff et al., 1998: 217).

ANALYSING MYTHS

The procedures applied to a general version of a myth by Lévi-Strauss follow these four steps:

1 Split the myth into its separate incidents/events, or mythemes.

2 Group together similar mythemes in the vertical columns of a table.

3 Find what themes contrast with one another (the binary oppositions).

4 Look at what meanings these could carry for the myth as a whole.

Lévi-Strauss's analysis of the Oedipus myth demonstrates this process more clearly. First of all, he breaks the myth up into elements in a syntagmatic chain. He also focuses on the significance of three of the characters' names:

I.   Kadmos seeks his sister Europa, ravished by Zeus.

II. Kadmos kills the dragon.

III. The Spartoi (men born as a result of sowing the dragon's teeth) kill one another.

IV. Oedipus kills his father Laios.

V.   Oedipus kills the Sphinx.

VI. Oedipus marries his mother Jokaste.

VII. Eteokles kills his brother Polyneikes.

VIII. Antigone buries her brother Polyneikes despite prohibition.

IX. Labdakos – father of Laios = Lame.

X.   Laios – father of Oedipus = Left Side.

XI. Oedipus = Swollen Foot.

(1963: 206–31)

He acknowledges that the choice of these particular elements is arbitrary; it is not the narrative that is important, but the structure. Lévi-Strauss's next step is to put similar mythemes together in a table (Table 8.1). Each of the columns represents a theme. Column I is the over-rating of blood relations, which in its most extreme form is incest. In contrast column II reflects an under-rating of blood relations, where offences are fratricide/patricide. The incidents in column III deny the autochthonous nature of man through the destruction of the monsters, and in column IV *show* the autochthonous nature of man through the limping Oedipus, symbolizing the emergence of man from the earth. It is clear that I is the opposite of II,

TABLE 8.1   GROUPING OF ELEMENTS OF THE OEDIPUS MYTH

I	II	III	IV
I. Kadmos seeks his sister Europa, ravished by Zeus.			
	II. Kadmos kills the dragon.		
	III. The Spartoi (men born as a result of sowing the dragon's teeth) kill one another.		
	IV. Oedipus kills his father Laios.		IX. Labdakos – father of Laios = Lame.
		V. Oedipus kills the Sphinx.	X. Laios – father of Oedipus = Left Side.
VI. Oedipus marries his mother Jokaste.			XI. Oedipus = Swollen Foot.
	VIII. Eteokles kills his brother Polyneikes.		
VIII. Antigone buries her brother Polyneikes despite prohibition.			

Source: Adapted from Lévi-Strauss, 1963: 213–4.

while III is the opposite of IV. Lévi-Strauss puts this into the structure I: II:: III: IV. What this means is that I is to II what III is to IV. From this Lévi-Strauss infers the function of the myth.

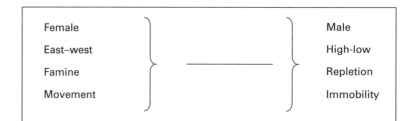

FIGURE 8.2   LÉVI-STRAUSS'S AXES OF INITIAL AND FINAL STATES OF AFFAIRS IN 'THE
STORY OF ASDIWAL' (LÉVI-STRAUSS, 1958: 164)

Greek religion maintained that man was autochthonous. Therefore, there is a
contradiction to be mediated: there needs to be found a satisfactory transition between
this theory and the knowledge that humans are really born from the union of man and
woman. This problem cannot be solved, but the myth provides a kind of logical tool
which relates the problem: born from one or two? Thus the myth sets up the contradiction and then, by an intellectual trick, mediates it (Lévi-Strauss, 1963: 216). This is just
one example of Lévi-Strauss's application of his methodology to myth. He carries out a
much deeper analysis of the myth of Asdiwal, but using the same techniques. Another
way of identifying binary oppositions, and from these inferring the meaning of the
myth's message, is to pinpoint the main themes found in the initial state of affairs to
identify how the scenes contrast with each other. In other words, placing the syntagmatic axis alongside the paradigmatic axis to see how the two are superimposed one
upon the other. He uses a diagram (shown in Figure 8.2) in *The Story of Asdiwal* to show
the main codes allowing us to infer a meaning from the myth.

Lévi-Strauss believes hidden meanings and structures are universal, a point he attempts
to prove in *Mythologiques (1964–1968)*. He studies 813 myths which appear to be
quite different on the surface, but which, he argues, contain the same themes such as
incest and patricide. Lévi-Strauss also maintains that behind all this there is a similar
message wrapped in code, and this shows that many different myths are versions of
the 'same' myth. As the message transcends the narrative, the repetition of this and
the underlying structure can be found in a wide variety of narratives. Leach demonstrates this in his extension of Lévi-Strauss's Oedipus myth, which attempts to show
that many different stories are simply 'permutations of a single plot': that 'Greek
mythology as a whole constitutes a single "system" (language) and that each individual
story is a syntagm of the "system"' (Leach, 1970: 69). He uses the schema shown in

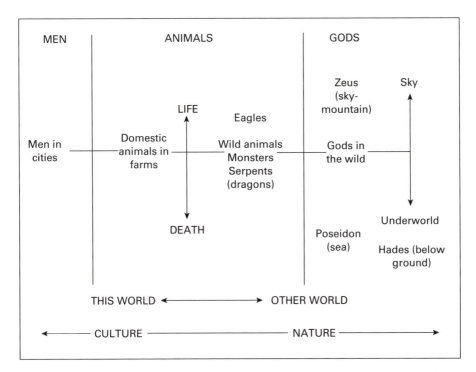

FIGURE 8.3   LEACH'S MATRIX OF OPPOSITIONS IN GREEK MYTHOLOGY (LEACH, 1970)

Figure 8.3 to show that different incidents or individuals in the myths can fit into the overriding, general binary oppositions.

SUMMARY OF LÉVI-STRAUSS'S ARGUMENT

If all these points are brought together an idea of Lévi-Strauss's overall argument emerges. Basically humans are both animal (Nature) and human (Culture), with a mediator in between to join the two. This idea is taken from Freud, whose own 'binary oppositions' are id (animal) and ego (human), which are mediated by the 'super-ego', the unconscious. For Lévi-Strauss the divisions go into further sub-sections if considered from the individual's point of view, with such examples as family or tribe. To him this process is dialectical, as humans express these categories in things like marriage and the structure of myth. Lévi-Strauss's fundamental interest is in looking at mediators which humans use to distinguish themselves as cultural, not animal.

The main thing that separates humans from animals is language. Rousseau commented that only when humans are capable of using metaphor for comparison and contrast can they realize they belong to a group (Glucksmann, 1974: 65). Hence the mediator for humans is metaphor. It is language that makes this mental operation possible, due to its symbolic categorizations (Leach, 1970: 39). All humans use this method to create an orderly universe, and by transforming the categories of nature into the social or cultural they themselves become mediators. Thus, it is the ability of humans to use metaphor to express their categorization of nature that makes them different from animals. To explain *why* humans are able to mediate, the difference between animals and humans must be considered more carefully. Both humans and animals can distinguish between things such as different species, dominance and submission, or what is and is not edible. Humans are able to distinguish further using the rules of their culture, and this is social status. This takes place within the unconscious, the *structure* of the brain, and is done to allow the individual to fit in to the particular culture. Hence the animal level of distinction is developed into *social* classifications (Glucksmann, 1974: 40).

As this behaviour is unconscious, humans are not aware of the constructions they are using to convey different meanings. Lévi-Strauss believes all the different possible combinations available in the unconscious are the equivalent of an algebraic matrix (Leach, 1970: 42). Therefore, through using language and metaphor, humans have become capable of symbolic thought, able to see signs, understand what they signify and use them as 'things' with which to think. Animals can only respond to signals. In society the binary pairs are full of cultural significances, and used in communication and exchange.

CONSEQUENCES OF LÉVI-STRAUSS'S STRUCTURALISM

In everything that Lévi-Strauss studied, his main concern is with the unconscious nature of collective phenomenon. His approach is about making an attempt to uncover the thought formation of human minds, which for him is universal. He is asking us to see his enterprise as a catalogue of the ordering principles of human cultures:

> The ensemble of a people's customs has always its particular style; they form into systems. I am convinced that the number of the systems is not unlimited and that the human societies, like individual human beings (at play, in their dreams, or in moments of delirium), never create absolutely: all they can do is to choose certain combinations from a repertoire of ideas which it should be

possible to reconstitute. For this, one must make an inventory of all the customs which have been observed by oneself or others. With all of this, one could eventually establish a sort of periodic chart of chemical elements, analogous to that devised by Mendeleev. In this, all customs, whether the real or merely possible, would be grouped by families and all that would remain for us to do would be to recognise those which societies had, in point of fact, adopted. (1961: 6)

All cultural items come from these universal principles operating in our minds, and it is only the particular environments and technology in which people find themselves that divide up human beings. Hence, the universal principles are the same in Westerners as in South American Indians, but Westerners, living in a technological environment, have overlaid *our* basic logic with special logics required by our artificial conditions. Therefore, Lévi-Strauss studied unsophisticated cultures such as South American Indians, whose thought processes were less hidden and whose chief way of communicating them was through myth. Hence the source of meaning is not an individual's experience or understanding, but the signs and grammars, binary oppositions and operations which govern language. The focus is therefore on the system that regulates and limits what any individual can do with it. Whatever we say can, accordingly, only be a part of a system we use. I can only say 'I' because I can use a system of language of which 'I' is a part.

Any analysis will not provide a description of the teller of the myth, but instead the *structure*, which is not a 'conscious contrivance' of the teller. Each teller gives their own partial version of the pattern of possibilities, so we can only understand the patterns and structure by seeing the way they are worked out over the whole range of myths. As Cuff et al. state (1998: 217–18), Lévi-Strauss is not looking to trace the cultural history of a myth, nor is he looking for patterns that result from one individual's ideas and beliefs. This would not be finding the *true* meaning; this only originates *from the system*, which tells us significant things about the structures of the human mind. He also believes that places, events, temporality and people in myths are the reverse of those found in society because the relationship between fact and myth is dialectical. Myths offer a way to contemplate the contradictions upon which society is formed; they do not *represent* society (Glucksmann, 1974: 78).

THE ISSUES

Lévi-Strauss's structural analysis rests ultimately on a version of realism. This is the idea that knowledge, ideas and language must have some 'real' basis in the world.

In its crude and main form ('empiricism'), it is the notion that our ideas and words refer to and get their meaning from the fact they 'correspond' to real objects 'out there' in the world. Lévi-Strauss's realism is much more sophisticated than this. He recognizes that reality can be 'cut up' in many different ways. Therefore it cannot be objects which determine our ideas. Yet our ideas must have some real basis. What is it that is 'real' if it is not the objects our ideas describe? Lévi-Strauss's solution (a development of Kant) is to focus on the *structure* of our ideas. The logical organization of our ideas is what, according to Lévi-Strauss, constitutes and guarantees their reality. But if structure is 'real', where is this reality itself located? It is not located 'out there', argues Lévi-Strauss, nor is it in language, for languages vary from one culture to the next. Lévi-Strauss needs some crucial repository in which to locate 'structure' as a real thing and he finds it in the *mind*. Therefore, in describing the structures of culture and language one is describing the 'reality' of the mind. It is the mind which is 'really real'; thus Lévi-Strauss has his absolute, his bedrock on which reality (as we can know it) rests. The main issue for us is about the assumption of this kind of realism. Does there have to be a bedrock upon which our ideas must rest, for those ideas to be possible in the first place? If we accept that there must be, then we must also consider how we can produce correct descriptions of this reality. Does the correctness of a description reside in its reflecting of the 'real structures' which constitute the mind or is it judged in relation to rules and standards for doing structuralist analysis? Lévi-Strauss's realism takes in some difficult but very interesting methodological questions; questions with which he was fully familiar and demonstrated throughout his empirical work. Hence we have a body of work which can show us, if we wish to follow his realist approach, how to conduct a structural analysis of culture.

Studies of the self in communities

Erving Goffman (1922–82), the Canadian sociologist, is known throughout the social sciences for his anthropological studies of how the 'self' adapts to the problems of different social environments. Strongly influenced by the ethnographic approach of the Chicago School of sociology, European anthropology, the philosophy of William James and the pragmatists, and the social psychology of George Herbert Mead, Goffman's interest was in how individuals managed information exchanges with others in a range of settings. For Goffman the individual self is engaged in the management and co-ordination of encounters with other 'selves' to define, and act in accordance with the situation (in an operating theatre or asylum).

Goffman gained his masters and doctorate in sociology and anthropology at the University of Chicago (1949–53), spending some of this time doing anthropological field studies in the Shetland Isles for his thesis and book, the *Presentation of the Self in Everyday Life* (1959), which is still in print and available in several languages. Before taking up a teaching post at the University of California (1958–62), he was visiting scientist at the National Institute of Mental Health, Bethesda; *Asylums: Essays on the Social Situation of Mental Patients and Other Inmates* was published in 1961. From 1962 until his death he taught at the University of Pennsylvania, Philadelphia. Goffman continued to write numerous articles and books of his studies, all of which are well known, including: *Stigma: Notes on the Management of Spoiled Identity* (1963); *Behaviour in Public Places: Notes on the Social Organization of Gatherings* (1963); *Interaction Ritual: Essays on Face-to-Face Behavior* (1969); *Relations in Public: Micro-Studies of the Public Order* (1971); and *Frame Analysis: Essays on the Social Organization of Experience* (1974).

THE SELF IN SITUATIONS

All of Goffman's studies share to a lesser or greater degree a concern to explicate the ways in which people manage, as individuals in a collective, the sense of who they are, their worth and identity. The self is a crucial part of human existence; it is about the self-worth one feels one has and the degree to which others recognize that worth (status, recognition, respect). The self, according to Goffman, needs to have something to belong to (community, collective, group, team) and also something to resist. Goffman's studies document the different ways persons construct a sense of their self in the course of an interaction. The waiter, for example, moves through the door separating the kitchen (back stage) from the diners and the dining area (front stage). The move through the door exposes the waiter to different definitions of their self, who they are. In the public arena the waiter becomes the 'waiter'; who they are becomes irrelevant to the diners; they expect, along with the waiter, that a particular pattern of social organization – an interaction order – will ensue. Diners ascribe to themselves a sense of greater importance, as persons to be served and shown respect. The servility expected of waiters does not mean they are accepted without some resistance from the waiter. In the backroom of the kitchen the waiters can mock the diners, telling stories and giving disrespectful impersonations of particular diners. This example highlights one of Goffman's analogies, the *dramaturgical analogy*. This describes social interaction as if it were a performance in a theatre. People are actors who take on roles according to the script; there are props, audiences and performances. In everyday life there are back stages, where we can be 'ourself', and front stages, where we perform to give the impression of being what we know will be expected (normative meanings). The individual is never alone as the self is social in its construction, development and use. Goffman says that there is the:

> ... back region with its tools for shaping the body, and the front region with its fixed props. There will be a team of persons whose activity on stage in conjunction with available props will constitute the scene from which the performed character's self will emerge, and another team, the audience, whose interpretive activity will be necessary for this enterprise. The self is a product of all of these arrangements, and in all of its parts bears the marks of this genesis. (1959: 253)

Goffman is therefore looking at interactions to explore the details of identities, group relationships and the impact of the environment on the self. The self-identity a person has is shaped by their interactions with others, through the exchange of information and environment, which allows changing definitions of identity to be managed. The process of establishing and knowing one's identity is closely related to situations and especially 'fronts', which are seen as relatively stable environments in which persons know what kind of information to project for others to understand as being in agreement with the normative expectation of the setting. Co-operation is collective representation which establishes the proper setting for appearances for the social roles assumed by the participants. The role a participant assumes is ascribed particular expectations and these are expected to be seen (communicated) by the others. Each actor (participant) produces a performance by controlling what information (impression management) they make available to be seen as exhibiting an appropriate role and attitude for the situation.

MANAGING THE SELF IN EXTREME SITUATIONS

In some extreme environments such as asylums for the mentally ill and disabled, prisons, hospitals, boot camps and other 'total institutions' the front/back stage distinction and sense of self is very different from that witnessed in everyday life. The total institution subjects the inmate to a series of degradations, humiliations, abasements and invasions of the body which show no concern for the person's sense of self. The process of becoming an inmate is about stripping away the person's self so that they will submit to the behaviour of the institution. The inmate is made to wear a uniform, is assigned a number and their behaviour documented in detail. There is no back stage, only front, so there is nowhere to be one's self. In *Asylums*, Goffman describes in a series of essays different ways in which inmates of different total institutions attempt to resist and protect their selves from stripping and transformation. He describes inmates managing the tension between themselves as a self and the pressure of definitions imposed upon them by the institution. Goffman's description of inmates' behaviour includes examples of hoarding mundane objects such as pieces of string, tinfoil, combs, toilet paper and letters – often carrying everything in their pockets – and having an obsessive preoccupation with privacy. Objects they own take on a sacred character and when these are threatened by other inmates or staff are defended beyond any 'normal' sense of their value. This kind of behaviour is interpreted as 'abnormal' and as a symptom of the inmates' mental illnesses.

Goffman, however, uses his descriptions to draw out the normality of the inmates' behaviour. Despite the seeming chaos of what they do, Goffman argues that from the inmates' position their behaviour makes sense:

> When patients entered Central Hospital, especially if they were excited or depressed on admission, they were denied a private, accessible place to store things. Their personal clothing, for example, might be stored in a room that was beyond their discretionary use. Their money was kept in the administration building, unobtainable without medical and/or their legal agent's permission. Valuable or breakables, such as false teeth, eyeglasses, wrist watches, often an integral part of body image, might be locked up safely out of their owner's reach. Official papers of self-identification might also be retained by the institution. Cosmetics, needed to present oneself properly to others, were collectivised, being made accessible to patients only at certain times. On convalescent wards, bed boxes were available, since they were unlocked they were subject to theft from other patients and from staff, and in any case were often located in rooms locked to patients during the day.

If people were selfless, or were required to be selfless, there would of course be a logic to having no private storage place, as a British ex-mental patient suggests:

> 'I looked for a locker, but without success. There appeared to be none in this hospital; the reason soon became abundantly clear: they were quite unnecessary – we had nothing to keep in them – everything being

shared, even the solitary facecloth which was used for a number of other purposes, a subject on which my feelings became very strong.'

But all have some self. Given the curtailment implied by loss of places of safe-keeping, it is understandable that patients in Central Hospital developed places of their own.

It seemed characteristic of hospital life that the most common form of stash was one that could be carried around on one's person wherever one went. One such device for female patients was a large handbag: a parallel technique for a man was a jacket with commodious pockets, worn even in the hottest weather. While these containers are quite usual ones in the wider community, there was a special burden placed upon them in the hospital: books, writing materials, washcloths, fruit, small valuables, scarves, playing cards, soap, shaving equipment (on the part of men), containers of salt, pepper, and sugar, bottles of milk – these were some of the objects sometimes carried in this manner. So common was this practice that one of the most reliable symbols of patient status in the hospital was bulging pockets. Another portable storage device was a shopping bag lined with another shopping bag. (When partly full, this ... also served as a cushion and back rest.) Among men, a small stash was sometimes created out of a long sock: by knotting the open end and twisting this end around his belt, the patient could let a kind of moneybag inconspicuously hang down inside his trouser leg. Individual variations of these portable containers were also found. One young engineering graduate fashioned a purse out of disregarded oilcloth, the purse being stitched into separate, well-measured compartments for comb, toothbrush, cards, writing paper, soap, small face cloth, toilet paper – the whole attached by a concealed clip to the underside of his belt.

The same patient had also sewn an extra pocket on the inside of his jacket to carry a book. Another male patient, an avid newspaper reader, invariably wore a suit jacket, apparently to conceal his newspapers, which he carried folded over his belt. Still another made effective use of a cleaned-out tobacco pouch for transporting food: whole fruit, unpeeled, could easily be put in one's pocket to be taken to the ward from the cafeteria, but cooked meat was better carried in a grease-proof stash. (1968: 222–4)

The inmates are struggling against the pressures of the institution to transform their identities by holding on to and preserving some portion of familiar objects. In doing so they are reacting to their environment by making adjustments to their self in ways that do not challenge the authority of the institution. By holding on to a familiar object, no matter how insignificant to the institution, they are maintaining a hold on to their own identity by exercising some (although small) control over their environment and the information they project. Possession of objects comes to stand for and communicates to other inmates their ability to resist the administration of the institution. If ownership signifies a sense of self, then even the most mundane objects take on a sacred value and are therefore protected; inmates, if they have nowhere secure to keep their 'things', carry them about in their pockets. The objects are given value by the inmates, as a collectivity. Having had control over their personal details, *their* information, taken away – often by close relatives and trusted significant others (betrayal funnel) – the inmate's progress towards social isolation (moral career) and acceptance of different standards by which to judge oneself and others is begun. Rather than assuming that such behaviours are symptoms and confirmation of illness, Goffman assumes they are rational reactions, what anyone would normally do in the situation and circumstances of institutional life.

CONSEQUENCES AND ISSUES OF GOFFMAN'S
METHODOLOGICAL BEHAVIOURISM

The way Goffman chooses to make the interaction order visible is in his story-cum-vignette-like descriptions. His stories are fascinating and carry the reader along, but he offers nothing in terms of proof for his observations. There are no hypotheses, research questions, inferences or a formulation of his research as a coherent project. The different books seem to be about the same thing, but do not provide any clear statements saying how they are related. For some people this can be frustrating, for they want to know just what all of this means and what value it has for research and understanding. Goffman could, therefore, be seen as providing little more than interesting, non-replicable, insights into human behaviour. As descriptions presented in a rhetorical style, they seem to lack objectivity and fail to meet any of the criteria of science. To go this way would be to make a major error of understanding of what Goffman's work is all about. A more accurate and sensible way to view his work is as a series of investigations of his primary interest in the ways in which the tensions between the self and society are managed in a variety of situations.

If we focus on how he did his investigations, we can see the systematic application of a methodological strategy. That strategy can be characterized as *methodological behaviourism*. Following the naturalist, who observes birds in various settings, aiming to understand the purpose of what seems to be chaotic behaviour, Goffman observed human behaviour – in particular what often seemed to be irrational behaviour. Where the naturalist may use a frame of reference derived from Darwin to describe the behavior of birds, classifying some behaviours as mating rituals, nesting or feeding, Goffman uses a different frame of reference to classify human behaviour. He is not interested in all human behaviour but in a specific sphere of behaviour that displays information exchange in social groups. So, like the naturalist, his reference point is the collective and not the individual. This is what makes his work sociological and not psychological. Hence, his methodological behaviourism does not commit him to methodological individualism. Calling Goffman's work methodological behaviourism therefore includes his choice to use ethnography as naturalistic observation to explore, from a particular frame of reference, the order of social life.

Misunderstanding is a risk Goffman takes by electing to use a story-like and rhetorical style. Its use would, in part, please the Popperian, who sees risk as a sign of good research. This style, especially the use of analogies and metaphors, provides some effective ways of understanding his stories, but there is no attempt to construct theoretical frameworks or models and hence there are no hypotheses to be falsified. Goffman's purpose in choosing this strategy is to provide a series of concepts which we can use to investigate common behaviours that display/exchange information in commonly known ways. The use of the concepts makes available for description aspects of the observed behaviour. The analogies do not provide an explanatory framework or a means of analysis to say what the behaviour 'really' means. His behaviourism is not the behaviourism of psychology, nor is it based on any theories of the mind; this is ensured by his observational strategy – it excludes everything that cannot be observed – and his focus on how behaviour is used, naturalistically, in terms of responding to problems of information exchange. This strategy therefore commits the researcher to discarding assumptions given, say by an organization, about the meaning of some behaviours, and to seek understanding through careful observation, often from the standpoint of those doing the behaviour. He assumes, therefore, that behaviour which may seem irrational is the exercise of rational choices, although limited, in order to maintain, even if tentative, a grasp on the capacity to make decisions and control what information is communicated about one's self. Goffman's descriptive portrayals provide us with understandings of how people resist the definitions imposed on them by others and thereby furnish explanations of what often seems odd behaviour.

Studies of practical actions

Harold Garfinkel (1917–) is the American sociologist known for founding a new approach to social science call 'ethnomethodology'. Ethnomethodology is a composite term invented by Garfinkel to describe how people accomplish and maintain the meaningful, patterned and orderly character of daily life through the methods of understanding and knowledge they apply to the multitude of encounters they are routinely a part of. 'Ethno' refers to people, while 'methodology' refers to the methods people use to routinely make decisions and inferences about what is what. According to Garfinkel, and in contrast to traditional social science, it is the shared methods and knowledge people use to accomplish social order that are the subject of sociology. This means that in place of theorizing, abstraction and generalization we need to describe carefully the methods we use, but rarely notice, to achieve the orderly patterns of social life. Ethnomethodology is not therefore a method but a careful study of the method*ology* – the logic of the methods – of a culture they employ for producing recognizable social order.

Prior to World War II, Garfinkel studied sociology at the University of North Carolina, where he was exposed to transcendental phenomenology. From 1942–46 he served in the US armed services before rejoining his studies at Harvard University. Among his teachers were Pitirim Sorokin, Robert Bales and Talcott Parsons, who was also his doctorate supervisor. During this time Garfinkel began to make visits to the phenomenological philosopher Alfred Schutz. Garfinkel's doctorate was entitled *The Perception of the Other* (1952, unpublished), which marked the beginning of his respecification of the problem of social order. During the late 1950s and 1960s he undertook research into medical and mental health care settings and into jurors that resulted in a new approach to specifying the phenomena of study. It was from his study of how jurors do being jurors that the term 'ethnomethodology' was born. It was also during this period that he began his conversations with Harvey Sacks, who was to establish the study of conversation as a means of analysing naturally occurring data. Garfinkel has published relatively little work but what he has produced, including *Studies in Ethnomethodology* (1967) and *Ethnomethodology's Program: Working out Durkheim's Aphorism* (2002), has had a substantial impact on the social sciences.

GARFINKEL'S STUDY OF AGNES

Agnes is the pseudonym of a patient of the Department of Psychiatry at the University of California (UCLA). In 1958 Agnes was a 19-year-old white woman. Garfinkel describes her as:

> ... a nineteen-year-old girl raised as a boy whose female measurements of 38–25–38 were accompanied by a fully developed penis and scrotum [that] were contradictory of the appearances that were otherwise appropriate ... Agnes was typical of a girl of her class and age ... There was nothing garish or exhibitionistic in her attire, nor was there any hint of poor taste or that she was ill at ease in her clothing, as is seen so frequently in transvestites and in women with disturbances in sexual identification. Her voice, pitched at an alto level, was soft and her delivery had the occasional lisp similar to that affected by feminine appearing male homosexuals ... convincingly female. She was tall, slim, with a very female shape ... She had long, fine dark brown hair, a young face with pretty features, a peaches-and-cream complexion, no facial hair, subtly plucked eyebrows, and no makeup except for lipstick. At the time of her first appearance she was dressed in a tight sweater which marked off her thin shoulders, ample breasts, and narrow waist. (1967: 117–19)

Agnes was born a male and until the age of seventeen was generally recognized as a male. Her goal was to have a sex-change operation that would change her fully developed penis and scrotum (Garfinkel, 1967: 117) into a vagina. Garfinkel summarizes Agnes's claim in the following way:

> ... compare Agnes' beliefs not only with those of normals but with what normals believe about persons whose genitals for one reason or another change in appearance, or suffer damage or loss, through aging, disease, injuries, or surgery we observe that it is not that normals and Agnes insist upon the possession of a vagina by females (we consider now only the case of the normal female; the identical argument holds for males). They insist upon the possession of either a vagina that nature made or a vagina that should have been there all along, i.e., the legitimate possession. The legitimately possessed vagina is the object of interest. It is the vagina the person is entitled to. (1967: 127)

At the UCLA medical centre, which was involved in a study of inter-sexed persons, psychoanalyst Robert Stoller, psychologist Alexander Rosen and Garfinkel were interested in Agnes's case to investigate the origins of her desire to be a women and what effects this had on the management of her self-identity. While Stoller and Rosen were primarily interested in her endocrinology, physiology and lifelong desire to be a 'proper' female, Garfinkel noticed something else, very different, in this case. After approximately 35 hours of tape-recorded conversation with Agnes about her life-story, prospects, problems of passing as a women and fears of disclosure and stigmatization (by society), Garfinkel formulated an analysis of sexual status as a 'situated accomplishment' and Agnes as a 'practical methodologist'. Garfinkel describes this in the following way:

> Agnes' practices accord to the displays of normal sexuality in ordinary activities a 'perspective by incongruity'. They do so by making observable *that* and *how* normal sexuality is accomplished through witnessable displays of talk and conduct, as a standing process of practical recognition, which are done in singular and particular occasions as a matter of course, with the use by members of 'seen but unnoticed' backgrounds of common place events, and such that the situated question, 'what kind of phenomenon is normal sexuality?' – a member's question – accompanies that accomplishment as a reflexive feature of it, which reflexivity the member uses, depends upon, and glosses in order to assess and demonstrate the rational adequacy for all practical purposes of the indexical question and its indexical answers.
>
> To speak seriously of Agnes as a practical methodologist is to treat in a matter of fact way her continuing studies of everyday activities as members' methods for producing correct decisions about normal sexuality in ordinary activities. Her studies armed her with knowledge of how the organized features of ordinary settings are used by members as procedures for making appearances-of-sexuality-as-usual decidable as a matter of course. The scrutiny she paid to appearances; her concerns for adequate motivation, relevance, evidence, and demonstration; her sensitivity to devices of talk; her skill in detecting and managing 'tests' were attained as part of her mastery of trivial but necessary social tasks, to secure ordinary rights to live. Agnes was self-consciously equipped to teach normals how normals make sexuality happen in commonplace settings as an obvious, familiar, recognizable, natural, and serious matter of fact. Her speciality consisted of treating the normal facts of life of socially recognized, socially managed sexuality as a managed production so as to be making these facts of life true, relevant, demonstratable, testable, countable, enumeration, or professional psychological assessment; in short, so as unavoidably in concert with others to be making these facts of life visible and reportable – accountable – for all practical purposes. (1967: 180)

Although the language may seem a little strange and difficult to understand, what Garfinkel is saying is very radical. We can understand how by looking at what we normally mean by sexual status. It has been traditional to treat the categories of 'man' and 'woman', 'male' and 'female' as facts given in nature that everyone knows is determined by biology. Transition between the two is normally prohibited except in temporary and playful situations, such as in the theatre. In the feminist literature (broadly speaking) the categories female and male are used as starting points for discussing the cultural, social, economic, political and psychological aspects of discrimination, exploitation and oppression, usually of women, in a patriarchal world. Traditional studies of gender typically select aspects from the features of sexual relationships, at an institutional level, as a resource to explain particular cultural, social, economic, political and psychological states of affairs – life-chances, outlooks, occupations, activities and so on in relation to social structures. Sexual categories are therefore taken for granted as the starting point for gender research and analysis. Garfinkel takes a very different view and starting point. Rather than being a *resource* for analysis and argue the phenomenon, the categories 'woman' and 'man' become the *topic* for investigation. Garfinkel aimed to *explicate* rather than explain, or take a moral standpoint, the features of sexual status to see how it was produced and reproduced to be recognized by others as a fact – remember, we do not normally see a person's genitalia in everyday encounters. Therefore where others began their studies, Garfinkel ended his. He distanced himself from the familiar, everyday (as used by sociologists) use of sexual categories and made them 'anthropologically strange'.

Agnes had a series of ever-present problems and fears, mostly due to her having a penis and scrotum. These were:

- distinguishing herself from transvestites, transsexuals and homosexuals, to present herself as being female all along, from the beginning and being a trick of nature;

- dealing with those who knew she had been a male and had a penis; and

- dealing with those who did not know and took her as a female.

Agnes was preoccupied with managing the details of the normally not noticed features which accomplish the recognition of a person as female. For Agnes the category could not be taken for granted; she had to work at producing and reproducing the details of the category for it to be recognized and applied to her as normal. Garfinkel notes that for Agnes, as for everyone else, the category of male or female is a practical achievement of doing *gender work*. You and I are no exceptions, nor are sociologists or psychologists, to this work for we too are incumbents of expected, taken-for-granted sexed categories and are taken to be normal, what we seem to be, without serious doubt:

> From the standpoint of persons who regard themselves as normally sexed, their environment has a perceivably normal sex composition. This composition is rigorously dichotomized into the 'natural', i.e. *moral*, entities of male and female. The dichotomy provides for persons who are 'naturally', 'originally', 'in the first place', 'in the beginning', 'all along', and 'forever' one or the other. (Garfinkel, 1967: 116)

We may not notice the work we do to achieve this, but Agnes did because she had to. In the myriad of everyday settings and encounters Agnes was fully aware of the practical management of her gender category as an account (observable, recognizable, reportable) others took for granted:

> In each case the persons managed the achievement of their rights to live in the chosen sexual status while operating with the realistic conviction that disclosure of their secrets would bring swift and certain ruin in the form of status degradation, psychological trauma, and loss of material advantages. Each had, as an enduring practical task, to achieve rights to be treated and to treat others according to the obligated prerogatives of the elected status. They had as resources their remarkable awareness and (un)common sense knowledge of the organization and operation of social structures that were for those that are able to take their sexual status for granted routinized, 'seen but unnoticed' backgrounds of their everyday affairs. *The work of achieving and making secure their rights to live in the elected sex status [of becoming, recognisably, a woman ...] I shall call 'passing'.*
>
> ... The experiences of these intersexed persons permits an appreciation of [the] background relevances that are otherwise easily overlooked or difficult to grasp because of their routinized character and because they are so embedded in a background of relevances that they are simply 'there' and taken for granted. (Garfinkel, 1967: 118)

If sexual categorization is therefore something we routinely accomplish and take largely for granted, then for Garfinkel the key question was what this work might consist of. Agnes provided an excellent case for understanding this work because for two years she had been a very sensitive and self-reflective ethnographer of 'femaleness' in order to furnish her own identity:

> Can you imagine all the blank years I have to fill in? Sixteen or seventeen years of my life that I have to make up for. I have to be careful of the things that I say, just natural things that could slip out … I just never say anything at all about my past that in any way would make a person ask what my past life was like. I say general things. I don't say anything that could be misconstrued. (Garfinkel, 1967: 178)

CONSEQUENCES OF GARFINKEL'S EXPLICATION

Garfinkel's explication of how sexual categories are accomplished has had relatively little measurable impact on the study of sexuality and gender and even less on feminist research. Very little has been done to systematically work out the details and implications of the Agnes study. This may be because his work is too radical, non-political and difficult to understand. The radical element is a respecification of the phenomenon: from resource to topic. His non-partisan stance contrasts sharply with many feminist studies: he has no academic interest in the position of women. This does not mean he is not interested in social structure. Part of his respecification is to look at social structure very differently from convention approaches. Sexuality is treated in everyday life as 'objective', 'normal' and 'routine' – as factual. These are core features we use, as members of society, to orientate our everyday actions. If we had to pay attention to every detail of social life, the *social* would become extremely difficult: typifying, classifying and categorizing enable us to take what we experience for what it is intended to be and sexuality is not excluded from this. As practical methodologists we, unlike Agnes, apply our skills in ways that are largely unnoticed, and in doing so we conform to (reproduce) and confirm (maintain) the order of sexual categories as given, permanent and natural: as a social structure we regularly partici-pate in but take for granted. Therefore as members we may, like Agnes, have a realist view of reality (believing in an objective social world), but as Garfinkel has shown it is embedded in our taken-for-granted assumptions about what things are to be taken to be and in our historically based practices for situating our experiences into common categories (orders). The main consequences are then:

♦ **There are no traditional research designs for the ethnomethodologists. Hypotheses, variables, measuring instruments and the like are all absent from ethnomethodological studies.**

♦ Where mainstream social science mostly uses features of a phenomenon to talk about a concept such as power, control and alienation, ethnomethodological studies pay close attention to the details of how the phenomenon is, what it is, and do not use it as a vehicle for explanation or argumentation.

♦ Ethnomethodological studies do not aim to explain but to explicate the details of the practices people routinely use, but rarely notice, to accomplish concerted social order.

♦ Ethnomethodology is not a theory, has no clear theories and is therefore different from mainstream social science. Its difference is often a cause for misunderstanding and difficulty in understanding and appreciating what it is about. Understanding ethnomethodology is like a revelation, after which the social world and research is never the same again.

THE ISSUES

Being a non-theoretical, descriptive and empirical approach sets ethnomethodological studies as an alternative to conventional social science and to such a degree that any study within social science has the potential for being respecified into an ethnomethodological study (Garfinkel, 2002). Many of the arguments about ethnomethodology are generated by ethnomethodologists themselves debating the emphases to be given to different aspects of the ways in which competent persons go about the taken-for-granted accomplishment of social order. Conventional social science has increasingly recognized ethnomethodology but still expects ethnomethodologists to engage in its kind of methodological debates – nature of reality, verification and falsification, operationalization of concepts, qualitative versus quantitative and so on. Conventional social scientists fail to see, often because of their misunderstanding of ethnomethodology and Garfinkel's original studies, what ethnomethodology is about and how its investigative programme is incommensurable with their own (Giddens, 1976). With its origins in phenomenology and Parsons's structure of social action, ethnomethodology is not the sum of these. It is not looking to define an ontological position for the social sciences or stipulate an epistemological method. Its focus is, as the study of Agnes shows, on how members do practical methodology in their everyday lives. The problem for ethnomethodologists is to describe adequately how members do what they do to achieve the sense of order they accomplish.

In the 'Appendix to Chapter Five', included in *Studies in Ethnomethodology* (1967: 285–8), Garfinkel informs the reader how eight years after the completion of the study Agnes made some revelations that she had lied to him and to others. The feminization of her body was not, she confessed, due to a medical condition but to her continued and pro-longed use of female hormones. Agnes had at the time strenuously denied taking any such hormones; in short, she lied. Does this revelation discredit Garfinkel's study? Some have claimed that Garfinkel was duped (Denzin, 1991) and comments by his co-worker Stoller (Hilbert, 1991: 266) seem to confirm this. In essence this revelation makes no difference to what Garfinkel makes visible about how everyday life is a matter of practical reasoning to accomplish social order. The reasons for this reside in the way in which he presents his explication of the phenomenon. Garfinkel's aim was to make visible for description the everyday practices we all use to make ourselves accountable (recognizable and reportable) and Agnes provided an ideal opportunity to do just this. Agnes was an artful ethnographer of gender categorization and this allowed Garfinkel to situate her as a woman in terms of the attributes commonly used to produce the category 'woman' and 'female'. This makes irrelevant the facts of her birth and yet at the same time he problematizes Agnes's place in the category of female by standing back, as an analyst, from taking the category for granted. He does this to focus on the details of how Agnes accomplishes femininity as a normal taken-for-granted category. It does not matter that Agnes lied or that this would be a serious matter for conventional sociology. Garfinkel was not using Agnes as a resource, as a source of data, Agnes *was* the data and the way he tells her story and analyses the use of categories achieves his goal of making visible for description the very details of how, *in situ*, Agnes accomplished femaleness for all practical purposes.

Matters of methodological relevance

In this chapter we have looked at only five examples of research in the social sciences. To some degree they are comparable because they are all concerned, at a basic level, with providing descriptions of human behaviour. As we have seen, this is no easy or straightforward matter. There are any number of ways in which we, as inquirers into human behaviour, can approach the aspect of human activities which we have selected for our topic. Lombroso and Goddard shared a concern with what were then seen as common social problems and in their largely reforming positivistic approach sought to explain the causes of what they defined as moral infringements. Their reformist motivations and generalizing theories can be traced back to many eighteenth- and nineteenth-century social philosophers such as Spencer and Comte and naturalists such as Darwin. Social ideals and generalizations, from whatever perspective and whosever standpoint, combined with confirmationalist inductive measurements, were regarded as scientific, as being in the interests of the greater number of 'civilized' society. That such measurements were not falsifiable in the *closed research paradigm* of searching for specific characteristics, excluding anomalies and ignoring social and economic conditions, was not, at this stage of development in social science, thought to be problematic. They sought to simplify the complex, undertaking detailed measurements, classifying data to produce typifications of behaviours, placing boundaries around what was to be taken as relevant, using the epistemology of empiricism and in the belief that this was *the* scientific way to the betterment of human kind (Smith, 1998: 46–65).

In a different mode the relative work of Lévi-Strauss, Goffman and Garfinkel is no less interesting, not for historical reasons but for their sheer complexity. Each, in his own way, has spent most of his professional life systematically working out some of the most complex and difficult methodological problems of the social sciences. Lévi-Strauss's realist ontology, when combined with an empiricist assumption of the availability of knowledge about the external world, typifies much of the sophistication, now often suppressed by later structuralists, of French structuralism. Lévi-Strauss's work does, however, have some connections with that of the early positivists. He believed it was the function of analysis to uncover the mechanisms which regulated and gave order to social life. His methodological approach may have combined quantification and qualitative interpretation, but it was ultimately aimed at producing descriptions based on correspondence theory: the notion that words and ideas get their meaning from the fact they correspond to real objects external to us. Of course, his work is not *as* moralizing as that of Goddard or Lombroso, though it *is* moralizing. This can be seen in many places in his writing when he advocates strongly for social science to be the protector of so-called primitive peoples. In some ways Goffman also looked to give voice to those persons (in a general sense of categories) who could not express their own views on their situation. Moreover, like Lévi-Strauss, Goffman employed anthropological methods in his research. His choice to make observational studies of persons in extreme environments expressed his value-relevance, what he thought important to say. In many places throughout his work we can read of his concerns for the underdog, for those persons who, for whatever reasons and biographical circumstances, have found themselves subject to the power of others to define them in ways which limit how they are understood and often restrict their interactions with the world at large. Goffman's work also looked to reveal aspects of the lives of such people which were not often understood by 'professionals' (for example, psychiatric nurses). He aimed to reveal the rationality of inmate behaviour hidden by the paradigmatic ideologies of interventionist services to show that seemingly odd behaviours labelled 'irrational' were rational from the standpoint of those doing the behaviour. His approach is one of an *open research paradigm* that takes into account the multiplicity and complexity of social reality as mutually co-existing *realities*. His neo-Kantian position (see the debate on internalists and externalists in Chapter 7) then has some, though very limited, connections to that of Lévi-Strauss. Therefore, although we can say both Lévi-Strauss and Goffman are neo-Kantians, they use the notions and assumptions of idealism in very different ways. The point of this observation is that although two or more theorists may have a common intellectual heritage, it cannot be assumed they will be easily comparable or can be pigeon-holed together.

Garfinkel's work has, on occasion, been categorized as a version of symbolic inter-actionism, as work based on the observation of human behaviour in natural settings. The latter part of this is largely the case, but Garfinkel's ethnomethodology is certainly not a version of symbolic interactionism or the same as Goffman's methodological behaviourism. Garfinkel emphasizes the need for empirical data which has been captured from natural settings. These settings have, through a succession of ethnomethodological studies by others, varied enormously and so too have the kinds of data captured. This has included audiotape and video recordings of people in work situations, hand-drawn sketches on paper of people queuing, collections of print materials such as personal advertisements and architectural designs. Ethnomethodologists do not have any prescriptions for what is to count as measurement because they do not measure anything through their data. Data for Garfinkel are what make the practical reasoning of people noticeable for analysis. Garfinkel is not trying to reveal or uncover anything in the ways in which Goffman and Lévi-Strauss are, but aims to make noticeable those methods we routinely use to determine what *is* what, which, due to its utter familiarity, goes mostly unnoticed. He is therefore doing a very different kind of social science from all the other social scientists we have looked at in this chapter and who are the mainstay of most texts on research. His work and that of other ethnomethodologists cannot therefore be easily categorized, but it certainly is not positivist in any conventional sense of the term. Its origins in the phenomenology of Alfred Schutz and in normative theories of social action, both of which trace their heritages back to idealism and neo-Kantianism, do not mean that ethnomethodology is idealist. It is, as it was designed to be, the careful observation of the empirical details of the things people do (deciding on what is what) to establish and maintain the facticity of social life (social facts). Dispensing with the need for theoretization to explain social order, Garfinkel also did away with the need for a distinction between the macro and micro, as social structure and institutions become things that are accomplished by the sense-making practices of members. It is this respecification of the conventional approach to social order that makes Garfinkel's work so methodologically radical.

SUMMARY OF THIS CHAPTER

In this chapter an attempt has been made to illustrate the rich diversity of methodological assumptions and research strategies in the social sciences. The following are some of the main points that have been made:

♦ The work of Goddard and Lombroso show us how early researchers attempted to incorporate the findings of experiments in biology and botany to explain human social conditions and how they embraced the positivist assumptions and mission to improve society through science.

♦ Lévi-Strauss demonstrated the logic of his neo-Kantian position in successive analyses of a range of cultural products. His structuralist approach allowed him to construct successive studies showing the relationships between categories imposed on nature and culture by the human mind.

♦ Goffman's descriptions of human behaviour show how what people do can be approached from the standpoint of a behavioural naturalist. He demonstrates that behaviour can be explained by describing the conditions which give rise to that behaviour.

♦ Garfinkel's ethnomethodology is a radical alternative in social science. His studies of practical reasoning show that social reality is far from fragile and is the accomplishment of people routinely seeking and confirming the social facts of their situations.

Further reading

Smith, M. (1998) *Social Science in Question*. London: Open University/Sage. Contains many diagrams and illustrations to show the consequences of different approaches.

Hughes, J. and Sharrock, W. (1997) *The Philosophy of Social Research*. 3rd edn. Harlow: Addison Wesley Longman. A sound companion to Smith (1998), providing a thorough overview of the complexities of the relationship between philosophy and social research.

Research ethics and standards

All research is based on a series of decisions about the nature of the topic, what research questions to ask, how to use the literature, how to give fair play to the arguments of others, how best to collect data so as to avoid bias, how to present the findings, what interpretations to give of the findings and many more. Research is therefore a decision-laden activity. It is also encompassed and shaped by the values we hold about the world around us. Many of these decisions are ethically based in that they require alternatives to be thought about and choices made. In both the natural and social sciences decisions are routinely made which have an ethical dimension, including: how to select a sample; what rights are to be respected on behalf of subjects (humans and animals); what counts as valid data; whether to collect data 'naturally' without subjects knowing, or to tell them and get their consent; what methods and theories are preferred; how to handle sensitive information; whether to tell subjects how the research may affect them or others; and whether to cite all disconfirming cases of your hypothesis. The purpose of this chapter is to examine the ethics of research by discussing the following kinds of questions:

1 What are ethics?

2 How are ethics related to doing research?

3 What is the function of ethical codes and ethics committees?

4 What are the consequences of ethical digressions in research?

5 How do you ensure your research is ethical?

In this chapter we are going to look at research ethics from a number of perspectives and standpoints. The aim is to develop critical awareness of the need for sound argument over ethical decisions and why codes may be regarded as guidelines rather than mandatory regulations. The intention is not to stipulate what counts as ethical research, but to help you understand the nature of research ethics and how all research has several ethical aspects which need to be addressed. This includes having an awareness of the debates about research ethics and the origins of these debates in philosophy.

Definitions and codes of ethics

The journal, conference and report literatures of the social sciences contain many citations that discuss, debate and define ethics. All social science disciplines have a code of ethics. How ethics is defined and the examples used to illustrate what is taken to count as ethical and unethical research would, one would expect, be in abundance in the literature and also in the codes. As we will see, this is not the case. In the social sciences there is only a handful of reported cases of what has been labelled 'unethical behaviour'. Before looking at the philosophical origins of research ethics and the principles to be found in codes of research, our starting point is the definitions in the secondary literature.

SOME DEFINITIONS OF ETHICS

In the secondary research literature one tends to find attempts to define ethics in general terms or with reference to decision-making when thinking about the use of methods and practices. Two popular textbooks on social research give the following definitions of ethics.

> Ethics is concerned with the attempt to formulate codes and principles of moral behaviour. (May, 2001: 59)

A distinction is sometimes made between ethics and morals. While both are concerned with what is good or bad, right or wrong, ethics is usually taken as referring to general principles of what one ought to do, while morals are usually taken as concerned with whether or not a specific act is consistent with accepted notions of right or wrong. The terms 'ethical' and 'moral' are subsequently used interchangeably in this text to refer to 'proper' conduct. (Robson, 2002: 66)

It is because research is context based and one cannot foresee what ethical dilemmas will arise that ethics in research in any generic sense is difficult to define. However, the kinds of dilemma which often arise can be categorized (loosely) as those affecting one or more of four stakeholders: the research itself; the researcher; the university (or sponsor); or the subjects. Some decisions will be based on 'expediency' in terms of what is needed for the research to continue as planned, others may be based on 'principles' you may hold about what you consider right or wrong. It is because research has many stakeholders with potentially different standpoints that makes it complicated and sometimes presents conflicting ethical positions to be dealt with. Whatever the issues you are faced with, it is ultimately your responsibility to deal with them and the ways in which you do so will say something about you as a person and as a researcher.

PHILOSOPHICAL ORIGINS

What constitutes right and wrong or good and bad behaviour has been a concern for most philosophers. It is the arguments of philosophers such as Thomas Hobbes (1588–1679), Jean-Jacques Rousseau (1712–78), Immanuel Kant (1724–1804) and Jeremy Bentham (1748–1832), among many others, that have shaped the ways in which we currently think about, debate and approach ethical issues in research. Summarizing their respective positions can never be easy as they involve sophisticated and sometimes equivocal arguments open to a range of interpretations. I therefore recommend that you read for yourself a selection of primary writings by some of these philosophers, in particular Kant's work on ethics.

In this section we will focus on Kant's *Groundwork of the Metaphysics of Morals* as it provides a way of typifying and understanding the two main positions in research, the 'deontological' and the 'consequentialist' approaches. Kant distinguishes between two kinds of things (actions, thoughts, sentiments and so on) – those which are unconditionally good in themselves and those which are good because they are qualified by their consequences (effect). This distinction can be seen in Figure 9.1.

From the deontological standpoint, ethical behaviour is that which is done out of a sense of what is good and this comes from a deep or inner respect for principles of right/wrong

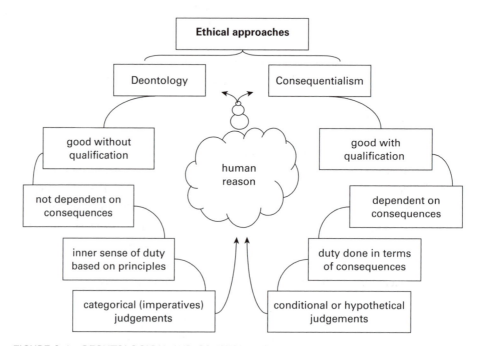

FIGURE 9.1   DEONTOLOGICAL AND CONSEQUENTIALIST APPROACHES TO ETHICS

and good/bad. The ethical value of behaviour is done from a duty that expresses respect for the behaviour itself without regard for its consequences or to produce an effect. In research terms such acts may include: self-reflection; self-control and discipline; empathetic understanding; discretion; honesty; and integrity. These are not qualities we get from experience (*a posteriori*), but are, according to Kant, concepts we have because we are rational beings; they are therefore *a priori* – concepts we bring to experience. Action that is based on principles is an action we could commend to others, such as *not* consistently lying to or deceiving others. There are, of course, situations when we are faced with temptations or opportunities in research which may be good for us. But Kant argues that in judging, as rational beings, that something may be good for us does not mean we will choose it, because this is insufficient in itself for choice. We know, he maintains, from our inner sense (that acts as a kind of command) what we ought to do even when we do not want to. Within us is this universal imperative, what Kant calls the 'categorical imperative', that tells us we are rational beings and should exercise our judgements based not on what we can gain from an action but whether such an action is morally right. If, therefore, there is no *purpose* in deceiving subjects, providing false information or engaging in actions which are not open and honest, then there is nothing contingent (dependent) on doing so, and such a stance would be unconditional and belong to categorical imperatives.

There are, however, situations which we may need to think about because we can imagine hypothetical events when ethical problems may arise. This is something we often do when writing our research proposal; we conjecture what conditions might arise which could possibly create ethical problems in the research. For example, we may be researching an online community and believe it right to obtain informed consent from the users, but how could we do this given that most users are anonymous or the group regularly changes its membership? Our purpose would therefore be best served by considering the reasons for not seeking informed consent. In doing this we would construct an argument that qualifies the situation and consequences to show how the interests of the research and our purposes would be best served by not following a general principle.

Consequentialism is not therefore against principles guiding actions, but recognizes that some ethical decisions are based on the ends (outcomes) we are aiming to achieve. To achieve some end we need to think about the possible means and how we may use these to address and overcome the technical and ethical problems we may encounter on our research journey. 'The hypothetical imperative' is the phrase Kant gives to the act of conjecturing what means may be necessary to achieve a particular end. The hypothetical imperative has a practical force in that it commands us to consider both means and ends together and as conditional (dependent) upon our selves being the cause of the situation, because it is our purposes (goals) which have created the situation and given rise to the need for the means and ends to be justified.

We also have less esoteric duties to fulfil as researchers and these include: facilitating; giving and receiving feedback; problem definition; record keeping; political awareness; attribution of ideas; and conflict resolution. These are some of the everyday expectations of the professional researcher and are carried out to satisfy the conditions of proper conduct in administering and managing a research project. They are not strictly means to achieve our ends except in that they are conditional imperatives which express our adherence to standards in research.

Even from this brief overview of deontology and consequentialism we can see the influence that philosophical argument has on contemporary research ethics. Principles of research, as stated by the various professional associations, belong more to the deontological approach, while codes of conduct lean more to the consequentialist approach. It is not necessary to see research principles as rules or to believe that anything goes so long as the ends are achieved. It is not a matter of either deontology or consequentialism, for most codes include statements like the following:

> Guarantees of confidentiality and anonymity given to research participants must be honoured, unless there are clear and overriding reasons to do otherwise. (*British Sociological Association Code of Ethics*, 1996: 3)

Whether one applies the exception or not, Kant may have argued that you should give the same kind of treatment to other persons as you would expect from them. This means that the categorical imperative does not rule out treating others as means to pursue your own ends, but that you should not treat them merely as means, as if their worth depends only on their use-value to your ends. You might want to remember this comment when we look at experiments done by Nazi doctors on concentration camp prisoners (we look at this later in this chapter).

PROLIFERATION OF CODES

During the later part of the twentieth century the number of research codes and the amount written about codes and ethics proliferated. For reasons we will look at later, there has been a perceived need by those in positions of control for codes of conduct and behaviour. The research code has become, in itself, a phenomenon of modern research and its growth can be illustrated using a simple comparative list such as this:

♦ *Ten Commandments* = 9.5 column centimetres (3.5 inches) of the Gideon Bible.

♦ *Oath of Hippocrates* = 224 words.

♦ 1969 *American Sociological Association Code of Ethics* (its first) = 1,200 words or approximately five pages.

♦ 1997 *American Sociological Association Code of Professional Ethics* = 15,247 words.

All professional bodies have, to my knowledge, a code that states how its members ought to conduct their professional activities and what procedures can be used to enforce the code. Interestingly, the research codes of the major associations of the social sciences in sociology, psychology and anthropology and the like do not include any references to the philosophical principles of ethics to be found in the works of Aristotle, Kant or Rousseau (among others) – key figures who made significant arguments about ethics.

What we often see in formal codes are statements of aspirations expressed as principles. Table 9.1 indicates what these principles are for some of the major research codes.

TABLE 9.1 ASPIRATIONAL PRINCIPLES OF ETHICAL RESEARCH CODES

American Psychological Association Ethical Principles of Psychologists and Code of Conduct	National Committee for Ethics in Social Science Research in Health (India)
Six general principles:	Four moral principles:
• Competence: provide only those services and use only those techniques for which you are qualified.	• Non-malfeasance: research must not cause harm to the participants in particular and to the people in general.
• Integrity: be honest, fair, and respectful of others – do not make statements which are false, misleading, or deceptive.	• Beneficence: research should make a positive contribution towards the welfare of people.
• Professional and scientific responsibility: uphold standards of conduct, obligations, accept responsibility for behaviour.	• Autonomy: research must respect the rights and dignity of participants.
• Respect people's rights and dignity: respect the fundamental rights, dignity, and worth of all people – privacy, confidentiality, self-determination.	• Justice: the benefits and risks of research should be fairly distributed among people.
• Others' welfare: respect the welfare of those with whom you interact.	
• Social responsibility: be aware of your professional and scientific responsibilities; apply and make public your knowledge to contribute to human welfare.	

Source: www.apa.org/ethics/code2002.html (accessed 15. 01. 04) and Aga Khan University www.aku.edu/bioethics/symp-press.html (accessed 15. 01. 04).

While reading these you may wish to consider how they relate to your own research and research with which you are familiar.

Why are research ethics important?

When we talk about ethics being about making decisions we need to know, in order to be prepared, what some of these decisions may look like. The illustrations which follow attempt to show the potential for conflict between the different stakeholders in a research project. The illustrations are based on a distinction between you, as the private person who is also a researcher with responsibilities to your research, and the public realm of research codes and the law.

ETHICS HAVE CONSEQUENCES

From our discussions so far we can now begin to appreciate through reflection that our actions when doing research can have an ethical dimension. It may be that the outcome of decisions some researchers have made about their ethical stance has resulted in studies which are 'authentic' in that they are rich in detail, but which would have otherwise been difficult or impossible to obtain had they taken a different stance. Humphreys's covert participant observational study of casual sex amongst men in public toilets (tearooms) is a case that illustrates this (this is described in the next section). But this study also generated a considerable amount of controversy over its methods and nearly resulted in sanctions on Humphreys. When completed, his research, done for his PhD, became known to the members of the department of sociology at Washington University. Staff petitioned the president of the university to rescind Humphreys's PhD. This did not happen, but the arguments it produced led to a fistfight among some staff, with about half of them leaving the university for other posts, some of whom made the case public by giving the details to a journalist. Humphreys's methods were severely criticized in the press on the grounds that he had invaded the privacy of individuals. He was compared to a 'peeping tom' who takes voyeuristic pleasure in knowing what people do in their private and secret places.

The outcome of this case (if there was an outcome) was that some of the professional sociologists at the university brought to the fore for academic and public debate the nature of ethics in the social sciences. As a discipline largely based on argument, Humphreys's research may be seen as contributing to the very nature of sociology, but in the world of careers and making a living from being a researcher the outcome could have been very different for Humphreys. He could have had his doctorate rescinded and therefore been effectively barred from the profession. Like Humphreys, we too must be careful because we could also, through carelessness, mistake or deliberate act, face any one or more of the possible consequences listed in Table 9.2 that a

TABLE 9.2   CONSEQUENCES OF RESEARCH MISCONDUCT

Institutional actions	Personal and career
• termination of employment • dismissal from school • repayment of grant funds or award • suspension with pay • supervised research • written reprimand • retraction and/or correction • ethics training • community service • notification to the relevant professional associations and regulatory bodies • suspension from course of studies and the university	• removal from a research post and loss of scholarly integrity • loss of respect of and recognition by peers • possible legal proceedings • end of academic career prospects • debarment from profession • supervised research • prohibition from service on advisory committees • certification of data • certification of sources • retraction and correction

Source: Adapted from the Office of Research Integrity (ORI) http://ori.dhhs.gov/.

professional association or university (or the media) can bring to bear on us. The Office of Research Integrity provides a list, shown in Table 9.2, of consequences and disciplinary actions for those proven (mostly in the bio-medical sciences) to have infringed ethical codes.

ETHICS AS DECISIONS

To illustrate the nature of the public versus private conflict generated by ethical problems, we will shortly be looking at some examples. When reading these, ask yourself what you would do, whether you would make your decision public and how you would justify your decision, if you decided to go public, to the research committee of your university, especially when it concerned illegal actions. You might also ask yourself about the consequences of going or not going public and who would possibly be affected by your doing so.

These situations raise many points for debate and argument but are largely about making ethical decisions during the course of your research. They illustrate that many of the dilemmas you will face cannot be foreseen at the beginning of your research.

It is for reasons such as these that most universities and all professional research bodies have codes for the conduct of research to guide your decisions.

Classic examples in the literature

Unlike in the natural, especially bio-medical, sciences (see Grayson, 1995) there are only a small number of cases cited as raising concerns about ethics in research in the social sciences. The concerns raised about these cases range from acts of deception (Cyril Burt on intelligence testing) to issues about the conduct of research in terms of disclosure (Laud Humphreys's covert participant observation of casual homosexual sex), conduct of the researcher (Alfred Kinsey having sex with colleagues), designing harmful experiments (Stanley Milgram on getting volunteers to administer electric shocks to another person) and purpose of the research (Project Camelot to destabilize foreign governments). In this section we will provide outlines of some of the most frequently cited cases and use one of them – the Burt Affair – to look at the nature of academic fraud.

RESEARCH WHICH HAS CAUSED ETHICAL CONCERNS

The cases that will be outlined are listed below. These have been chosen because they are among the most cited examples in the literature and are readily available in most academic and some public libraries and because they concern the actions of individuals. Before reading these you need to note that no comments or evaluations are made about them. As far as possible they have been presented in a way that is non-judgemental. The intention of this is to let you think about them, using, if you wish, the scheme employed to assess Cyril Burt – his research and as a man – that follows the third case. The four cases are:

♦ **Stanley Milgram (1974),** *Obedience and Authority.*

♦ **Laud Humphreys (1975),** *Tearoom Trade: Impersonal Sex in Public Places.*

♦ **Alfred C. Kinsey (1948),** *Sexual Behaviour in the Human Male.*

♦ **Cyril Burt (1966), 'The genetic determination of intelligence: a study of monozygotic twins reared together and apart'.**

Case 1: Giving electric shocks to people

Stanley Milgram (1933–84) was a social psychologist who aimed to demonstrate the following hypothesis: Germans are different from other nationalities in that they are more obedient and this difference explains why they obeyed orders to systematically exterminate Jews and others such as trade unionists, Catholics, homosexuals and the mentally disabled. Milgram's reasoning for this was that mass extermination involves many thousands of other people to implement the actions required and this must be based on a shared characteristic to obey authority.

Milgram developed a research design based on a series of experiments which would systematically measure obedience. His plan was to compare the results of his experiments between American and German subjects. If he could show that there was a difference, then he could vary the experiment to try and find out what it is that makes some people more obedient than others. In itself this is a reasonable research puzzle to pursue, but it was how Milgram designed and conducted his experiments that are the issue. Milgram never undertook any experiments in Germany. His main subjects came from New Haven. The reason for this was that his first experiments showed that Americans (Milgram made this generalization) are generally obedient people. He therefore reasoned there was no need to take the experiment to Germany.

The experiment went something like this:

♦ Classified advertisements were taken out in a local newspaper and some people mailed direct asking for volunteers for an educational experiment.

♦ The job would take approximately one hour and would pay $4.50.

♦ Interviews were held at the Yale Interaction Laboratory.

♦ Jack Williams, the experimenter, greeted the volunteers wearing a white laboratory coat.

♦ He told them they would be paid no matter what the outcome of the experiment.

♦ The experiment, he tells the volunteers, is about identifying the conditions under which people learn and it will be about negative reinforcement – being punished in some way when you do something wrong.

- On a table for the volunteers to see is a book titled *The Teaching—Learning Process*.

- Also in the room is another man who looks nervous and mild-mannered.

- The volunteer and the man each select a piece of paper from a hat.

- The mild-mannered man apparently chooses 'learner' and the volunteer 'teacher'.

- The learner is asked to sit in a chair, his arm is strapped to the chair and electrodes are attached to the arm. Care is taken to apply a gel to the arm before attaching the electrode so as not to cause a burn or blister.

- With the teacher present, the learner is asked if he has any medical condition and replies he has a heart condition and should avoid shocks.

- The teacher is asked to read out a series of paired words, for example, nice—day, fat—neck and so on. When finished they say the first word again and the learner is asked to choose from four possible answers.

- If the learner gets the wrong answer, the teacher is asked by the experimenter to administer an electric shock.

- The device for shocking the learner clearly shows increments starting at 15 volts going up to 450 volts. At the high end of the scale there are labels saying 'intense shock' and 'danger: severe shock'.

- For each successive wrong answer the teacher is told to increase the voltage by 15 volts.

- The teacher is given a shock of 45 volts so that they know how much it hurts.

- If the teacher hesitates, the experimenter tells them to continue.

This is the experiment. The objective is to find out at what shock level the teacher will disobey the command of the experimenter. Milgram made a prediction based on talks with Yale psychology students that most 'teachers' would disobey on or before they reached the mid-point of the shock scale. Milgram found in his pilot study, however, that most teachers would obey the experimenter and increase the voltage all the way to the end of the range. Milgram therefore altered the experiment and tried to generate disobedience. He did this by playing a tape recording of the protests from the learner ranging from 'hey that hurts' to 'I can't stand the pain' and included screams at 285 volts. The teachers could no longer see the learners and after 315 volts the tape was stopped so there was apparent silence from the learner.

The results showed that 65 per cent of teachers obediently kept on administering shocks to the learner — a mild-mannered man with a heart condition — all the way to 450 volts. Milgram continued with variations on the experiment to see just what would reduce the levels of obedience. Even with more extreme protests from the learner and the feigning of a heart attack, some 30 per cent of teachers continued to obey the experimenter.

Case 2: Not telling people that they are your subjects

This second case of research undertaken by Laud Humphreys is easier to describe than the previous case but no less significant in the debates it has subsequently generated about its ethics. Humphreys, an American sociologist by training and education, started with the proposition that authorities concerned with law enforcement hold simplistic and stereotypical views and beliefs about men who engage in impersonal sexual acts with one another. Tearooms, as they are known to these men, are public toilets (restrooms) and tearoom sex is fellatio in the toilets. Humphreys's aim was to study the realities rather than the stereotypes of why these men seek quick, impersonal sexual gratification in tearooms with other men.

His research formed the basis of his doctorate at Washington State University. Humphreys's research design was a field study based on participant observation and structured interviews. In the first stage of his research he took the role of 'watchqueen', a person who keeps watch for the police and coughs when the police or a stranger comes near. This role Humphreys played while observing acts of fellatio in the tearooms. With some of the men he observed he disclosed his real purpose and identity as a researcher in order to gain their confidence and to persuade them to talk about their lives and motives. Those willing to talk to him tended to be among the better educated and more prosperous users of the tea-room trade. However, Humphreys secretly followed some of the men he had observed and recorded the license numbers (index numbers) of their cars.

In stage two of his research, approximately one year later, Humphreys used the license plate numbers to identify a sample and obtain their addresses. This information he obtained from a policeman. This he used and in disguise visited their homes and, claiming to be a health-service interviewer, interviewed them about their marital status, job, ethnicity ('race' in the original study) and other features of their lives.

Humphreys's research generated a significant amount of understanding about the tearoom trade. The following is a summary of his findings:

♦ 44 per cent of his subjects were married and living with their wives.

♦ 38 per cent of subjects were neither bisexual nor homosexual, but men whose marriages were characterized by tension.

♦ Most of the 38 per cent were Roman Catholic or their wives were and conjugal relations were rare, hence:

  – impersonal sex was an alternative source of quick, inexpensive gratification; and

  – impersonal sex did not threaten their marriage or standing in the local community as husband and father.

♦ 24 per cent of the subjects were bisexual, married, well educated, economically successful and exemplary members of their local community.

♦ 24 per cent were single and covert homosexuals.

♦ 14 per cent of subjects were primarily homosexual and were interested in homosexual relationships.

Case 3: Having sex with your colleagues and subjects

Alfred C. Kinsey (1894–1956) was an entomologist trained and educated in biology who spent 20 years studying the Cynipidae — a wasp. He spent a considerable amount of his time travelling across the United States collecting 52,000 specimens of the wasp. Having written a definitive monograph on it he, possibly by accident, came to teach a course on marriage. He adapted his entomological fieldwork methods to study human biology to collect, measure and count sexual activity among humans. He used his training and expertise in naturalism to study sexual behaviour.

The result of Kinsey's research was an 800-page book derived from thousands of case histories made up from over 18,000 face-to-face interviews. The book, *Sexual Behaviour in the Human Male*, provided data which showed that sexual behaviours commonly branded as wrong were widely practised in America. The results included:

♦ 90 per cent of men interviewed had masturbated;

♦ 85 per cent of men had premarital coitus;

♦ 40 per cent of men had engaged in extra-marital affairs;

♦ nearly 40 per cent of men had had some homosexual experience; and

♦ 17 per cent of farm hands had buggered livestock.

Few, if any, of these findings are shocking in the way they were over 50 years ago to the American media and public. However, it is not the findings of the Kinsey Report with which we are concerned, but his relationships with his subjects and colleagues. In a thorough biography of Kinsey (Jones, 1997), we read testimony on how for him his research was a source of his own sexual fulfilment. From interviewing students on campus to being a participant in sex in the gay zones of New York and Chicago, Kinsey filmed 2,000 subjects masturbating to answer the question, does sperm spurt or dribble? As participant-observer Kinsey established the Kinsey Institute where he had sex with almost all of the staff, both male and female alike. He is widely reported to have initiated awareness and conscious-raising by exposing himself and masturbating in front of colleagues and encouraging bed-hopping. The only stipulation made was that Kinsey himself had to be informed and give permission for all sexual activities.

Case 4: The Burt Affair

In this case Cyril Burt's standing and academic pedigree is outlined before we go on to discuss the criticisms which have been made of his work.

Cyril Lodowic Burt (1883–1971) was a leading figure in British and international psychology for several decades. His curriculum vitae is very impressive and includes such highlights as:

♦ Oxford graduate (1906), studied in Germany for a couple of years before returning to Oxford to study mental philosophy as a John Locke Scholar.

♦ From 1908 to 1913 he lectured in experimental psychology at Liverpool University and from 1913 until 1930 was chief psychologist for the London County Council.

♦ Between 1931 and 1950 he was professor and chair of education at the University of London.

♦ He was also employed by the National Institute of Industrial Psychology, Industrial Health Research Board and as an advisor to government on educational psychology.

♦ He was the founder of educational psychology in Britain, editor of the *British Journal of Statistical Psychology* and president of the British Psychological Society (1942).

♦ He developed tests that were used to measure intelligence of children (IQ tests or 11+) and these were used as the basis for differentiating children in order to allocate them to one of three type of schools — grammar, technical or secondary modern.

♦ He wrote more than 300 articles and a dozen books mainly on mental measurement, abilities and differences in intelligence.

♦ He reported in his articles and books that 85 per cent of intelligence as measured by intelligence tests was hereditary.

♦ He was knighted in 1946.

This curriculum vitae shows that Burt was productive, influential and held in such high regard by his academic peers and government that he was widely honoured. Burt apparently had all the academic pedigree possible for the positions and influence he was given. However, within a year of his death in 1971 suspicions were aroused about the validity and integrity of his work. By 1976 suspicions had become accusations and he was found to have fabricated data to prove that intelligence was inherited. But as with all accusations against the dead, new interpretations are often brought to bear and in 1989 the case against Burt was reopened. Joynson (1989), MacKintosh (1995) and Tucker (1997) resurrected the debate and since then the whole issue has generally become known as the 'Burt Affair'.

The reported research: Burt's most famous work was on a study of twins. His aim was to show that intelligence was due largely to hereditary factors rather than environmental ones. The outcome of this was a series of articles and books on an increasing number of twins reared apart, which included correlations showing a positive relationship (coefficient) between similar intelligence levels that could be attributed to inherited genes and not to their environment because they were reared separately. Burt reported coefficients of: 0.77 (1943) based on 15 pairs of monozygotic twins; 0.771 (1955) based on 21 pairs of twins; and 0.771 (1966) based on 53 pairs of twins. This series suggests a very strong relationship between heredity (genetics) and intelligence levels.

The accusations: There have been two main stages in the accusations levelled against Burt's reported research and the counter-accusations: the first stage from his death in 1971 until the mid-1970s and the second from 1989 to the late-1990s. We will focus primarily on the first stage by briefly outlining the findings of four main players in the affair – Leo Kamin, Arthur Jensen, Oliver Gillie and Leslie Hernshaw.

Kamin, a Princeton psychologist, examined the published writings of Burt on monozygotic twins and suspected that so many sets of twins would have been difficult, if not impossible, to find. Between 1955 and 1966 Burt doubled his population of twins reared in separate environments. Kamin suspected that this population was suspiciously large and non-verifiable. He concluded these amounted to flaws in the verifiability and reliability of Burt's findings and consequently were unworthy of serious scientific consideration. While Kamin was giving presentations on his suspicions about Burt, Arthur Jensen, another psychologist and like Burt a hereditarian, published a paper finding fault with Burt's data. In 1974, Kamin published *Science and Politics of IQ*, a critique and denunciation of the hereditarian position.

In 1976 Burt was publicly labelled a fraud by the *Sunday Times* medical correspondent Dr Oliver Gillie. After reading Kamin's book he investigated Burt by trying to find two of his research assistants, a Margaret Howard and a Jane Conway. After talking with people who had known Burt since the 1920s and advertising in *The Times*, Gillie was unable to find any tangible evidence that either existed. He concluded that both were fictions made up by Burt. Added to this, Gillie talked with others working in the field of intelligence and hereditability and was told that there had been suspicions about Burt's statistics and his data. Gillie was told that Burt's results were scientific fraud.

In 1979 Leslie Hernshaw, who had delivered an address at Burt's memorial service, published a biography of Burt. Hernshaw began his readings of Burt's public and private papers with the intent to clear Burt's name and to show that he was a man of integrity. Hernshaw, however, reports that he found contradictions and lies in Burt's work which were not mistakes but deliberate acts to cover up research he had never undertaken.

We can summarize this by saying that the main concerns with Burt's work are focused on three elements:

1 The number of twins reared apart: the number was exceptionally high and not verifiable.

2 The statistical correlations: Burt reported coefficients of 0.77 (1943), 0.771 (1955) and 0.771 (1966). As the population of twins was increased it would be normal to expect the degree of variability between the coefficients to increase rather than stay almost the same.

3 The research assistants: Howard and Conway could not be found and no verifiable evidence located to prove they had ever worked with Burt.

Assessing Burt as a researcher: When we come across such widespread and damning accusations as those levelled at Cyril Burt how can we, as researchers, assess those accusations in order to jugde the work of, in this case, Burt? The starting point is the literature and this will include the accusations and counter-accusations, works by Burt himself, biographical works, editorials in the relevant association journals and newsletters and works by other significant figures who have relied on Burt's work to substantiate their own research. This kind of assessment is a mini-literature review in itself. If we take the main players in the controversy – Kamin, Hernshaw and Jensen – (excluding Gillie, but recognizing that he did confirm some of the evidence) as representing and displaying generally high levels of scholarship, trustworthiness and integrity, then we can begin an assessment of Burt. The tool we can use is Table 9.3 (introduced in Chapter 1).

TABLE 9.3 ASSESSMENT OF CYRIL BURT ✓ = YES ✗ = NO

Skills		Capabilities		Attitudes		Qualities	
Succinctness	✓	Synthetical thinking	✓	Proactive	✓	Integrity	✗
Classifying	✓	Analytical thinking	✓	Responsive	✓	Objectivity	✗
Drafting and editing	✓	Argument analysis	✓	Trustworthiness	✗	Honesty	✗
Innovator	✓	Managing projects	✗	Responsible	✗	Leadership	✓
Communicator	✓	Intuition	✓	Persuasive	✓	Self-confidence	✓
Letter writer	✓	Aware of principles	✗	Self-awareness	✓	Adaptability	✗
Negotiation	✓	Self-management	✗	Visionary	✓	Assertiveness	✓
Networking	✓	Self-marketing	✓	Cultural awareness	✗	Openness	✗
Statistical ability	✗	Self-teaching	✗	Reflective practice	✗	Determination	✓
Oral presenter	✓	Issues awareness	✗	Anthropological	✗	Finisher	✗
Position paper use	✓	Receiving feedback	✗	Research orientation	✗	Self-discipline	✗
Record keeping	✗	Aware of actions	✗	Self-development	✗	Sociability	✓
Fluent writer	✓	Theory application	✓	Self-control	✗	Self-evaluative	✗
Report writing	✓	Data management	✗	Inter-disciplinary	✗	Storytelling	✓
						Consistency	✗

In Table 9.3 a tick has been used to indicate the skills, capabilities, attitudes and qualities Burt exhibited in his writing or personality as reported in the secondary literature, while a cross indicates skills, capabilities, attitudes and qualities Burt did not display. After reading the 'Burt literature' for yourself you may disagree with some of these, which is good, but remember to give reasons for your disagreements. As we can see in Table 9.3, Burt displayed many positive attributes: we have given him 30 ticks. But note that these are mainly for such activities as personal promotion (for example, sociability, networking, self-confidence) and, as a part of this, communication (for example, writing and presenting). We have also given him ticks for being intuitive, applying theory and being a visionary. We could, on the basis of this assessment, characterize this face of Burt as the flamboyant academic (not gentleman scholar) who promoted his intuitive assumptions through persuasive writing and talking rather than actual empirical research. The negatives we have attributed, some 27 in total, increased as we moved from skills to capabilities to attitudes and to qualities. The poor state, in terms of verifiability, of Burt's record-keeping and his incompetence with analytical statistics is evidenced in his articles and books. With the higher-level attributes such as trustworthiness, self-control, honesty and objectivity we have failed Burt. These attitudes and qualities are, we have argued throughout this book, essential characteristics of the research scholar. Burt therefore falls far short of the minimum standards expected of anyone engaged in research. Burt may have been convincing, but to those scholars who praise modesty, self-reflection and debate, Burt, it would seem, was conspicuously suspect and this in itself is an example we should remember when assessing the work of our contemporaries.

Ethics and your research

Figure 9.2 provides an overview of the main ethical issues you should be aware of for your research. The figure attempts to show that ethical issues can arise during all stages of your research, from the design stage through to the reporting stage, including the authorship of articles for journals and presentation of papers at conferences. Most of the issues included in 'design of the research' and 'implementing the research' in Figure 9.2 are self-evident in that if you have worked your way through his book you will be at the stage in your research to appreciate many of these issues. The amplification that follows therefore assumes that you already have an understanding of what would normally be right and what would normally be wrong in terms of research. Using Figure 9.2 as our reference point, we can look at each section in turn.

Designing your research: when you begin to design your research the main issues include:

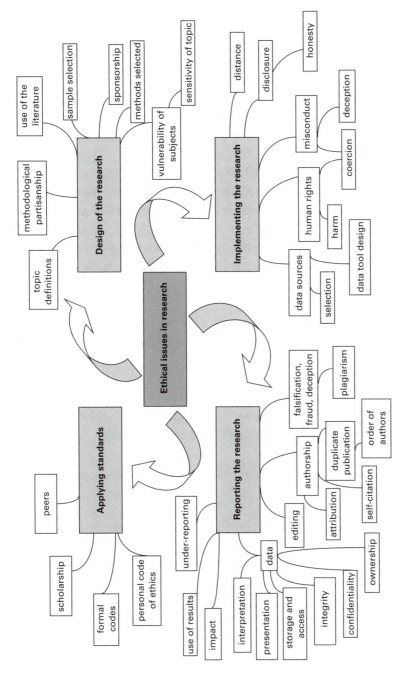

FIGURE 9.2   ETHICAL ISSUES IN RESEARCH

◆ *Have clear definitions*: failure to construct a definition or critically examine pre-existing definitions of a topic or phenomenon can compromise the validity of the data collection instrument; and inadequate definitional scoping of the boundaries of a project can be regarded as disguising preconceived assumptions which inherently bias the results.

◆ *Be open to all methodologies*: failure to consider and evaluate alternative methodologies and tools for the collection of data may be regarded as partisanship resulting in a biased study.

◆ *Employ all of the literature*: an inadequate search and review of the topic and methodological literature is bad practice; and not giving fair and balanced assessments of other people's ideas and arguments amounts to bad scholarship.

◆ *Ensure a sound sample*: selection of a biased sample will invalidate the findings and be regarded as deliberate tampering with the design to achieve a predetermined result.

◆ *Be independent*: failure to demonstrate a non-partisan and detached standpoint from the topic and subjects may be a cause to question the findings and methods of a piece of research.

◆ *Justify your methods*: selecting methods without considering their ability to obtain data with appropriate breadth and depth may be regarded, at best, as naïvety, at worst, a deliberate ploy to avoid collecting data.

Implementing your research: when you begin to implement your research the main issues include:

◆ *Having respect for others*: failure to obtain consent for data collected from a person or group, which may impact on them, may be regarded as a breach of human rights; coercing subjects, colleagues or students to engage in particular behaviours is a form of bullying and an abuse of position with potential for litigation; exposing subjects to actual or potential stressful situations without consent or safeguards may be regarded as infringing safety laws and human rights acts; and failure to treat all subjects regardless of their demographicvariables in ways which are fair and consistent may be seen as an act of prejudice.

♦ *Avoiding mistakes*: not taking all reasonable steps to ensure the accuracy of data and information, to check and verify the proper use of statistical calculations and the presentation of data may be regarded either as incompetence or as a deliberate act to allow unchecked sources to be included in the results; presenting incomplete data, either quantitative or qualitative, as if adequate, amounts to deception; and having no means to verify data because no detailed records exist may invalidate the value of a piece of research or be regarded as a deliberate act to hide the source of, or lack of, data.

♦ *Being self-reflective*: failure to reflect upon your role and status as a researcher, including your own choice of affiliations to a methodological position, may be regarded as a form of methodological myopia; and omitting to articulate your own methodological assumptions and beliefs while using them as the basis for interpretation might be regarded as a deliberate ploy to present an interpretation as based only in the data and this amounts to deception.

Reporting your research: when you write up your research into the dissertation the main issues include:

♦ *Full and proper attribution of ideas*: presenting the words, data or ideas of another person as your own without properly citing them, and thereby showing the attribution, amounts, in varying degrees, to plagiarism. This is not only misconduct, but can also be an infringement of copyright and therefore a criminal act.

♦ *Ensuring the integrity of your data*: falsifying, fabricating or omitting data constitute misconduct — any of these acts is unacceptable because to varying degrees they are either lies or distortions of the truth; using some techniques of presentation which give a biased impression about the significance of the data constitutes misconduct; ownership of and access to data and knowledge generated by a research project done in a public institution needs to be clarified before the beginning of a project; and destroying data generated by a project within five years of the completion of a project is bad practice as it prevents any subsequent interpretation or challenge.

♦ *Safeguarding confidential information*: use of information about a person or group without their permission may violate laws covering data protection and be regarded as a breach of trust; revealing or selling confidential data to a third party will violate data protection laws; and making known the identities of subjects who have been given assurances of confidentiality is a breach of their trust and integrity.

♦ *Maintaining standards of authorship*: failing to acknowledge all persons and organizations involved in a research project constitutes bad practice; publishing duplicate or nearly duplicate articles of the research in multiple journals distorts citation indexes and is therefore bad practice; and including the name(s) of persons who had little or nothing to do with the research for an article constitutes deception.

DETECTING UNETHICAL RESEARCH

As a researcher you may come across research that you suspect has involved some form of misconduct. I cannot advise you on what to do if you do have suspicions about a piece of research because much will depend on your own personal ethical principles and your specific circumstances. What I can do is give an indication of some practices in reporting which can lead you to suspect misconduct. These include:

1 *The data is too perfect*: the data gives perfect correlations; therefore it may have been made up or some anomalies in it not included, as, for example, with Burt's correlations on hereditary and intelligence.

2 *Part or all of the text is plagiarized*: you have read the same article under someone else's name published earlier than the one you are reading, as in the case of Bettelheim's (1976) plagiarism.

3 *There are unexpectedly high instances of the phenomenon*: there are too many subjects with a particular characteristic than is known in reliable data, and therefore some or all of them may be fictitious, for example, Burt's incidence of twins.

4 *The work could not have been achieved with the methods reported to have been used*: there are data which could not have been obtained using the methods reported, and so there is a question of where this data came from.

5 *The timescale is inconsistent with the work that has been done*: the work should have taken much more time than it is reported to have taken; some of it, therefore, may not have been done but been fabricated.

6 *The data sets are too large for the size of the project reported*: there are far too many returns for the size of project, and therefore some may be false.

7 *The author may not be capable of this level of research*: the author is not known for research in this field at this level, and therefore it may be someone else's research.

8 The data is incomplete: the author may have published other parts of the study elsewhere, in other journals, and may therefore be trying to hide something.

QUESTIONABLE RESEARCH PRACTICES

There is substantial room for debate over what is and is not an intentionally criminal action. Using the definitions of the Office of Research Integrity (US Public Health Service), the following three-part definition has been constructed to encompass most of the major definitions of research misconduct:

1 Fabrication, falsification, plagiarism or other practices which seriously deviate from those that are commonly accepted within the research community for proposing, conducting and reporting research.

2 Failure to comply with statutory regulations for the protection of human subjects, their personal information and use of that information.

3 Failure to meet regulations in the use of resources and status as a researcher in ways which are accountable, non-discriminatory or non-exploitative.

Even this adaptation does not fully encompass the range and relative severity of different kinds of unethical behaviour. Savan (1988), however, provides a list of questionable behaviours arranged in descending order according to seriousness. Some of the behaviours she identifies fall within the definition of fraud, such as the falsification of data, while some others are not criminal, such as interpreting results so that they point in one rather than another direction. Table 9.4 attempts to categorize Savan's list to show the distinctions which currently exist between questionable and criminal behaviours in research.

TABLE 9.4   QUESTIONABLE AND CRIMINAL BEHAVIOUR IN RESEARCH

Questionable behaviour in research	Criminal behaviour in research
• Suppression of projects, hypotheses or rejection of findings, manuscripts or grant applications for personal rather than academic reasons.	• Invention of entire experiments and research, complete with fictitious results (fraud).
• Suppression or deletion of inconvenient data by omitting it from calculations, tables and graphs.	• Fabrication of the data, artefacts or other research materials (false representation).
• Designing research so that the results are inevitable.	• Altering data to fit a hypothesis (misrepresentation).
• Using unwarranted or invalid methodological or other invalid assumptions which bias the research and its results.	• Using the words, data and tables of another and passing it off as one's own (plagiarism and copyright infringement).
• Using for your own work ideas, data or arguments from a research proposal or article under review.	• Making malicious allegations against another researcher (defamation) or acting so as to sabotage their work.

Source: Based on Savan, 1998.

The ethics of codes of research

During the last two decades, most organizations and associations which have anything to do with research have developed or adapted codes of research conduct. Most of these codes are much more than mere guidelines because they attempt to put into place statements on how research should be conducted and in what circumstances. From an epistemological and ontological viewpoint, some codes influence what can be studied, by whom and how. The reason for these codes is often to be found in a small number of examples of research which had the potential to do harm to the subjects and the reputation of the researcher and their sponsoring organization. Potential harm, along with the possibility of litigation, is a serious consequence for any researcher. But if we take a step back to look at codes as ethical standpoints, then we may be better able to understand and then engage in ethical issues. In this section we will look at two positions on codes of conduct for research, known respectively as the 'liberal' and 'humanist' positions.

LIBERALISM AND CONTROL

What is commonly referred to as the liberal position on codes tends to hold the view that ethics and moral behaviour are not things to be left to the individual. What is to count as moral behaviour can and should be stated in formal codes of conduct so that all researchers can be aware of what is and is not acceptable. Researchers ought to behave, it is assumed, in similar ways so that there can be an assured sense of the continuity and predictability of research. There are a number of issues about this view and most can be explored by asking why it is deemed necessary to systematically develop and impose quasi-contractual codes on researchers. Below is a selection of commonly available examples of research codes from some of the major American associations:

♦ **American Sociological Association: http://www.asanet.org/members/ecoderev.html**

♦ **American Psychological Association: http://www.apa.org/ethics/code.html**

♦ **American Political Science Association: http://www.apsanet.org/pubs/ethics.cfm**

Originating in the tradition of positivism, the aim that we could have a set of procedures for doing science is the methodological basis for most codes. We are not referring to the method of research, but to the behaviour of researchers. The idea is that research requires standards and these standards can be stated. Many of them are about formalizing the behaviour of researchers so as to prevent them from committing an ethical digression that could bring themselves and others into disrepute. Written codes of acceptable and unacceptable behaviour will, it is assumed, standardize the conduct of researchers and provide associations, funding bodies and universities with the means to censure digressions from the code. In support of codes, cases such as the *Tearoom Trade* (Humphrey, 1975) and *Project Camelot* (Horowitz, 1967) are often cited as illustrations of the potential harm some ways of, and reasons for, doing research can have. Given that such research was done prior to the spread of codes is regarded as illustrating the need for codes to prevent such happenings in the future. Codes therefore attempt to pre-empt intentional and unintentional infringements of acceptable behaviour, proper use of data and legitimate reasons for doing research.

Probably the clearest example and motivation for codes was the evidence given during the Nuremberg War Crimes Trials following World War II. During the trials 23 German doctors were charged with crimes against humanity for performing medical experiments upon concentration camp inmates and other living human subjects, without their consent. People like you and I were subjected to a range of experiments including: freezing to measure patterns of death and effects of cold; injections of malaria, typhus and epidemic jaundice to test for vaccines; application of phosphorus and mustard gas to the skin, causing burns, to test for the healing value of treatments; and investigating the effects of high altitude on motor co-ordination. Translated into the language of crimes, these doctors committed murder, brutality, torture and cruelty in ways which were systematic in that they were planned as experiments and justified by recourse to their 'scientific value'.

An outcome of the trials was *The Nuremberg Code* (1947). As a part of this the court specified some rules for 'permissible medical experiments' and these include: voluntary consent; benefits outweighing risks; and the ability of the subject to terminate participation. What happened in Nazi-controlled

> For further information see: http://ohsr.od.nih.gov/nuremberg.php3, http://www.ushmm.org/research/doctors/indiptx.htm and http://www.gpc.peachnet.edu for full transcripts of the trials.

Europe is a stark reminder of the need for regulation and standards. In the codes we have for the social sciences, what is emphasized either implicitly or explicitly are the consequences of digression from the codes. The codes point out that infringements can have consequences for a number of stakeholders but especially for the researcher, who could face a range of sanctions and even criminal prosecution.

One of the core principles underpinning most research codes is judicial potential. By this we mean that many of the codes share a common concern for the potential legal implications if a researcher can be shown to have deviated from their intended research. It is for this reason that many institutions require the researcher to specify in their research proposal the ethical issues and

> For examples of codes for research from a wide range of academic associations and professional bodies, see *Codes of Conduct* compiled by J. Berleur in Further Reading to this chapter.

dimensions of their intended research. To help make the researcher aware of the codes and specific applications, the research proposal is often employed as an imaginary exercise in 'what if' such and such ethical issues should arise. If we were to characterize the liberalist position, we could do so by saying that: it is based on a standpoint that looks for possible consequences, mostly legal; it values an openness to subjects about research; it requires researchers to be professional by drawing clear boundaries around their research projects and not taking sides or holding values which may introduce bias; and it believes that research and its findings can be influential in both impact and use.

HUMANISM AND AUTHENTICITY

Humanists do not disagree over the need for standards of behaviour from researchers and others who may have a stake in a research project. Where they differ from the liberalist position is that they look at codes for research ethics (in the social sciences) as having few tangible benefits which can be substantiated with examples. To this they add that codes in themselves, as a set of regulations, may prevent the researcher benefiting from opportunities which may arise during the research. We can examine the humanist position on codes by asking the question: 'Whose and what interests do codes serve?' When one begins to read the contributions of the humanist approach to codes of ethics we see that they are not about what ought to be or should be, but are critical evaluations and arguments about the ability of institutions to control what research is done, by whom and how. For humanists the issue of codes is about much more than infringements of position or misuse of data. They seriously question the benefits to research of codes and the part codes play in attracting sponsors for research (Abbott, 1983); the restrictions codes may impose on studying the disadvantaged as well as the powerful (Duster et al., 1979); the need for centralized control; the morality of codes themselves; and the assumptions made about the power of research (Hammersley, 1995).

The humanists regard the proliferation of codes as part of a tendency towards greater control of research. Control that is increasingly centralized is based on the assumption that researchers have specialist knowledge and expertise which can, if not regulated, cause harm to others. The cases of potential harm are questioned. Cases such as *Project Camelot* and the *Tearoom Trade* did not cause harm. Camelot was halted and Humphreys revealed nothing about his research, subjects or data. What such cases did was to create 'what if?' conjectures based on fears of litigation and disrepute. Anticipatory fear became real in its consequences in that some research is now only possible because the actual details are not reported. In other words, the more regulations there are, the less what actually happens in the field is reported. Codes may therefore have ironic consequences, in that rather than assuring openness they encourage deception. This is not to argue for, or advocate deception in not reporting what actually happens in the course of research. It is merely a suggestion that has its origins in classical sociology about the unintended consequences of bureaucracy, and hence it is something to think about when considering codes as bureaucracy (Weber, 1948; Michels, 1949).

If the cases of potential harm cannot be substantiated, it may be that their ritualistic function is more important than their exposed role. As a researcher you have to have your research proposal with its section on ethics approved. Your imaginary ethical 'what ifs' show your required compliance with the code and its expectations. When considering your research proposal, a research degrees committee judges your compliance and in particular your appreciation of the possibilities of litigation from your research. In giving consent they admit you to and sign you up to an implicit contract for the protection of themselves, your subjects and yourself.

The availability of codes and the ritualistic judgement of a researcher's intentions (as described in their research proposals) is, to borrow Goffman's (1961) phrase, a form of impression management. Having a code of ethics in the social sciences and human studies is good for business; it attempts to say that the research 'we' do can have consequences and that 'we' are responsible. It may be for these kinds of function that codes in the social sciences tend, in many ways, to be similar to codes in the biomedical disciplines. They may be trying to impress upon funding bodies and new entrants into the subject that their research is professional and can produce knowledge that is powerful. Such an impression would have its advantages when applications are made for research grants and other resources. Research centres and subject associations would be better placed against the competition if it is generally believed they need such elaborate codes of conduct so as to control what may be powerful research potential.

In addition to this, that neither *Tearoom Trade* nor *Project Camelot* caused harm may not be the major point. What may be important is that studies such as *Tearoom Trade* demonstrate the epistemological authenticity that is possible when responsible researchers take their position, knowledge and craft seriously in a professional manner and do not reveal personal details of subjects. What Humphreys reported on was real life, real relationships and contacts as lived by real people in real situations. Some of it may be, to some people, distasteful, but to others a revelation. From a research point of view the study shows the casual, almost ephemeral and sometimes absurd comicness of this group of people. It also shows – and this may be a worry to those who seek to control research – that social life is unpredictable as is what often presents itself during the course of a research project. Humphreys's work, like that of others such as Goffman (1961), who passed himself off as an assistant to the athletic director to study inmate life in asylums, Gans (1963), who told his respondents he was doing a history in order to undertake an ethnography of life among residents of the West End of Boston, and Garfinkel (1967) whose breaching demonstrations involved him being deliberately rude to people, might not have been allowed if there had been codes for research.

Following on what we have said so far about codes, we need to reiterate that humanists are not against open research, professionalism or the need for sanctions against those who wilfully deceive for their own gain. What we have introduced are some of the debates about the social organization, and through this the control, of research.

Making ethical decisions in your research

Ethics in research, as in everyday life, are a combination of socialization, instinct, discretion and being able to put ourselves in the position of others to reflect on and see our actions as others may do. When faced with an ethical problem that requires a decision, there are a number of steps you can take which will help you 'work' the problem without making more problems for yourself. These include:

1 Define, as clearly as possible, the problem.

2 Determine whether it is or is not an ethical problem.

3 Isolate the ethical issue.

4 Analyse the issue, determining whether it is a problem of right or wrong or of a conflict of interests.

5 Determine whose problem it is — is it personal or related to the sponsor, supervisor, institution or subjects?

6 Identify who will be affected by the problem; normally the person with the ethical problem will not be the one(s) affected by the decision to deal with it.

7 Look at the alternative courses of action; be realistic with time, resources and involvements.

8 Assess the input required for each alternative and its consequences.

9 Evaluate the alternatives in terms of legality, moral principles, professional custom and practice.

10 Select the best course of action for all concerned based on the kind of person you would like others to see you as.

By following this kind of systematic process you will most likely use reasoning rather than rationalization to explore the possible consequences of your actions. This means you should avoid doing something and then trying to find a rationalization for having done it.

PROFESSIONAL VALUES AND QUALITIES OF THE RESEARCHER

Ethical issues in research can arise at any time and in many forms. The spread and increased use of information communications technology has exacerbated some of the ethical problems that we, as researchers, face, especially in terms of 'informed consent' (Jones, 1994). When we discussed Humphreys's research we saw how some decisions can be very real in their consequences. This is because the ethics we may hold as a person and a researcher do not always accord with those of our peers, supervisors, professional associations or institutions. There is a great deal of potential for conflict between these and other stakeholders in research over all aspects and stages of any research project. Figure 9.3 represents this potential, while the list in Box A indicates what we would normally expect as a minimum in terms of professional values for a researcher.

> **Box A   Professional values:**
>
> ♦ pursuit of knowledge and understanding;
> ♦ access to information and knowledge;
> ♦ impartiality in research and presentation of findings;
> ♦ service to the community, including social responsibility;
> ♦ continuing self- and professional development;
> ♦ respect for standards of scholarship;
> ♦ intellectual freedom, including free speech for all; and
> ♦ respectful scepticism.

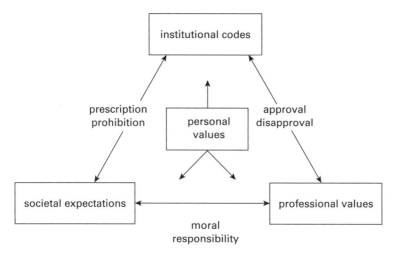

FIGURE 9.3   PARADIGM OF POTENTIAL ETHICAL CONFLICTS

When a situation arises that has ethical implications, your considerations and reflections are likely to be influenced by your skills, capabilities, attitudes and personal qualities. Figure 9.3 shows one way of understanding this in terms of placing ethics within this framework. Using these will help you to conceptualize the problem and its possible consequences within scenarios based on likely events. In asking what you 'should do' you will be doing ethics in ways which may help you to demonstrate your knowledge of the principles of ethical behaviour. Among such principles is respect for the freedom of researchers to choose for themselves what courses of actions they take and the range of such choices, as indicated in Figure 9.4. It is your duty, as the researcher, to take responsibility for your choices and this means choosing well. This aspect has a symmetry as it will also apply equally to others who have a stake in your research. If you have the freedom to choose, then so too must others. This symmetrical respect focuses our attention, as researchers, to see others as we would like ourselves to be seen; it emphasizes our commonalities as rational beings rather than our differences; and this discussion has, you may have noticed, taken us back to Immanuel Kant via *existentialism* – a twentieth-century philosophy of existence that you may look at for yourself.

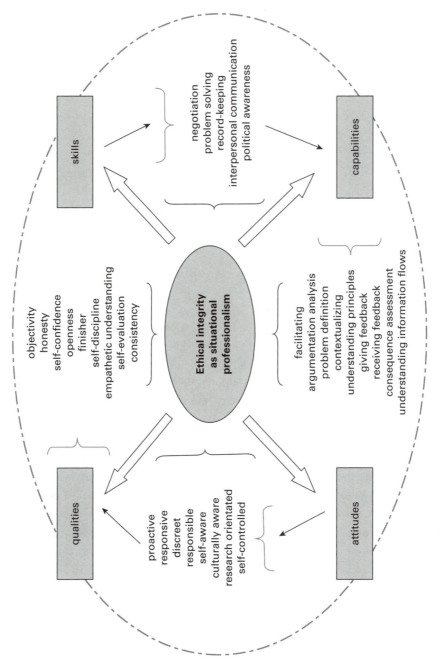

FIGURE 9.4   ETHICS AS SITUATIONAL PROFESSIONALISM

SUMMARY OF THIS CHAPTER

In this chapter an attempt has been made to introduce ethical issues that research makes us think and take decisions about. The emphasis has been on the following points:

♦ Looking beyond codes to see ethics from the researcher's standpoint within an institutional context.

♦ Explaining why an understanding of research ethics and one's own ethical position is important.

♦ Showing how ethical decisions are a part of all the stages of a research project.

♦ Arguing that all researchers need to know what integrity is in order to practise it in their research.

Further reading

Codes of Conduct, Practice and Ethics from Around the World. Compiled by J. Berleur, and held at Virginia Technical University. http://course.cs.vt.edu/~cs3604/lib/WorldCodes/WorldCodes. html. Accessed 03/12/03.

Grayson, L. (1995) *Scientific Deception.* London: British Library. An excellent and thorough research and review of the literature (based on the natural sciences) on the definitions, nature, causes, consequences and policy implications of deception in research. Hundreds of citations with long annotations. Also the 'update' (1997).

http://ethics.edu/theories/ provides on-line the books/texts of most philosophers, including Kant, along with excellent discussions.

10 Research design

Thinking about the choices you have to make in order to undertake a coherent piece of competent research you will have considered, amongst other matters, the literature, the nature of your topic, definitions, methodological traditions and approaches and their consequences, and the ethical dimensions relevant to your research idea. Research is, to repeat something we said earlier in this book, a decision-laden activity and not something that can be done without thought and interpretation. In this chapter we will look at how to bring together your decisions into a design for your research. This means looking at what it means to have a coherent design in terms of ensuring that your research has a logical strategy with tactics which are consistent with that strategy. Hence this chapter is not about 'how to collect data' or 'what to do with data', though it does list some methods for doing this. It will not do this because there are many excellent books and other sources dedicated to the details of the different methods of data collection and analysis; some of these will, as a matter of course, be cited. The main questions this chapter will discuss are:

1 What is the relationship between methodological traditions, methodological approaches and tools to collect data?

2 What is research design and its place in research?

3 What are the elements needed to construct a design for a research project?

4 What kinds of research need sampling, and how do I construct a sample?

5 How can I ensure that my research is valid, reliable and objective?

The purpose of this chapter is to show you the relationships between methodological traditions and standpoints, methodological approaches, cultures and data collection tools. We will look at how these can be arranged into a research design that is capable of producing reliable and valid findings and from which, if required, generalizations can confidently be made. We begin, however, with the most obvious question.

What is research design?

Research design and the methods you use to collect your data are not the same thing. Data collection and its analysis are parts of research design. There are a number of ways of thinking about what research design is. The first is to think of it as the structure that holds together your research and enables you to address your research questions in ways that are appropriate, efficient and effective (reliable and valid). The structure of your design acts, and can also be thought of, as the scaffolding that supports the purpose of your research. As such it needs to be put together with care so that it does not let you down by being unable to support your research when needed. In this section we will look at the methodological logic of research design, showing how the major parts should be linked together into a strategy for your research and at how the tactics you decide on to implement your strategy are linked to the type of research you intend to undertake.

THE METHODOLOGICAL LOGIC OF RESEARCH DESIGN

Achieving a methodological logic in your research design involves making coherent and reasoned connections between the choices you have made and which methodological tradition to follow, which approach and which data collection methods you use. Figure 10.1 shows the logic of research design in terms of these major choices.

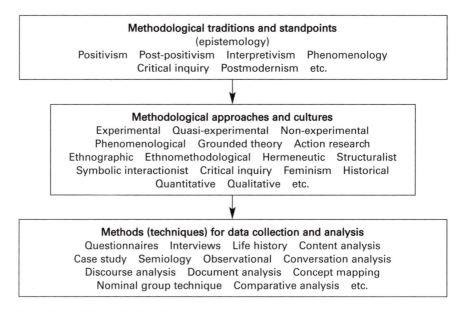

FIGURE 10.1   THE METHODOLOGICAL LOGIC OF RESEARCH DESIGN
Source: Adapted from Crotty, 1998: 3–11.

What are implicit in Figure 10.1 are the different research cultures often used as standpoints for approaching and framing your research design. These include critical, ethnographic, feminist, theoretical, action, evaluative, hermeneutic, behavioural and ethnomethodological research cultures among others (Bentz and Shipiro, 1988). These often have their own particular histories which give them their specific heritage, linking them to a methodological tradition and methods of data collection. They also provide a starting point for understanding the discourse (language) that acts as the frame of reference for defining and describing your topic and puzzle, your research design and findings.

THE PLACE OF RESEARCH DESIGN IN THE RESEARCH PROCESS

Research design is, like other forms of design, the stage where what you have defined is made possible in a detailed specification. Producing a design specification means making choices between a range of alternatives, some of which are not easily, if at all, comparable. Figure 10.2 shows the four Ds (define, design, do and deliver) of research that we have used in this book. In Chapter 3 we looked largely at how to identify and define a research puzzle. In Chapter 5 we looked at different types of dissertation (traditional, work-based and literature review) and research (applied, theoretical, evaluative and so

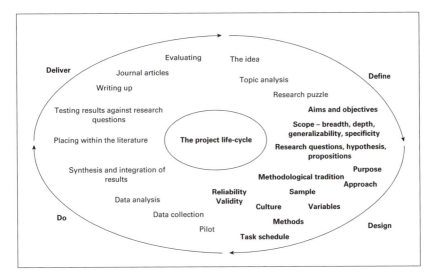

FIGURE 10.2   THE PLACE OF RESEARCH DESIGN IN THE RESEARCH PROCESS

on). This provided a bridge to selecting an approach to research based on our purposes (explain, describe and so on). Chapter 6 showed the importance of using the topic and methodological literature. It showed how the literature is an essential reference point for subsequent research and analysis. Chapters 7 and 8 took us into the space between defining and designing, and also helped us to understand methodological standpoints and appreciate some of their relative consequences. Finally, Chapter 9 highlighted the importance of ethics in research. It encouraged us to think about the nature of ethics in research and how general principles could become specific issues in our own research. Chapters 11 and 12, yet to come, will show us how to deliver some of the products of our research: the research proposal and dissertation. It will be the essential elements of our design that will be formulated into a single document – your research proposal. Figure 10.2 therefore represents much of the work required to produce the proposal.

Deciding on the type and purpose of your research

As with the design of anything, you will need to make choices by investigating (researching) the options available to you given the constraints on your time and other resources. In this section we will look at the broader choices in terms of different types of research.

DIFFERENT TYPES OF RESEARCH

One way of thinking about research design has just been outlined; another way is to ally it with different types of research. Figure 10.3 categorizes research into three main types: experimental, quasi-experimental and non-experimental. This threefold categorization is merely a useful device for identifying some of the main elements you need to bring together in your design to do your research. This categorization will also help to make clear what is involved when selecting elements to include in a design. There are, of course, other ways of categorizing research, including using the 'quantitative–qualitative' dichotomy. In some ways this simplifies comprehension. It signals the fact that qualitative approaches often involve descriptive statistical data and identify and isolate variables for discussion and interpretation, though of course for different purposes from those of experimental research (Milgram, 1974). Using Figure 10.3 as our frame of reference, we will take a brief tour around its constituent parts. The figure shows some of the constituent choices which face researchers when thinking about their research project. In some cases your discipline will influence which of these choices you make. For example, behavioural psychology tends to favour the experimental and quasi-experimental type of research, involving hypothesis testing through to the controlled measurement of variables, while anthropology favours the descriptive and ethnographic type involving immersion in the culture of those people being studied. Figure 10.3 also tries to show that there are overlaps between the types of research as they have been characterized here.

This means you will sometimes find that qualitative data has been employed to make recommendations on interventions into a situation or programme, as in the case of emancipatory research, and that quantitative data is evident in interpretivistic studies. There are no strict rules on which kinds of data should be collected for which types of research except that it should be the most appropriate to address the research questions set. The other thing to note in Figure 10.3 is the discourses commonly used by adherents of the approaches. Although only indicative they have been included to remind us that between as well as within the different traditions and approaches there are different frames of reference researchers can use to describe what may seem the same thing. You may remember we looked at this issue in Chapter 7 when we discussed the different ways the contents of a woodyard could be categorized, and that such differences were a matter of purpose based on what you intended your description to describe (for example, types of wood, wood products, properties of different woods, and so on).

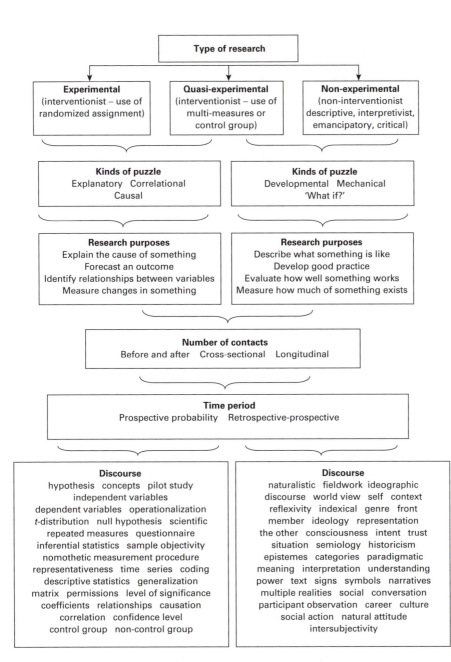

FIGURE 10.3   DIFFERENT TYPES OF RESEARCH AND ASSOCIATED STUDY
DESIGN ELEMENTS

Experimental and quasi-experimental studies aim to make an intervention in a situation to see what variable(s) cause an occurrence. The aim is to identify and determine the degree to which a relationship exists between two things: the degree to which one thing, the independent variable, causes another, the dependent variable (Field and Hole, 2002). If, given certain conditions and processes, one thing is found to cause another, then a causal relationship has been found. The two main types of experimental design are the randomized experiment (true experiment) and the non-randomized experiment (quasi-experiment). Randomization refers to how cases and controls for a study were *selected* and then *assigned* to samples from a larger population. This brings up the matter of sampling and the degree to which a sample can be said to represent (confidence in generalizability, also known as *external validity*) a population. We look in more detail at sampling later in this chapter. Random selection and assignment works like this. Say you have a population of 1,000 athletes and draw 100 randomly from this: you have a random sample. If you further randomly assign 50 of these to be cases exposed to some motivational counselling and the others, as controls, to no counselling, you have a random assignment. What this means is that anyone in the population group has an equal chance of being assigned to either a case or control (or left in the population).

EXPERIMENTAL AND DESCRIPTIVE RESEARCH DESIGNS

In aiming to state the variable that causes an outcome to happen, experimental approaches use many forms of design to study the effects of an intervention. These include looking at post-experimental outcomes, pre- and post-outcomes and at differences between a case and a control group. In the post-experimental study, subjects who are known to have been exposed to some variable (intervention) in the past are the source of data and information to see if the exposure can be said to be the cause of their current state. Subjects are often asked to recall their situation prior to the intervention and to describe the intervention. Personal interviews, questionnaires and documentary records are often the source of data and information. The key problems with this kind of study include relying on documents to be accurate and sufficiently detailed and the ability of people to be able to recall past states of being and not miss extraneous variables which may have intervened over the time period. In the pre- and post-design, the 'before' is constructed and the intervention introduced, usually under controlled conditions, and its effects measured. The time lapse between the two main measures is also a problem with this design. Subjects may have changes in behaviour, attitudes and opinions, due to variables outside the control of the research design.

This design is, however, suited to evaluation studies where the aim is to evaluate the effectiveness of a programme. If evaluation is built into the programme (for example, an educational programme to raise literacy rates among a population), then the before and after can be evaluated, but only if sufficient and accurate data was collected on a sample of the population before the programme is implemented. With a case and control group it is normal for the design to use at least two samples from two populations. Measurements are made on both groups to provide base-line information on each group before the randomized cases are subject to an intervention. The difference, if any, caused by the intervention between the case and the control is then quantified using analytical statistics.

Descriptive non-experimental research is also interested in identifying variables and relationships between them. There are, of course, different degrees of association and different ways of describing a phenomenon. The most common form of statistically based descriptive study aims to quantify the extent of a phenomenon to answer questions of 'how much?', 'how frequently?' and 'how many on average?'. The design is usually based on a *case* where the subject is measured only once; a *cross-section* of some behaviour is observed based on a sample from a population. A case is someone (or thing) that exhibits the attributes (for example, behaviours) you are interested in. Other people not exhibiting the behaviours are known as the *control group*. If the attribute is measured more than once, the series is called a *case series*.

Descriptive studies measure the occurrence of phenomenon without intervening, that is, making changes to behaviour. In some cases it would be difficult and unethical to intervene. For example, Raine et al. (1997) studied the brains of people found guilty of murder and compared them with those of 'ordinary' people; there was no way they could have randomly assigned participants to groups or made any other kind of intervention. In behavioural analysis the descriptive strategy may involve something like the following. A particular behaviour is selected, a phenomenon, that occurs relatively frequently among a subject group in a particular setting. The behaviour of subjects is observed for at least three sessions and in three ways, that is, whole-interval, partial-interval and momentary time-sampling. Observations are also done by other researchers rotating across the types of observation. When the particular behaviour occurs it is scored on the record sheet. Each type of observation should have at least one inter-observer whose observational record agrees with another's to a degree of at least 80 per cent. The observations can then be analysed and presented as a graph. Measures are often done through a survey, interviews and observations. Ideally, comparison is made between a case and control group over time; this is called the longitudinal study (Koluchova, 1972; Hodges and Tizard, 1989). Descriptive studies are also used to identify attitudes, needs and differences between people. In the management litera- ture, for example, we see studies looking at the differences between leaders (cases) and non-leaders (control) which aim to identify what variables lead to individu- als becoming leaders. Comparison between the two is often made on the basis of testing different theories through a hypothesis such as leadership is innate or situa- tional. Researchers look to see what leaders have been exposed to in the past (genes, situations), causing them to become leaders. These are called retrospective studies because they aim to identify common factors that may have influenced the subjects to become cases rather than controls. Alternatively (and even at the same time), you can look to select potential variables at the start of a study (for example, lack of expo- sure to sunlight) to measure the degree to which they are the cause of something (for example, depression) after a period of time. These are called prospective or cohort studies.

INTERPRETIVIST AND DESCRIPTIVE RESEARCH DESIGN

Just as it is a mistake to say that experimental and descriptive research is wholly quan- titative, so too is it a mistake to say that interpretivist research is wholly qualitative. Much of the debate about interpretivist research is largely from within the tradition itself (Hammersley, 1992) and is about the methods used to capture qualitative data, the contextual and historical influences (for example, gender, ethnicity), and how much emphasis to give to which version of idealism (for example, Kant, Hegel). The debate over methods rather than methodology misses many of the more interesting and pro- ductive points of what humans are about, which is their constant search for under- standing, and this means making interpretations about what something means and what is going on (Cicourel, 1964). In many ways an interpretivist research design can be far more difficult to construct than one based on the measurement of variables. This is because there are many more issues and problems to be addressed in the course of doing the research than in experimental studies. Taking an open-systems approach raises problems of data type, quality and variety, reproducibility, validity and reliabil- ity and involvement with the setting and subjects. However, it is the character of inter- pretivist research that often makes it challenging and the findings worth the effort. While Table 10.1 summarizes two main strands of interpretivism, you are strongly recommended to read some of the literature and examples for yourself to gain a much

TABLE 10.1   SUMMARY OF INTERPRETIVIST RESEARCH DESIGNS

Empirical orientation	Hermeneutic orientation
Pragmatism Taking the view that action is creative and reflexive, used when routine behaviour is found to be problematic in pursuing everyday understanding.	**Wholes to parts** Using the assumption that different cultural things are parts, and therefore accountable, because of larger meaning structures (wholes).
Ideography Careful and detailed description rather than explanation of particular cases. Focusing on individual phenomena to identify key principles of understanding; regarding the production of description as an achievement in itself.	**Underlying meaning** Assumption that cultural products and processes have, and are a part of, underlying patterns which makes them understandable and meaningful. The underlying pattern is made visible by elevating interpretation beyond the particular and commonsense level.
Exploration Use of an open, flexible approach combined with introspection and continued revision of initial concepts. Works by taking the stance that research is an interaction with theory and the empirical – that any rational basis to research is a question for reflection rather than a procedure of research itself.	**Empathy** Employing internal intuitive understanding to see the original intention of something, thereby going beyond the mere external facts; but using the facts as the means to re-enact and recover meaning.
Sensitizing concepts Use of concepts derived from analogies such as the dramaturgical frame of reference (Erving Goffman) to orient the focus and description. The concepts guide rather than lead investigation and exploration.	**Contextuality** Viewing everything as existing within a context – historical, religious, political – so that particular artistic or cultural works are explainable with reference to the context (as texts) of their creation. Originality of perspective is possible by placing a text within a new context.

(Continued)

TABLE 10.1 (CONTINUED)

Empirical orientation	Hermeneutic orientation
Social action Focus on the social interactions between actors, especially their intersubjective use of symbols, gestures and behaviours to convey information about their selves. May be contrasted with a concern for abstract social structures.	**Text** Data whether quantitative or qualitative is text: it has context in terms of its relationships to how it was produced and to larger social structures. Facts are thus the outcome (results) of interrogating data within broader systems of meaning.
Inductive case study Preference for studying a particular social phenomenon within definite social settings, over time, among a particular group of actors. Involves looking to see what categories and concepts emerge from the data rather than imposing a theory on it beforehand.	**Metaphor** Claiming correspondence between two things based on systems of meaning, a feeling and an object, e.g. love and a rose. Language provides the parameters constraining images to create similarity from difference.
Empirical materials Extensive use of field notes, video, audio and other tools to capture naturally occurring social interactions in the analysis.	**Authenticity** Employing evidence to provide (convince) beyond all reasonable doubt that a thing is what it is claimed to be. Involves questioning the thing and its provenance to get to the essential condition to establish it as genuine.

deeper understanding before making any choices on whether or not to employ them in your own research.

Characterizing the interpretivist approach cannot be done as simply as with the experimental approach. This is because the characterizations tend to have recourse to the history of the tradition, citing the Chicago School (Bulmer, 1984), and exemplars from the symbolic interactionist (Goffman, 1961, Becker, 1953) tradition along with ethnographic studies (Geertz, 1973), to hermeneutic analysis (Ricoeur, 1981) and emancipatory studies (which aim to bring about change) associated with critical theory and feminist analysis. A common feature of the references used in characterizations (such as the ones just cited) is a concern for a methodology these researchers believe produces results in ways which answer the questions of what is going on in a situation and how people do what they do.

Researchers such as Goffman and Becker are not concerned with technical procedures such as the operationalization of concepts or with procedural protocols such as internal validity. Their concern is with producing adequate descriptions that answer their research questions in ways which are a logical consequence of following through a methodological set of assumptions about the nature of the social world and how it is able to be described. Their results are essentially descriptions of the formal properties people exhibit in their behaviours and accounts of those behaviours. They are not re-formulations of what people do or theorize about (Gilbert and Mulkay, 1983). The aim is to identify and describe the knowledge people need to have in order to do what they do and be seen to be doing what they do by those relevant to them in their situation. An interpretivist design is not therefore a matter of 'anything goes', but is rooted in the kinds of methodological assumptions and argument we encountered in Chapter 7 when we looked at the debate Schutz and Parsons (Grathoff, 1978) had over the nature of social reality and how it might be known for analysis. Interpretivism is not then about saying how people 'see', 'understand' or 'interpret' the world, but is about identifying what procedural state of affairs (Sharrock and Watson, 1988) needs to exist in order for people to 'see' something like this rather than that which gives rise to the behaviours (courses of actions) they consequently follow (exhibit). This strategy can be used to design empirical investigations as well as critical evaluations of theories, concepts, arguments and discourse.

Interpretivist research design therefore has, like that of experimental design, a broad remit from the highly empirical, such as conversation analysis, to the extremely theoretical, such as hermeneutics. The central design features of the former usually include a combination of pragmatism, descriptive (ideographic) exploration, social action, sensitizing concepts, inductive case studies and an overriding concern for empirical materials (Alvesson and Sköldberg, 2000: 13–15) collected through data-oriented methods. The design features of the latter include intuition, relating parts to wholes, looking for underlying meanings, empathy, contextuality, text and authenticity (2000: 52–109). Among the empirically oriented typical approaches include those labelled 'grounded theory' (Glaser and Strauss, 1967), Chicago ethnography (Bulmer, 1984), 'symbolic interactionism' (Rock, 1979), 'phenomenological method' (Moustakas, 1994), 'ethnomethodology' (Heritage, 1984), 'conversation analysis' (Psathas, 1995) and 'inductive ethnography' (Fetterman, 1989). In hermeneutic-orientated research typical approaches are labelled objectivist, alethic, historicist, existentialist, poetic and ethnographic (Alvesson, and Sköldberg, 2000; Packer and Addison, 1989). What this classification shows is the many positions and standpoints within the broad category 'interpretivist'.

DIFFERENT RESEARCH CULTURES AND PURPOSES

The type of research you choose should be capable of addressing your research questions. It may, on occasion, reflect your own ontological, epistemological and moral preferences, for example for a realist or idealist ontology and for experimental, interpretivist or emancipatory research. One of the problems you may face is the overwhelming range of research cultures and standpoints. Few people, if any, can gain sufficient knowledge to practise all kinds of research. Therefore try to select which kind of research orientation and culture accords with your research questions and stance as early as possible. This will still involve substantial reading, but this can be limited by focusing in on key studies and debates. Table 10.2 provides a brief overview of some approaches commonly used in masters research, along with an indicative list of readings and sources, sufficient to allow you to undertake a reconnaissance into that 'field' of research.

Designing in quality: generalizing, validity, sampling, reliability, measurement, triangulation and objectivity

Quality in research can mean a number of things, including: that the tools used to collect the data were the right ones; the data collected was the right kind and quantity; the observations made were the right kinds of observations; and the interpretations made were clear and transparent. It is often assumed that the experimental method can be the model for other kinds of research, in that it sets the standards of quality all research should emulate. This is largely a myth. This section will look at designing, to a sufficient degree, quality in your research project. We will look at what it means to be objective and neutral, how to assure reliability and how to produce valid findings.

TABLE 10.2 EXAMPLES OF AND SOURCES ON DIFFERENT RESEARCH STANDPOINTS AND CULTURES

Types of research	Brief description	Indicative print and Internet sources and resources
Experimental (*positivist and post-positivist*)	When the aim is to identify causality, independent and dependent variables are identified and defined, subjects randomly assigned to control and experimental groups and exposed to effects. The three main conditions for causality to be established are: (1) association between two or more variables; (2) the time and order of the effect is controlled; and (3) the effects of confounding variables are systematically eliminated. Quasi-experimental research can only identify relationships between variables in terms of correlations. Associated with positivism and realist methodological assumptions.	Campbell and Stanley, 1963; Field and Hole, 2002; Kitto, 1989; Bandura, Ross and Ross, 1963; Lazarsfeld and Rosenberg, 1955; Loftus and Palmer, 1974; Piliavin, Rodin and Piliavin, 1969; Rosenthal and Jacobson, 1966; Greenacre, 1993; <u>A primer on experimental and quasi-experimental design.</u>
Ethnographic (*interpretivist*)	Direct observation, either as participant or non-participant, of the activities of a group over time, describing their routine behaviours including such things as beliefs and social relations (culture), consists of ethnography: 'graph' as in description and 'ethno' as in people. Data can also include objects, art, dress, documents etc. An approach associated with Malinowski, Radcliff-Brown and Lévi-Strauss.	Agar, 1985; Atkinson, 1990; Becker, 1970; Bulmer, 1982; <u>Center for Ethnographic Research: Center for Urban Ethnography;</u> Clifford and Marcus, 1986; Denzin, 1997; Fetterman, 1989; Fielding, 1981; Geer, 1964; Goffman, 1989; Green and Wallats, 1981; <u>Handbook of Ethnography;</u> McCall and Simmons, 1969; Stewart, 1998; van Maanan, 1988; Whyte, 1943.

Note: Titles underlined mean Internet source or resource; URLs and full citations can be found in Appendix 3.

(*Continued*)

TABLE 10.2 (CONTINUED)

Types of research	Brief description	Indicative print and Internet sources and resources
Phenomenological (*interpretivist*)	The structuring of experiences of the social world is demonstrably heterogeneous. Research approaches are very varied from the highly empirical, as with conversation analysis, to the more abstract, as with hermeneutic interpretation. The aim is to describe the essence of ways in which experiences of everyday life are structured to be meaningful and sharable. An approach associated with Husserl, Schutz and Merleau-Ponty.	Binswanger, 1967; Casey, 1987; Cavalier, Lectures on Heidegger's 'Being and time'; Frick, 1990; Giorgi, 1970; Holstein and Gubrium, 1998; Ihde, 1986; Laing, 1965; Moustakas, 1990 and 1994; Packer and Addison, 1989; Phenomenology; Psathas, 1989; Seamon and Mugerauer, 1989; Spiegelburg, 1976; van Manen, 1990; Wagner, 1983.
Grounded theory (*interpretivist*)	An emphasis on achieving in-depth, initially ideographic, studies of particular cases firmly based on the systematic exploration and categorization of empirical materials. The aim is to bridge the gap between deductive theory and statistical abstraction and empirical data to achieve a balance between theory generation and verification. Categories are developed out of the data, are saturated with other data from similar cases to test relevance, and then used to develop more general analytical frameworks for transfer to other settings. An approach strongly associated with Glaser and Strauss with its origins in symbolic interactionism and statistical positivism.	Glaser and Strauss, 1967; Goulding, 2002; Hutchinson, 1988; Locke, 2001; Pandit, The creation of theory: a recent application of the Grounded Theory method; Strauss and Corbin, 1990, 1994, 1997, 1998.

(Continued)

TABLE 10.2 (CONTINUED)

Types of research	Brief description	Indicative print and Internet sources and resources
Surveys (*positivist and post-positivist*)	The use of mailed, self-administered questionnaires and interviews to gather large amounts of data on a topic from a large number of people. Normally based on sampling, the survey is often used to describe frequencies of behaviours and attitudes and sometimes to identify relationships between variables (correlation) and test hypotheses. Often associated with the poverty research of Booth and Rowntree and statistically based opinion generalization studies.	Aldridge and Levine, 2001; Bourque and Fielder, 1995; Cartwright and Seale, 1990; Dale, Arber and Proctor, 1988; de Vaus, 1991; Fink, 1995; Foddy, 1993; Fowler, 2001; Hoinville and Jowell, 1987; Home Office, 1983; Hyman, 1955; Kish, 1965; Marsh, 1982; Moser, 1971; Oppenheim, 1992; Petersen, 2000; ResearchInfo.com; Rowntree, 1901; Salant and Dillman, 1994; Sampling guide; Sapsford, 1999; Statistical good practice guidelines; Statistics Glossary; Tacq, 1997; Trochim; University of Wisconsin Cooperative Extension; Wells, 1935.
Case study (*positivist and post-positivist or interpretivist*)	A focus on a single case (person, group, setting etc.) allows investigation of the details, including contextual matters, of a phenomenon. Usually ideographic the emphasis is on explication and illumination rather than variables. In psychology often used to explore the exceptional case and in conversation analysis the deviant case. Historically associated with Freud's psychological studies and with sociological community studies.	Abramson, 1992; Feagin, Orum and Sjoberg, 1991; Gomm, Hammersley and Foster, 2000; Hamel, Dufour and Fortin, 1993; Merriam, 1988; Ragin and Becker, 1992; Stake, 1995; Travers, 2001; Yin, 1993.

(Continued)

TABLE 10.2   (CONTINUED)

Types of research	Brief description	Indicative print and Internet sources and resources
Action research (*emancipatory*)	When a problem is faced by a group in a common situation a researcher, who may be a member of the group, may act as an agent to encourage understanding of the situation and identification of lines of action to bring about change and improvement. Group members are encouraged to take an active (action oriented) role in the research itself, to identify changes, implement changes and conduct subsequent evaluation. The approach is often associated with management and organizational research.	Action research: an electronic reader: Argyris, 1993; Argyris, Putnam and McLain, 1985; Carr and Kemmis, 1986; Collaborative action research network; Dick, 1997; Heron, 1996; Oja and Smuljan, 1989; Whyte, 1991; Coghlan and Brannick, 2000; Greenwood and Levin, 1998; Reason and Bradbury, 2000; Action Research International; Center for Action Research in Professional Practice.
Critical theory (*emancipatory*)	An interdisciplinary approach to social analysis and evaluation based on the early works of Marx and later works of Freud. The premise that multiple realities are shaped by historical, social, ethnic, gender and disabilities values as well as economic ones is used to suggest *what ought to be* over what is. Focus is on places in society where forces for emancipation can be actualized, especially in discourse which is regarded as distorting and restraining. Associated with the Frankfurt School and Habermas.	Adorno, 1991 and 1994; Braaten, 1991; Boyle, 1996; Burawoy, 1979; Calhoun, 1995; Connerton, 1976; Deetz, 1992; Ewert, 1991; Fay, 1987; Forester, 1993; Habermas, 1984; Haraway, 1991; Held, 1980; Kincheloe and McLaren, 1994; LaCapra, 1989; Lasch, 1978; Leiss, 1978; Marcuse, 1964; Morrow and Brown, 1994; Radnitzky, 1970; Thompson and Held, 1982; Young, 1990.

(Continued)

TABLE 10.2 (CONTINUED)

Types of research	Brief description	Indicative print and Internet sources and resources
Feminist methodology (*emancipatory*)	The application, using a range of methods and approaches, of women's perspective and standpoint to explore critically and document the position of women relative to men (and other women) in terms of income, health, status, career, domesticity etc., in order to critique and suggest what ought to be; an emancipatory and critical approach. Women's oppression, discrimination and exploitation are examined in all forms of analysis including statistical, discourse and ethnographic. Often associated with Mary Wollstonecraft, J.S. Mill, Simone de Beauvoir, Kate Millett, Germaine Greer, Sheila Rowbotham and Foucault.	Feminist research methods; Fonow, and Cook, 1991; Hammersley, 1992 and 1995; Humphries and Truman, 1994; Jaggar and Struhl, 1978; Keohane, Rosaldo and Gelpi, 1981–82; Maynard and Purvis, 1994; Reinharz, 1992; Roberts, 1981; Stanley, 1990; Sydie, 1987; Warren, 1988; Sociological Research Online.
Virtual phenomena (*post-positivist* or *interpretivist*)	Studies of how people use, understand and interact with virtual reality (software, Internet, World Wide Web), especially in chat groups, have established a new research orientation often referred to as 'computer mediated communication'. Various approaches have been adapted to unobtrusive observation and analysis of behaviour in cyberspace, including network analysis, ethnography and ethnomethodology.	Birnbaum, 2000; Center for Electronic Commerce; Coomber, 1997; Dourish, 2001; Hine, 2000; Jones, 1999; Murray, 1997; Journal of On-line Behaviour; Resources Centre for Cyber-culture; Cybersociology; Journal of Computer Mediated Communication.

(Continued)

TABLE 10.2 (CONTINUED)

Types of research	Brief description	Indicative print and Internet sources and resources
Evaluation (*post-positivist or interpretivist or emancipatory*)	Specific assessment for the purposes of making recommendations for change to a policy, programme or product. Uses whatever data collection tool and approach is appropriate, including attitude measurement, performance indicators, ratings scale, questionnaires and unobtrusive measures. The aim of action change makes evaluation inherently political. Summative evaluation aims to evaluate 'effectiveness and need' so as to provide data for decisions on the continuance, changes to, or merger of a policy or programme. Formative evaluation is mostly done to provide evidence on design decisions during the development of a policy or programme.	House, 1993; Hadley and Mitchell, 1995; Fetterman, 1994; Scriven, 1991; Green, 1994; Madaus, Stufflebeam and Scriven, 1983; Chen and Rossi, 1992; Stake, 1983; Denzin and Lincoln, 1994; Patton, 1990; Popham, 1988; Posavac and Carey, 1992; Rossi and Freeman, 1993.

Before we do, however, you need to know that your methodological allegiances and that of any particular discipline often influence understandings and practical approaches to research quality. For instance, if you believe that an empirical world exists independently of human reason and that research methods are able to penetrate that world, then you may also believe as a consequence that a neutral descriptive language is a possibility. This position may lead you into making estimates, based on statistical calculations, of the degree of reliability your methods may have. Conversely, though not necessarily opposed, if you believe that the empirical world is knowable through such things as the language used to describe it, then you may have a very different understanding of what it means for a method to be valid. It follows that if language shapes or even constitutes reality and the ways in which a reality may be known, then objectivity and validity become matters dependent upon the particular discourse used in a research project. Taking these two possible positions as starting points, we will now look at what is assumed about research.

GENERALIZATION

Not all research is compelled to aim for, or produce, generalizations. Even in randomized experiments and quasi-experimental research, maintaining reliable generalizations is difficult. A generalization is a statement normally made about a population based on a study of a sample of that population. The basic formulae are that when X then Y, or when X, your chances of getting Y are Z times as high under conditions P and Q. In everyday life generalizations (making inferences) are routine and normal and this expectation is often carried over into research. Following on the critique of Fielding and Fielding (1986) of social research, Silverman (1989) in a study of two social science journals found a tendency for authors to select data which matched their preconception of the phenomenon and to select exciting and dramatic data for discussion and argument. Citing Bryman (1988: 77), Silverman (1997: 153) contends that these practices, along with the seeming disregard for validity, are grounds for concern about the representativeness and generalizability of some social science research. In this section we will look at the options and related issues concerning generalizations in research and at what you will need to consider when justifying your position and choices to do with compromises between generalization and specificity and between breadth and depth. Figure 10.4 provides an overview of this in terms of the broad methods of data collection associated with these.

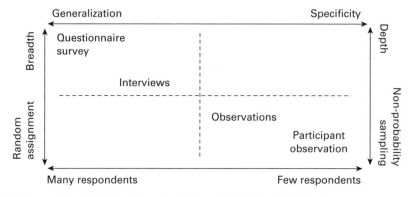

FIGURE 10.4   GENERALIZATION, SPECIFICITY, BREADTH AND DEPTH

As an initial starting point, following Ragin (1994), we will make a distinction between three equally valid kinds of generalization in social research. The most common type of generalization, often sought by experimental research, is *statistical generalization*. By statistical generalization is meant the use of standard statistically based random sampling methods and statistical analysis where either a causal or correlational relationship is produced, within a closed-systems approach. Hence when X then Y, or when X, your chances of getting Y are Z times as high under conditions P and Q. The second kind is *comparative generalization*, of the type often sought in evaluation and cross-national studies. Comparative studies aim to generalize using an open-systems approach by selecting criteria, applying them and evaluating them using comparative cases. The outcome is usually the identification of conditions which give rise to certain consequences. The third kind is *concept generalization* (or analytical generalization), of the type sought by ethnomethodological and conversation analysis studies. The aim is to use general concepts to analyse instances (specimens) to see if general formulations of devices, methods and principles can be used to inform the analysis of other specimens (ten Have, 1999: 135). The outcome is normally the replication of analysis with other, often 'deviant cases', instances of naturally occurring interaction to make visible an aspect of the 'procedural infrastructure of interaction' (Schegloff, 1992: 1338, quoted in ten Have, 1999: 136). Whatever kind of approach to generalization is taken, the problem nearly always seems to be that we are expected to address generalization in terms of the discourse of the experimental and the closed-systems approach. The main elements of this discourse an be classified as discussions about measurement, validity, sampling, reliability, objectivity and triangulation. It is taken as a matter of course that all research

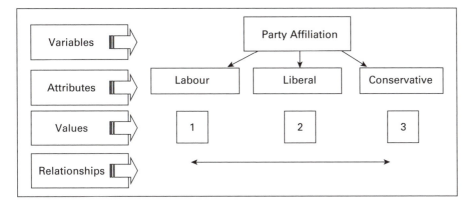

FIGURE 10.5   VARIABLES, ATTRIBUTES, VALUES AND RELATIONSHIPS

seeks to produce learning which can be transferred to other contexts and research problems. It is in this sense, the learning one, that being knowledgeable about the nature of generalization is important.

LEVELS OF MEASUREMENT

In many cases research involves assigning a value to attributes which are variable amongst a population. Figure 10.5 shows this in terms of affiliation to mainstream political parties in the UK.

We have already described the relationship between concepts, definitions and variables in Chapter 3, but it is also important to know what kind of measurement you are using and what you can do with the data it produces. If you do not know these, then you cannot design your research properly as you will not be able to fulfil its design purposes, know what kinds of analysis will be possible and what kinds of relationships between variables can be investigated. In the case of party political affiliation, shown in Figure 10.5, the values assigned are merely shorthand. In themselves these mean nothing and certainly not that 3 is higher, better or superior to 1 and 2. We call this shorthand the *nominal* level: the level at which a numerical value is assigned to an attribute. We do this because in a typical questionnaire we may have several dozen attributes and will need a unique shorthand descriptor for each. There are no statistical tests you can do to nominal values and you certainly cannot rank them. Surveys and interview schedules therefore employ other levels of measurement. In ascending order these are: the ordinal, by which attributes can be ordered; the interval, by which attributes can be given meaningful distances between them; and the ratio level, which allows an absolute zero to be used. Appendix 2 summarizes what you can do with which level of measurement.

VALIDITY

Validity is not about measurement in the same way, as we will see, that reliability is. Validity is about ensuring that you build into your research sufficient robustness to have the confidence to make generalizations. Designing research that is robust in these terms means paying careful attention to integrating a number of elements within your research. Although some complex approaches have been developed for establishing validity in research, such as the 'nomological net' (Cronbach and Meehl, 1955) and 'multitrait-multimethod matrix' (Campbell and Fiske, 1962), for most purposes such a level of design is to over-engineer and provide far more than is usually necessary and sufficient for masters research, though more is said about this in the section on triangulation. Figure 10.6 outlines the main elements of validity, showing the relationships between them, and indicates which can be built into the overall research design.

Using Figure 10.6 and Table 10.3 as reference points, we can briefly explain through an example (based on those given in Judd et al., 1991: 30–36, and van Dalen, 1979: 135–8) the main elements and principles of validity. In educational policy research there is a longstanding concern to be able to measure educational achievement accurately. In the UK this concern is allied with that of class sizes. It is assumed by many parents and teachers that the higher the number of pupils in a class (class size), the lower will be the overall educational achievement of pupils in that class. A correlation is assumed, and can be hypothesized, to exist between the independent variable, class size, and the dependent variable, educational achievement. Looking at Figure 10.6 we can divide validity into three main parts – construct, internal and external validity – which are described in Table 10.3.

What Table 10.3 shows is that validity is about carefully constructing definitions of your concepts, hypotheses or propositions so that they can be translated clearly and predictably into detailed operational methods, down to the level of specific questions and observations. It is about ensuring that there are strong transparent relationships between the conceptual or theoretical part of your research, the phenomenon you

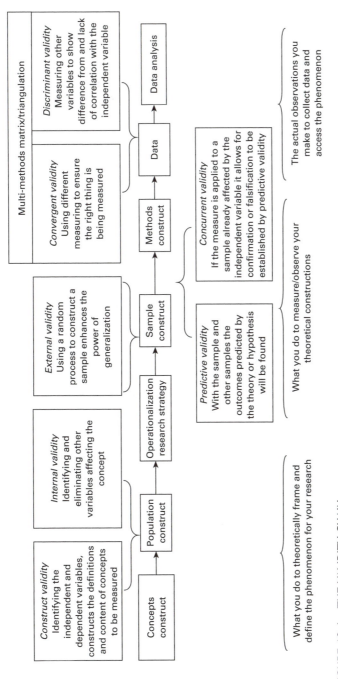

FIGURE 10.6   THE VALIDITY CHAIN

TABLE 10.3   CONSTRUCT, INTERNAL AND EXTERNAL VALIDITY: CLASS SIZE AND EDUCATIONAL ACHIEVEMENT

Types of validity	Educational achievement/ large class size	Issues to be addressed
Construct validity	Defining the meaning of the variables and deducing certain consequences which should be observable if the construct hypothesized does exist: using the literature, experts, teachers, etc., to construct definitions. Classifying what is meant by a large class and small class, educational achievement and under-achievement.	Different experts and people will have different views on what counts as a large class and educational achievement. We can rarely measure just one construct of a variable. A test will also measure test anxiety, motivation, reading ability and concentration levels. Test marking will measure grading decisions (teachers' biases) and classifications. Multi-measures are often used (multi-operationalizations) to argue that the same thing and the right construct (as defined) is being measured.
Internal validity	Identifying the degrees of relation-ship between all sensible variables on the phenomenon (gender, weight of pupils, height etc.), using random assignment to select pupils for different class sizes and overcoming threats to accuracy and effects of measurement.	Identifying a relationship between variables is not sufficient to claim causality. A number of threats to internal validity need to be addressed. You need to know (amongst other things): how pupils were selected to be in the classes you are measuring (selection threat); what effect time has on pupils in different classes (maturation threat); the effect of being included in the research (Hawthorne effect). To establish causality different class sizes need observing whose pupil cohorts have been randomly assigned. If using different operational definitions of the concept, e.g. written tests, testimony of the teacher and interviews with pupils, and there is a high degree of overlap (convergence validity) between the different measures, then it is assumed we are measuring the same construct.

(Continued)

TABLE 10.3 (CONTINUED)

Types of validity	Educational achievement/ large class size	Issues to be addressed
		The number of agreements will give us the correlation between them. Ideally, the same measures should show a difference and fail to correlate with other constructs, e.g. height of students (discriminant validity).
External validity	The extent and warrant we have to make generalizations from our study to the wider population from which our sample(s) were selected. Generalizations are also predictions, i.e. the larger the class size the lower the educational achievement will be and conversely the smaller the class size the higher the educational achievement of pupils. The extent to which we can extrapolate from the data depends on how we have been able to control the sampling process.	The ability or warrant to generalize is determined by the type of research possible and the limits we place on the population we wish to generalize, too. If pupils cannot be randomly assigned to classes of different sizes, then we cannot have a causal explanation but can have a test of correlation. The population, setting and behaviour should be defined as precisely as possible. What pupils, in which kinds of schools, at what ages, of which gender and ethnicity, in what kinds of villages, towns or cities, doing which subjects, are the kinds of things that need specifying. Using a random sampling technique to select a sample increases the degree of external validity, i.e. the confidence in generalizations. Using random assignment to select who goes in which class increases internal validity, i.e. confidence in establishing a causal relationship between the variables.

have identified for investigation and the method you intend to use to get access to that phenomenon. Your methods operationalize your concepts and so provide a bridge to 'reality' – as you have assumed it to be from your particular methodological standpoint (remember, methods do not provide a bridge to 'truth'). The assumption is that if you correctly integrate these elements, which include appropriate sample construction, you will have the basis for making generalizations beyond the sample of subjects you have researched.

While an understanding of these three main types of validity is important in evaluating the research others have done, their relevance is relative to the kind of research you intend to do. If you are able and are aiming to undertake experimental research, then the technical details of Cronbach and Meehl's (1955) 'nomological net' and Campbell and Fiske's (1962) 'multitrait-multimethod matrix' may be relevant. If you are unable to control your research to this degree, yet are interested in identifying relationships between variables or applications of classifications and categories, you may wish to focus on construct validity. This means looking to examine or test prior constructs of variables to see if replication is possible in a different setting at a different time.

SAMPLING: SIGNIFICATION AND CONFIDENCE

One of the most common questions students ask is 'How large should my sample be?' The answer depends on the type of research you are doing and the degree of confidence you are aiming to have for your generalizations. For these reasons, in this section we will try to answer many of the most common questions about sampling at masters level, but in a way that explains the methodological assumptions sampling is based on. There are numerous excellent textbooks on sampling and statistics which should be used to acquire more knowledge of the technical details of calculations and sample size determination.

WHAT IS SAMPLING AND WHEN IS IT NECESSARY?

Sampling is a procedure for generalizing about a population (people, organizations, behaviours and so on) without researching every unit (person, organization, behaviour and so on) in that population. All kinds of research, not just experimental and quantitative studies, can use some form of sampling procedure. It is, however, not a necessary requirement that all research uses sampling as part of its design. For example, if you are studying behaviour amongst your peer students and there are

50 of them, you could survey all 50. In which case, sample selection would be largely irrelevant if you could show that these students were your population and that you did not want to generalize about other students outside of your class. Sampling then, of some type, is necessary in varying degrees if you are aiming to make inferences about a phenomenon based on a study of instances of that phenomenon when the popula-

> **Definition**
> Sampling is about carefully selecting a sub-set (sample or samples) of a specific population that can be shown to share the properties or variables of the population. Findings from the sample can then be employed to make inferences, to varying degrees of confidence, about the larger population.

tion is too large for all units to be studied. If, however, you are aiming to analyse a phenomenon, say in a piece of conversation, then generalization is not likely to be a part of your research design and sampling would be irrelevant, though not the issues of validity of the data and reliability of your technique for analysis (see ten Have, 1999 for a sound discussion of these issues). Sampling is an intentional activity rather than prerequisite based on the needs of your research and is not a necessity for all research. When used it involves applying procedures in ways which are transparent in order to identify sufficient sources of data for the study of the phenomenon and selection of appropriate techniques to analyse measurements. This allows judgements to be made about relationships between values and inferences and predictions to be made about other members of the population who were not part of the research.

THE ASSUMPTIONS OF SAMPLING

Although many textbooks on sampling and statistics fail to mention it, the methodological idea of sampling is simple. It is based on the assumption that a population (a theoretical category of things) will have a mean value and a deviation from this (standard deviation) will be dispersed about its mean. It you are unfamiliar with standard deviation, its principles are easy to pick up from most standard statistics textbooks, but you should be able to grasp the idea from the figures and text that follow. If a sub-set of the population is carefully selected, it too will have a mean value and a standard deviation. The assumption is that, even though there is no way of knowing for certain about the characteristics of the entire population, there will be a correspondence between the mean of the sample and that of the population. On this basis inferences can be made about the population based on the sample. This basic

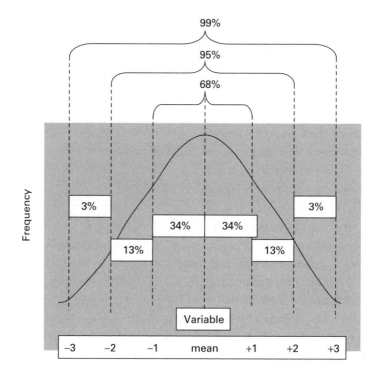

FIGURE 10.7   APPROXIMATE AREAS UNDER THE NORMAL DISTRIBUTION

assumption is the foundation of what is detailed in most of the literature and one main aspect of this is the principle of confidence in generalization.

THE PRINCIPLES OF CONFIDENCE LEVELS

One of the keys to understanding sampling is to grasp the implications of the normal distribution. Figure 10.7 shows an idealized normal distribution. Do not worry if what it is about is unclear: I will soon explain things. The normal curve has some properties which, once you understand them, can have some powerful uses in making inferences and predictions about a population. To understand these properties a simple example may help. If we take 100 students whose assessed course work has a mean (average) mark of 62 with a standard deviation of 17, then we can do some basic calculations which will allow us to predict what percentage of students will attain a mark within a given range. We do this by calculating the standard error of the mean by dividing the standard deviation (17) by the square root of the population, which looks like this:

$$17/\sqrt{100} = 17/10 = 1.7$$

Taking our mean mark of 62, we use the standard error of 1.7 to produce a range like this:

$$62 + 1.7 = 63.7 \qquad\qquad 62 - 1.7 = 60.3$$

This means 68 per cent of the sample will have a mean mark within the range of 60.3 to 63.7 and that 32 per cent will not. That is, there is a 16 per cent chance that the mean is greater than 68 per cent and a 16 per cent chance that it is less than 68 per cent (on Figure 10.7 this is 13% + 3%). Is a 68 per cent probability good enough or would you need to reduce the chance of 32 per cent falling outside this range? You can increase the range within which the population can fall and hence reduce the probability of some student marks falling outside the range. You can increase the level of confidence to 95 per cent and 99 per cent. You do it like this:

for a 95 per cent confidence level:

$$1.7 \times 2 = 3.4$$
$$3.4 + 62 = 65.4 \quad 62 - 3.4 = 58.6$$

This means 95 per cent of students will have a mean mark within the range of 58.6 to 65.4 for a 99 per cent confidence level:

$$1.7 \times 3 = 5.1$$
$$5.1 + 62 = 67.1 \quad 62 - 5.1 = 56.9$$

This means 99 per cent of students will have a mean mark within the range of 56.9 to 67.1.

You should now be able to see that what is represented in Figure 10.7 is an idealization. The image of the curve is useful as it reminds us of the relationship between the mean value and the standard deviation. The points showing plus or minus represent plus or minus standard deviations from the mean (usually represented by the Greek letter μ for the mean and σ for the standard deviations). Where they dissect the curve is where the curve changes. So $-1\ \sigma$ and $+1\ \sigma$ dissect the curve immediately where it changes from very steep to steep and $-2\ \sigma$ and $+2\ \sigma$ dissect it where it changes from steep to shallow. This gives us the proportion of a population that will be below and above the mean within the values of the standard deviations. Hence plus or minus one standard deviation from the mean covers 68 per cent of the population and means there is a 0.68 probability of a unit (say student mark) falling within the range (one-third will be found within the range of minus one standard deviation from the mean). It does not matter whether the shape of the curve is tall or shallow or if the population is not distributed symmetrically about the mean. The same principles apply to the area under the curve. In doing these simple calculations you can extend the range to increase confidence that the mean of the population will be within certain limits. However, it is not calculations such as these which will give accuracy to your results, but the way in which you selected your sample in the first place. If your sample is randomly selected and is of a relevant size (usually more than 30), then the mean value is not likely to change significantly even if the sample size were doubled or increased even higher.

WHAT SIZE SHOULD A SAMPLE BE?

Before you calculate what size your sample should be, it is important that you understand the context of sampling. Figure 10.8 represents this, showing in the right-hand column the elements of sampling and in the left-hand column what these mean for your sample design.

Although Figure 10.8 is mostly self-explanatory, the source you use for selecting your sample – the sampling frame – must be clearly explainable. This means you must be able to show that it is accurate, current, complete and free of duplicates and biases in the way in which it was constructed. It must not favour a particular group over another relevant to your study. As a list the sampling frame must also be legally usable, that is, not subject to laws covering data protection. However, it may not always be possible to meet all these criteria fully due to the nature of your population. If you were studying homelessness in a particular city, then whatever lists exist will, by the very nature of the populations' lifestyles, be constantly changing as subjects move in and out of the area and in and out of homelessness. For reasons such as these you need to have knowledge about your subjects that goes beyond available statistics that you can use for gathering up-to-date intelligence about the current state of affairs. So before determining what size of sample is needed, you need to understand the nature of your population in general and the peculiarities of the sampling frame. Once you know these things about the population you will be able to access, then you are ready to estimate the size of your sample. There are various calculations you can do to find the appropriate size of sample. Some resources on the Internet, called calculators,

THE THEORETICAL POPULATION This is the universe of possible and potential units, e.g. all teachers everywhere in the world	THE POPULATION YOU ARE AIMING TO GENERALIZE TO The population, people, organizations, behaviour, that exhibit the phenomenon you are researching, e.g. secondary school science teaching to girls
THE POPULATION FOR THE STUDY This is the population you know to exist and can get access to, e.g. teachers working in secondary schools in Manchester	THE POPULATION YOU HAVE ACCESS TO Those teachers and classes you can collect data about, e.g. six schools in Manchester over a term
MEANS OF SELECTING THE SAMPLE These are the reference sources you can use to identify individuals from the accessible population, e.g. employee work numbers held by the local education authority	THE SAMPLE FRAME FROM WHICH TO SELECT UNITS A list of local schools, teaching timetables, curriculum from which you can select a sample that is representative of most on the list, e.g. information from the local education authority
UNITS FOR THE STUDY The individuals selected for inclusion in the research, e.g. named teachers	THE SAMPLE FOR THE STUDY The actual schools and timetabled classes you will research, e.g. three scheduled classes per week in six schools over a 12-week period.

FIGURE 10.8   THE CONTEXT OF SAMPLING

can help you to do the mathematics. But as a rule of thumb Table 10.4 will give you a good indication of what you need.

There are now a number of readily available references for estimating sample size, such as the one shown in Table 10.4. The main point to bear in mind is that they work because of the assumptions made to produce them. Most make the assumption that a 95 per cent or 99 per cent level of confidence will be required and estimate the standard deviation. Using these resources is easy, but remember that you will need to achieve the sample number and calculate the actual standard deviation.

TABLE 10.4   RECOMMENDED SAMPLE SIZES FOR A GIVEN POPULATION
(DEGREE OF ACCURACY 0.05)

Population N	Sample S	Population N	Sample S
10	10	220	144
15	14	240	149
20	19	250	153
25	24	270	160
30	28	300	172
40	36	325	180
50	44	350	187
60	52	375	194
70	59	400	201
80	66	425	207
90	73	450	212
100	81	480	216
125	96	500	222
150	110	550	233
160	114	600	239
175	122	650	247
180	124	750	258
190	128	800	264
200	134	1000	286

SAMPLING IN PRACTICE

What has so far been indicated is that sampling is a purposeful activity and one which requires some thinking about. This can be seen in Figure 10.9, which shows the logic of sampling again, but this time in terms of the relationships between the different elements of the research process. What you can see in Figure 10.9 is the movement from the general to the particular and back from the particular to the general via the application of a range of statistical techniques. This brings us back to the logic of sampling in terms of the relationship between the population and the sample. The variables looked at in the sample, it is assumed, will be similarly distributed among the larger population. The sample, if chosen carefully, will bring the variations from the population with it. How this is to be achieved is dependent upon what type of research you

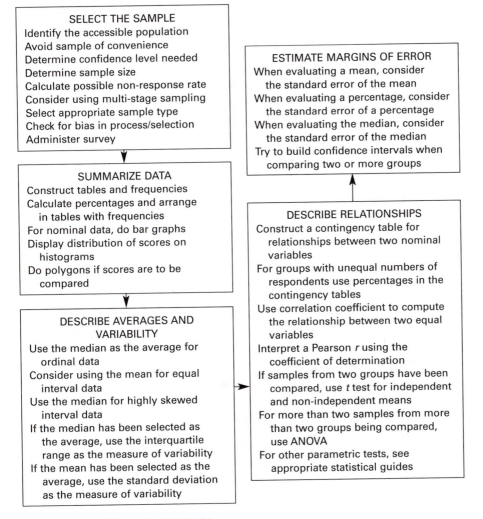

SELECT THE SAMPLE
Identify the accessible population
Avoid sample of convenience
Determine confidence level needed
Determine sample size
Calculate possible non-response rate
Consider using multi-stage sampling
Select appropriate sample type
Check for bias in process/selection
Administer survey

SUMMARIZE DATA
Construct tables and frequencies
Calculate percentages and arrange
  in tables with frequencies
For nominal data, do bar graphs
Display distribution of scores on
  histograms
Do polygons if scores are to be
  compared

DESCRIBE AVERAGES AND VARIABILITY
Use the median as the average for
  ordinal data
Consider using the mean for equal
  interval data
Use the median for highly skewed
  interval data
If the median has been selected as
  the average, use the interquartile
  range as the measure of variability
If the mean has been selected as the
  average, use the standard deviation
  as the measure of variability

ESTIMATE MARGINS OF ERROR
When evaluating a mean, consider
  the standard error of the mean
When evaluating a percentage, consider
  the standard error of a percentage
When evaluating the median, consider
  the standard error of the median
Try to build confidence intervals when
  comparing two or more groups

DESCRIBE RELATIONSHIPS
Construct a contingency table for
  relationships between two nominal
  variables
For groups with unequal numbers of
  respondents use percentages in the
  contingency tables
Use correlation coefficient to compute
  the relationship between two equal
  variables
Interpret a Pearson r using the
  coefficient of determination
If samples from two groups have been
  compared, use t test for independent
  and non-independent means
For more than two samples from more
  than two groups being compared,
  use ANOVA
For other parametric tests, see
  appropriate statistical guides

FIGURE 10.9   SAMPLING IN PRACTICE

are doing. If you are conducting true experiments, then you will most likely need to use some form of probability sampling technique involving random selection, then random assignment of units. If your research is not experimental, then a non-probability sampling technique will be a likely option.

It is not always necessary, or even desirable, to use probability sampling techniques. The purpose and type of research you are doing, allied with your research questions, should be the main determining factors for which type, if at all, of sampling technique you employ in your research design. Purposeful sampling is not, then, an inferior approach to research than probability sampling. In many cases you will find that not using a probability technique will be far more difficult than using one. Identifying and selecting information-rich subjects can be very time-consuming and require substantial energies in managing the contact and relationship regardless of what kind of people are involved. Whatever type of sampling technique you use it will, as a matter of course, need full justification in terms of an explanation in your methodology. It may be the case that you need to explain why and how you employed more than one technique, such as a systematic stratified sample. Multiple sampling techniques can be used, but select which ones on the basis of what your research needs. Figure 10.10 gives an overview of the different types of sampling which can be used and more can be found in most textbooks on sampling, such as Patton (1990, 182–3).

Finally, although we have only touched on some of the main issues and procedures of sampling we would like to place sampling into the broader context of a research project. Figure 10.9 attempted to show the place and role of data produced through using samples. It takes for granted the initial stages of formulating research questions and hypotheses and defining concepts. Once the sample has been selected and research instrument applied, data will have been produced. For the sample you can then start to apply a number of summations and calculations on the data before finding the averages and degrees of variability. It is from these descriptive statistics that relationships can be tested and identified, such as Z scores, t-tests and correlations. The significance of any relationship is, as I have said, dependent on the quality of the data and any inference made is similarly dependent upon the validity of the sample.

RELIABILITY

If you wanted to measure a length of a piece of paper you might use a standard ruler to find out its length in millimetres. The same ruler will, on every occasion it is used to find the length of something, produce consistent results. A ruler is a tool that will, if used properly, give consistent measures of length which are free of bias and error and which are accurate within the limitations of the degree of precision of the ruler itself and taking into account that the length of what you want to measure is within the scope of the ruler's normal usage. Table 10.5 shows the three main types of reliability.

In research the tools or instruments we use to make measurements and observations need to be as free of bias as possible within known limitations. An observation of a test can be

| Experimental (interventionist – use of randomized assignment) | | Quasi-experimental (interventionist – use of multi-measures or control group) | | Non-experimental (non-interventionist – use of random selection) |

Probability sampling

Simple random	From the population each unit has an equal chance of being selected.	Statistically regarded as the most bias-free and best for reducing error. May not always represent sub-groups within the main population.
Systematic random	Units are selected from the sampling frame systematically according to a particular criterion, e.g. place on list	Can be quick and easy to select units, but degree of distance between units on a list may hide extraneous variables.
Stratified random	Units are selected from different groups, e.g. male/female that exhibit the variables under examination.	Useful technique to avoid bias towards one group. Need for both groups and samples to be of equal size.
Cluster sampling	Selection of samples from within a larger sample of a population. Can be used with other techniques.	Useful when the parameters of the population are wide or not clear. The more samples the greater the likelihood of increased error.

Non-probability sampling

Convenience	Selection of the nearest units for inclusion in the sampling frame and selection of sample, e.g. your own student cohort.	Very convenient, but may be highly unrepresentative of any larger population and therefore not a basis for generalization.
Quota	Quotas are used from a range of groups within a population when that population has an opportunity to engage in a common action, e.g. voting.	Ensures a wide spread of responses from sub-groups stratified across a population. Needs reliable, accurate and timely information on each sub-set of the population.
Purposeful	Units are hand-picked on the basis of how they represent a population or category to which they belong. Useful in case-study and critical path analysis.	Needs a minimum of 15 to generalize in terms of averages. Never any assurance that subjects will be representative of their category.
Criterion sampling	Useful when a particular action or feature is being studied that is regarded as normal but which subjects fail to do or do not exhibit.	Good for identifying instances, making comparisons and suggesting continua. Problems with defining normal and deviant will arise.

FIGURE 10.10   PROBABILITY AND NON-PROBABILITY SAMPLING

TABLE 10.5   TYPES OF RELIABILITY

Inter-test reliability	Test and re-test reliability	Parallel-forms reliability
Sometimes called inter-observer reliability, which means calibrating the ways in which two or more observers do observations. This can be done in a series of pilot applications where you calibrate, bring closer together, the degree of similarity between observers. In lone ethnographic studies and textual analysis this may mean practising making notes in different settings and keeping a research journal with a record of issues and problems, along with analysis. The idea being to practice explaining how one observation and use of categories (or criteria) can be treated as having been done in a similar way to another. This can be supplemented by making your data available to others to see if the interpretations you have made are concurrent with what they can also see.	This technique deals with the issue of ensuring that observations of the phenomenon are similar when done over time. Making observations at different times will allow you to make comparisons. In quantitative studies this may mean you can make correlations between statistical data. With interviews, piloting the schedule will help to reduce variability and equivocality. It will also minimize inter-rating of categories, allow confirmation to be perused between initial and later responses and follow-up questions to gain more depth. The time gap in between re-test (interviews) will normally be a variable; the longer the gap the less likely will be a similarity in responses. In terms of analysis re-testing will allow for the researcher to test out interpretations with respondents.	When you have access to different units of analysis in different locations, say in different organizations, then it may be possible to select samples which parallel each other. If the data collection instrument is administered at, or about, the same time, then the results may be comparable, allowing you to identify contextual variables for further analysis. Samples can be randomly selected or assigned and the data collected over similar time periods using data tools which are equivalent or the same. Additionally, a sample may be split in half to see if the test, once administered to both groups, has measured the same property. The degree of reliability between the halves can be estimated using correlation.

said to be reliable if it results in the same or very similar outcomes each time it is applied to the same unit of analysis under the same or very similar conditions. If, for example, a student receives a score of 99 in a test, then she should be able to achieve a similar score in a subsequent test if done within a relatively short time of the first test. If an observation or a test can be repeated and it consistently results in very similar outcomes, then it can be said to be reliable. Reliability is not something that can be calculated precisely. In some kinds of research involving multiple observations over time, however, it is possible to estimate the degree of similarity between outcomes to give a measure of the consistency and variability of a research instrument. Such calculations are much more prevalent in experimental research than non-experimental research. Hopkins (2000) provides a reasonably clear introduction to the statistics of reliability in experimental research. The key principles of reliability are, however, relatively easy to grasp and build into any research project.

TRIANGULATION: MYTHS OF CONVERGENCE AND CONFIRMATION

In navigation it is possible to plot location by taking measurements of distance and angle using a sextant or global positioning system. Three measurements triangulate to give an accurate position. Triangulation is often used as a metaphor in the social sciences for recommending the use of multiple methods (sometimes referred to as multiple operationalism, multitrait-multimethod matrix and convergent validation) to increase the validity of a construct and to evaluate the accuracy of a measurement tool (Campbell and Fiske, 1962; Garner, 1954; Garner et al., 1956).

Triangulation assumes that the use of more than one method will confirm the validity of the concept by converging data from the different methods and give a more complete description (Knafl and Breitmayer, 1989: 237) of the concept than can be had from using a singular method (Denzin, 1970; Smith, 1975; Hammersley and Atkinson, 1995; Mathison, 1988). It also assumes that the accuracy and reliability of the different methods can be assessed and measured against each other. Remembering our discussion of positivism and realism (Chapters 7 and 8), this idea of convergence assumes there to be a single reality which multiple measures can corroborate to give us a more accurate correspondence to it in descriptions of it. If one takes a realist position, then the mechanics and the assumptions on which triangulation are based make sense. But triangulation will not bring us any closer to 'reality' than a single method. If we do not accept the realist position, then social reality is not something that may be interpreted in different ways, but is what an interpretation can legitimately make it to be (Blaikie, 1991: 120). Hence, it is not a simple matter of 'if not one, then the other' or if not convergent validity then 'anything goes'.

In assuming that validity is essential in terms of construct definitions and operationalization, then the purpose of triangulation is to build accurate definitions and reliability of measurements. This, of course, is not done when we use a sextant or satellite navigation system. Using them is not a test of them as instruments to give reliable measures of location or as tests for constructs of position: topographers would not attempt to give the location of a feature without knowing first that their instruments worked, how the data they give is to be interpreted and where the exact locations are from which measurements are to be taken. The metaphor of triangulation using notions of intersection is a poor one for the social sciences. This is because, unlike the map-maker, the social scientist does not know the exact locations of a variable, whether their instrument is actually measuring the concept it is supposed to and if the measurements are accurate. From the position of a realist, we can build maps of concepts and look to measures to identify relationships between these concepts to show convergence (and express this in correlations) and divergence, but this does not mean we will have discovered 'truth' or validity of the construct. What is at issue here is the belief that measurements from one method can confirm those of another, and conversely that any agreement between the two methods proves the validity of the second one, that is, mutual confirmation. The nonsense (or fallacy) of this is like saying A is valid because B is valid and B is valid because A is valid. For either A or B to be valid, the measurements must be assumed to be accurate measures of the construct. Showing divergence between measures goes against the whole assumption of triangulation – that all measures will intersect. Divergence has been seen as a strength of multiple methods (Mitchell, 1986). It has been argued that the weaknesses in one method can be off-set by the strengths in another (Jick, 1983: 138; Denzin, 1970: 300) and enhance research strategies such as ethnography. This entails the assumption that some methods and designs are epistemologically better than others, but, if we do not know which, then how can comparative assessments be made without an agreed standard? Hence there is no purposeful outcome to debates comparing qualitative and quantitative approaches or experimental with non-experimental unless it can be done within, and in terms of justifying, a theoretical position. Even then different kinds of data cannot be easily, if at all, weighted or ranked – especially if they result in different 'findings'. The best we can hope for is that they illuminate aspects of the phenomenon each has identified or more sensibly use them to show there are different frames of reference which can be used (remember the example of the woodyard in Chapter 7?) to broaden the interpretive repertoire.

Triangulation may then be inappropriate if not carefully considered because each method used will produce its own unique data. That data will not be a representation on the world *as it is*, but one way of seeing it among other ways. Hence the aim for convergence and completeness should not be taken at face value, for what is to count as convergence and completeness (or correspondence and literal description) are beyond meaningful delimitation (see Sacks, 1963 and Garfinkel, 1967: 24–34). This does not mean our research design should lack a concern for validity and reliability, but does mean we think carefully about what they mean. This may help us to avoid the trap of using mixed methods and traditional assumptions about validity which often lead researchers to find, and thereby create, the connections between different data types so that they fit a plausible frame of reference. Ironically, this will lead the realist further away from the reality they are so keen to get close to.

OBJECTIVITY AS CONFIDENCE

Students are often heard to remark that one of the features that distinguish the natural from the social sciences is that the social sciences are largely based on interpretation while the natural sciences are based on objective and neutral methods. When asked where did they get this assumption from, they often say their textbooks on research make a distinction between positivist and non-positivist approaches and do so using a dichotomy between scientific and interpretivist research. Scientific research is assumed to be that from which generalizations can be made with a measurable degree of confidence. But not all research can employ random selection and assignment to attract the label of science and confidence in generalization. This does not mean that generalization is impossible and that such research will not be systematic and valid. To dispel this myth we often point them in the direction of studies in the sociology of science, specially ethnographies of scientists doing science (Mulkay, 1979; Latour, 1987; Woolgar, 1988; Knorr-Cetina, 1981). This quickly shows them that science and any kind of research activity, no matter what the popular conception or ideal type, is based largely on people (in the role of researchers) attempting to understand and make sense of their data and at the same time reflect on and justify the methods they use to collect that data. We will therefore begin by looking at a definition in a popular research textbook:

> There are two notions related to the idea of objectivity that, traditionally, have been very influential on research. First, there is the idea of some external vantage point from which to gain a better view and, second, there is the idea of approaching matters in a fair and unbiased manner. Both facets of objectivity help social researchers to claim that their findings are better than those based on common sense or received wisdom. (Denscombe, 2002: 160)

It would seem Denscombe is claiming that objectivity is about being detached, having no relationship to the research topic itself or the subjects or having an influence on the way in which the data are to be collected. He also seems to be saying that objectivity is about an attitude to other theories, interpretations and ideas; that the researcher ought to be open-minded in terms of being impartial, unbiased, neutral and having no vested interests. This position goes against many of the positions taken by researchers doing emancipatory research. It also takes us back to the debates and issues surrounding value-neutrality (see Chapter 7). There is no clear-cut way in which non-experimental studies can claim to be able to generalize with the statistical confidence of experimental studies. But both experimental and non-experimental research does require that it exhibits relevance and confidence. Relevance is about showing how the research makes a real contribution to understanding, including the development of a methodological approach. Relevance can sometimes be associated with importance, but this should not be taken to mean the impact on change or application such research can have. Importance is a matter for a discipline and a particular research programme to determine, given the kinds of puzzles they are working with. Confidence is related to relevance in that we need to be able to clearly demonstrate that our research was done systematically, without prejudice. Confidence is about ensuring that the procedures for designing and implementing our research are reasonable and transparent. This extends to writing up the research, where what was done needs to be explained and the data made available for others to read and assess the reasonableness of our interpretations of it.

It is therefore possible and often desirable to look for functional equivalents between procedures for ensuring reliability, validity and confidence in experimental studies and non-experimental research. Bauer and Gaskell (2000: 342–9) recognize that some researchers reject any such attempts by interpretivist researchers at establishing functional equivalents with experimental research. Such researchers, they argue, reject procedures aimed at constructing measures of reliability, internal validity, sample confidence and external validity on the grounds that they are elements of dominance and control. In place of rejection Bauer and Gaskell (2000: 342–9) argue for interpretive approaches to develop their own criteria for quality based on relevance and confidence. Throughout this book a position similar to that of Bauer and Gaskell (2000) has been advanced and in terms of actual research practice means the following:

♦ **using methods which are accountable and transparent;**

♦ **being completely open about one's relationship to the topic;**

♦ **ensuring that subjects are fully aware of the nature and implications of the research they are participants in;**

- ◆ taking into account alternative theories, arguments and interpretations;

- ◆ not delegating the views of subjects to a form of reasoning that is regarded as inferior;

- ◆ developing the ability to reflect on the research, data, your role and the research itself; and

- ◆ not using restricted frames of interpretation without first subjecting them to critical evaluation and comparing them, where possible, against potential alternatives.

Research that lacks objectivity will exhibit such things as partisanship for a cause, bias towards particular methods and theory, and commitment to a narrow interpretive framework. It will therefore also lack critical engagement with the data and lead to pre-assumed interpretations. Alvesson and Sköldberg summarize this kind of research myopia:

> The particular interpretive options open to the researcher are crucial in this context. One condition for reflection in the interplay between empirical material and interpretations is thus the breadth and variation of the interpretive repertoire. If someone has dedicated almost all her academic career to a particular theory, then their repertoire will be restricted. Pre-structured understandings dominate seeing. The capacity for reflection, if not altogether eliminated, is at least reduced. Something which strongly overlaps with such a cognitive bias is the researcher's own emotions. If one has worked a lot on a particular theory, one becomes, as a rule, emotionally attached to it. The empirical material will tend by and large to confirm the theory. Alternatively, recalcitrant data can always be dismissed by referring to the need for more research. (2000: 250)

Alvesson and Sköldberg (2000: 251, 247–86) recommend that the problems associated with the researcher can, in part, be overcome through the collection of rich data from multiple sources. Like Bauer and Gaskell (2000: 345–6), they are not referring to traditional understandings of triangulation. Their argument is that different types of data will encourage greater effort from the researcher to produce various interpretations of the data. The researcher will need to look beyond a simple interpretive repertoire and engage in a process of exploration and elimination that is based on a reflective dialectic with their own preferences and methodological assumptions. This recommendation resonates with that of Popper, who claimed that:

> What categorizes the empirical method is its manner of exposing to falsification, in every conceivable way, the system to be tested. Its aim is not to save the lives of untenable systems but, on the contrary, to select the one which is by comparison the fittest, by exposing them all to the fiercest struggle for survival. (1959: 42)

It is interesting to note that, in most arguments about quality in research, a common position is taken on common sense – it is relegated as something which needs correction. They give to the researcher a privileged position by which and through which common sense and common knowledge are regarded as inferior, partial and often irrational. You may wish to return to the discussion of the work of Harold Garfinkel in Chapter 8 to remind yourself of how one major theorist takes common sense as the topic for his research.

What is data?

All research needs data. Data can be whatever you deem necessary to address your research questions. There are no types of data which are naturally better than others, though some may be preferable, but not available, and therefore other data have to be used. For example, a positivist may hold the view that consciousness and the mind are reducible to material operations in the brain. From their materialist standpoint a range of tests could be devised to measure levels of consciousness; what a person is able to do is used as a measure of their consciousness. It may even be used as a measure of their intelligence. Concepts such as consciousness and intelligence, along with behaviours such as grief and happiness, can be proceduralized into a deductive approach using tests and comparative measures. The data in such cases would be the result of the tests (solving mathematical problems and physical puzzles) normally undertaken in controlled conditions. More sophisticated versions have aimed to test, through experimentation, the impact of social expectancy and labelling as independent variables on the academic performance (dependent variable) of schoolchildren (Rosenthal and Jacobson, 1966). Some researchers hold that there is no need for this kind of proceduralization to render such things as the mind available for observation and analysis (Coutler, 1989). They would argue that the operations of the mind can be observed in what people do in their natural settings. As people, researchers are able to recognize other people exhibiting grief, happiness, surprise, anger and many

TABLE 10.6   THE PLACE OF DATA COLLECTION TOOLS IN RESEARCH DESIGN

Design orientation	Data tools	Data analysis
Case study	Focus groups	Content analysis
Comparative study	Interviews	Structural analysis
Sample survey	Questionnaires	Semiological analysis
Panel survey	Video recording	Coding and indexing
Observational	Audio recording	Concept mapping
Ethnographic	Diaries	Conversation analysis
Experimental	Drawings	Discourse analysis
Evaluation	Tests	Category analysis
Action learning	Delphi	Correlational analysis

other behavioural modes. So-called subjective dispositions (as if there were also objective ones) are what people do; they are a defining characteristic of being human and an animal. The key problem is how to capture these as data for analysis. The method most commonly used is observation: watching people do what they do in the setting in which they do it. Hence the approach is often called 'naturalism' (Kirk and Miller, 1986). This means studying people's actions in their own environment, which can be done using audio and video recordings, as well as examining many other things which allow the phenomenon to be analysed, such as cinema film, television programmes, autobiographies and fiction. One could even include in this watching behavioural psychologists administer a test because they would be in their natural occupational setting. Similarly, these can also be sources for the behavioural approach in that the behaviour of people on video can be used to measure the frequency of a behaviour, personal biographies used to construct a scale to measure stress caused by particular life events (Holmes and Rahe, 1967) and drawings used to say what the experience of menstruation is like for adolescent girls (Koff, 1983). While the methodological tradition does have an influence on the kinds of data a researcher tends to select, of greater influence are the research questions, the orientation of the research design, and the kinds of data they require in order to be properly addressed. Table 10.6 indicates this in terms of the tools commonly used to collect and capture data and techniques for its analysis.

There is no direct relation between many design orientations, tools to collect data and techniques to analyse it. But there are conventions. For example, experimental studies tend to use correlational and regression analysis to ascertain the degree of the relationship between the independent and dependent variable (Bryant et al., 1989). Correlational analysis is not always based on experiments. Saying what data is, is not a straightforward matter, but it certainly includes the following: letters, books, architecture, diaries, photographs, video, scripts, advertisements, posters, signs, fashion, talk, bibliographies, jokes, plans, statistics, interviews, questionnaire responses, software design, myths, art, stories, comics, magazines, charts, diagrams and many other things. Data is what people produce (artefacts), what they do (actions/behaviours) and how they do what they do with the things they produce, which include beliefs, attitudes, opinions, customs, science and culture.

COLLECTING DATA

Having identified possible sources for the type of data you will need, think about just how the data can be collected systematically, in sufficient quantity and of the necessary quality. In this section we will look briefly at some of the most common ways in which data is collected as part of masters research. There are many other books and articles and Internet sources which cover data collection in far greater detail than there is space for here. To help you pursue possible methods, citations to some of these sources have been provided at relevant points in the text.

Just as there are many forms of data, so there are many ways in which data can be collected for analysis. Table 10.7 summarizes some of the methods for data collection. A useful way of thinking about methods is that of seeing them as gateways to phenomena. Some phenomena suggest obvious gateways. For example, if you are interested in turn-taking in everyday conversation, you will need audio recordings of people engaged in everyday conversation. With concepts which are more elusive and abstract, surrogates for the concept are sometimes needed and both the methods and data are used to stand for or stand in as representing a phenomenon. For example, intelligence is not something that can be easily defined or categorized. Tests on the ability to perform a given range of predetermined puzzles opens up the potential to access the concept as it has been defined for the sake of the test being applied. Therefore, the more abstract the concept the more likely that the method of data collection acts as, at best, a surrogate gateway to the phenomenon and, at worst, as means of demonstrating the instrument (test) can measure the definition rather than the phenomenon.

TABLE 10.7   METHODS FOR DATA COLLECTION AND ANALYSIS

Method	Brief description	Sources
Interviews	Talking to selected respondents on a specific topic to find answers to research questions is the basis of interviewing. There are many kinds of interviewing, including structured, semi-structured, unstructured or focus group interviews. Interviews are an obtrusive method which can generate substantial in-depth qualitative information usually from a small number of respondents. Interviews can follow from questionnaires, adding depth to breadth, or be a part of an ethnographic study or oral history. The results of interviews are analysed by looking to find similarities and differences between responses from respondents. The researcher looks to relate individual responses hermeneutically to the 'big picture' set by the research questions.	Arksey and Knight, 1999; Bell and Roberts, 1984; Bourque and Fielder, 1995; Brenner, Brown and Canter, 1985; Dexter, 1970; Douglas, 1985; Flick, 1998; Foddy, 1993; Fontana and Frey, 1994; Fre and Mertens, 1995; Gubrium and Holstein, 2001; Holstein and Gubrium, 1995; Hyman, 1975; Kahn and Cannell, 1983 [1957]; Kvale, 1996; Lavrakas, 1993; McCracken, 1988; Merton, Fiske and Kendall, 1990; Mishler, 1991.
Questionnaires	Questionnaires are a series of structured questions which address a specific topic or issue and are used as the basis of the survey approach. Used to find out what, how much, how many, and how often (e.g. as in what/who will you vote for surveys), the questionnaire survey can be administered personally, via post or e-mail. The questionnaire is usually an operational instrument to measure a number of variables of a concept by sampling respondents from a larger population in order to make generalizations about that population. They can be used to measure attitudes using various scales (e.g. Likert scale)	A primer on experimental and quasi-experimental design: Electronic textbook: PA 765: Foddy, 1993; Oppenheim, 1992; Statnotes: an online textbook: Petersen, 2000; Sampling guide: Statistics glossary: Statistical good practice guidelines: The little handbook of statistical practice: University of Wisconsin Cooperative Extension.

Note: Titles underlined mean Internet source or resource; address and full citations can be found in Appendix 3.

(Continued)

TABLE 10.7 (CONTINUED)

Method	Brief description	Sources
	and will provide information from a large number of people, which can be followed up with interviews to gain more depth. As an obtrusive instrument, depending on how the questions are constructed responses can be analysed at nominal, ordinal and interval levels, making possible tests of significance (e.g. chi-square) and association (e.g. correlation) between dependent and independent variables.	
Focus groups	Based on interviewing, a focus group is a carefully selected group of people brought together in the same place to discuss a particular topic or issue relevant to them. The researcher may use stimulus materials (e.g. pictures, objects, quotes etc.) to encourage conversation on a topic, but as with all interview methods the interactions are artificial, obtrusive and may be subject to 'group think'. Focus groups tend to be used in marketing research, action research and for research on social issues. Multiple responses are usually unstructured and therefore can create difficulties in transcribing recordings (audio/video).	A manual for the use of focus groups: Agar and MacDonald, 1995; Banks, 1957; Barbour and Kitzinger, 1999; Bion, 1961; Bloor, Frankland, Thomas and Robson, 2000; Fern, 2001; Goulding, 2002; Greenbaum, 2000; Krueger, 1994 and 1997; Locke, 2001; Market Navigation: Morgan, 1993; Myers, 1988; Social Research Updates: Stewart and Shamdasani, 1990; Using focus groups to create excellence: Vaughn, Schumm and Sinagub, 1996; Wilkinson, 1998.
Delphi Technique	Delphi Technique (DT) was developed by the RAND Corporation in the 1960s as a method to make forecasts to aid corporate problem solving, planning and decision-making. Along with the Nominal Group Technique (NGT), it	Delbeq and van de Ven 1971; Fink, Kosecoff, Chassin and Brook, 1984; Fowles, 1978; Gerth and Smith, 1991; Pill, 1971.

(Continued)

TABLE 10.7   (CONTINUED)

Method	Brief description	Sources
	is a method for identifying points of consensus among a group of people with common concerns. Respondents do not have to be physically co-present to suggest alternatives to a problem or make selections from a range of alternatives. The DT and NGT can be used in action research where their aim is to get the group to take responsibility for identifying issues relevant to them and making recommendations they can act upon to bring about change and address their common issues.	
Document, discourse and conversation analysis	Documents come in many formats and include official documents (e.g. reports, minutes, statistics), personal documents (e.g. diaries, letters), literary (e.g. poems, novels) and many forms of ephemera (e.g. posters, advertisements, e-mails, electronic discussions). Documents often define who we are and what rights we have, who someone was, what we take as knowledge (e.g. bibliographies) and leave traces of the past. Documents can be contemporary accounts of an event, secondary reconstructions and organizing tools (e.g. catalogues) to documents. Use of documents is usually unobtrusive but involves issues of what the purpose of a format may be, how it is to be understood outside its context of	*Personal documents*: Cooper, 1991; Malinowski, 1989; Webb, Campbell, Schwartz and Sechrest, 2000 [1966]. *Discourse analysis*: Edwards and Potter, 1992; Cazden, 1988; Faircloth, 1992; Foucault, 1977; Gumperz, 1982; Gill, 1996; Potter, 1996. *Content analysis*: Ang, 1991; Bauer, 1998; Berelson, 1952; Glasgow University Media Group, 1976; Holsti, 1969; Kaplan, 1943; Krippendorff, 1980; Leiss, Kline and Jhally, 1986; Neuendorf, 2002; Riffe, Lacy and Fico, 1998; Rosengren, 1981; West, 2001. *Rhetorical analysis*: Cole, 1991; Gross and Keith, 1997; McCloskey, 1994; Meyer, 1994;

(Continued)

TABLE 10.7 (CONTINUED)

Method	Brief description	Sources
	production, and how it was constructed. Typical modes of analysis applied to the contents of documents include conversation, content, discourse, rhetorical and semiological analysis.	Nelson, Megill and McCloskey, 1987; Toulmin, 1958. *Semiological analysis*: Barthes, 1977 and 1986; Gottdiener, 1995; Hawkes, 1992; Saussure, 1974; Williamson, 1978. *Conversation analysis*: Atkinson and Heritage, 1989; Button and Lee, 1987; Sacks, Schegloff and Jefferson, 1974; ten Have, 1999.
Narrative/life history	Personal experiences are a major source for the study of social, economic, cultural and technological events. Based on the past of a person or group, as remembered, capturing temporal experiences is the main challenge to this approach. Such experiences are captured using a wide range of sources including diaries, in-depth interviewing, episodic interviewing, school reports, letters, photographs and objects. Various strategies have been developed across many disciplines (sociology, feminism, economics, anthropology, psychology, biographical literature) to systematically record and analyse the processes of remembering and structures of experience, including oral history, narrative studies and biography. Topics are wide-ranging, including experiences of immigration, poverty, adolescence, schooling, motherhood and war.	Cortazzi, 1993; Lee, 1994; Lieblich and Josselson, 1994; Narrative resources; International Conference on Narrative; Oral history: techniques and procedures; Oral History Society; Reinharz, 1992; Riessman, 1993; Rubin and Rubin, 1995; Spradley, 1979; Weiss, 1994; Werner and Schoepfle, 1987; Yow, 1994.

SUMMARY OF THIS CHAPTER

This chapter has attempted to give an overview of the main standpoints and cultures available to you for your research. The main points which have been made in this chapter are:

♦ Research can be categorized into three main types — experimental, quasi-experimental and non-experimental — and each has an equal place in understanding the social world.

♦ Generalization is, but does not always have to be, the goal of valid and reliable research.

♦ Sampling can be a part of all types of research, but not all types of research require sampling techniques to be included.

♦ Triangulation is a much misused metaphor in the social sciences and should only be used if the methodological assumptions on which it is based are fully understood.

♦ Designing a research project is about making choices from many alternatives that are not always comparable, and so methodological assumptions play a major role in shaping those choices.

Further reading

Bentz, V.M. and Shapiro, J.J. (1998) *Mindful Inquiry in Social Research*. Thousand Oaks, CA: Sage. Useful chapters on positivism and interpretivist and different research cultures.

Mertens, D.M. (1998) *Research Methods in Education and Psychology: Integrating Diversity with Quantitative and Qualitative Approaches*. Thousand Oaks, CA: Sage. Very competent and clear instructional text on all the approaches mentioned in this chapter.

Judd, C.M., Smith, E.R. and Kidder, L.H. (1991) *Research Methods in Social Relations*. 6th edn. Fort Worth, TX: Harcourt Brace Jonanovich. An older textbook, but still packed with details on many approaches to research.

Seale, C. (ed.) (1998) *Researching Society and Culture.* London: Sage. Provides a clear introduction to a range of approaches.

AAPOR Resources on the Web, http://www.aapor.org/. This has resources on public opinion research.

Statistical Calculators, http://www.calculators.stat.ucla.edu/. This site contains almost every conceivable calculating tool for all levels of analysis.

Internet Society for Sport Science, http://www.sportsci.org/resource/stats/. Comprehensive resource on choosing statistical tests.

Part Three   Doing the Writing

Writing your research proposal

The development and writing of a proposal is an essential part of all research. Research supervisors and research committees, along with research funding bodies, often insist that before you begin your research you develop, over a short period of time, a proposal for your research. Often this developmental period consists of you examining ideas for research, analysing possibilities and drafting a research proposal. An important part of this stage is consulting with and taking advice from your supervisor. Remember that your supervisor will have more experience than you with research and will therefore be able to guide you, in ways which will save you time and effort, to a workable topic for research. The purpose of this chapter is, therefore, to look at the following questions about research proposals:

1 What is a research proposal and why is it necessary?

2 What does a research proposal look like?

3   What are the contents of a proposal and how should they be arranged?

4   How is a research proposal normally judged?

Your research proposal will be based on your suggested design for your research (Chapter 10). Your research design will have been based on defining your topic, stating the research questions (Chapter 3), a search and review of the literature (Chapter 6), selection of an appropriate methodological approach (Chapters 7 and 8), identification of the possible ethical issues (Chapter 9) and selection of tools to collect, and techniques to analyse, your data (Chapter 10).

What is a research proposal?

A proposal is a *plan* that you have chosen to follow in order to achieve your intended outcomes – the completion of your research. A proposal is like a map that will help you navigate your journey along the research process. It will:

♦ give directions on what needs to be done, when and how and in what order;

♦ show you what transport is best suited for your research journey in terms of which methodological assumptions to use and which data collection techniques will be reliable; and

♦ provide milestones for measuring how far you have gone with your research and how far you have to go to complete it.

You research proposal is therefore a working document that shows to others what decisions you have made about:

♦ defining your topic to limit its scope (definitional analysis);

♦ what methodological assumptions you intend to use and those you have rejected (argumentation analysis and argument construction);

♦ what approaches to research you intend to employ and those you will not (methodological analysis);

♦ your choice of data collection techniques and how they will result in reliable and valid findings (instrument analysis);

♦ the existence of the data and its accessibility (source analysis); and

♦ potential problems and ethical issues (risk analysis).

Your proposal will have argumentative and persuasive elements because you are required to demonstrate that you can analyse a topic (topic analysis) and argue for the need to study that topic (justification) in the ways you have suggested (methodological assumptions and approaches). At this stage in your research this argument is largely based on an *indicative* analysis of the literature (current research and theory) on your topic. In Chapter 6 I showed your how to do a search and review of the literature.

WHAT ARE THE FORMAL REASONS FOR WRITING A RESEARCH PROPOSAL?

There are a number of very good practical, personal and intellectual reasons for writing a proposal for your research. Your research proposal will help you to:

♦ *explain* to your supervisor and research committee what you intend to research, why you believe the research needs to be done and how you intend to research the topic (research design);

♦ *demonstrate* to your supervisor that you have developed the necessary skills of literature analysis and argumentative analysis to analyse a topic and find a gap in our knowledge requiring research (skills and capabilities);

♦ *construct a plan* for your research that will enable you to *imagine* the process as a logically interconnected series of tasks which are based on reliable and valid research techniques, recording of activities and analysis; and

♦ *understand* the importance of ethics and risk analysis and provide a justifiable, workable position and contingency plans.

Your research proposal should reflect the thought and analysis you have done to pose questions capable of being answered by the research you are proposing, in the ways you have identified. As a map it is your guide, and

The what, why, how, when, where and who of a research proposal:

What	you intend to research
Why	the research is needed
How	the research will be done
When	the research will be done
What	resources are needed
Who	you will talk to
Where	the data is
How	to access the data
How	the data will be analysed
What	the outcomes may be

as the reader and creator of this map you are responsible for its implementation. This means using it properly in ways which do not compromise your integrity and honesty. It also means adapting it to accommodate the circumstances and opportunities you encounter on your research journey. Like all maps there is a certain amount of latitude for changes in the route; alternative ways of reaching a destination, even for changes in the destination itself. All research proposals are open to change, change that is often demanded by the realities of everyday life. Any change must, however, be thought about and the opportunities weighed against what will be lost and, importantly, must be justified not only in terms of your personal objective but of the ethical standards expected of a professional researcher. Hence we can say that a research proposal is a document that explains to others and yourself what you intend to research, how, why and when you will research it, and what you will do if something goes wrong.

THE ELEMENTS OF A RESEARCH PROPOSAL

All research proposals demand time to ensure that they exhibit a coherent, integrated and structurally sound argument to answer fully the 'what', 'why', 'how' and 'when' questions. My approach to the research proposal is one of construction through reflection, analysis and discussion with others. This approach involves looking to identify what elements are required, working on them, arranging them and then integrating their contents to ensure the whole has coherence. Figure 11.1 indicates the main elements of a typical research proposal. It attempts to show the interrelatedness of the elements and the ways in which you should aim to link the contents to achieve integration and coherence.

Achieving coherence in any kind of writing in no small achievement. A research proposal is constructed incrementally and is a process of collecting materials, drafting, writing, editing and rearranging. This in part explains why this chapter is where it is in this book; you need to know about research and methodology and have done some analysis, thinking and reflection before you begin your proposal. You may note that there are some elements not shown in Figure 11.1, such as ethics, risk analysis, a timetable and resources. This is because I want to get across the relationships between the elements shown in terms of the justification and title. You may want to add boxes on ethics, risks and a timetable for yourself to see what kinds of relationships they have with the others. In the sections which follow we will look at these, providing examples from research proposals. Before we do, however, something needs to be said about the common questions often asked about research proposals.

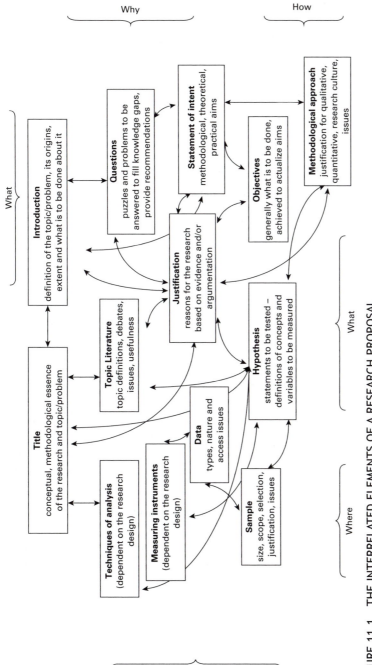

FIGURE 11.1   THE INTERRELATED ELEMENTS OF A RESEARCH PROPOSAL

TABLE 11.1   INDICATION OF LENGTH FOR A RESEARCH PROPOSAL

Criteria	Length
Introduction	1 page
Aims and objectives	Half page
Topic justification	1–2 pages
Scope and limitations	Half page
Literature review and citations	3–6 pages
Methodology and data collection	2–4 pages
Ethical considerations	1–2 pages
Risk analysis	1–2 pages
Schedule	Half page
Resources	Half page
References	As required

HOW LONG SHOULD A PROPOSAL BE?

The question of how long your proposal should be depends on the requirements of your university. Table 11.1 provides an indication of how much in page space using 12-point type and single-line spacing can normally be expected from a research proposal. As you can see from the table, and from some of the extracts included in this chapter, you have very little space to communicate clearly, coherently and succinctly the pre-research and analysis you have been doing for two or more months.

Table 11.1 presupposes, for the sake of clarity, a typical structure for a proposal. The thing to notice is that the contents should be as brief as possible, without the loss of meaning.

DIFFERENT TYPES OF RESEARCH PROPOSAL

Although I have said that the research proposal you write will depend on your topic and the conventions for your university, there are some working structures you can

TABLE 11.2 TWO QUANTITATIVE AND QUALITATIVE RESEARCH PROPOSALS

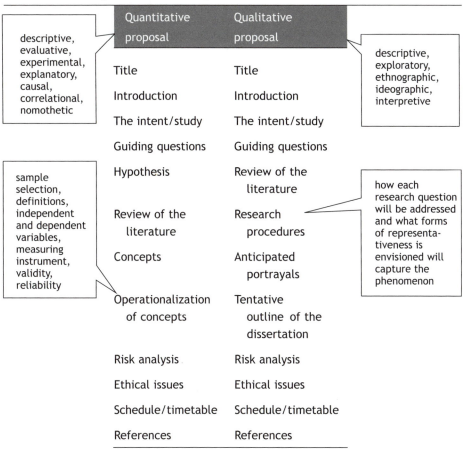

	Quantitative proposal	Qualitative proposal	
descriptive, evaluative, experimental, explanatory, causal, correlational, nomothetic	Title	Title	descriptive, exploratory, ethnographic, ideographic, interpretive
	Introduction	Introduction	
	The intent/study	The intent/study	
	Guiding questions	Guiding questions	
sample selection, definitions, independent and dependent variables, measuring instrument, validity, reliability	Hypothesis	Review of the literature	how each research question will be addressed and what forms of representativeness is envisioned will capture the phenomenon
	Review of the literature	Research procedures	
	Concepts	Anticipated portrayals	
	Operationalization of concepts	Tentative outline of the dissertation	
	Risk analysis	Risk analysis	
	Ethical issues	Ethical issues	
	Schedule/timetable	Schedule/timetable	
	References	References	

use to get started. In some of the chapters in this book, and in some tables and figures, ideas for structuring your writing can be found. In Table 11.2 two typical structures for research proposals are outlined. They represent ideal form and content and should therefore be used as you deem best to suit your topic and intention.

The structures shown in Table 11.2 are based on the typical content for proposals that are strongly quantitative or strongly qualitative. In the boxes attached to Table 11.2 there are reminders of the kinds of purposes, intentions, orientations, methods and the like often associated with the two main approaches. It is quite possible to have content from both approaches. Qualitative research can have a hypothesis, while quantitative research can have in-depth portrayals based on capturing the understandings of those being researched. Similarly, it can be useful to include an indicative outline of your dissertation if doing quantitative research. Whatever final structure and content you decide on, however, must be a coherent expression of your overall research design.

THE VOICE OF YOUR RESEARCH PROPOSAL

As you work on your research proposal, writing and editing it (often adding more text than you take out!), you may find that you and your research become 'one'. What I mean by this is that you begin to see how to do the work. There is a certain pleasure and excitement in being able to see what you can achieve and this gives you owner-ship of your research, often in ways which become, for the time being, a means of defining yourself – a *masters* research student. You become a part of the picture that you have drawn, that is, of your research proposal; you too are in the frame. The voice you give to this position and relationship may become a problem. As a piece of writing crafted by you, do you write in the third person, divorcing yourself from the very thing you are creating, using such phrases as 'the researcher', or do you use 'I will'? The choice is not, in practice, an either/or. Using the first person, especially 'I will', can be repetitive and uses up valuable space. Using the third person often adds a sense of the ridiculous and certainly does not make a proposal 'scientific'. The problem is often caused by explaining where your research topic originated in the past tense, and combining this with saying what you intend to do in the future tense. When explaining the origins of your topic, especially if it is based on a personal observation, then some use of the first person is, I suggest, legitimate. There are many famous examples of this, but one of the most famous is that given by Albert Einstein on how he thought up a theory that changed the world. Einstein did not develop his theory of general relativity by careful observation, experimentation or testing of hypotheses, but while lying back on a hill on a summer's day. Looking up at the sky with half-closed eyes, he noticed that the sunlight broke into thousands of tiny beams through his eye-lashes. He wondered what it would be like to take a ride on one of those sunbeams and imagined himself taking a journey, at the speed of light, through the universe. Of course, you cannot travel on a sunbeam at the speed of light, but his imaginary journey was one of his starting points for the mathematics he subsequently worked out to describe the physics of light and time. Einstein could do little other, if he wished to tell the truth, than say, 'I imagined …', to explain the origins of his theories. In other sections of your proposal a neutral tense can be employed. Here is an example to illustrate this:

Popular romantic novels may not be literary fiction but those who dismiss them often do not recognize that there is more to them than a love plot and happy ending. Jay Dixon (ex-employee of Mills and Boon) argues that popular romance 'come out of the oral storytelling tradition rather than the tradition of the written word ... literary style is irrelevant ... this kind of writing is, for the most part, intuitive'. (Smullen, 1999)

The voice here is relatively neutral and is being used to imply the nature of the argument for the research. The same kind of voice can be used in the title to give a strong indication of any argument or methodological position. Figure 11.2, for example, indicates a possible bias against popular romantic fiction by public librarians, yet has a sense of research to find out, even test, if the statement in the title has any validity:

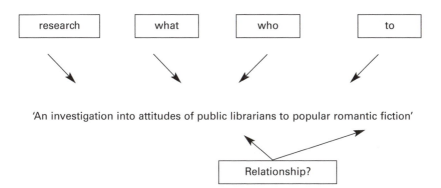

FIGURE 11.2   PUBLIC LIBRARIANS' POSSIBLE BIAS AGAINST ROMANTIC FICTION

It is a matter of using a little common sense to achieve an appropriate balance between sounding ridiculous and sounding egotistical. Words and phrases to avoid therefore include 'I hope to ...', 'the research ...', 'in my opinion', and 'I wish to ...'.

Crafting your research proposal

Some university research committees hold to the belief that a research proposal ought to follow a definitive structure explaining a methodology based on hypothesis testing and written in the third person. The only reasons I can give for this imposition is the belief that a certain structure, methodology and style is equated with 'science'. Such beliefs may be traced to the academic research socialization of members of research committees, but such an imposition is a *belief* and, from my own experience, can exhibit all the restraints and closing down of critical and creative thought of a fundamentalist religion. If you intend to use a methodological approach that is not common to a department, be prepared for resistance. Hybrid approaches, adding some qualitative elements to a predominantly quantitative approach, are usually accepted but again, from my experience, there are serious gaps in knowledge among the social science community of the spectrum of methodological debate and positions; the emphasis is still, in some institutions and disciplines, on maintaining a belief in the methodology of positivism, especially hypothetico-deductivism and its variants. This often manifests itself in simplistic renditions of the objective/subjective, quantitative/ qualitative dichotomies and criticism of proposals which do not adhere to the formula. If these comments are taken as criticism, it may also be taken that there is something to criticize. In this section I will outline typical arrangements for two kinds of research proposal, but I want to make it clear that, whatever arrangement you decide on, it should be appropriate for your topic and research methodology. It is your research and your research proposal and therefore your responsibility to craft it and defend it against preconceived notions. For these reasons I emphasize that a research proposal is crafted, rather than written to a formula. In what follows, some of the key sections, not covered elsewhere in this book, have been selected for further explication.

THE TITLE

From the title 'An investigation into attitudes of public librarians to popular romantic fiction' we can tell 'what kind' of librarians and 'what kind' of fiction. The title might also have an added sub-title to say from what country and possibly region the librarians would be selected – for example, 'A questionnaire survey of West Midlands branch librarians'. This says there will be a questionnaire survey, presumably postal, of public librarians working in branch as opposed to central libraries. The reasons, it will be expected, will be found in the main body of the proposal. The aim is to arrive at a title that describes what your research is about in the fewest words possible. To some degree your title is a 'working one'; one that at this stage in your research works to describe what you are intending to do. Whatever title for your research you start out with may, of course, change by the time you finish your research and have written it up into your dissertation. It may be the case that any change in title has to be approved by your supervisor or research committee.

THE INTRODUCTION

All research proposals should start with a short introduction giving the proposed topic for research. This may seem obvious, but so many sections labelled 'introduction'

TABLE 11.3   INTRODUCTION TO A RESEARCH PROPOSAL
FOR A TRADITIONAL DISSERTATION

Introduction	Comments
Women's magazines have been traditionally regarded as ideological ephemera which have little or no information content (1). Magazines aimed at women have been published for over 300 years and approximately 7.4 million women's magazines are sold each week, with about 150 different titles available each month. It is not surprising that they are one of the most significant yet least studied social institutions of our time (2). An indicative search of the literature seems to confirm that the informational role of women's magazines is almost wholly ignored and this is despite titles such as *Cosmopolitan* (3) and *Red* being aimed at working women. It could be proposed that women's magazines post-feminist movement (4) would be less ideological and more informational. This research will, therefore, aim to examine the proposition that women's magazines are devoid of *verifiable* information content and examine, through a sample-based comparison, the assumption that women's magazines prior to the late 1960s were more ideological than are current titles.	The summary of the gap in the literature is not always possible at the beginning. The topic 'information' is implicit at this stage. The scale of the phenomenon is shown through basic statistics. The Vancouver system of numerical citing of ideas and sources is used. Lack of understanding of the phenomenon is stated again and backed by reference to the literature search. The assumption that there would be differences between pre- and post-feminist movement magazines is introduced as a framework for comparison and as an assumption to be investigated. What is meant by 'information' and 'verifiable' will need clarification. The final sentence states that this is historical comparative research. Note that we are being asked to consider looking at something familiar in a new way.

Source: Adapted from Oliver, 1998 ('Health information in women's magazines').

often fail to do just this. An introduction should be a broad overview of your main argument, hypothesis (if you have one) or problem, and show, establish or define the problem, give examples of it and its extent, say what solutions were tried and why they failed, and indicate what research might be done and how. In Table 11.3 you can see an introduction to a traditional dissertation based on the analysis of information content in popular women's magazines.

The arrangement you use for your introduction is a matter for you to decide but, as we have just indicated, it needs to have a logical sequence. One way of determining an appropriate sequence is to think about and decide on what kind of problem you are researching. Are you trying to show that some problem exists and are therefore attempting to argue for research into it, or attempting to say that solutions to an established problem have, in some ways, failed and therefore require a different kind of approach, or claiming that definitions of an existing problem or phenomenon are inadequate, and therefore a different definition (respecification) is required? There may be elements from each of these in your research and in such a case you will need to distinguish them from each other. In Table 11.4 you can see an introduction to a work-based dissertation that argues for the need for reliable evidence in clinical decision-making. Although a little too brief, it combines elements from two of the orientations by referring to an existing problem and focusing attention on a possible solution. The need to make choices between competing priorities and forms of treatment are identified and a solution is suggested in the form of information which is accurate, timely and valid.

THE SCOPE AND LIMITATIONS

The degree of breadth and depth you intend to include in your research is a part of your scope. This means weighing up what you can do with how much time you have – include in the calculation your own skills development needs. In a piece of masters research you will only have time to do a limited number of things, so therefore you must acknowledge the constraints of time and your skills. In order to do these, think about including a short section on the scope or parameters you have identified for your research. This may mean you limit your research to a particular sample, geographical region, language, or time-frame and in particular set the themes you identified in your research questions. By setting out the scope of your research you are letting your reader know what you will and will not include in your research. In different parts of your proposal you will be able to explain further the reasons for the limitations you have placed on your research. Your scope should answer, as a minimum, the 'who' and 'where' questions. The extract in Table 11.5 is an example of a scope that says who will and who will not be included, where the research will be done and on what topic.

JUSTIFICATION FOR THE RESEARCH

The research you are undertaking is being carried out for a primary purpose and this is to contribute to your masters degree. But as a piece of research, what is it you want

TABLE 11.4   INTRODUCTION TO A RESEARCH PROPOSAL
             FOR A WORK-BASED DISSERTATION

Extract	Comments
It is acknowledged (1) that one of the main problems confronting health care professionals remains the huge body of available evidence and the lack of time to read, and the skills to assess the value of, this information. For example, a general physician would currently need to examine 19 articles a day, 365 days a years, to keep up to date with his or her speciality. In a nationwide study of 600 clinicians and 100 opinion leaders in the United States (2), only 5.3 per cent searched computerized information sources regularly, although more than a third said they searched occasionally. In the United Kingdom (3) general practitioners may see an average of 125 patients per week and, during each consultation, several queries concerning diagnosis, prognosis and treatment might arise. Thus a practitioner could make some 25,000 clinical decisions each year. However, because of lack of time, GPs generally fail to keep up with the research literature and change their practice as a result (4). For hospital medical staff, reading time per week has been reported as 90 minutes for medical students, zero minutes for house officers, 20 minutes for senior house officers, 30–45 minutes for registrars, 45 minutes for consultants and 30 minutes for older consultants (5). As a result, it has sometimes taken many years for important new research findings to become established and for patients to see the benefits. One example is the long delay before the proven advantages (in the late 1980s) of thrombolysis following a heart attack were recognized and the treatment became established practice.	The scale of the information problem confronting medical practitioners is established through a series of illustrations from the literature. The literature is used to show common agreement about the nature and cause of the problem. The illustrations are grounded with reference to actual groups of practitioners. An example of the effects of the problem is given, which is effective. It indicates the consequences for other advances if nothing is done.

(Continued)

TABLE 11.4 (CONTINUED)

Extract	Comments
Even once this treatment became established, and despite definitive and confirming results, several studies in the 1990s found that many eligible patients still failed to receive thrombolysis (6). Clearly, if doctors are to keep up to date, information must be clear, succinct and easy to access from their workplace. This will necessitate a change to the delivery and form of research information to medical practitioners. What is needed are bulletins, in text and electronic formats, of statements and evidence supporting them which will give succinct information on the benefits of new practices. This may provide health professionals with the confidence to change established practices in the light of proven research findings so that patients can benefit sooner rather than later from research.	A recommendation is made to address the problem. The benefits of this proposed solution are outlined for practitioners and patients alike.

Source: Adapted from Weightman, 1998 ('Evidence into practice: A study of the professional attitudes to the "Health Bulletins" in Wales').

to achieve? We have already said that masters research is not strictly about making a discovery or adding new knowledge, but there is, for many masters students, a clear conviction that their research should *do something*. Clough and Nutbrown (2002: 6–14) looked at this commitment research students have to their research. They grouped the reasons given by their students for doing research into the following:

♦ **researching to bring about change;**

♦ **researching for self-development; and**

♦ **researching for understanding.**

What we are looking at here is an important part of any research proposal, and this is answering the 'so what' and 'for whom' questions. These questions mean: 'What is the point or purpose of your research and who may benefit and how.' The students

TABLE 11.5   STATING THE SCOPE OF YOUR RESEARCH

Extract	Comments
The project will focus on library and information services for qualified information agents working within the NHS community Trusts, general medical practices and dental practices in South West England. Services to postgraduate medical and dental practitioners are also included. Where acute and community trusts have merged only the library services to community staff will be included. Library and information services to nursing and medical students will be excluded as will be services to primary care professionals funded directly by local authorities (e.g. psychologists). Medical information services for patients are also excluded.	The range of occupations which could possibly be included in such a study are wide, due to the complex structure of health services. The focus for inclusion is allied to services to specified and identifiable practitioners within the NHS trust in the region. An explanation somewhere else in the proposal may be helpful to map the structure of services within the health care sector in order to show its complexity.

Source: Adapted from Fowler, 1996.

Clough and Nutbrown talked to have a clear sense that their research should answer questions about the relevance of their research. The core feeling Clough and Nutbrown bring out of their discussion is that research students want their research to bring about some changes to practice, policy, professional development or to doing research itself.

In Table 11.6, Evans's justification for her research attempted and succeeded in saying a lot about her intentions in a very limited space. Her argument is fairly clear due to its structure and the use of conventional devices to establish a situation. That situation being the need to do more if a current policy initiative is to be successful. Her purpose is to do research to develop an understanding among professional information workers of the key concepts on which major national and local policy developments are based. If this is done, she argues, her profession will be better placed to implement effective change through better informed interpretations of policy for organizational

TABLE 11.6 IDENTIFYING THE RELEVANCE OF YOUR RESEARCH

Extract	Comments
The public library system in the United Kingdom is one of the most extensive and developed in the world. Visiting the public library is the fifth most popular activity in the United Kingdom, making it much more popular than visiting the other cultural institutions such as museums and art galleries.	The size, scale and importance of the public library system is established.
However, a number of high-profile pieces of research and government reports agree that public libraries and information professionals have missed many opportunities relating to the library's role in a sophisticated, complex, multicultural country.	References to recent research literature provide the foundation for the argument that an opportunity is being lost.
The research shows that the advent of information communications technology, changing industrial, commercial, and educational patterns, has not been addressed by the public library.	The changing and increasingly complicated nature of the problem is indicated.
In particular the research suggests that public libraries have an insufficient strategic direction because of the absence of a National Steering Organization, given the primacy of the cultural and educational role they are generally expected to fulfil.	What is missing to address change is stated.
The sector has, it is agreed, benefited from the formation of the Library and Information Commission in 1995. In the same year the review undertaken for the Department of National Heritage reported an improved sense of purpose and direction and status of the public library system.	Developments already in place are mentioned but found insufficient.
The cultural role, however, has, arguably, received very little attention and in particular lacks clarity and definition yet it is considered extremely important by many professional librarians and government bodies.	The insufficiency is attributed to a lack of understanding of a major concept, that is culture.
Government policy on the cultural role of the public libraries will have an important influence on the future of the library system and professional librarians' understanding of their role. This research will explore the understanding and interpretations professional librarians have of the present and future cultural work of public libraries in the West Midlands in the UK.	The benefits of a focus on the understandings of culture are outlined.

(Continued)

TABLE 11.6   (CONTINUED)

Extract	Comments
This will be placed in the context of the national government agenda for public information. This research will make a timely and relevant contribution to understanding the ways in which a major government centralized policy is understood and interpreted by a local library system during a time of transition and change both within the organization of the public library system and in the status of professional information workers.	The reasons for the research are formulated and the context given. The benefits are reformulated in terms of national, local and professional outcomes.

Source: Adapted from Evans, 2000 ('The cultural role of public libraries').

strategy. Notice there is a political element in Evans's justification. Her intent to bring about change is essentially political: she aims to make an impact on how a group of professionals 'see' something and therefore change how they may devise and enact courses of action based on their changed understandings. Therefore the management of this project would require careful consideration and sensitivity not only to avoid overt bias, but also to ensure that all relevant ethical matters are clearly accounted for. So we can see how Evans employed a structure to establish a problem, identify some attempts to deal with the problem, find fault with those attempts, identify a cause of the fault, state what would need to be done and what the benefits of her research might be. She does all of this and also manages to place her research into a contemporary organizational and political context.

One way of thinking about your justification is to examine what you intend to achieve by doing your research. Evans wanted to bring about change to professional practice through understanding an important concept. Change is a common element of most justifications. You may intend to bring about a better or a different understanding of a theory or concept, or bring change to certain actions and behaviours. These two general intentions are not mutually exclusive, as though the former is characteristic of the academic dissertation and the latter of the work-based dissertation. The example in Table 11.6 shows that the understanding and investigation of interpretations of a concept often have a direct impact on the implementation of an organizational strategy. The key questions for your justification include:

- ◆ **What is the nature of the problem?**

- ◆ **How extensive is it?**

- ◆ **When and where did it begin?**

- ◆ **What will happen if nothing is done about it?**

- ◆ **What are its possible causes?**

- ◆ **What can be done about these causes?**

- ◆ **What will the benefits be of doing something?**

You are attempting, in addressing these questions, to make a persuasive case which establishes that you have a real problem for your research and that the research you suggest will have benefits. These benefits do not, of course, have to be practical. Intellectual outcomes are equally legitimate and in many cases are the foundation for many others.

THE INDICATIVE LITERATURE REVIEW

In Chapter 6 we looked at reviewing the literature on your topic. In this section I want to show you three examples of indicative reviews from the main types of dissertation. The first extract (Table 11.7) is from a literature-based research proposal. The researcher, Kellie Snow, had a deep and longstanding interest in the legend of King Arthur. She took this interest to identify her general topic, turning it into an analysis of the bibliographic sources on the legend. As you can see, this kind of research places high demands on the researcher. Knowledge and familiarity with an extensive and sometimes difficult literature is required and this sometimes means, as in Snow's case, having the ability to read and translate from a number of languages. But as you can also see from Table 11.7, the elegance of her knowledge is more than adequately expressed in her indicative review of the literature.

In Table 11.8, the second extract is from a review of the literature for a traditional dissertation. Ellen Smullen, who wrote this review, turned her pre-existing attitudes on popular romantic fiction into her topic and looked to survey her peers on their attitudes to the genre.

TABLE 11.7   LITERATURE REVIEW FROM A LITERATURE-BASED RESEARCH PROPOSAL

Extract	Comments
The earliest *recorded* mention of an Arthur comes in *The Gododdin* by bard Aneirin, which probably dates back to the seventh century. However, it only mentions a great British warrior, and as the earliest manuscript still in existence is from the thirteenth century, the true value of this is debatable. The first significant mention comes in the *Annales Cambriae* (*The Welsh Annals*) and *Historia Brittonum* (*History of the Britons*) in the eighth or ninth centuries, but in both cases yet again he features only as a leader of battles, who 'perished' at Camlann along with Medraut (Mordred). The bard and prophet Merlin also appears in these, but is not related to Arthur in any way. Geoffrey of Monmouth's *Historia Regum Britanniae* (*History of the Kings of Britain, c.* 1136) is the first work to portray Arthur as a *king*, and also to feature other characters which are still popular in the myth today. He wrote the first 'story' of Arthur, *claiming* to have gained the information from an ancient book given to him by his patron, and from the *Historia Brittonum*. Geoffrey followed this work with *Vita Merlini* (*Life of Merlin, c.* 1150) focusing on the bard's adventures from Welsh literature and further developing his character. The degree of historical proof in these works is debatable because, as Snyder remarks, 'Geoffrey's writings rely on an immense body of vernacular tradition and outright fable which is impossible to date and authenticate', plus there are his own probable frequent exaggerations. However, his works make Geoffrey key to the development of the Arthurian 'myth'. The focus of this project is English language literature, but in these early cases others must be included as they are fundamental to the origins of some of the features of the myth.	As with many pieces of research that involve an analysis of biographies, this one is also a chronology. An attempt is made to identify key historical works and to say, briefly, what each contributed to the development of the myth. It is common also with this kind of research to state the names of authors and their publications. Most of these works will not, of course, be available for consultation in your local academic library. It is more the case that you would have to make special arrangements with organizations like the British Library to consult such rare documents. However, it is increasingly possible to consult these kinds of documents in electronic format.

(Continued)

TABLE 11.7 (CONTINUED)

Extract	Comments
The French writer Wace was the next significant author of Arthurian material. His chronicle *Brut* (1155) follows that of Geoffrey of Monmouth, but the Round Table and the hope of Arthur's return from Avalon are also introduced. Layamon translated *this* into English between 1199 and 1225, but made his own additions by bringing the focus back to Arthur's struggle against the Saxons, probably to appeal to the British audience. Various Welsh and Breton works exist from around this time also, recording the oral traditions of their people and providing references for writers such as Geoffrey and Wace. Stories related to that of Arthur such as Culhwch and Olwen, Tristan and Iseult and particularly Merlin emerge from these. The characters Guinevere, Mordred, Bedivere and Kay also first appear in Welsh writings, though not in the specific guise in which they are now known. French romance writers added more episodes and angles to the Arthurian story, turning its appeal to tales of 'love, magic and manners' as well as military accomplishments. However, in this group of writings Arthur becomes a benevolent leader who fades into the background to allow for the stories of other characters, and his problems are also no longer foreign invasions, but enemies that are within. Chrétien de Troyes, the most significant of the French writers from this time, tells in particular the stories of Eric and Enid, Lancelot and his affair with Guinevere, and the story of Perceval. He is also the first writer to mention Arthur's court, 'Camelot', and the 'Grail' that the knights went in search of. All of these stories bring out the idea of chivalry that later writers would focus on.	To some degree the writer expects the reader to know something of the legend or myth. In a similar way, some of the characters and authors are also expected to be known about. Although the purpose of this research is not stated, its indication is present in the review – being to map and analyse the development of the myth in what has become a substantial corpus of writings.

Source: Adapted from Snow, 2002 ('Structural analysis of sources on Arthurian legend').

TABLE 11.8   AN INDICATIVE REVIEW OF THE LITERATURE FROM A TRADITIONAL
RESEARCH PROPOSAL

Extract	Comments
Arguments expressed in the literature against public libraries stocking romances are numerous and complex, but mainly focus on their literary quality, formulaic style and the fact that they are mass-produced commodities, belonging to a 'consumer society, not to a truly Literate and Literary society (1)'. Romance novelist and former librarian Jane Anne Krentz believes that to criticize romances on these grounds is to criticize them for all the reasons that they work (2). Krentz argues that many who criticize romances have never attempted to read one, so their assumptions and bias are not based on a sound understanding of the conventions and complexities of the genre (3). Librarian Kristin Ramsdell has done a great deal of work on romance fiction in an effort to legitimize the genre and encourage greater understanding among the library profession (4). She believes that romances are often judged as substandard because of their immense popularity, and because they differ from literary texts which place importance on language, characterization, and thematic complexity (5). Mosley et al., (6) in their award winning article in defence of the romance novel, state that many librarians conveniently overlook the fact that classic authors such as Charles Dickens produced serialized novels specifically aimed at the lower-paid masses, novels that in our culture are considered to be great literary works:	This review begins by stating a common argument and position against popular romantic fiction. It also highlights some contrary views against this argument. Positions which have a positive attitude towards popular romantic fiction are succinctly summarized.
Sometime, somewhere, somehow, someone drew an imaginary line and created 'lowbrow' and 'highbrow'. Occasionally, an author who's been dead long enough can cross from 'lowbrow' to 'highbrow', as is the case with Charles Dickens, who wrote serialized novels in his day (7).	The notion of high and low culture is introduced as a basic cause of prejudice against this genre. The case of Dickens is highlighted to show the historical origins of popular fiction and that he was quite well aware of its popularity.

(Continued)

TABLE 11.8 (CONTINUED)

Extract	Comments
Individual taste in novels and perception of what accounts as cultural enrichment are very subjective, and are subject to change. Supporters of the romance genre believe that it is not the place of the librarian to 'judge cultural relativity, but ... to provide a service relative to our culture'(8), and that to judge romances against literary works is ridiculous, as romances, such as those produced by Mills and Boon 'have never claimed to be classical literature' (9). Jay Dixon (10), in her text, *The Romance Fiction of Mills and Boon 1909–1990s*, believes that it is unfair to dismiss series romances as trash purely on the basis of their literary style, and that romances should be judged by their own criteria rather than compared against literary novels. Frances Whitehead, ex-editorial director for Mills and Boon agrees, asserting that the novels do not need to apologize for what they are, and that they keep countless women amused and happy regardless of their apparent lack of literary merit (11).	Key words and phrases are introduced to indicate the problems of making judgements about any kind of literature and implicitly about readers of popular fiction.
Criticism of romances on the basis of their literary style originates from the belief that these types of novels, if read exhaustively, could limit people's knowledge, moral outlook and language skills. Social historian Richard Hoggart agrees with this criticism, and has stated that it is a common myth that readers of romances will move on to reading more 'improving' literary texts, as they are far more likely to keep reading more of the same (12). Hoggart is strongly in favour of libraries returning to their educational role and increasing their stock of literary texts (13). Politician Roy Hattersley is not so convinced, and has expressed the concern that if libraries exclusively stocked literary and 'improving' texts, they would lose the accessibility that they currently enjoy (14).	Further examples from literature of positive attitudes to popular fiction are now introduced and show there is a research literature that runs counter to the popular view that popular fiction is sub-standard. A number of points and observations are briefly mentioned, which can form the basis of further detailed argument.

Famous cultural critics are introduced and their competing arguments summarized in terms of the high and low culture debate. |

(Continued)

TABLE 11.8 (CONTINUED)

Extract	Comments
Public library borrowers would ultimately vote with their feet and go elsewhere for the books that they want to read, and it will be the public library that would suffer. Hattersley also believes that public libraries should be working towards '… demolish(ing) the myth that books are the preoccupation of a cultural elite. Reading was meant to make us glad … all of us'(15). Librarians tend to protect works of classic fiction, and concentrate cutbacks on popular fiction, but Hattersley believes that there is danger in this logic, as the popular genres do a great deal in keeping communities reading and turning the pages (16). Peter Mann (17) has conducted a lot of research into books and their readers/borrowers, and his research reveals that there is a great deal of misconception about the readers of romances and that the novels play an important part in keeping people interested in reading:	The role of the librarian is now introduced. Based on initial statements in this review, librarians are seen as holding the high-culture position.
The fact that while we all declare the way TV has ousted the printed word, it is Mills and Boon with their print run of millions who are in the front line of keeping people reading and off the breadline. (18)	Given that popular romantic fiction is the most borrowed of items from the library, librarians' reasons for stocking it are indicated.
Part of the justification for stocking popular fiction in public libraries has been that it brings in borrowers who can then be encouraged into reading other types of fiction (19). This is an important point, especially in an age where libraries are actively involved in reader development schemes (20), and are aware of the important position they have in encouraging literacy among their communities. Rachel Van Riel's consultancy firm Opening the Book has been particularly important in this area, helping librarians to encourage borrowers to explore beyond their usual reading, and diversify tastes beyond genre and brand loyalty (21).	Further research on reading is now introduced. The focus librarians have is shown to be on developing readers' reading abilities. This implies that readers of popular romantic fiction are unable to read high-brow fiction.

(Continued)

TABLE 11.8 (CONTINUED)

Extract	Comments
Opening the Book has also been influential in helping libraries recognize that readers of popular fiction are not passive, but are voracious readers with very specific needs and tastes. Stuart Hannabus (22) has commented on the dangers of librarians overlooking the complexity of the romance genre in his article *Resources for Love*, and Kristin Ramsdell has worked towards raising awareness of the importance of stock selection and reader advisory work when dealing with romances and their readers (23). Concern has been voiced in the literature about reader development schemes that librarians will be tempted to promote only 'good' literature, but Van Riel (24) insists that the manipulation is not to shape individual tastes, only to open up access to a greater variety of books. It is still up to the reader whether they like the books recommended or not. Culture Secretary, Chris Smith, also believes that libraries are well placed to encourage reading, but should be careful in their approach, avoiding condescension and paternalism and opting for encouragement:	The emphasis therefore from the library, librarians and government is to encourage reader development. The general view that popular fiction is sub-standard has therefore been reiterated and shown to be institutionalized. A number of dissenting voices from within the library profession are identified, but not before the general attitude of the library profession has been reiterated.
If the library or librarian is wagging a metaphorical finger at the reader saying: 'you are reading rubbish, you really shouldn't be. Here is a good, improving book — we think you ought to be reading this', that is the worst possible way of getting people to appreciate the wonders of great literature. (25)	
Librarian attitude has been pinpointed as vitally important when advising readers on their choice of fiction (26). Kristin Ramsdell notes that the condescending attitude of librarians can seriously affect their borrowers, and that despite disparagement of romance being a 'time honoured tradition in many library circles' (27) this is no reason to continue unethical bad practice. The romance novel is still hugely popular and is unlikely to disappear (28), despite the suggestion that many librarians would like to see 'bibliographic euthanasia' for the genre (29).	The critical view of a popular romance is developed by looking at sources from outside the library and information profession, at critics who see the genre as promoting serious unwanted outcomes in readers.

(Continued)

TABLE 11.8   (CONTINUED)

Extract	Comments
Cathie Linz, Mary K. Chelton, Kristen Ramsdell and Shelley Mosley, are just a few of a growing number in the library profession who believe that it is time to legitimize this outcast genre, and give dignity to the reading choices of romance readers (30). However, some criticisms about stocking popular romances in public libraries go beyond concerns of literary merit, and are much more sinister in nature (31). Series novels, such as those published by Mills and Boon, have been criticized for promoting sexual stereotypes (32), and are acknowl-edged as being racist and homophobic (33) even by those who enjoy them. In recent years there have been attempts to rectify these problems, and new sub-genres have emerged (such as ethnic and multicultural series) to reflect more realistically today's society. Supporters of series romances insist that the books are very important in com-municating the changing values of society to people who would read very little else, and that as a medium of com-munication, this is justification enough for stocking them in the library (34). Some disagree with this point, insisting that by stocking series romances, libraries are legitimizing and reinforcing the dubious values that such books include:	Such critics see librarians as actively promoting sexual and racial stereo-types and homophobia because they stock popular romances. The 'popular' from the point of view of such critics is equated with rubbish. Popular romances are said to be rubbish because they are not considered to reflect real life (whatever that is). Ironically, the critics are calling for popular romance to be censored. The basis for the research is therefore established: to examine the views of public librarians to popular romantic fiction.

> Rubbish is popular, and it is necessary to state why it is lethal: it provides an escape from the real and actual world. It depicts a two-dimensional world in which there is no poverty, unemployment, vandalism, drug dependence, failing family relationships and injustice before the law. It is an opiate; it positively undermines the determination to change the status quo. (35)

This statement reveals that, for some, popular romantic fiction has had an all too convincing victory over the censors, and that a stronger line in stock selection is believed to be necessary and justified.

Source: Adapted from Smullen, 2002 ('Survey of librarians' attitudes to popular romance books').

TABLE 11.9 AN INDICATIVE REVIEW FROM A WORK-BASED RESEARCH PROPOSAL

Extract	Comments
The existing structure of library support for the NHS has developed over the past 30 years (1). Many of the regional library services were put in place to support postgraduate medical and allied education during the 1960s (2). Health service libraries were furthered by the government recommendation (3) which stated services should be multi-disciplinary and available to all professional groups. At this point libraries were funded by hospitals as part of their contribution to a postgraduate and continuing medical education of their staff. Education, training, research and development in the NHS are funded by a 17 per cent levy on health authorities and postgraduate medical education, and the funding for libraries has been largely derived from this route.	This review begins by giving a brief chronology of information service provision within the NHS. It attempts to show that NHS library services developed in an ad hoc way and that funding for them has been provided from within and from other programmes.
Library services in the South Western regions developed largely along parallel tracks, in line with the national initiatives just described. The first postgraduate Medical Centre librarians were appointed in the early 1970s. Very early on the libraries in each region joined to form inter-lending networks, and document-supply mechanisms were also established. These mechanisms resulted in semi-formal arrangements which were based on reciprocal need for access to extended resources. Since the original merger in 1994 the two major library networks have begun to integrate some of their activities. Eight joint operating frameworks combined to form the South and West Regional Library and Information Network in 1996. This merger has highlighted a number of ongoing issues and problems in the provision of library and information services. These include information for research and development, information for non-medical education and, training, resource sharing, and, most importantly, financing of information services.	The nature of the problem is to look from a regional perspective based on the researcher's place of work. Some of the key issues and problems perceived in the workplace are listed and seen as general issues and problems facing health care libraries at a national level.

(Continued)

TABLE 11.9 (CONTINUED)

Extract	Comments
A number of independent, NHS-generated and government reports have also highlighted these major problems, not least those of providing and financing a co-ordinated information service within the NHS and to those working in public health, social care, and other professions related to health care. To date very little detailed information has been gathered on the resource and management issues related to specific library and information services, in order to identify responsibilities for funding and management of services. The situation today is one of general confusion over which department, unit or sector within health care is ultimately responsible for library and information services. This is exacerbated by the problem of how this information can best be obtained, given the wide variety of libraries and their geographical spread.	The problem is then summarized, with an additional point being made that solving the problem will have difficulties in itself in terms of conducting the research.

Source: Adapted from Fowler, 1996 ('Library and information service provision to NHS community-based staff').

In the third extract, shown in Table 11.9, you can see a literature review for a work-based dissertation. Christine Fowler, an information worker in the NHS, took as her topic the provision of information by NHS information services to health practitioners. Her basic premise was that all organizations need information and that those based on research need it even more. The literature review she did for her proposal was long and complex, looking at the literature on recent changes in the NHS, government policy and at the arguments for the role of information to health care professionals. The extract in Table 11.9 shows the literature related to health care libraries.

THE METHOD SECTION

The purpose of this section is to demonstrate the reasons behind your choice of methodological tradition, approach, procedures and tools for the collection and analysis of your data. There is often some confusion over what some of these terms mean and how they should be used. In this book I have used the following terms and phrases in the following ways:

- by *methodological tradition* I mean the choice you have made between positivist and non-positivist traditions;

- by *methodological approach* I refer to a choice and balance between experimental and non-experimental and qualitative and quantitative;

- by *research culture* I refer to choices between historical, feminist, comparative and other cultures of research;

- by *technique of analysis* I refer to types of analysis such as content, discourse, category and other forms of analysis.

The problem with writing this section is attempting to describe your overall approach, the methods and procedures you will use and at the same time show how you arrived at the decision on which combination to employ.

> We looked at research questions along with hypotheses and propositions in Chapter 3.

This is often called the *logic of justification*. If you go back to Chapters 7 and 8 where we looked at the logical assumptions and the consequences of methodological choices, you will see just how important it is to explain the reasoning behind your choices. It is not sufficient simply to describe what you will do; you need to explain how you elected to take one approach rather than another and at the consequences this might have for the research. This involves looking at the design of your research as a whole and not just at the collection of data but at what kinds of data you have, and how it can be managed, sorted, analysed, presented and interpreted, in terms of your overall methodological approach. It is often your research questions which guide the inquiry process and not the data or data collection tools or analysis itself. Your research questions are the hub or the centre of your research and of your research proposal; the ways in which they are worded give direction to your methodological assumptions, methodological approach, kinds of data you deem necessary and form of analysis. Your research questions form a frame or skeleton which hold the rest of your research proposal and research together. In the extract shown in Table 11.10 you can see the part of the section that deals with how the data is to be collected.

The extract in Table 11.10 is a paraphrase. We could reasonably expect the actual dissertation to run to about four pages and include summaries of, and citations to, debates about the pros and cons of the survey approach, the validity and reliability of questionnaires and interviews, along with political sensitivity when using senior

TABLE 11.10   METHODS SECTION OF A RESEARCH PROPOSAL

Extract	Comments
It is proposed that this research is based on a survey approach: a survey of the relevant literature, a questionnaire of key decision-makers and follow-up interviews (1). The combination of these three techniques is designed to get an appropriate balance between breadth and depth in order to achieve a valid description of the current state of understanding and interpretation of the concept of culture (2). The organization and execution of the postal survey will be undertaken in July and responses are expected within four working weeks. The use of a standardized questionnaire will avoid the problem of varying quality of interview data (3). They will also provide an opportunity to gather some quantitative data which can be used to construct questions for follow-up interviews (4). The literature on questionnaire surveys (5) is generally agreed that questionnaires alone are an insufficient technique for gathering valid data even though they may be reliable if properly constructed and conducted.	Three main sources of information and data are identified, including the literature. The issues of balancing breadth against depth is mentioned. Timing and reasons for a structured questionnaire are given. Note the citations, which will presumably be used in the dissertation with others to provide fuller explanations for the method.
There is no need for a sample of key decision-makers because at the national and the local level all relevant persons have agreed to take part in this research. This includes all the senior management teams of public libraries in the West Midlands region, chief executive of the Library Association and his senior management team, and a representative from the policy formation unit of the Department for National Heritage. In this respect the population will be a purposeful sample and will require the techniques developed to interview elites (6).	Access to subjects is explained along with who they will be. Sampling issues are dealt with and the nature of the status of subjects is mentioned – possibly to indicate that certain techniques may have to be employed.
Having established, from the literature review, the subject areas to be explored, the postal questionnaires will allow a close examination of the subject based on a combination of specific and general questions. Questions would be either of the closed or open type and based on the guiding questions for this research project (7).	

(Continued)

TABLE 11.10 (CONTINUED)

Extract	Comments
A pilot questionnaire (8) has already been tested in the field and a final design of the questionnaire is nearly ready. Given that the chief executive of the Library Association will be acting as my sponsor for this research and has already contacted the subjects it is anticipated that the questionnaire will have a high if not 100 per cent response rate. A coding frame for the questionnaire has been constructed and is appended to this proposal (9). The total number of questionnaires expected to be completed is 24 therefore it is not expected that software will be required to analyse the results.	The form of the questions is stated along with the pilot. A key person for the research is identified by post and organization because they are important for gaining sufficient access to subjects.
Based on three pilot interviews (with staff from my department) it is feasible to conduct interviews with all 24 subjects in the time available. An opportunity to conduct most of the interviews over a week period has presented itself in the form of a national conference for public librarians. Twenty of the respondents will be attending the conference and have agreed via my sponsor to set aside up to two hours during the conference. The final version of the interview schedule will not be prepared until all questionnaires have been analysed (10). The interviews will be, however, structured, to allow	Levels of response rate are mentioned and there is therefore no need to explain what will be done if the rate is too low. When the subjects will be interviewed is stated, but the problems this may create are not mentioned.
some control of the course of the conversation, to maintain the focus on the relevant issues and problems surrounding the concept of culture (11). It will be possible for respondents to explain their understandings and interpretations, and will be encouraged to base these on their own organizational policies and courses of action (12). There will also be an opportunity for a second round of interviews, should this be necessary, with a much smaller group (13), approximately six subjects, to follow up further issues raised in the questionnaires and the first round of interviews.	Reasons for using interviews are indicated and relate back to the need for depth, which is augmented by the mention of the possibility for further interviews.

Source: Adapted from Evans, 2000 ('The cultural role of public libraries').

persons in organizations as a source of your data. In your dissertation you will have an opportunity to amplify on your methods and to discuss the methodological approach you chose to use. In your research proposal, however, you will only have the space to give an indication of what data collection tools you intend to use, how you will get access to the data/subjects, what some of the technical problems might be and how you will analyse the data.

THE ETHICS SECTION

In Chapter 9 we looked at ethics in terms of doing research and emphasized that an analysis of your personal ethical standpoint and the needs of your research are important parts of the whole research process. Your proposal should include a set of brief statements on how you intend to conform to accepted ethical codes, and should detail what particular ethical issues and problems you will need to deal with in your research. In Table 11.11 you can see such a statement.

There is, as you can see in Table 11.11, a certain number of 'usual ethical issues and problems' and this represents the basic contents to be included in your ethics section. The main point is to state what the specific ethical issues are in terms of your research. More details could have been included in this statement, linking each problem to a specific part of the research. You may want to look back to Table 11.6, where we introduced Ceri Evans's research, and think about what kinds of ethical issues and problems might emerge from her research.

THE TIMETABLE

In Chapter 2 we looked at how you can begin to identify the tasks and estimate the time needed to complete your research. This timetable or schedule should be included in your proposal to show your supervisors that you have made a realistic estimation of the time your research will take you. Your schedule should also include time for writing up your dissertation and, importantly, time for unforeseen happenings – like illness, relatives visiting and holidays. A typical way of presenting your schedule is shown in Figure 11.3.

There are other ways to present your timetable, such as in a Gantt chart or by using various kinds of software such as *Project Manager*. But whatever way you choose, it must indicate the sequence and relationships between the major groups of tasks to be achieved to meet the target dates.

TABLE 11.11   STATEMENT OF ETHICAL ISSUES AND PROBLEMS

Extract	Comments
This research will need to attend to the following ethical issue and problems: confidentiality of subjects and protection of their identities and places of work; maintaining independence from possible attempts by interested parties/bodies to bias results; ensuring security of data during and after completion of the research. These key issues and problems will be addressed by: using the university's formal procedures including sending standard agreements and letters of consent on confidentiality to all subjects; sending a copy of this research proposal to all parties so that they are fully informed about the intent of this research; ensuring non-disclosure of subjects by using numbers in place of names, and of their respective organizations by using letters in place of names; only myself and my dissertation supervisors will have access to the data. Subjects will have the right, as stated in the letter of consent, to withdraw from this research but will not have the right to edit or censor the final dissertation so long as their identity/organization has not been revealed nor has there been any other breach of the agreement.	The key issue and problems are stated. These may become problematic in the course of the research or change altogether. Therefore they are largely the 'obvious' matters for attention. Using the university's or a professional organization's formal code can be an effective way of conforming to accepted standards. How you ensure non-disclosure needs to be determined in advance. The rights of subjects are indicated, but so to are your rights. Is it ethical for a key informant to withdraw near the end of your research, perhaps making it impossible to complete, when you have not infringed any ethical code or agreement?

You may have noticed that the schedule in Figure 11.3 allows time for slippage, when you take more time than expected on a task, and allows ample time for writing up and doing production jobs in the three to four weeks prior to the handing-in deadline. A key piece of advice I annually give to my masters students is to expect the unexpected – whatever can go wrong has gone wrong for your predecessors. Moreover, do not think you can print off your dissertation in an afternoon. The pagination, printing and checking page numbers and all the other minor jobs take, on average, about three days. Plus, of course, you will have to get at least two copies bound and, if you do not hand them in yourself, you should allow plenty of time for the post – twice the normal delivery time.

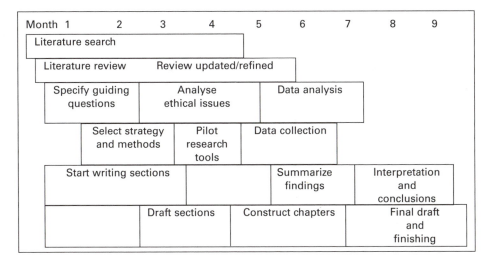

Month 1	2	3	4	5	6	7	8	9
Literature search								
Literature review		Review updated/refined						
Specify guiding questions		Analyse ethical issues		Data analysis				
	Select strategy and methods		Pilot research tools	Data collection				
Start writing sections					Summarize findings		Interpretation and conclusions	
	Draft sections			Construct chapters			Final draft and finishing	

FIGURE 11.3   SAMPLE TIMETABLE FOR YOUR RESEARCH PROPOSAL

SHOWING COHERENCE

If your proposal has been carefully crafted, then it should have a logical structure; this means it will have coherence between the different parts and their contents. The discourse is the language and vocabulary of your methodological approach, your research design, and your approach to specifying a topic or problem. The discourse (or vocabulary) is not an empty shell of phrases and words (buzz terms) to be included, but a set of tools to be used in ways which can demonstrate your proficiency at applying them appropriately. To do this is to display your reasoning in a way that allows the reader – and you – to see the flow, sequencing and logic of your overall approach. One way of achieving this is to lay out your initial proposal as shown in Table 11.12.

Table 11.12 shows a logical sequence of questions about a puzzle. It shows three chapters of a dissertation in outline form. Each chapter attempts to attend to a related problem through the guiding questions which you have stated to help you construct a topic or problem for your research. The fourth column on process and product highlights the kinds of skills, capabilities, qualities and attitudes you will need to synthesize 'doing–thinking–doing', in order to make decisions on how best to move forward and further into your research. Although this practice is not common in all universities, envisioning your dissertation in this way can be very useful. It can give you a clearer idea of the dissertation you will be taking to your research committee and the research journey you will be undertaking. In summary it will help you to:

TABLE 11.12   SHOWING COHERENT THINKING ABOUT YOUR PROPOSAL

Issues	Guiding questions	Explication/ explanation	Process/products	Chapter in dissertation
Starting out, uncertainty	How can I understand the range and variety of definitions and uses of the concept 'culture'? What has the literature to say?	During this initial stage I see the main task as identifying the meaning of the concept through its use in the literature, especially in anthropology and sociology. Immersion in the literature in the literature will be needed across the social sciences.	Close reading of key texts in anthropology (e.g. Malinowski, Evans-Pritchard) should contextualize the use of the concept as a phenomenon for research/description rather than for simulative definition. An analytical review of the concept as used in the literature will be the main tangible product.	Chapter 2 will be the review of the concept culture as used in the literature. It will focus on how culture as a phenomenon has been researched and described and what methodological assumptions have been made by researchers (ethnographers).
Equivocality about the concept	In what ways do key government policy documents use the concept 'culture' when talking about public library services? How do these uses relate to those in the academic literature?	This stage will involve analysis of policy documents relevant to the cultural agenda of public libraries. The emphasis will be to extract the intent of the concept in the context of its use.	Using rhetorical analysis/reading techniques, the review of policy documents should result in the usage of the concept. This will provide a major part of the relevant discourse for constructing relevant questions for the interviews.	Chapter 4 (Chapter 3 was an explanation/explication of the methodology and research procedures) will describe the use of the concept in policy documents. The focus will be on extracting the discourse of the documents to see if there are any assumptions being made about what culture is or should be.

(Continued)

TABLE 11.12 (CONTINUED)

Issues	Guiding questions	Explication/ explanation	Process/products	Chapter in dissertation
Problems of gathering reliable and valid understandings	What kinds of understandings do senior figures in the library profession have of the cultural role of public libraries? How do these understandings relate to those in policy documents?	The challenge in this stage will be to get access to senior figures in the information profession. My contacts – chief executive of the Library Association and member of the LIC – have agreed to arrange introductions. I will be guided by the tacit uses of culture in the literature/policy documents to construct appropriate discourses for interviews.	Using my 'sponsor' – arrangements will be made to interview key figures in the library world including the sponsors themselves. Their understandings and interpretations will be recorded and probed and any documents/policies/ programmes initiated will be collected for analysis.	Chapter 5 will report on the interviews with senior figures in the information and library profession. It will present an aggregated set of responses based on the themes which emerged from the analysis of the documents and the literature. Documents collected in the field will be listed and subject to comparative analysis in Chapter 6.

♦ identify what things and tasks you may encounter on your way;

♦ arrange the literature into sections to deal with different issues, concerns and problems;

♦ narrow down your research to make it manageable;

♦ identify key landmarks and risks;

♦ identify key stakeholders and groups; and

♦ identify different approaches and specify the logical connectivity of your approach.

Assessment of a research proposal

In most cases the research proposal is part of the assessment for an accredited course of study. For this reason the ways in which your research proposal will be assessed need to be taken into account when you prepare your document. This has certain problems, not least that the assessor may have preconceptions as to what structure should be used. I have already said, quite strongly, that the structure should be a matter for you to decide. This means there is potential for conflict between what your supervisors expect and what you deem necessary. The main way to address this is to be clear from the outset with your supervisors about what kind of research you intend to do. As you work on your proposal, consult with them on a regular basis about the reasons for the structure you are intending to use for your proposal. This should encourage you to explain and justify your choices in ways which help you to incorporate all the necessary elements to meet the assessment criteria.

TYPICAL CRITERIA FOR ASSESSING THE PROPOSAL

In this section I want to suggest some criteria that are often used to assess a research proposal, my purpose being to orient your work towards meeting them in ways which suit your research and the bureaucracy of a research committee. Table 11.13 provides a snapshot overview of the formative criteria that could be used for the overall assessment of your proposal.

TABLE 11.13 OVERVIEW OF CRITERIA FOR A RESEARCH PROPOSAL

Criteria	Description
1 Aims and objectives	Aim(s) and objectives form a coherent set. Aim(s) show clear intention and can be actualized by the objectives which are logically sequenced.
2 Literature review and citations	Identification of key sources, authors and arguments to place the topic in an historical perspective. Summarizing and evaluating different ideas and arguments. Showing a command of the subject/topic vocabulary. Citations are consistent, correct and detailed.
3 Topic rationale	Use of argumentative structure with sufficient evidence and data to justify and provide a rationale for the topic. Use of the literature to provide authority or/and indicate direction of the topic.
4 Methodology and data collection	Overview of methodological approach with identification of appropriate data collection techniques which are briefly assessed. Justification is provided by reference to the literature and the definition and scope placed on the topic.
5 Argumentation and critical awareness	Argumentation analysis shown in rationale, literature review, scope set for the topic and justification of methodology and data collection techniques.
6 Presentation and succinctness	Clear, systematic and structured with very good grammar, spelling and clear arrangement.

READER'S QUESTIONS TO BE ANSWERED IN YOUR PROPOSAL

Another way of approaching this problem is to think about it from the standpoint of a person assessing your proposal, asking yourself whether it answers the basic questions the reader will raise. Using your peers as proxi-assessors can be a useful way of gaining the kind of insight and understanding of assessment necessary to meet the criteria set. It will also provide you and your peers with an important learning opportunity from which you can acquire a much broader and deeper understanding of what makes for a good research proposal. Here are some possible questions to help you begin this exercise:

♦ *Title*: Does it indicate the topic, approach and key concept?

♦ *Introduction*: Does this seem complete? Is the topic established, are facts given and the approach justified? Is it clear and succinct?

♦ *Statement of the problem*: Is the problem clearly stated and its parameters defined? Is the background clear and used to show the nature of the problem?

♦ *Research questions*: Are these clear and systematic? Are they fully related to the problem statement? Are they answerable with research?

♦ *Justification*: Is this clear, well argued, using evidence and data? Are the research questions logical outcomes from the justification? Is the problem statement consistent with the conclusions of the justification? Is it appropriate for the definition of the problem?

♦ *Indicative literature review*: Is there a clear structure? Are citations correct? Are key concepts, theories and findings identified? Does it make logically, justified conclusions for research?

♦ *Feasibility*: Is there enough time to do the research? Has the student the necessary skills and abilities? Is the data accessible and able to be analysed appropriately?

♦ *Risk analysis*: Have the risks been identified? Are contingency plans identified? Are these realistic?

These are the kinds of questions most readers would address to a research proposal even though the criteria for assessment may be expressed as shown in Table 11.13 or Table 11.14. What you need to try and achieve is an assessment of your proposal in terms of seeing if it 'hangs together'. This means looking to ensure that the different elements are integrated and all focused on researching the topic/problem.

TABLE 11.14   ASSESSING THE JUSTIFICATION FOR THE TOPIC

Topic justification	Grade
Excellent use of argumentative structure and evidence to demonstrate, through analysis, the importance of the topic, the need for research, kinds of questions requiring answers and what benefits such answers may bring. Effective and efficient use of the literature to provide authority and backing to claims.	Excellent
Good justification of the topic but *may* lack full use of argumentative structure *or* evidence to demonstrate a thorough topic analysis. Importance or benefits of the research *may* require a small amount of clarification. More *or* better use should have been made of sources to provide authority and backing.	Satisfactory
Relevant topic identified but lacks convincing argument to link analysis with research questions or hypothesis stated. Little use of sources to provide authority and backing.	Poor

The proposal should be:

♦ *rational,* to show the research has been reasoned out;

♦ *informative,* in that it provides enough detail for the reader to understand the proposal;

♦ *persuasive,* to gain support for the research;

♦ *demonstrative,* to show the appropriateness of the work proposed; and

♦ *realistic,* to show that it is capable of being achieved.

In Table 11.14 a particular element of a proposal has been selected for attention – the justification of the topic. There may be similar tables of criteria for 'argumentation', 'presentation', 'risk analysis' and so on. The problem for assessors is that the more specific the criteria, the more mechanical the assessment is, leaving little latitude for interpretation and exercise of professional judgement – something some people see as an advantage. The more formative (open) the criteria, the more scope there is for innovative and creative research proposals.

Using the various assessment criteria can be a way to constructing a good research proposal. It is, however, very difficult to interpret and meet formative assessment criteria in any literal way. The various tables of criteria in this chapter will help you express the vision you have for your research. Use them to give substance to how you have envisioned your research. In this way you will have a better idea of exactly what it is you will be doing, what tasks, issues and problems you may encounter on your way, how to manage what you produce, including developing contingency plans for what may go wrong and, of course how to specify the logical connectivity of your research design.

SUMMARY OF THIS CHAPTER

The purpose of this chapter has been to bring together many of the elements required for designing a research project. The focus has been on constructing a proposal for research. The key points which have been made include:

♦ A research proposal is the map which will help you to navigate on your research journey because it contains all your analysis, preparation and pre-emptive planning.

♦ There is no definitive structure or content for a research proposal. Each proposal is a unique document crafted by an individual; your proposal says something about you as a potential researcher.

♦ A good research proposal is clear, structured, succinct and answers a series of key questions. To achieve some of this you need to think about the reader of your proposal.

♦ Most research proposals require several drafts, edits and re-writes before a satisfactory one is ready. There is no such thing as the perfect research proposal.

Further reading

Clegg, B. and Birch, P. (2000) *Imagination Engineering*. London: Prentice-Hall. An introduction to using your imagination to make imaginary journeys like those of Einstein.

Piantanida, M. and Garman, N.B. (1999) *The Qualitative Dissertation: A Guide for Students and Faculty*. Thousand Oaks, CA: Corwin. Two good chapters on crafting the research proposal with examples of anticipated portrayals.

Walliman, N. (2001) *Your Research Project: A Step-by-Step Guide for the First Time Researcher*. London: Sage. Chapter 8 is a useful introduction to writing a research proposal.

12 Writing your dissertation

CHAPTER CONCEPTS

● THE UNIVERSITY AS THE CONTEXT ● REPORTING OR WRITING YOUR RESEARCH? ● *DIFFÉRENCE* MAKES THE DIFFERENCE ● OBJECTIVIST AND CONSTRUCTIVIST DISSERTATIONS ● WRITING LONG DOCUMENTS ● PREPARATION AND PLANNING ● SETTING UP TEMPLATES ● VERSION MANAGEMENT AND CONTROL ● SAVING PAPER AND INK WHEN PRINTING ● WHAT STYLE OF WRITING TO USE ● USING THE PERSONAL PRONOUN ● AVOID INAPPROPRIATE LANGUAGE ● CONSTRUCTING A PLAN AND MAP FOR YOUR DISSERTATION: THE MACRO-LEVEL ● THE HYPOTHESIS GENRE ● THE ANALYTICAL GENRE ● THE MYSTERY GENRE ● ORGANIZING CHAPTER CONTENTS: THE MICRO-LEVEL ● PLANNING THE STRUCTURE, CONTENTS AND EVIDENCE OF A CHAPTER ● USING QUOTATIONS AS EVIDENCE ● THE INTRODUCTORY CHAPTER ● THE LITERATURE REVIEW CHAPTER ● THE METHODOLOGY CHAPTER ● THE FINDINGS CHAPTER ● THE ANALYSIS AND DISCUSSION CHAPTER ● THE CONCLUSIONS AND RECOMMENDATIONS CHAPTER ● OTHER PARTS OF THE DISSERTATION ● THE TITLE ● THE ABSTRACT ● THE EXECUTIVE SUMMARY ● ACKNOWLEDGEMENTS ● THE CONTENTS PAGE ● FIGURES AND TABLES ● APPENDICES ● FINAL THOUGHTS ● FURTHER READING

Writing a dissertation is a major undertaking, but because many people manage to produce masters dissertations each year it is an undertaking many of us are capable of. Successful dissertations are not, however, products which can be done without much thought, planning and time. A masters dissertation is a long document. Being somewhere between 12,000 and 20,000 words, a dissertation will take time to write. During this time a considerable amount of thought and sometimes anguish will be spent working through just how it should be constructed. Architecturally speaking, a dissertation needs to have an appropriate structure so that as a whole it has sufficient coherence to hang together. This is because it has to do many things in many places and some simultaneously and not always in linear sequence. A dissertation has to tell the reader why, how and when the research was done, what was found and what this means, and show how it relates to previous studies in the literature. A dissertation is more than the sum of its parts. Although usually made up of individual chapters, a dissertation is not a bound collection of these chapters. Each chapter should be part of an integrated whole, providing a coherent account of a research project. Each chapter should be grounded in making a logical and evident contribution to addressing the research questions set for investigating a specific puzzle. The task as a whole can be summarized in these general questions:

1   How can you write a dissertation that has a logical structure, is clear, and demonstrates that you have acquired and put into practice the range of skills, capabilities, attitudes and qualities expected of a masters student?

2   How do you do all of this in a way that is explicit, provides justification for the definition of the topic, selection of methodology and research design, shows all relevant findings and relates them to previous research and theory?

3   How can all of this be done in a way that communicates what and how you did your research, demonstrating that you understand the process with all its problems?

You will appreciate from this list that a dissertation has a number of tasks to perform. How you go about doing these is a matter for you to decide. Of course, your supervisor will help, as will examples of other dissertations done in your field of study. A key factor in this will be showing particular audiences that you have been on a research journey and have come back with a good story to tell. This normally means addressing your research questions in ways that match the expectations of more than one audience (Fish, 1989). It is this appreciation with which we start, before moving on to look at some of the technicalities that can be employed to meet the challenges of writing your dissertation.

The university as the context

The research you have undertaken will have been done within the context of an academic institution, usually a university or similar institution of higher education. As such, your course will be subject to a set of formal regulations which govern quality through written procedures. There will be a number of professional expectations particular to the institution and to the academic discipline in which you have undertaken your research. At the beginning of your research journey, like most masters students you will have been eager to establish just what is expected and just what a masters dissertation should look like for this university and department. This is a normal and natural part of the process on the journey to becoming a master. Your university and academic department is the cultural environment, maintained by staff and students together, to provide the impetus for doing your research in the way that is expected (Said, 1982). This means doing research that is in line with how research in that university department has evolved, usually over several decades. Your research will normally be expected to embody the standards, modes and look of research previously done in the last five to ten years. This is a reality for most research students. As such, your particular 'habitus' is a major resource for you to use. It will provide you with much of the information and guidance you will need to produce a competent dissertation. By the time you have reached the major writing-up stage, you should have already immersed yourself in the 'habitus' (Bourdieu, 1990/1980: 52) of the department and in the particular position and approach you have taken within your subject discipline. Your course of study should have shown you (through a process of exposure to examples) what your department expects and regards as an acceptable format for a masters dissertation. In practice, at the technical level, this often means meeting the stipulated standards of presentation, which may include such things as the typeface and type size to use. It will also mean, at the academic or scholarly level, that you understand the options available to you in terms of maintaining coherence between the methodological assumptions you employed in your research and the way in which you present that research.

REPORTING OR WRITING YOUR RESEARCH?

When thinking about the dissertation as a large document it may, at first, seem that your main problem is how to write such a large document. But looking at and thinking about the kinds of questions below, you will soon realize that a 12,000–20,000-word document may not be enough to say all the things you think are relevant about your research.

♦ **How do I provide sufficient information so that another researcher could do what I have done in my research?**

♦ **How do I show the link between my choice of methodological position regarding positivist/objectivist or constructivist/interpretivist approaches to show the rationale of a quantitative or qualitative method of data collection?**

♦ How do I explain how the data was collected or produced, and how much actual data should I make available to the reader?

♦ How do I make a convincing argument for the interpretation of the data and its role in addressing my research questions?

These questions may seem general, but when writing a dissertation they become important starting points for deciding on what kind of dissertation to write. How you approach these questions is a matter for you to decide. If you believe that your research has uncovered facts out in the world, and that the means you used were free from values and merely found 'truths' about your phenomenon, then you may well have used an *objectivist* approach. Alternatively, if you believe your research and the methods you used have engaged with and shaped the way you understand your phenomenon, then you may well have used a *constructionist* approach. The objectivist approach is an epistemological position which holds that meaning exists apart from consciousness. A tree in a forest exists objectively, regardless of its being seen and categorized. Its 'tree-ness' is intrinsic to it as an object. When seen by humans its tree-ness is available for them to see empirically, categorize as such and take to be a tree. Many of the features of a positivist position on the nature of reality (ontology) are linked to the epistemology (ways of knowing) of *objectivism*. If you have taken a position within these traditions, it would most likely be that your dissertation 'reports' on your research. By this is meant that it may take a *realist* approach to reporting your research as 'the research' in a way that separates it from you as a conscious subjective person. This typically involves using the third person to represent *the* research as being objective, having found the truth about facts out in the world, through methods that were presented as reliable, valid and able to be replicated by others. Alternatively, if you hold the view that reality is inseparable from the mental categories we use to understand it, by taking a position within the *idealist* (ontological) approach, and regarding your methods as constructing the data, then it is likely you will be taking a *constructionist* approach to epistemology. Believing that theory cannot be separated from observation, nor facts from values, it is likely your dissertation will be *written* as an experience of doing research. In both of the main ontological and epistemological positions just sketched out there are many variations which give differences of emphasis. The main point, however, is that the format and style of your dissertation may be strongly influenced by the choices you made in the design of your research. Whatever design you used for your research, it will have been based on a position within the main methodological positions regarding reality and how that reality is knowable.

DIFFÉRENCE MAKES THE DIFFERENCE

In terms of style and expression there are two main choices. One is to use an objectivist style. This may mean writing your dissertation in the third person, distancing yourself from your research. The typical format (shown and discussed in Chapter 4), consisting of chapter headings, is used of 'introduction', 'literature review', 'methodology', 'findings', 'discussion' and 'conclusions'. Within this the research is reported from a distance, as if separated from the person who did it and from those involved. Little contextual information is given or discussed, and findings are presented as facts. This is a characterization and I do not claim that all realists would have no problem with this format and style. But in its presentation and style this characterization is the most common one used in masters dissertations. An alternative approach might be to acknowledge that reality is not predictable or able to be subject to unproblematic mechanical research. Your dissertation might acknowledge or make a virtue of regarding social reality as constituted through interactions; as a phenomenon made meaningful by the place and time in which a particular person-researcher applied the research methods they had constructed (Derrida, 1987/1980). This may mean you construct an account of your research as a journey written, when necessary, in the first person and past tense. The aim, by doing this, is to get across to your reader how you experienced your research and describe to them just what the process actually involved.

Being aware of this choice means that you can decide on how to write your dissertation. This choice will be shaped, as I have just said, by the ontological and epistemological positions you take and also by your willingness to tell your reader just what really happened during your research. In practice even the most detailed research plan will need minor (sometimes major) adjustments once the research is underway. Research is an activity that is rarely unproblematic or transparent (Bingham, 2003: 148), but is an experience highly contingent on solving a successive stream of problems and dealing with ethical issues. It is also the case that any kind of writing is problematic for most of us. There are, regardless of the type of approach we take with our dissertation, numerous and continual problems and decisions to be made. You will find yourself asking: In what tense should I write this section? How much should I include? How can I express this as a graph? How much detail is needed? Should I mention the hunches I had at the beginning of the research? – and so on. Some of these are technical questions concerned with how to do something, like a graph. Others are questions about how much of 'yourself' you reveal as having been a part of your research. Whatever decisions you make will mark the *'différence'* (Derrida, 1987/1980) between your dissertation and others. This will be seen in the ways you balance description, explanation and discussion of your research as a managed performance of your skills, capabilities, attitudes and qualities.

OBJECTIVIST AND CONSTRUCTIVIST DISSERTATIONS

The distinction between the objectivist and constructivist dissertation is merely a useful contrast. It is borrowed from Michael Crotty (1998: 8–9), who uses it to help organize his exposition of the many ontological and epistemological positions in social research. Its use here is an adaptation that can allow us to understand the relationship between the methodological strategy a researcher has used and the way in which this is embodied in how they have written-up their research. Table 12.1 attempts to encapsulate the main differences between the objectivist and constructivist dissertation. The example I have chosen to illustrate the objectivist approach is that of a work-based dissertation. Other kinds of research characteristic of this approach would typically include experimental, quasi-experimental and correlational studies.

The objectivist example in Table 12.1 is produced in more detail in Chapter 5. Its contents listing shows the apparent flow from the introduction and aims through methodology, data collection to conclusions and recommendations. Comparisons between the two library services and the methods used to collect data on the phenomenon of 'change' are reported as if unproblematic. That is unproblematic to the research. As a consequence, conclusions are reached and clear recommendations made. This is possible because, on the one hand, change is treated as something external, 'out there', able to be measured and thus reported about. On the other hand, this contents page also illustrates the process model used by the student. What is meant by this is the way in which practices and processes have been applied that have allowed the main issues of the research to be highlighted. There is a strong inference that the student has paid close attention to the procedures believed necessary for producing the research to look like research done according to conventional expectations. This is what Bruno Latour terms 'circulating reference' (Latour, 1999: ch. 2). This kind of chapter arrangement and sectioning allows for appropriate references to be made at appropriate places. This has involved many operations which have transformed the practices and processes and data collected into 'findings' about the phenomenon (1999: 60–71). There are no alternative standpoints or frames of reference employed to give different descriptions. Nor is there any indication, except in the student's name, of why this topic was chosen; why they felt sufficiently committed to it for masters research.

In the other example (provided by Maria Piantanida and Noreen Garman (1999) in their excellent book on qualitative dissertations) of a contents page in Table 12.1 we see a different kind of approach. Some familiar chapters can be seen and the arrangement of them is conventional. In many ways this also exhibits as a performance the kinds of procedures and processes of the first one. But in the sectioning we see the differences. Initially these

TABLE 12.1   DIFFERENCES BETWEEN THE OBJECTIVIST AND CONSTRUCTIVIST
DISSERTATION

Objectivist dissertation	Constructivist dissertation
Chapter 1	*Chapter 1*
Introduction	Introduction
Setting the scene	Intent of the study
Aims and objectives	Importance of the study
Benefits and justification	
	Chapter 2
Chapter 2	Drama definitions: a selected review
Background information	of the literature
Structure of academic libraries in Romania	Definitions of drama in education
Current state of development of academic	Drama as subject and as a process
libraries in Romania	Types of educational drama
Problems in academic libraries in Romania	Classroom drama situated in educational
	contexts
Chapter 3	
Literature on Western/UK academic	*Chapter 3*
libraries	Drama data, the study process
Literature on Eastern/Romanian	Narrative inquiry
academic libraries	Description of the school setting
Conclusions	The children
	Duration of the study
Chapter 4	The data collection process
Methodological overview	Data analysis procedures
The literature – Delphi Technique –	The narrative genre of the study
the panel – questionnaires vs.	
interviews – questionnaire design	*Chapter 4*
Conclusions	Drama depictions: the narratives of our
	classroom
Chapter 5	Drama as pedagogical practice
Implementation	A dramatic picture
Response rates	Dramatic teacher performance
Round 1	The drama of daily classroom routines
Round 2	Drama and plans – the beginning of the
	drama process
Chapter 6	Drama and unexpected events
Results	Drama and the home–school connections
Priority areas of change in your library:	Drama in the elementary content areas
targets	Dramatic thinking
Major ways forward: how to achieve	
targets	
General strategy	

(Continued)

TABLE 12.1 (CONTINUED)

Objectivist dissertation	Constructivist dissertation
Chapter 7	*Chapter 5*
Discussion and analysis	Drama disclosures: drama as analogy
The current state of developments in Romanian academic libraries	Drama as knowing
	Drama as discourse
Priority area of change in your library: targets	Drama as narrative
	Drama as synectics
Major ways forward: how to achieve targets	
	Chapter 6
General strategy – general library environment	Drama as pedagogy, observations for the elementary school educator
	A final observation
Chapter 8	
Conclusions and recommendations for change	
Priority areas of change in your library: targets	
Major ways forward: how to achieve targets	
General strategy	
Recommendations	

Source: Adapted from Piantanida and Garman, 1999.

can be seen in the vocabulary where such words and phrases as 'intent', 'as subject and process', 'contexts', 'narrative genre of the study' and 'picture' are used. Further differences are observable in that multiple descriptive frames of reference are used based on differing standpoints to drama. There are five main standpoints given sections in Chapter 5. Finally, the last chapter does not have conclusions or recommendations, but observations. There is a strong inference that this dissertation is based on an interpretivist approach and that the student has constructed it to embody this and to achieve a sense in which findings are definitely not to be seen as 'facts', but as understandings.

Writing long documents

Although you may find, once you start to write, that 15,000 words is not enough for all you want to say, a dissertation of this length is a *long* document. In this section we will briefly look at some basic things you can do to make this more manageable and relatively risk-free. For more guidance on the technical skills of the production process and standards stipulated by your university, see your supervisor and course handbook. The handbook, in particular, should specify such things as page size (margins and headers), font size, line spacing, title pages and how to bind your dissertation. The following is therefore some basic advice derived from what my students find useful and what I use when writing chapters for books.

PREPARATION AND PLANNING

Whatever software you use, make sure that you know the basics of what it can do. This does not mean reading the whole manual or obtaining lots of books on it. It means knowing your way around the menu screen and how to do such tasks as setting up a page, making words bold or italics, drawing tables and inserting figures. Do not be afraid to 'play and experiment' with your computer. Also look back to Chapter 2, where you will find guidance on setting up a document management system for your research.

SETTING UP TEMPLATES

Your university will have standards for how wide margins should be for their dissertations. Use these to create a set of standard blank documents. Using pen and paper, roughly sketch out the number and titles of the main parts of your dissertation. These can be the chapters. For each chapter create identical templates on separate disks or memory sticks. The standard template should save you time because you can specify the font and size so that it will be the same throughout your dissertation. It is usual to use Times New Roman or Arial, with a 12-point size for all text and 14 or 16 for main headings. Do these things to save time later on. You want to avoid having to go back to each section of each chapter to do formatting. Near the end of your research time you will be under pressure with other tasks, and re-doing headings, sub-headings, line spacing, quotations and the like will take a lot of time.

VERSION MANAGEMENT AND CONTROL

Most people generate a number of versions of a document. This is normal. No one I know can start off with a blank page and write a perfect (or even acceptable) chapter in one go. Writing chapters is about arranging the contents, deciding on the contents and re-working sentences, paragraphs and whole sections once you have had time to reflect on them. This book, largely thanks to development editors, went through a number of revisions and changes. Doing changes is more than correcting grammar; it is about looking to say things as clearly as possible without losing the sense of your intention. In some cases, you may want your readers to 'think' about what they have read.

For feedback you have your tutor and peers. Showing your tutor what you have written, no matter how rough it may seem to you, is usually an effective way to obtain regular feedback. This will mean, of course, revisions. One way to manage these is to be very clear and precise in the use of names for your document files. Have separate document files for each chapter and part of your dissertation. Keep a notebook on what these are. Keep all your files in one folder so you will know where they are. If you need to keep more than one version of a document file, then give it a consecutive name, for example, ch1v1, ch1v2. Your word-processing software will also help you keep track of versions. Most will tell you when a file was created and last used.

Do not rely on your hard drive to store your work. Keep multiple copies of your files on other devices. Memory sticks are becoming very useful for this, given how much you can save on them. For information on such things as endnotes and footnotes, page numbering and the like, refer to the help facility on your word processor.

SAVING PAPER AND INK WHEN PRINTING

If, like me, you like to handle what you have written, then you will be doing a lot of printing. Whether you use an ink-jet or laser printer, the cost of doing this can be high. There are two effective ways of saving ink and paper. One is to set your print command to the 'save toner' mode. You can save up to 50 per cent. The other is to print two or more pages on one sheet of A4. Two pages are still readable and useful for identifying where corrections are needed. More than two pages per sheet is useful for checking margins and page layout. It is also useful to put the date on your printout to avoid mixing-up different versions of the same document.

What style of writing to use

Among the main issues which often arise at this initial stage in dissertation writing is the matter of academic style. The purpose of academic writing is to present the research clearly and succinctly and this includes constructing argument, providing evidence, citing sources and avoiding pompous use of technical and obscure terminology. You should aim to develop a preciseness in your writing so that your expression is as clear, coherent and as systematic as you can possibly make it. The goal is to write in a straightforward style that uses unadorned English and avoids cliché, colloquialism and informality. Remember that academic writing is not meant to be entertaining.

Some of the materials and arguments you encounter will be complex and some will be poorly expressed. Others, however, will be expressed clearly in a style that makes them comprehensible. Look out for examples of clear writing in the books and articles you read and make notes on any useful stylistic techniques you can employ to make your own work clear. In particular look at the purpose of the writing you think is good – is it an argument, an analysis, a description, explaining a point, criticizing an idea, examining evidence, providing an introduction? Collect examples of good and bad writing which have been used for different purposes, so that when you have a problem expressing yourself you have some examples to inspire you.

USING THE PERSONAL PRONOUN

In some disciplines it is expected that the personal pronoun is not used. The exact reasons for this are not usually stated, but some institutions believe that not using 'I' somehow gives greater objectivity to the research reported. Not using 'I' does not add objectivity to academic writing – it is merely a convention. In many parts of a dissertation the issue rarely arises, but in an introduction where you are explaining the impetus for your research, the use of 'I' often seems more appropriate than using the words 'the author' or 'the researcher'. If it is the convention not to use 'I', then try not to substitute its use with 'us' or 'we', and strictly limit the pompous circumlocutions such as 'author' and 'researcher'. In this book the 'we' and 'you' have generally been used because I, as the author, see doing a dissertation as a collaborative task. Because you are reading and using this book it means that *we* have a relationship. It also acknowledges 20 years of working with other people, masters students and colleagues, and much of what has been said echoes conversations we (our community of shared interests) have had.

AVOID INAPPROPRIATE LANGUAGE

A dissertation is a formal document and as such is normally written using a combination of the formal and middle register. The term 'register' refers to the style, tone and language a document uses, given its purpose and audience. The formal register is used for legal, official and scholarly documents. The middle register is used for articles in newspapers, magazines and ephemeral publications. There is also the informal register, which is used in documents where the normal standards of grammar and tone can be largely ignored. For the formal and middle registers the conventions of standard grammatical English are expected. Words should not be used in an abbreviated form, for example, 'ain't'; clichéd expressions, for example 'drunk as a Lord', sexist language, for example 'old wives' tale', or offensive terms, especially expletives, for example 'moron' should be avoided. Do not worry too much if you believe your written English could be better. Many people believe this about their writing. We could all write better if we had the time. There are now many excellent and accessible guides to grammar and writing. The more you write, the better your writing will become.

Constructing a plan and map for your dissertation: the macro-level

There are two broad levels on which a dissertation, like most other documents, is planned. One is the macro-level and the other the micro-level. At the macro-level you make a map and a plan. Your map should determine what kind of dissertation you intend to write. We have already seen that there are two broad approaches, the objectivist and constructivist, which will give you a guide to the overall structural arrangement of your dissertation. Looking at the examples shown in Table 12.1, both of these approaches tell a story. They are both accounts telling the reader the 'what', 'why', 'how', 'when' and 'where' of the research. You can do this using a range of genres, including the hypothesis, analytical, and mystery genres. These genres are patterns or conventions for organizing what you have to stay. All of them should be considered as the basis for telling the story of your research journey. It is not the case that a particular type of research corresponds with a particular genre or that only one genre should be used. The choice of genre should reflect, on the one hand, the way in which your puzzle was set up, research questions framed and research planned. On the other hand, it should be capable of telling what actually happened during the research.

THE HYPOTHESIS GENRE

If you have tested a hypothesis as your research, then a conventional structure may be appropriate for your dissertation. This could consist of three main parts: the hypothesis

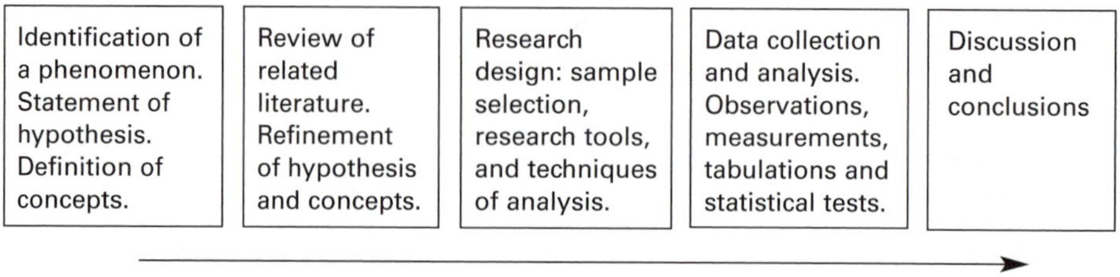

| Identification of a phenomenon. Statement of hypothesis. Definition of concepts. | Review of related literature. Refinement of hypothesis and concepts. | Research design: sample selection, research tools, and techniques of analysis. | Data collection and analysis. Observations, measurements, tabulations and statistical tests. | Discussion and conclusions |

FIGURE 12.1 TYPICAL STRUCTURE OF THE HYPOTHESIS DISSERTATION

and concepts; the data and analysis; and the discussion and conclusions. The conventional structure is shown in Chapter 4. It consists, as shown in Figure 12.1, of chapters which sequentially focus on a presumed relationship between an independent and dependent variable.

This genre usually uses a 'report' template to present the research. As a research report it is written in the third person, in the passive voice. The first chapter is usually very short, providing only a brief description of the phenomenon and statement of the hypothesis. The second chapter is usually long; it examines the major concepts relevant to the phenomenon from previous studies. The third chapter is short'; the methods, sample and measurements are described. The forth chapter presents the data and calculations without comment. The final chapter presents the calculations on the degree of relationship between variables and discusses the relevance of this. This is usually related to previous research and generalizations are suggested based on the degree of external validity.

THE ANALYTICAL GENRE

Most research involves looking at something complicated and then breaking it up into its constituent parts. This process of analysis is therefore a generic part of research. How you approach and frame your analysis will give you a particular story to tell. That story will *tell and show why* (rather than just tell how) you selected the properties, features or characteristics of a phenomenon for attention in your analysis. This means that you need to achieve a number of things in your story. One is to make an assertion that is your own about the phenomenon. You may be asserting that previous approaches have failed in some respect and you are therefore arguing for the need to respecify the nature of the phenomenon. This implies that you have

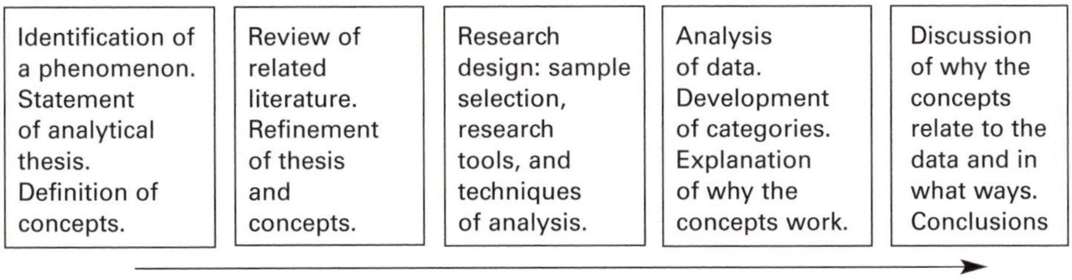

Identification of a phenomenon. Statement of analytical thesis. Definition of concepts.	Review of related literature. Refinement of thesis and concepts.	Research design: sample selection, research tools, and techniques of analysis.	Analysis of data. Development of categories. Explanation of why the concepts work.	Discussion of why the concepts relate to the data and in what ways. Conclusions

FIGURE 12.2 TYPICAL STRUCTURE OF THE ANALYTICAL DISSERTATION

a justifiable alternative approach. You will also need to show why your proposed alternative is relevant by answering the 'so what?' kind of question. This implies that you have a sound knowledge of previous analyses of the phenomenon, what assumptions they used and what their results were. You will need to tell and show what is going on in previous analyses, what they sought to achieve, and how the issues you are raising are an effect of previous forms of analyses. Once you have shown the consequences of previous approaches and reached some justifiable conclusions about how an alternative may be constructed, you then have an analytical thesis statement. This should explain what you are to analyse, the main parts of the phenomenon you will analyse, and the general order in which you will present the analysis. Your analytical statement is usually the starting point, stated in Chapter 1, for your dissertation. Figure 12.2 provides an indicative structure for the analytical dissertation.

Figure 12.2 is based on the assumption that the analytical dissertation can be used across the social sciences, employing most traditions, approaches and research cultures. It can be used for making detailed arguments, evaluations and expositions. However, it is usually associated with theory and concept-led research, in which research is undertaken to explore or investigate the power of a concept to contribute to an approach or research tradition. The 'report' template is not always used. In place of 'telling', the dissertation aims to show the reader, through the use of evidence, the relevance of the concepts analysed.

The presence of the researcher is much more evident in many forms of analytical story. This is because the assertions made about relationships and contexts for understanding why concepts work in the way they do are personal. Hence an active voice is often used to show why you made the statement and why you chose to examine related concepts in the ways you did. However, avoid over-use of the active and first-person voice. Only use the personal pronoun when strictly necessary, or you will distract your reader from your main points and the evidence you are offering to support them. Also avoid doing too much analysis. Keep the number of concepts and categories you use to a minimum. Use the same categories, when possible, to examine different aspects of your phenomenon. Use of too many concepts can often lead to confusion and a very 'bitty' and incoherent story.

THE MYSTERY GENRE

According to Alasuutari (1995: 183), research starts with a set of questions pointing to a mystery about some phenomenon. The mystery, or what is not known about the phenomenon, is framed by a series of questions that form the basis of the first chapter. These questions are usually based on some phenomenon you bring to your reader's attention; something you find a puzzle. These questions are then used as the main reference point and developed through investigation in succeeding chapters. The relevance of the mystery is further shown as a problem of understandings, data or methodology. Hence you could: tell and show how the problem in a corpus of literature is due to the general methodological approach used; or tell and show the need for concepts to explain a behaviour; or tell and show the need to explain a process. Whatever the purpose of your research, the dissertation will normally proceed by developing questions and possible answers. Figure 12.3 provides a generic overview of the mystery dissertation. It shows the progression from the puzzle (mystery) through the collection of data, its categorization and a gradual process of elimination until only one explanation seems possible.

Notice that the arrangements shown in Figure 12.3 suggest an inductive approach to research. The mystery genre can be an effective one when an inductive (rather than deductive) approach has been used, but it is not always necessary.

The mystery genre is not the easiest to use to tell your story. Like all mysteries the telling and showing how the puzzle was solved requires the skills of a storyteller. This means you will need to be able to show how the questions framing the puzzle are related not only to each other, but also to the evidence you collected. Keeping focused on the puzzle is necessary to ensure coherence throughout the different chapters. Finally, the 'solution' to the puzzle needs to be shown as logical and evident, especially when there is conflicting evidence.

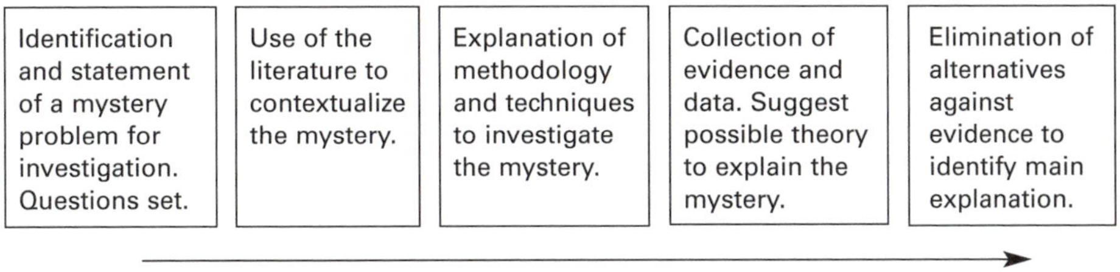

Identification and statement of a mystery problem for investigation. Questions set.	Use of the literature to contextualize the mystery.	Explanation of methodology and techniques to investigate the mystery.	Collection of evidence and data. Suggest possible theory to explain the mystery.	Elimination of alternatives against evidence to identify main explanation.

FIGURE 12.3   TYPICAL STRUCTURE OF THE MYSTERY DISSERTATION

Organizing chapter contents: the micro-level

You already know a great deal about what a dissertation can look like and about writing. We looked in Chapter 5 at different types of dissertation and in Chapter 11 at writing a research proposal. In this section we will look in a little more detail at what the different chapters may be used for, how to structure them and what should be included. The headings used are ones of convenience; they are not recommending any particular arrangement for your dissertation. As you already know, there are different kinds of research including theoretical, action, applied, evaluative, ethnomethodological (Mertens, 1998); different methodological positions including interpretivist, positivist, realist, idealist (Crotty, 1998); different research cultures including feminist, critical, postmodernist (Alvesson and Sköldberg, 2000); and different types of dissertation including, empirical, literature review, work-based, methodological and theoretical. This means your dissertation will have a quality that is unique. This will be an outcome of making choices from the possible alternatives and it is the resulting synthesis that will make your dissertation unique.

PLANNING THE STRUCTURE, CONTENTS AND EVIDENCE OF A CHAPTER

Although you may spend some time deciding on the arrangement of a chapter and writing the contents, it does not mean your reader will spend the same amount of time reading what you have written. A well-structured and clearly signposted chapter will help you convey to your reader the essence of what you have done. Figure 12.4 gives an overview of what to do before you start to write. Begin your planning by stating what you need to achieve in a chapter: this is its purpose. Use no more than a few short sentences for this. When you start to write the initial drafts, these can be expanded a little to introduce the chapter. Next list the points you want to make in the chapter. This can be done by saying to yourself, 'I need to tell them about this, this and this ...', and also

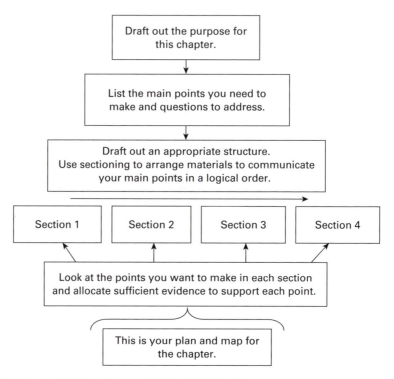

FIGURE 12.4   THINKING AND PLANNING THE WRITING

by asking yourself, 'What else will they need to know to fully understand my points?' Your answers to these questions will help you to see your writing from two standpoints: from yours, as the researcher-cum-storyteller, and from that of the reader. It is important, therefore, to tell your reader what a chapter is about, what it aims to achieve and how it is arranged. All of this can be done in a short introduction. In the main body of the chapter follow the agenda you have set out in your introduction: your reader will expect this. Clear side-headings will allow your reader to see the sequence you have set out in your introduction. Before you get to this stage, draft out the main sections for the chapter. For each section identify what point(s) you will make in it. Then allocate your evidence to each point. This may include references and quotes from the literature. Every statement or claim you make needs as much substantiation as possible.

Among things to avoid is having too many sections and sub-sections. As you only have between 2,500 and 3,000 words for each chapter, five sections means about 600 words per section. Sub-dividing a section with only 600 words into further sections may mean you create a very fragmented chapter. This will distract from your points and may negate any coherence you were aiming to achieve.

USING QUOTATIONS AS EVIDENCE

Some of the evidence you use will be quotations from the literature and from respondents (if an interview schedule was used to collect data). Quotations are normally used to give backing to what you have to say, especially to an argument you are aiming to make. Using your sectioning, select the most appropriate quotation for your purpose. Do not over-use them or it may give the impression you are 'padding-out' your dissertation, hoping to disguise the fact you have little to say. Quotations would normally make up no more than one quarter of a chapter unless there are very good reasons for doing otherwise. The remaining three-quarters should be your own analysis and argument. As general 'rules of thumb' the following points about quotations should be used as a guide.

+ Use quotations to support, not make a point.

+ Select quotations which are clear, distinctive or authoritative.

+ Do not use quotations which summarize what you have already said.

+ If someone has said something better than you can, or in a way that para-phrasing would only reproduce the essence of the quote, use the quote.

+ Always cite, giving proper attribution, to every source you quote or paraphrase.

+ Never quote out of context; distorting another's sense is unethical behaviour.

Quotations which are less than four lines long should be set out in the text. Longer quotations should be separated from the main body of the text and indented. Use quotations marks for quotes used in the text, but not for those indented. For guidance on which method of attribution to use, see Chapter 6 and the style manual of your university.

THE INTRODUCTORY CHAPTER

Many masters students often claim that the introductory and concluding chapters are the most difficult ones to write. It is common to find that they leave both chapters until the very end of the writing period. It is not necessary to do this with either

TABLE 12.2   HEADINGS FOR ARRANGING THE INTRODUCTORY CHAPTER

Objectivist approach	Constructivist approach
Chapter title	Chapter title
Introduction	Introduction
Rationale	Rationale
The intent of the study	The intent of the study
Guiding questions	Guiding questions
Hypothesis	Indicative review of the literature
Objectives	Objectives
Concepts	Research procedures
Operationalization of concepts	Nature of portrayals
Ethical issues	Ethical issues
References	References

chapter as you can make observations on possible points you may want to make as you write other chapters. This way you will have thoughts already written down to get you started. With the introduction, your first chapter, you already have your research diary and your original research proposal. Both of these will also be of use, as we will soon see, for your conclusion.

The basic structure of your research proposal can be recycled to construct the introductory chapter. This chapter is not, however, your research proposal. Some things will have to be changed for this to be the case. Where your research proposal would have been written in the future tense, the introductory chapter will be in the past tense. The examples used in Chapter 11 should, however, still be useful as guides to what to include in your introductory chapter. The main headings a reader will expect to see are shown in Table 12.2.

How you arrange this chapter is a matter for you to decide. The two templates shown in Table 12.2 are merely suggestions. You may also want to include a section on reliability and validity or give an outline of the chapters to follow. Your reader, however, will need all the help you can give, in determining the answers to the following questions:

♦ **What is this dissertation about?**

♦ **What are the reasons for this research?**

- ◆ **What kind of research is it?**

- ◆ **How was it done?**

- ◆ **Where was it done?**

The introductory chapter therefore has a particular purpose. It provides the reason for your research and an overview of what the reader can expect to find in more detail in the succeeding chapters. It may therefore be appropriate to begin this, as with the other chapters, with a brief paragraph on the purpose of the chapter and what it contains.

While your primary purpose is to provide information, this is normally done in terms of an argument from within a particular frame of reference. The aim is to let your reader know from the outset your methodological position and preferred research culture. The language you use will indicate some of these things, especially your methodological approach. Another indication will be the side-headings you have used. Within this analysis there will be the argument from your proposal. This is a combination of information, claims backed by data and some discussion. The introduction usually provides information in the form of the terms of reference, what the research is about, followed by the identification of a puzzle or problem situation.

The rationale section builds on this, using a structured argument to say what the need for the research was. It may be appropriate here to look back at your proposal to see how, now that you have the benefit of having done the research, you can comment on the justification you gave some 9 to 16 months ago. Various kinds of support and backing are usually used here, such as statistics, quotes and brief examples. Hence you will find yourself using sources which may not have been available to you when you did your initial proposal. The structure you use to do this needs to be logical. Table 12.3 shows some examples of possible structures.

The templates shown in Table 12.3 illustrate the suggestion that a recognizable argumentative structure is used to construct a logical rationalization for your topic. The problem-awareness template aims to make the reader think about something they may not have previously noticed or understood in a particular way. Methodologically it may consist of showing that a particular set of assumptions can be used differently or that some data can be seen as the outcome of some social process. A 'problem' is thus identified and possible consequences inferred. In the cause and effect rationalization, the cause of some phenomenon is hypothesized. Possible alternative causes and/or

TABLE 12.3 STRUCTURES FOR CONSTRUCTING A RATIONALIZATION

Problem awareness rationalization	Cause and effect rationalization	Possible solution rationalization
Describe the character of a problem (or behaviour):	Establish the existence of a behaviour (or problem):	Evaluate approaches to a situation (behaviour, problem):
• Give examples of its properties (prevalence, variables, locations, structure). • Develop a definition. • Show the relevance of the problem for a situation, understanding or methodology. • Explain the consequences if nothing is done. • Recommend a course of action to examine the problem.	• Give examples of the behaviour. • Define the behaviour, identifying key concepts. • Propose potential independent variables as the cause or as related to it. • Provide evidence for preferred potential relationship between variables. • Suggest a hypothesis for investigation.	• Outline the situation. • Give examples of approaches already applied. • Identify an aspect not addressed by existing approaches. • Show why they have failed in this aspect. • Identify relevant factors requiring action. • Recommend an alternative approach to those already tried.

relationships with independent variables are criticized, usually on the basis of inadequate data. A preferred and measurable relationship between independent and dependent variables is identified for experimentation. In the possible solution rationalization of the implementation of an intervention is critically evaluated and alternatives are considered for failures in performance. Recommendations are then made for a possible change to the intervention. These approaches are not mutually exclusive. Elements from any of them can be adapted to suit the particular needs of your type of research.

Finally, do not use (unless absolutely necessary) diagrams in your first chapter. Reserve diagrams for the other chapters where you may need to illustrate your thinking.

THE LITERATURE REVIEW CHAPTER

Depending on your research, you can have one or more chapters dealing with the literature and, in some cases, none. It is not necessary to have only one literature review chapter or to see it as a precursor to the methodology chapter. What you have taken from the literature, what issues you have with previous research and how it was done should be made clear throughout your dissertation. The literature on your topic may be the basis of a literature review chapter; it should also be used in your introduction, discussion and conclusions. Similarly, the methodological literature will form at least one chapter, but also be a source for discussion. The literature on your topic and methodology is therefore an essential part of your research. Searching, selecting, analysing and evaluating what has already been done on a topic is, in itself, research. Regrettably, it is only recently that some of the major research councils in the UK have recognized this, while many respectable refereed journals rarely publish reviews. What they seem to overlook is the fact that the synthesis you create from bringing together different elements of the literature can often bring a new and unique understanding to a topic.

You started the process of searching and evaluating relevant publications during your initial analysis of your topic and for your research proposal. Your evaluations then may or may not be what you finally include in your dissertation. This is because you will be writing evaluations of publications in different chapters of your dissertation almost up until the final few weeks. The most significant part of these evaluations will not be done until after you have collected and analysed your data. Your data will help you to identify what, from the literature, is actually relevant to you. It is an iterative process of going back and forth between your data and your literature to identify connections, similarities and differences. In this way you will produce much more than a description of what is in the literature. This process will encourage an interrogation of theories, concepts, definitions and findings already published.

Hence there are a few major mistakes to avoid. One is writing your literature review chapter before you collect any data. There is the danger of getting bogged down with searching and reading, meaning you lose time to collect data. This will also mean that you produce a literature review that 'stands largely alone', and no matter how thorough it is may not all be relevant to what you find. Identifying ways in which your phenomenon has been defined, researched and what has been found out about it are all necessary requirements prior to doing your data analysis. They form the current knowledge base on your topic. Thus it is your notes and initial evaluations of these which can form the resources for looking to see where your research stands in relation to what has gone before. A second point to note is that it may be your research which stands in direct contrast to the traditional literature; that it is too different to say anything meaningful in terms of the existing treatment of the topic. In which case the literature will be of little use to you. This is mostly the case with studies using an ethnomethodological approach.

What I have so far said means that you look to see how your research relates to what has already been done. This will give you an opportunity to make sound inferences on how your research has contributed to further our understanding of a phenomenon. In this way you will be producing specific knowledge which contributes to a general knowledge and understanding of the phenomenon. Following this line of reasoning, Wolcott (1990: 17) argues that the convention of having a literature review chapter before the data chapter should be dumped and that research thought to be related be discussed after the data chapter. For many kinds of research, especially ethnographic, Wolcott's suggestions make a lot of sense. But going against convention would take a lot of nerve and determination.

You have then a number of choices to make concerning where to place the bulk of relevant literature in your dissertation. You can have a literature review 'chapter' before or after the data analysis. As a general guide, there are two sets of questions we can pose; the first set relates to justifying your topic and approach, and the second to assessing the relevance of implementing your recommendations:

♦ **How has the phenomenon been defined?**

♦ **What are the main concepts which have been used?**

♦ **How have these framed the approaches to the phenomenon?**

♦ **What are the strengths and weaknesses of previous studies?**

♦ **How does your research propose to address some of these?**

♦ **What difference will doing your research make, and to whom?**

This first set of questions are the kind which you would normally aim to address in your introduction to justify your research. They can also form the basis of an initial literature review chapter if you follow the conventional format. The second set of questions is more suited to an assessment of the relationships between your research and what has already been done by others.

◆ How does your definition of the phenomenon relate to others? What differences did you find?

◆ What are the similarities and differences between previous research designs and yours? What are the consequences of this?

◆ What problems and issues did you face that were not mentioned in the literature?

◆ What do your findings say about claims made in the literature? What support do they give (or not) to previous findings and how do prior findings support yours?

The templates we looked at in Table 12.3 can be adapted to structure your review of the literature. The pre-data-collection literature review would, as indicated by the first set of questions, be concerned to deal with the first two or three points given for each type of rationalization. The final part of the review chapter could draw conclusions based on the problems identified in terms of a gap in our knowledge of some phenomenon.

THE METHODOLOGY CHAPTER

In the methodology chapter (or chapters) you describe how you did your research and explain why and how you did it. The number of chapters, structure and contents of the 'methodology' will be unique to your research. The main factors shaping your methodology chapter(s) will be:

◆ type of dissertation, for example, traditional, literature review or theoretical;

◆ methodological approach and culture, for example, feminist, action oriented, critical, ethnographic and so on;

◆ type of research, for example, experimental (correlational, causal), non-experimental (descriptive, analytical);

◆ methods, for example, qualitative, quantitative: and

◆ type of story, for example, hypothesis, analytical and mystery.

All but the last of these influences represent the choices you made when designing your research. By type of story is meant the overall structure you use to 'tell' others about your research – your dissertation's macro-structure. Within the main types of dissertation most approaches and types of research are possible. The main difference, from the student standpoint, is epistemological: it is likely your research will be predominantly either qualitative or quantitative in use of methods.

While the empirical dissertation normally has one main methodology and methods chapter, the theoretical dissertation may have two or more methodology chapters and the literature (or methodological) dissertation may have three or more such chapters. In the empirical (traditional and work-based) dissertation you tell and show the reader how you planned to do your data collection and analysis and how it was actually done. Having only 2,500–3,000 words means you can only provide a brief account. Much of your thought about alternative courses of action and showing your reasoning are formulations of what you actually did. In the theoretical dissertation, because you have more space, possibly two or three chapters, you are able to reveal more of the methodological basis of your analysis. In the literature review dissertation, where most chapters are focused on analysing related corpuses of literature, you are able to display many more of the details of your methodology and reasoning. In many cases the theoretical and literature review dissertations make the methodological reasoning and analysis on which they are based much more visible than the empirical dissertation. This is not a failing of the empirical dissertation, but a constraint imposed by its structure.

Whether you have one or more chapters for methods, one useful way of arranging your materials is to address your readers' questions. Initially, the main things your reader will want to know are:

♦ **What data did you not collect (type, scope, problems)?**

♦ **Why this data and not other types (alternatives, relevance, issues)?**

♦ **How was it collected (methods, tools, levels of measurement, sampling procedures)?**

♦ **How reliable and valid were the methods used (reliability type, construct and internal validity)?**

♦ **What are the limitations of the data and methods (scope, quantity, depth)?**

♦ **What were the techniques used to analyse the data (content, semiology, conversation analysis and so on)?**

♦ **What claims (inferences) can be made about the data (external validity, generalization)?**

You need to provide enough information for your reader to be satisfied that you have a thorough understanding of research design and its implementation. They will be looking to see if you have sound reasons for your design and for the claims you make for it. In many ways your methodology tells and shows what you have done, whereas your research design and research proposal told what you intended to do. Hence methodology chapters are often written in the past tense, using hindsight gained from experience. This may mean that you include in the telling what actually happened, letting the reader know the problems you faced (technical, ethical) and how you overcame them. You can do this in all types of dissertation.

Your institution and discipline will have expectations about how you write up your methodology. Check these out before you start and discuss your ideas with your supervisor. With the report style it is usual to use the third person and describe as briefly as possible the research design. With the constructivist dissertation it may be expected that you provide a developmental account of the research from your standpoint. This may mean highlighting some of the main problems, saying how you felt about these, how you solved them and how this affected your research and learning. The latter element, what you learnt, can form a section in your conclusions in which you reflect on your research experience.

In practical terms you will be restricted by the word limit. This may mean you adapt a conventional template to meet your particular needs. Table 12.4 shows a conventional template for the single methods chapter of a dissertation based on quantitative methods. The order in which you present your account is a matter for you to decide.

Table 12.4 can easily be adapted to meet the needs of researchers using qualitative methods. In Chapter 10 we looked at some of the functional equivalents to procedures used to assure confidence. These can be used, substituting, where necessary, the procedures normally associated with experimental and quantitative methods. Depending

TABLE 12.4   GENERIC TEMPLATE FOR THE METHODOLOGY CHAPTER

Method	Description
Introduction, purpose and outline of the chapter	Let your reader know what the chapter is about, what will be covered and in what order.
Research questions, proposition or/and hypothesis	What research puzzle the methodology, as designed, was intended to address.
Key concepts	Statement of key concepts and frame of reference; reasons.
Definitions of concepts	Statement on what the concepts are taken to be; reasons.
Indicators of concepts	Attributes and properties corresponding to the concepts; reasons.
Measures/observations required	Measures of the attributes and properties; levels of measurement; reasons.
Data required	Type, scope, access, sources, quantity, issues and reasons.
Sampling procedures	Population, sample frame, selection, issues and reasons.
Research instrument	What will be used to collect the data; issues and reasons. Piloting of the instrument. Full copy of the instrument administered.
Reliability checks	Inter-test, re-test and parallel forms; issues and reasons.
Validity procedures	Construct, internal, external validity, issues and reasons.
Analysis techniques	Type of analysis to be used on the data, issues and reasons.

on your institution and discipline, how much is needed to justify your methodology will be a matter for you to determine. In many of the enlightened institutions the use of qualitative methods is as acceptable as quantitative ones. Such institutions generally acknowledge that neither is better than the other and that there is no need to make a special case for a qualitative approach. In both cases, however, it will be expected that your reasons refer to the methodological literature. Use previous discussions and arguments on methodology, method and techniques to show how your design is a continuation of and contribution to an existing corpus of research.

THE FINDINGS CHAPTER

Depending on what kind of research you have done and the nature of your data, there may not be the need for a separate 'findings' chapter. If you have conducted interviews or analysed a text, then your findings may be combined with your analysis and discussion chapter. If you have administered a questionnaire survey, then a findings chapter may be appropriate. Always consult with your supervisor, who will guide you on this.

A findings chapter should present your data and nothing else. This means presenting the data you collected from your questionnaires in tables. The responses from each question of your questionnaire should be tabulated. These should show how many respondents answered this question, how many are missing and what the range of responses was. If you had a 20-question questionnaire, you will have 20 tables. Each table should be numbered consecutively, using whatever coding you assigned to the responses. Your reader should be able to identify which table reports responses on which question. Some brief notes can be attached to a table explaining why the data has some feature. Other than these, no comment or observations should be made about the data. As far as possible include all the data which was collected. This will allow the reader to make an informed assessment of how you analysed it and came to the interpretations you did. While most books on statistics will show you how to construct tables, here are some of the key things to follow.

- ◆ **Use tables not graphs. Graphs such as pie charts should only be used in the discussion and interpretation chapters.**

- ◆ **Use whole numbers and not percentages. The use of percentages can distort the power of the data, making a low response rate seem more significant than it really is.**

- ◆ **Number each table consecutively. The tables and figures in this book follow the expected standard for those to be used in a dissertation.**

The above are recommendations and are not universally adhered to by all institutions or disciplines. As a supervisor and researcher, I always recommend that the research student include, either in their dissertation or in an attached volume (including electronically), all of their data. This may mean submitting audiotapes of interviews, videos or full paper copies of texts analysed (this can now be done on CD-ROM). The reasons for this are transparency and confidence. By being able to look at all the data collected, especially before it has been repackaged in tables and the like, others can see for themselves and understand just what was collected, under what conditions. They can also see more of the processing done by the student to make their data presentable and understandable to their readers. Providing such data may be an added task, but it will ensure a greater degree of confidence in what you say about your findings than would be the case if you *only* selected extracts as illustrative.

THE ANALYSIS AND DISCUSSION CHAPTER

In broad terms your research will have one of three outcomes: what you predicted in your hypothesis or proposition will have been found; what you predicted will partially have been found to be the case, but there are anomalies; and what you predicted will not have been found. Each one of these three outcomes demands discussion. Do not worry if your research results in the latter of these outcomes. Negative outcomes are also findings, in that you will have largely eliminated a possible relationship or approach to a puzzle.

Your analysis or interpretation chapter should be based only on the data you have collected. This means no extraneous data or evidence or assumptions should be used to bolster your data. The data, however, will not 'speak for itself'. The interpretation of all data needs a frame of reference. The research method (quantitative or qualitative) and research culture and approach you have employed will give you a frame of reference. It will enable you to make particular sense of specific and aggregated data. Meaningfulness is therefore a product of your frame of reference and standpoint, constructed in your research design, which you bring to your data. It is not, then, a mechanical process of merely 'writing up' your data. Analysis and subsequent interpretation means a process of iterative cogitation. The more of an open-systems approach you have taken, the more time is usually needed for interpretation. Conversely, the more of a closed-systems approach you have taken, the more straightforward the analysis. This is because statistical correlation calculations are routine and made easy with the use of statistical software. Saying what the result means and implies can be more difficult. All kinds of research have this interpretative element.

It is very difficult to explain what interpretation is and how one does it. At the most general level, interpretation is a cognitive process consisting of making sense of something, in your case your data in relation to your research questions and research puzzle. By doing interpretation you are aiming to employ a frame of reference known to your readers that they can also use to understand your intention and to assess your interpretation. This process is normally one of elucidating the significance of the data in terms of your research questions. This may involve translating your data and its analysis into probabilities, generalizations and/or explanations.

Your interpretation will not 'come from nothing'. It is not a matter of merely looking at the data to see what it says. From your research questions and the way in which you framed your research puzzle, you have a substantial amount of 'material' for constructing your interpretation chapter. In the three possible structures for constructing a rationalization (shown in Table 12.3) you have, for example, points of reference from which you can begin an assessment of your data. If your aim was to evaluate a policy, then the *possible solution pattern* could act as your template. You could examine the ways in which a policy and situation could be changed, given what you have found. To do this the interpretation of your data should show: how it is valid and relevant to the situation; how it is different from existing data; how it has addressed or made visible behaviours or effects not otherwise noticed or subject to adequate explanation; how and why it addresses your research questions; and, importantly, what the limitations are to your findings. Interpretation is therefore a systematic process of using the data to assess your research questions, hypotheses or propositions in a way that is progressive.

It begins with a pen and paper. Initially it is good practice to sit with your data and research questions. Whether or not your data has been analysed and presented using a computer package, having it on pieces of paper has the advantage of allowing annotations and scribbling down of 'first thoughts' to be made. Successive sweeps and mining of the data soon build into stories to be told. Some of these may be routine, others may be exciting. Whichever, it progresses from presentation of the data to arranging it into ascending levels of abstraction. The lower levels consist of 'actuals' – concrete examples of what was found, along with basic relationships between variables and categories. Intermediate levels normally look to explore relationships within the data and to identify interesting issues. This may be based on posing successive questions to the data and using extracts to explore in more detail the implications of those questions. Higher-level interpretation will normally look to make inferences based on the data sample about the situation as a phenomenon and its explanation in terms of theoretical constructs.

THE CONCLUSIONS AND RECOMMENDATIONS CHAPTER

In the final chapter there are many things still to do. The problem usually faced, however, is one of little time or energy to write a good final chapter. By this stage in your research and writing your creative energy will probably be nearly exhausted. It is for this reason I recommend to our students that they keep a reasonably detailed research diary. The entries in it often provide many observations that would have otherwise been forgotten. Such observations are usually generated, ad hoc, as you work on some task. They can be problems you encountered, possible recommendations you would make to others doing similar research, and ideas for further research. It does not mean that they will be used, just that they may be useful aide-memoires when you are mentally tired. Do not introduce anything new in your conclusions chapter. Everything you have to say in it should be based solely on the contents of the preceding chapters. If you have a section, therefore, on further research, such research should have been alluded to in other parts of your dissertation, such as the scope, literature review and methodology.

The purpose of this final chapter is to demonstrate to your examiners that you have done research worthy of a masters categorization. It is the part of your dissertation where you can tell your reader what you have achieved and point to the places in your dissertation where the evidence of your achievements can be found. The sections often found in the conclusions chapter are:

♦ **Main findings of the research; a series of statements evaluating the degree to which the research objectives have been fulfilled. This includes saying what changes to the original research design were necessary, and why.**

♦ **The relationship of your research to the literature; saying how your research findings contribute to understanding and/or explaining the phenomenon. This may include a brief critique of the interpretations given in the literature, and the concepts or theories used as the frame for explanations.**

♦ **Further research; identification of other research questions and puzzles revealed by your research. This may mean identification of concepts, practices and behaviours not within the scope of your research but which you consider relevant to a more comprehensive understanding of the phenomenon.**

♦ Recommendations for policy or practice; brief systematic statements on courses of action for an organization or researcher. This may include constructing recommendations for an organization saying, on the basis of your research, what they could do to improve a practice or address a problem. Recommendations should state what could be done, what benefit it would bring to whom and what resources would be needed. You can also make recommendations or observations about existing recommendations and about the research on which they are based.

♦ Reflections on the learning experience; statements on your experience of doing the research. This is often said by students to be a difficult section to write. It consists of making a few points about your research as a learning experience. It is the part where you can look back on your research journey and say a little about the skills, capabilities, attitudes and qualities which were demanded of you. Consider also including a few points on your role as the agent constructing the knowledge that is in your dissertation. As a subjective-interpretative being, what assumptions did you have prior to doing your research, how did these change during it, and how did this help you to understand the process of knowledge creation?

The final chapter is much more than conclusions about your findings; it is a systematic set of informative observations on what you have done. It therefore aims to tell and show that your research is credible, has integrity and makes a contribution to knowledge and understanding. These are the kinds of things which will constitute your performance – a performance that shows you have acquired the necessary skills, capabilities, attitudes and qualities expected of the masters candidate.

Other parts of the dissertation

In terms of the overall presentation of your dissertation, you should aim to produce a clearly organized document. This means using your title, abstract, acknowledgements, contents page and other labelling to ensure a clean, professional look for your work.

THE TITLE

Deciding on the title for your dissertation can be a challenge. This is because you have only a limited number of words to formulate what your research is about. Although

TABLE 12.5   TITLES AND DIFFERENT KINDS OF PUBLICATION

Form of publication	Title	Purpose of title
Conference paper	' "By gum pet, you smell gorgeous": representations of sexuality in perfume advertisements'. British Sociological Association Annual Conference, *Sexualities*, Preston, March 1994.	To grab attention; be mildly humorous; play on local vernacular; announce the topic; show relevance to conference theme; indicate data sources and form of analysis.
Textbook	*Dissertations from Start to Finish: Psychology and Related Fields*. Cone, J.D. and Foster, S.L. Washington, DC: American Psychological Association, 1999.	Topic; process; practicality; relevance to audience; academic discipline.
Monograph	*Ethnomethodology's Program: Working out Durkheim's Aphorism*. Garfinkel, H. Oxford: Rowan & Littlefield, 2002.	Methodological approach; theoretical; argumentative; origins; relevance to audience.

some people may believe titles should be entertaining, humorous or even eye-catching, I believe they should be none of these. A dissertation is a serious piece of work and as such demands a title that embodies this. Titles are also important for other reasons. Your title will, along with your abstract, contain words and phrases which may be used by professional abstracting and indexing services. This means that if you want other people to be able to find your dissertation on electronic databases such as *Dissertation Abstracts*, then you need to give it a title that is a description of it. Different types of publication tend to employ different kinds of title to indicate what kind of publication they are and what they are attempting to achieve. This is something you can explore by looking at the references in this and other books. Table 12.5 shows examples of what is meant by this.

Conference papers are ideal vehicles to play with ideas in order to elicit feedback from the other delegates. In the case of ' "By gum pet, you smell gorgeous": representations of sexuality in perfume advertisements', my intention was to use a phrase from a popular television commercial for Boddington's beer. The expectation was that most people attending the conference (if from the UK) would know this phrase and want to come along to hear my paper. You can, of course, turn your dissertation into a conference paper and do likewise. For the novice scholar this can be a way of getting your research noticed. 'By gum pet, you smell gorgeous' worked very well and was even used by a daily broadsheet to comment on the conference. Textbooks, as you can see from the one in Table 12.5, usually employ a practical title to communicate their purpose and relevance to a specific audience. Monographs sometimes come out of dissertations and theses. Garfinkel's *Ethnomethodology's Program: Working out Durkheim's Aphorism* (2002) is a very descriptive title. Knowing only a little about ethnomethodology means you will probably know it is an approach invented by Garfinkel. Therefore a book by Garfinkel will be important and is not likely to be a textbook. Significant theorists are not usually known for writing textbooks. Garfinkel's title is the kind most closely associated with that suggested for a dissertation. It is descriptive, non-sensational, announces the theory, and then its purpose.

Writing a title is about playing with words and phrases. A good place to start is by writing down on separate pieces of paper all the words and phrases which could be used in a title. Look to assemble a collection that covers your topic, purpose, methodological orientation, theoretical position, subjects, place and time of the research, and type of dissertation. Only choose words used in your dissertation, especially in your statement of aims, hypothesis and research questions. This collection will probably be large, possibly in excess of 50 words. The next stage is to sort your words into categories. Place words that are theoretical, conceptual and analytical into one category. Words that are empirical, about subjects and the time and place of the research can be placed into another category. The next thing to decide is whether your research is predominantly theoretical or empirical. If it is predominantly theoretical, then words from this category can be used to construct possible alternatives for the first part of your title. The words designating the empirical element and scope of your research can be used to construct the second part of your title. In this way your title will be in two parts.

The words you select from your two sets can now be arranged to form alternative titles. Play with the words to see how many different titles you can make, looking at each for clarity and succinctness. You may want to ask some of your peer students and tutors what they think of your titles. Whichever one you finally select, ensure that it encapsulates what your research is about. It must use the same words as the reader will find in your abstract, aims and research questions. In this way you will be adding to the coherence of your dissertation.

THE ABSTRACT

In order for abstracting and indexing services to make your dissertation available to others, you need to provide an abstract and set of key words. You will have come across abstracts during your literature search and should look to some of these for further guidance as to what an abstract consists of. It should attempt to provide a summary of the research. It must say something about the purpose, literature, methodology, data, findings and conclusions of the research. There are two main types of abstract you can use: the indicative and the informative. Indicative abstracts are usually, though not always, written by someone else to convey the intention of an author. The purpose is to provide a reader with sufficient indication of the nature of a piece of research for them to decide if obtaining and reading the full document is worthwhile. An informative abstract is usually written by the author of a piece of research. It attempts to provide a summary of the principal elements of their research and will usually follow the structure of the original dissertation by:

♦ *stating the purpose of the research*: saying what the author was attempting to achieve; their aims, hypotheses, research questions;

♦ *stating the methodology employed*: mentioning which research tradition and culture were used;

♦ *stating the methods*: outlining what data collection tools were constructed and applied; and

♦ *stating the findings*: brief sentences on what was found, normally with little or no evaluation of the relevance of the findings, as matters of relevance and interpretation are for the reader to determine.

In other publications you may use a combination of indicative and informative abstracts. Conference papers often use a combination to state what the author has done and how they see its relevance to a topic or issue.

THE EXECUTIVE SUMMARY

In many work-based dissertations it is becoming more common to see an executive summary in place of the conventional informative abstract. The executive summary is commonly regarded as a tool for management. It is usually placed at the beginning of a document to state the main findings from a research project. The facts, as found by the

TABLE 12.6   EXAMPLES OF EXECUTIVE SUMMARIES

Local community groups and facilities at the library	Historic vehicles in the UK
Terms of reference.	Terms of references.
38 groups in the area hold on average three to four meetings each month.	£1.6 billion is generated by the historic vehicle movement in the UK.
Thimblemill library is the second busiest in the borough – it issued 150,000 items last year.	In excess of 25,000 people earn their living providing services to the historic vehicle movement.
Sandwell Metropolitan Borough is the seventh most deprived in England and this has worsened since 1981.	More than 650,000 vehicles made before 1977 still exist.
An average of 27.3% of pupils in Smethwick attained 5+ GCSE grades between A and C. The average for England was 43.3%.	Over 64% of vehicles owned by members of historic vehicle clubs are roadworthy and licensed.
15% of the local population are from ethnic minority backgrounds. This excludes persons of Irish descent who make up an undisclosed proportion of the local population.	Libraries and archives in the UK were visited over 270,000 times by historic vehicle owners seeking information about historic vehicles last year.
Most groups in the area rated the facilities at Thimblemill library as 'poor' or 'inadequate'.	Over 33,000 members of historic vehicles clubs drive a contemporary vehicle that is of the same marque as a historic vehicle they own.

Source: Adapted from Hart, 1997 and 2000.

research, are simply stated without interpretation or comment. Table 12.6 shows two executive summaries; one from a survey of historic vehicles and the other from a survey into the needs of local community groups. In both cases the executive summary gave the terms of reference for the research. This included saying briefly what the research was about and why it was done, followed by the main findings.

Both of the executive summaries shown in Table 12.6 are typical for applied research of this type. They give the main findings in a logical order, are brief, to the point and are easily reproducible by others.

ACKNOWLEDGEMENTS

Whoever has helped you in your research should be acknowledged. This includes people who have enabled access to subjects, advised on writing, given direction and provided guidance to resources and sources of information. Among such people will be your supervisor and the university librarian; if a family member or friend has done some proofreading they certainly need mentioning.

Acknowledgements help to show that research is based in a context of personal and institutional realities. It is not only good manners, therefore, to acknowledge the help you have received, but also to show the support you have had from others. If you have had financial assistance with your research, say from a funding body, it is common practice to give details of this.

THE CONTENTS PAGE

This may seem obvious; a contents page is a listing of the contents. The variety of ways in which the contents pages of dissertations differ each year is something my colleagues and I often remark on. Even though we give examples of good practice, authors of dissertations often do things differently. This book has several contents pages; there is one at the beginning that provides an overview of the chapters and each chapter has a detailed one at its beginning to show just what is in that chapter. We recommend you have only one contents page. It should be sufficiently detailed to provide information on what the chapter is about and how its contents are arranged. For example, if Chapter 8 of this book was a dissertation the format for listing its contents might look like this:

Contents

List of figures and tables

Acknowledgements

Chapter 1 Studies of feeble-mindedness

1.1 Goddard's study of the Kallikak family
1.2 Goddard's recommendations
1.3 Consequences of the Kallikak family study
1.4 The issues

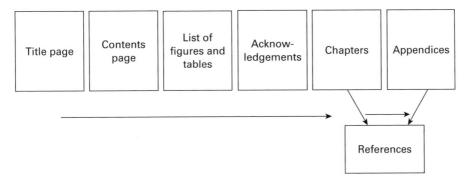

FIGURE 12.5   SEQUENCE OF PARTS IN A DISSERTATION

Chapter 2 Criminal types

2.1 Lombroso's research and theory

2.2 Consequences of Lombroso's theories

2.3 The issues

Chapter 3 The universality of mind

3.1 Structural study of cultures

3.2 The structure of myth

3.3 Analysing myths

3.4 Summary of Lévi-Strauss's argument

3.5 Consequences of Lévi-Strauss's structuralism

3.6 The issues

Appendix 1: The research proposal

References

Each chapter would be consecutively numbered and its contents double-numbered. Try to avoid taking multiple numbering too far. That is, avoid numbering all sections and having a number like 3.1.1.2.

Another way of looking at the parts of a dissertation is shown in Figure 12.5. This shows the sequence normally used. Note that the references (works you have cited in the text) can be placed after each chapter, as endnotes, or after the appendices, as a references section.

FIGURES AND TABLES

List your figures and tables on a separate page. Use the heading 'List of figures and tables' and list them continuously with figures first. Note that the ones below are from Chapter 10 of this book, and so they all begin with 10. Figures and tables are normally numbered by chapter. For example, figures in Chapter 1 begin with 1, figures in Chapter 2 with 2, and so on. So Figure 10.2 is the second figure in Chapter 10.

Figures

Figure 10.1 *The methodological logic of research design*
Figure 10.2 *The place of research design in the research process*
Figure 10.3 *Different types of research and associated study design elements*

Tables

Table 10.1 *Summary of interpretivist research designs*
Table 10.2 *Examples of and sources on different research standpoints and cultures*
Table 10.3 *Construct, Internal and External Validity*

APPENDICES

The contents of the appendices are not normally included in the word count for a dissertation. This does not mean that you can put a lot of material here which you would have liked to have had in the main body of your dissertation. The appendices are reserved for materials pertinent to the research. This may include a copy of your questionnaire, a printout of a website you analysed, letters you received from organizations, and the like. The way to format an appendix is like this:

Appendix 1: Letters of consent
Appendix 2: Portrait of Jane Austen

Final thoughts

I have, I hope, shown you that you have choices in research and that to be able to exercise them you need to know what they are, what each commits you to and what kind of consequences for understanding may follow. The choice is far greater and much more consequential than that between quantitative or qualitative. It involves asking big or little questions, looking to theorize or describe, aiming to produce recognizable descriptions which connect with reality (realism) or produce ways of picturing the world (conventionalism), making choices about value-relevance and value-neutrality, and understanding some of the implications of using a closed- or open-systems approach. Some disciplines or research programmes will have largely made the choices for you by making clear in their literature the ontological and epistemological parameters of their research. Feyerabend would advocate that you challenge these, but if you are happy with a particular frame of reference a research programme implies, and know what it entails, then get on with your research and 'work your problem'. After all, we are not attempting to address big questions such as the size of the universe or how consciousness works. We are interested, in the main, in formulating little questions (Geertz, 1973) which, through the design strategy of our research, we may be able to answer in some way. This requires that we collect relevant materials and data and pay close and careful attention to the details (Putnam, 1975; Hacking, 1983) so that we can apply our frame of reference in ways which display our knowledge. Doing research is, we contend, far more interesting and more productive than talking about it. At the end of the day research is not philosophy, any more than economics is psychology, and none is reducible to a single discipline or cause. They are forms of knowing and understanding and have things to learn from each other, but have differences at their cores which set them apart. Investigating what these cores are and what they mean are ways of exercising our intellects which help us develop our capacity for understanding and for tolerance towards other ways of knowing, and enhance our cognitive abilities as 'professional' researchers and people.

Further reading

Colinson, D., Kirup, G., Kyd, R. and Slocombe, L. (1992) *Plain English*. 2nd edn. Buckingham: Open University Press. Advice on making your writing clear.

Schwartz, M. (1995) *Guidelines for Bias-free Writing*. Bloomington, IN: Indiana University Press. Gives sound advice on what terms to use in order to avoid sexist, racist and other discriminatory forms of writing.

Schön, D. (1983) *The Reflective Practitioner: How Professionals Think in Action*. London: Basic Books. One of the earliest formulations of reflective practice in research.

Appendix 1   Skills, capabilities, attitudes and qualities of the masters

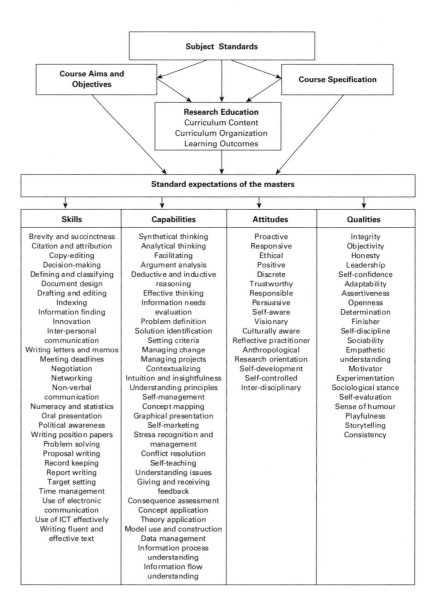

Skills	Capabilities	Attitudes	Qualities
Brevity and succinctness	Synthetical thinking	Proactive	Integrity
Citation and attribution	Analytical thinking	Responsive	Objectivity
Copy-editing	Facilitating	Ethical	Honesty
Decision-making	Argument analysis	Positive	Leadership
Defining and classifying	Deductive and inductive	Discrete	Self-confidence
Document design	reasoning	Trustworthy	Adaptability
Drafting and editing	Effective thinking	Responsible	Assertiveness
Indexing	Information needs	Persuasive	Openness
Information finding	evaluation	Self-aware	Determination
Innovation	Problem definition	Visionary	Finisher
Inter-personal	Solution identification	Culturally aware	Self-discipline
communication	Setting criteria	Reflective practitioner	Sociability
Writing letters and memos	Managing change	Anthropological	Empathetic
Meeting deadlines	Managing projects	Research orientation	understanding
Negotiation	Contextualizing	Self-development	Motivator
Networking	Intuition and insightfulness	Self-controlled	Experimentation
Non-verbal	Understanding principles	Inter-disciplinary	Sociological stance
communication	Self-management		Self-evaluation
Numeracy and statistics	Concept mapping		Sense of humour
Oral presentation	Graphical presentation		Playfulness
Political awareness	Self-marketing		Storytelling
Writing position papers	Stress recognition and		Consistency
Problem solving	management		
Proposal writing	Conflict resolution		
Record keeping	Self-teaching		
Report writing	Understanding issues		
Target setting	Giving and receiving		
Time management	feedback		
Use of electronic	Consequence assessment		
communication	Concept application		
Use of ICT effectively	Theory application		
Writing fluent and	Model use and construction		
effective text	Data management		
	Information process		
	understanding		
	Information flow		
	understanding		

Appendix 2 Levels of measurement and use

	Nominal Numbers are shorthand	Ordinal Attributes can be ordered	Interval Distance is meaningful	Ratio Absolute zero
Method of presenting data	tabulation		graphs	
Measures of association between variables	Coefficient of contingence			Chi-squared
		Ordinal correlation		
			Pearson's r correlation ANOVA	
			Regression and factor analysis	
Averages	The mode			
		The mean		
			Arithmetic mean	
Measures of dispersion		Quartile deviation		
		The range		
			Standard deviation	

Appendix 3   References for Tables 10.2 and 10.7

Experiments

A primer on experimental and quasi-experimental design. http://ericae.net/ft/tamu/Expdes. HTM.

Bandura, A., Ross, D. and Ross, S.A. (1963) 'Imitation all for film mediated aggressive models'. *Journal of Abnormal and Social Psychology*, 66: 3–11.

Campbell, D.T and Stanley, J.C. (1963) 'Experimental and quasi-experimental designs for research'. In Gage, N.L. (ed.), *Handbook of Research on Teaching*. Chicago, IL: Rand McNally.

Field, A. and Hole, G.J. (2002) *How to Design and Report Experiments*. London: Sage.

Greenacre, M.J. (1993) *Correspondence Analysis in Practice*. London: Academic Press.

Kitto, J. (1989) 'Gender reference terms: separating the women from the girls'. *British Journal of Social Psychology*, 28: 185–7.

Lazarsfeld, P.F. and Rosenberg, M. (1955) *The Language of Social Research: A Reader in the Methodology of Social Research*. Glencoe, IL: Free Press.

Loftus, E.F. and Palmer, J.C. (1974) 'Reconstruction of automobile destruction: an example of the interaction between language and memory'. *Journal of Verbal Learning and Verbal Behaviour*, 13: 585–9.

Piliavin, M., Rodin, J.A. and Piliavin, J. (1969) 'Good Samaritanism: an underground phenomenon?' *Journal of Personality and Social Psychology*, 13: 289–99.

Rosenthal, R. and Jacobson, L. (1966) 'Teacher's expectancies: determinants of pupil's IQ gains'. *Psychological Reports*, 19: 115–18.

Ethnography

Agar, M.H. (1985) *Speaking of Ethnography*. Sage University Paper Series on Qualitative Research Methods, Volume 2. Beverly Hills, CA: Sage.

Atkinson, P. (1990) *The Ethnographic Imagination: Textual Constructions of Reality*. London: Routledge.

Becker, H. (1970) *Sociological Work: Method and Substance*. Chicago, IL: Aldine.

Bulmer, M. (ed.) (1982) *Social Research Ethics: An Examination of the Merits of Covert Participant Observation*. London: Macmillan.

Center for Ethnographic Research. University of Missouri. http://iml.umkc.edu/cer/goals.html.

Center for Urban Ethnography. Graduate School of Education, University of Pennsylvania. http://www.gse.upenn.edu/cue/.

Clifford, J. and Marcus, G.E. (eds) (1986) *Writing Culture: The Poetics and Politics of Ethnography*. Berkeley, CA: University of California Press.

Denzin, N.K. (1997) *Interpretive Ethnography: Ethnographic Practices for the 21st Century*. Thousand Oaks, CA: Sage.

Fetterman, D.M. (1989) *Ethnography: Step by Step*. Newbury Park, CA: Sage.

Fielding, N. (1981) *The National Front*. London: Routledge and Kegan Paul.

Geer, B. (1964) 'First days in the field'. In Hammond, P. (ed.), *Sociologists at Work*. New York: Basic Books.

Goffman, E. (1989) 'On Fieldwork'. *Journal of Contemporary Ethnography*, 18(2): 123–32.

Green, J.L. and Wallats, C. (eds) (1981) *Ethnography and Language in Educational Settings*. Norwood, NJ: Ablex.

Handbook of Ethnography. http://www.comp.lancs.ac.uk/sociology/VSOC/handbook.html.

McCall, G.J. and Simmons, J.L. (eds) (1969) *Issues in Participant Observation: A Text and Reader*. Reading, MA: Addison-Wesley.

Stewart, A. (1998) *The Ethnographer's Method*. Thousand Oaks, CA: Sage.

van Maanen, J. (1988) *Tales of the Field: On Writing Ethnography*. Chicago, IL: University of Chicago Press.

Whyte, W.F. (1943) *Street Corner Society: The Social Structure of an Italian Slum*. Chicago, IL: Chicago University Press.

Phenomenology

Binswanger, L. (1967) *Being-in-the-world*. (Trans. and ed. J. Needleman). New York: Harper and Row.

Casey, E.S. (1987) *Remembering: A Phenomenological Study*. Bloomington, IN: Indiana University Press.

Cavalier, R. Lectures on Heidegger's 'Being and time', Department of Philosophy, Carnegie Mellon University. http://caae.phil.cmu.edu/CAAE/80254/heidegger/SZHomePage.html.

Frick, W.B. (1990) 'The symbolic growth experience: a chronicle of heuristic inquiry and a quest for synthesis'. *Journal of Humanistic Psychology*, 30: 64–80.

Giorgi, A. (1970) *Psychology as a Human Science: A Phenomenologically Based Approach*. New York: Harper and Row.

Holstein, J.A. and Gubrium, J.F. (1998) 'Phenomenology, ethnomethodology, and interpretive practice'. In Denzin, N.K. and Lincoln, Y.S. (eds), *Strategies of Qualitative Inquiry*. Thousand Oaks, CA: Sage.

Ihde, D. (1986) *Experimental Phenomenology: An Introduction*. Albany, NY: State University of New York Press.

Laing, R.D. (1965) *The Divided Self*. Harmondsworth: Penguin.

Moustakas, C. (1990) *Heuristic Research: Design, Methodology and Applications*. Newbury Park, CA, Sage.

Moustakas, C. (1994) *Phenomenological Research Methods*. Thousand Oaks, CA: Sage.

Packer, M.J. and Addison, R.B. (eds) (1989) *Entering the Circle: Hermeneutic Investigation in Psychology*. Albany, NY: State University of New York Press.

Phenomenology www.connect.net/ron/phenom.html.

Psathas, G. (ed.) (1989) *Phenomenology and Sociology: Theory and Research*. Washington, DC: Centre for Advanced Research in Phenomenology and University Press of America.

Seamon, D. and Mugerauer, R. (1989) *Dwelling, Place and Environment: Towards a Phenomenology of Person and World*. New York: Columbia University Press.

Spiegelburg, H. (1976) *The Phenomenological Movement: An Historical Introduction*. Vols. 1–2, 2nd edn. The Hague: Nijhoff.

van Manen, M. (1990) *Researching Lived Experience: Human Science for an Action Sensitive Pedagogy*. Albany, NY: State University of New York Press.

Wagner, H.R. (1983) *Phenomenology of Consciousness and Sociology of the Life-World: An Introductory Study*. Edmonton: University of Alberta.

Grounded theory

Glaser, B.G. and Strauss, A.L. (1967) *The Discovery of Grounded Theory: Strategies for Qualitative Research*. New York: Aldine.

Goulding, C. (2002) *Grounded Theory: A Practical Guide for Management, Business and Market Researchers*. London: Sage.

Hutchinson, S.A. (1988) 'Education and Grounded Theory'. In Sherman, R. and Webb, R.B. (eds), *Qualitative Research in Education: Focus and Methods*. New York: Falmer.

Locke, K.D. (2001) *Grounded Theory in Management Research*. London: Sage.

Pandit, N.R. The creation of theory: a recent application of the Grounded Theory method. http://www.nova.edu/ssss/QR/QR2-4/pandit.html.

Strauss, A. and Corbin, J. (1990) *Basics of Qualitative Research: Grounded Theory Procedures and Techniques*. Newbury Park, CA: Sage.

Strauss, A. and Corbin, J. (1994) 'Grounded Theory methodology: an overview'. In Denzin, N.K. and Lincoln, Y.S. (eds), *Handbook of Qualitative Research*. Thousand Oaks, CA: Sage.

Strauss, A. and Corbin, J. (eds), (1997) *Grounded Theory in Practice*. London: Sage.

Strauss, A. and Corbin, J. (1998) *Basics of Qualitative Research: Techniques and Procedures for Developing Grounded Theory*. 2nd edn. Newbury Park, CA: Sage.

Surveys

Aldridge, A. and Levine, K. (2001) *Surveying the Social World*. Buckingham: Open University Press.

Bourque, L.B. and Fielder, E.P. (1995) *How to Conduct Self-Administered and Mail Surveys*. London: Sage.

Cartwright, A. and Seale, C.F. (1990) *The Natural History of Survey: An Account of the Methodological Issues Encountered in a Study of Life Before Death*. London: King's Fund.

Dale, A., Arber, S. and Proctor, M. (1988) *Doing Secondary Analysis*. London: Unwin Hyman.

de Vaus, D.A. (1991) *Surveys in Social Research*. London: Routledge.

Fink, A. (1995) *The Survey Kit*. Thousand Oaks, CA: Sage. Nine volumes.

Foddy, W. (1993) *Constructing Questions for Interviews and Questionnaires: Theory and Practice in Social Research*. Cambridge: Cambridge University Press.

Fowler, F.J. (2001) *Survey Research Methods*. 3rd edn. Newbury Park, CA: Sage.

Hoinville, G. and Jowell, R. (1987) *Survey Research Practice*. London: Heinemann.

Home Office (1983) *The British Crime Survey*. London: HMSO.

Hyman, H. (1955) *Survey Design and Analysis*. New York: Free Press.

Kish, L. (1965) *Survey Sampling*. New York: Wiley.

Marsh, C. (1982) *The Survey Method*. London: Allen and Unwin.

Moser, C.A. (1971) *Survey Methods in Social Investigation*. 2nd edn. Aldershot: Gower.

Oppenheim, A. (1992) *Questionnaire Design, Interviewing and Attitude Measurement*. London: Pinter.

Petersen, R. (2000) *Constructing Effective Questionnaires*. Thousand Oaks, CA: Sage.

ResearchInfo.com http://www.researchinfo.com/docs/software/index.cfm.

Rowntree, B.S. (1901) *Poverty: A Study in Town Life*. Basingstoke: Macmillan.

Salant, P. and Dillman, D. (1994) *How to Conduct Your Own Survey*. New York: Wiley.

Sampling guide. http://www.fantaproject.org/publications/sampling.shtml.

Sapsford, R. (1999) *Survey Research*. London: Sage.

Statistical good practice guidelines – overview http://www.rdg.ac.uk/ssc/dfid/booklets.html.

Statistics glossary http://www.stats.gla.ac.uk/steps/glossary/sampling.html.

Tacq, J. (1997) *Multivariate Analysis and Techniques in Social Science Research*. London: Sage.

Trochim, W.M. The research methods knowledge base, 2nd edn. http://trochim.human.cornell.edu/kb/index.htm http://trochim.human.cornell.edu/kb/survey.htm

University of Wisconsin Cooperative Extension;. http://www.uwex.edu/ces/pdande/evaluation/evaldocs.html.

Wells, A.F. (1935) *The Local Social Survey in Great Britain*. London: Allen and Unwin.

Case study

Abramson, P.R. (1992) *A Case for Case Studies: An Immigrant's Journal*. Newbury Park, CA: Sage.

Feagin, J.R., Orum, A.M. and Sjoberg, G. (eds) (1991) *A Case for the Case Study*. Chapel Hill, NC: University of North Carolina Press.

Gomm, R., Hammersley, M. and Foster P. (eds) (2000) *Case Study Method: Key Issues, Key Texts.* London: Sage.

Hamel, J., Dufour, S. and Fortin, D. (1993) *Case Study Methods.* Vol. 32. Qualitative Research Methods, ed. by John van Maanen, Peter K. Manning, and Marc L. Miller. Newbury Park, CA: Sage.

Merriam, S.B. (1988) *Case Study Research in Education: A Qualitative Approach.* San Francisco, CA: Jossey-Bass.

Ragin, C.C. and Becker, H.S. (eds) (1992) *What is a Case? Exploring the Foundations of Social Inquiry.* Cambridge: Cambridge University Press.

Stake, R.E. (1995) *The Art of Case Study Research.* Thousand Oaks, CA: Sage.

Travers, M. (2001) *Qualitative Research Through Case Studies.* London: Sage.

Yin, R.K. (1993) *Applications of Case Study Research.* Vol. 34. Applied Social Research Methods, ed. by L. Bickman and D.J. Rog. Newbury Park, CA: Sage.

Action research

Action Research International. http://www.scu.edu.au/schools/gcm/ar/arhome.html.

Action research: an electronic reader. http://www.beh.cchs.usyd.edu.au/narow/Reader/.

Argyris, C. (1993) *Knowledge for Action: A Guide to Overcoming Barriers to Organisational Change.* San Francisco, CA: Jossey-Bass.

Argyris, C., Putnam, R. and McLain, S.D. (1985) *Action Science: Concepts, Methods and Skills for Research and Intervention.* San Francisco, CA: Jossey-Bass.

Carr, W. and Kemmis, S. (1986) *Becoming Critical: Education, Knowledge and Action Research.* London: Falmer.

Center for Action Research in Professional Practice. http://www.bath.ac.uk/carpp/carpp.htm.

Coghlan, D. and Brannick, T. (2000) *Doing Action Research in Your Own Organization.* London: Sage.

Collaborative action research network. http://cpca3.uea.ac.uk/menu/acad_depts/care/carn/welcome.html.

Dick, B., A beginner's guide to action research, 1997. http://www.scu.edu.au/schools/sawd/arr/guide.html.

Greenwood, D.J. and Levin, M. (1998) *Introduction to Action Research: Social Research for Social Change.* London: Sage.

Heron, J. (1996) *Co-operative Inquiry: Research into the Human Condition.* London: Sage.

Oja, S.N. and Smuljan, O. (1989) *Collaborative Action Research: A Developmental Approach.* London: Falmer.

Reason, P. and Bradbury, H. (2000) *Handbook of Action Research: Participative Inquiry and Practice.* London: Sage.

Whyte, W.F. (1991) *Participatory Action Research.* Newbury Park, CA: Sage Publications.

Critical theory

Adorno, T.W. (1991) *Culture Industry: Selected Essays on Mass Culture.* (Trans. S. Crook and J.M. Bernstein). London: Routledge.

Adorno, T.W. (1994) *The Stars Come Down-to-Earth and Other Essays on the Irrational in Culture.* ed. by S. Crook. London: Routledge.

Braaten, J. (1991) *Habermas's Critical Theory of Society.* Albany, NY: State University of New York Press.

Boyle, J. (1996) *Shamans, Software, and Spleens: Law and the Construction of the Information Society.* Chicago, IL: University of Chicago Press.

Burawoy, M. (1979) *Manufacturing Consent: Changes in the Labour Process under Monopoly Capitalism.* Chicago, IL: University of Chicago Press.

Calhoun, C. (1995) *Critical Social Theory: Culture, History, and the Challenge of Difference.* Oxford: Blackwell.

Connerton, P. (ed.) (1976) *Critical Sociology.* Harmondsworth: Penguin.

Deetz, S. (1992) *Democracy in an Age of Corporate Colonization: Developments in the Communication and the Politics of Everyday Life.* Albany, NY: State University of New York Press.

Ewert, G.D. (1991) 'Habermas and education: a comprehensive overview of the influence of Habermas in educational literature'. *Review of Educational Research,* 61(3): 345–78.

Fay, B. (1987) *Critical Social Science.* Cambridge: Polity Press.

Forester, J. (1993) *Critical Theory, Public Policy, and Planning Practice.* Albany, NY: State University of New York Press.

Habermas, J. (1984) *The Theory of Communicative Action.* Vol 1. Boston, MA: Beacon.

Haraway, D. (1991) *Simians, Cyborgs, and Women.* New York: Routledge.

Held, D. (1980) *Introduction to Critical Theory: Horkheimer to Habermas.* Berkeley, CA: University Press of California.

Kincheloe, J.L. and McLaren, P.L. (1994) 'Rethinking critical theory and qualitative research'. In Denzin, N.K. and Yvonna, S.L. (eds), *Handbook of Qualitative Research.* Thousand Oaks, CA: Sage. pp. 138–57.

LaCapra, D. (1989) *Soundings in Critical Theory.* Ithaca, NY: Cornell University Press.

Lasch, C. (1978) *The Culture of Narcissism.* New York: Norton.

Leiss, W. (1978) *The Limits of Satisfaction.* London: Marion Boyars.

Marcuse, H. (1964) *One-Dimensional Man.* Boston, MA: Beacon.

Morrow, R.A. and Brown, D.A. (1994) *Critical Theory and Methodology: Interpretive Structuralism as a Research Program.* Thousand Oaks, CA: Sage.

Radnitzky, G. (1970) *Contemporary Schools of Metasciences.* Vols I–II. Göteborg: Akademiföraget.

Thompson, J.B. and Held, D. (eds) (1982) *Habermas: Critical Debates.* London: Macmillan.

Young, R. (1990) *A Critical Theory of Education.* New York: Teachers College Press.

Feminist methodology

Feminist research methods: A guide to library and internet resources. http://libweb.uoregon.edu/uo/libhome/instruct/womenst.html.

Fonow, M. and Cook, J. (eds) (1991) *Beyond Methodology: Feminist Scholarship as Lived Research*. Bloomington, IN: Indiana University Press.

Hammersley, M. (1992) 'On Feminist methodology'. *Sociology*, 26(2): 187–206.

Hammersley, M. (1995) *The Politics of Social Research*. London: Sage.

Humphries, B. and Truman, C. (eds) (1994) *Re-thinking Social Research: Anti-discriminatory Approaches in Research Methodology*. Aldershot: Avebury.

Jaggar, A.M. and Struhl, P.R. (1978). *Feminist Frameworks: Alternative Theoretical Accounts of the Relations between Women and Men*. New York: McGraw-Hill.

Keohane, N.O., Rosaldo, M.Z. and Gelpi, B.C. (eds) (1981–82) *Feminist Theory: A Critique of Ideology*. Chicago, IL: University of Chicago Press.

Maynard, M. and Purvis, J. (eds) (1994) *Researching Women's Lives from a Feminist Perspective*. London: Taylor and Francis.

Reinharz, S. (1992) *Feminist Methods in Social Research*. New York: Oxford University Press.

Roberts, H. (ed.) (1981) *Doing Feminist Research*. London: Routledge and Kegan Paul.

Sociological Research Online. 'Feminist research processes: practices, issues, debates'. www.socresonline.org.uk/threads/femres/femres.html.

Stanley, L. (ed.) (1990) *Feminist Praxis: Research, Theory and Epistemology in Feminist Sociology*. London: Routledge.

Sydie, R.A. (1987) *Natural Women, Cultural Men: A Feminist Perspective on Sociological Theory*. Milton Keynes: Open University Press.

Warren, C.B. (1988) *Gender Issues in Field Research*. London: Sage.

Virtual phenomena

Birnbaum, M.H. (ed.) (2000) *Psychological Experiments on the Internet*. San Diego, CA: Academic Press.

Center for Electronic Commerce. *Rules of procedure for conducting the virtual focus group*. http://www.erim.org/cec/conduit/rules.htm.

Coomber, R. (1997) *Using the internet for survey research in sociological research online*. http://www.socresonline.org.uk/socresonline/2/2/2.html.

Cybersociology. www.cybersociology.com.

Dourish, P. (2001) *Where the Action Is: The Foundations of Embodied Interaction*. Cambridge, MA: MIT.

Hine, C. (2000) *Virtual Ethnography*. London: Sage.

Jones, S.G. (ed.) (1999) *Doing Internet Research: Critical Issues and Methods for Examining the Net*. Thousand Oaks, CA: Sage.

Journal of Computer Mediated Communication. http://www.ascusc.org/jcmc/.

Journal of On-line Behaviour. http://www.behavior.net/JOB/.

Murray, P.J. (1997) 'Using virtual focus groups'. *Qualitative Health Research*, 7(4): 542–9.
Resources Centre for Cyber-culture. http://www.com.washington.edu/rccs/.

Evaluation

Chen, H., and Rossi, P.H. (1992) *Using Theory to Improve Program and Policy Evaluations*. New York: Greenwood.

Fetterman, D. 'Empowerment evaluation: collaboration, action research, and a case example'. http://www.aepro.org/inprint/conference/fetterman.html.

Fetterman, D.M. (1994) 'Empowerment evaluation'. *Evaluation Practice*, 15(1): 1–15.

Green, J.C. (1994) 'Qualitative program evaluation: practice and promise'. In Denzin, N.K. and Lincoln, Y.S. (eds) *The Handbook of Qualitative Research*. Thousand Oaks, CA: Sage.

Hadley, R.G. and Mitchell, L.K. (1995) *Counseling Research and Program Evaluation*. Pacific Grove, CA: Brooks/Cole.

House, E. (1993) *Professional Evaluation: Social Impact and Political Consequences*. Newbury Park, CA: Sage.

Madaus, G.F., Stufflebeam, D.L. and Scriven, M.S. (eds) (1983) *Evaluation Models*. Boston: Kluwer-Nijhoff.

Patton, M. (1990) *Qualitative Evaluation and Research Methods*. Newbury Park, CA: Sage.

Popham, W.J. (1988) *Educational Evaluation*. Englewood Cliffs, NJ: Prentice-Hall.

Posavac, E.J. and Carey, R.G. (1992) *Program Evaluation: Methods and Case Studies*. Englewood Cliffs, NJ: Prentice-Hall.

Rossi, P.H. and Freeman, H.E. (1993) *Evaluation: A Systematic Approach*. Newbury Park, CA: Sage.

Scriven, M. (1991) *Evaluation Thesaurus*. 4th edn. Newbury Park, CA: Sage.

Stake, R.E. (1983) 'Program evaluation, particularly responsive evaluation'. In Madhaus, G.F., Scriven, M. and Stufflebeam, D.L. (eds), *Evaluation Models. Viewpoints on educational and human social services evaluation*. Boston/The Hague: Kluwer/Nijhoff: 101–115.

Interviews

Arksey, H. and Knight, P.T. (1999) *Interviewing for Social Scientists: An Introductory Resource with Examples*. London: Sage.

Bell, C. and Roberts, H. (eds) (1984) *Social Researching*. London: Routledge.

Bourque L.B. and Fielder E.P. (1995) *How to Conduct Self-administered and Mail Surveys*. London: Sage.

Brenner, M., Brown, J. and Canter, D. (eds) (1985) *The Research Interview: Uses and Approaches*. New York: Academic Press.

Dexter, L.A. (1970) *Elite and Specialized Interviewing*. Evanston, IL: Northwestern University Press.

Douglas, J.D. (1985) *Creative Interviewing*. Vol. 159, Sage Library of Social Research. Beverly Hills, CA: Sage.

Flick, U. (1998) *An Introduction to Qualitative Research*. London: Sage.

Foddy, W. (1993) *Constructing Questions for Interviews and Questionnaires: Theory and Practice in Social Research*. Cambridge : Cambridge University Press.

Fontana, A. and Frey, J.H. (1994) 'Interviewing: the art of science'. In Denzin, N.K. and Lincoln, Y.S. (eds), *Handbook of Qualitative Research*. London: Sage.

Fre, J.H. and Mertens, O.S. (1995) *How to Conduct Interviews by Telephone and in Person*. London: Sage.

Gubrium, J.F. and Holstein, J.A. (eds) (2001) *Handbook of Interview Research: Context and Method*. London: Sage.

Holstein, J.A. and Gubrium, J.F. (1995) *The Active Interview*. Thousand Oaks, CA: Sage.

Hyman, H.H. (1975) *Interviewing in Social Research*. Chicago, IL: University of Chicago Press.

Kahn, R.L. and Cannell, C.F. (1983 [1957]) *The Dynamics of Interviewing: Theory, Techniques and Cases*. Malabar, FL: Krieger.

Kvale, S. (1996) *Interviews: An Introduction to Qualitative Research Interviewing*. Thousand Oaks, CA: Sage.

Lavrakas, P.J. (1993) *Telephone Survey Methods: Sampling, Selection, and Supervision*. 2nd edn. London: Sage.

McCracken, G. (1988) 'The Long Interview'. Vol. 13. Qualitative Research Methods Series ed. by J. van Maanen. Beverly Hills, CA: Sage.

Merton, R.K., Fiske, M. and Kendall, P.L. (1990) *The Focused Interview: A Manual of Problems and Procedures*. 2nd edn. New York: Free Press.

Mishler, E.G. (1991) *Research Interviewing: Context and Narrative*. Cambridge, MA.: Harvard University Press.

Questionnaires

A primer on experimental and quasi-experimental design. http://ericae.net/ft/tamu/Expdes.HTM.

Electronic textbook. http://www.statsoft.com/textbook/stathome.html.

Foddy, W. (1993) *Constructing Questions for Interviews and Questionnaires: Theory and Practice in Social Research*. Cambridge: Cambridge University Press.

Oppenheim, A. (1992) *Questionnaire Design, Interviewing and Attitude Measurement*. London: Pinter.

PA 765 Statnotes: an online textbook. by Garson, G.D. http://www2.chass.ncsu.edu/garson/pa765/statnote.htm.

Petersen, R. (2000) *Constructing Effective Questionnaires*. Thousand Oaks, CA: Sage.

Sampling guide. http:gsociology.icaap.org/methods/sampling/html.

Statistical good practice guidelines – overview. http://www.rdg.ac.uk/ssc/dfid/booklets.html.

Statistics glossary. http://www.statsoftinc.com/textbook/glosfra.html.

The little handbook of statistical practice. http://www.tufts.edu/~gdallal/LHSP.HTM.

University of Wisconsin Cooperative Extension;. http://www.uwex.edu/ces/pdande/evaluation/evaldocs.html.

Focus groups

A manual for the use of focus groups. http://www.unu.edu/unupress/food2/UIN03E/UIN03E00.HTM.

Agar, M. and MacDonald, J. (1995) 'Focus groups and ethnography'. *Human Organization*, 54: 78–86.

Banks, J.A. (1957) 'The group discussion as an interview technique'. *Sociological Review*, 5(1): 75–84.

Barbour, R.S. and Kitzinger, J. (eds) (1999) *Developing Focus Group Research: Politics, Theory and Practice*. London: Sage.

Bion, W.R. (1961) *Experiences in Groups*. London: Tavistock.

Bloor, M., Frankland, J., Thomas, M. and Robson, K. (2000) *Focus Groups in Social Research*. London: Sage.

Fern, E.F. (2001) *Advanced Focus Group Research*. London: Sage.

Goulding, C. (2002) *Grounded Theory: A Practical Guide for Management, Business and Market Researchers*. London: Sage.

Greenbaum, T.L. (2000) *Moderating Focus Groups: A Practical Guide for Group Facilitation*. London: Sage.

Krueger, R.A. (1994) *Focus Groups: A Practical Guide for Applied Research*. Thousand Oaks, CA: Sage.

Krueger, R.A. (1997) *Analysing and Reporting Focus Group Results*. London: Sage.

Locke, K.D. (2001) *Grounded Theory in Management Research*. London: Sage.

Market Navigation, Inc. http://www.mnav.com/qualitative_research.htm.

Morgan, D.L. (ed.) (1993) *Successful Focus Groups: Advancing the State of the Art*. Newbury Park, CA: Sage.

Myers, D.L. (1988) 'Displaying opinions: topics and disagreement in focus groups'. *Language and Society*, 27: 85–111.

Social Research Updates. http://www.soc.surrey.ac.uk/sru/SRU19.html.

Stewart, D. and Shamdasani, P. (1990) *Focus Groups: Theory and Practice*. London: Sage.

Using focus groups to create excellence. http://child.cornell.edu/army/focus.html.

Vaughn, S., Schumm, J.S. and Sinagub, J.M. (1996) *Focus Group Interviews in Education and Psychology*. London: Sage.

Wilkinson, S. (1998) 'Focus groups in Feminist research: power, interaction, and the construction of meaning'. *Women's Studies International Forum*, 21(1): 111–25.

Delphi technique

Delbeq, A. and van de Ven A. (1971) 'A group process model for problem identification and program planning'. *Journal of Applied Behavioural Sciences*, 7: 467–92.

Fink, A., Kosecoff, J., Chassin, M. and Brook, R.H. (1984) 'Consensus methods: characteristics and guidelines for use'. *American Journal of Public Health*, 74: 979–83.

Fowles, R.B. (ed.) (1978) *Handbook of Futures Research*. Westport, CT: Greenwood.

Gerth, W. and Smith. M.E. (1991) 'The Delphi Technique. Background for use in probability estimation'. *Human Health Economics MHHD*. Merck and Co., 8 September.

Pill, J. (1971) 'The Delphi method: substance, context, a critique and an annotated bibliography'. *Socio-economic Planning Science*, 5: 57–71.

Personal documents

Cooper, J.E. (1991) 'Telling our own stories: the reading and writing of journals and diaries'. In Witherell, C. and Noddings, N. (eds), *Stories Lives Tell: Narrative and Dialogue in Education*. New York: Teachers College Press.

Malinowski, B. (1989) *A Diary in the Strict Sense of the Term*. Stanford, CA: Stanford University Press.

Webb, E., Campbell, D., Schwartz, R. and Sechrest, L. (2000 [1966]) *Unobtrusive Measures: Non-reactive Research in the Social Sciences*. London: Sage.

Conversation analysis

Atkinson, M. and Heritage, J. (1989) *Structures of Social Action: Studies in Conversation Analysis*. Cambridge: Cambridge University Press.

Button, G. and Lee, J.R.E. (eds) (1987) *Talk and Social Organization*. Clevedon: Multilingual Matters.

Sacks, H., Schegloff, E.A. and Jefferson, G. (1974) 'A simple systematics for the organization of turn-taking in conversation'. *Language*, 50: 696–735.

ten Have, P. (1999) *Doing Conversation Analysis: A Practical Guide*. London: Sage.

Content analysis

Ang, I. (1991) *Desperately Seeking the Audience*. London: Routledge.

Bauer, M.W. (1998) 'Guidelines for sampling and content analysis'. In Durant, J., Bauer, M.W. and Gaskell, G. (eds), *Biotechnology in the Public Sphere*. London: Science Museum.

Berelson, B. (1952) *Content Analysis in Communication Research*. Glencoe, IL: Free Press.

Glasgow University Media Group (1976) *Bad News*. London: Routledge and Kegan Paul.

Holsti, O.R. (1969) *Content Analysis for the Social Sciences and Humanities*. Reading, MA: Addison-Wesley.

Kaplan, A. (1943) 'Content analysis and the theory of signs', *Philosophy of Science*, 10: 230–47.

Krippendorff, K. (1980) *Content Analysis: An Introduction to its Methodology*. Beverly Hills, CA: Sage.

Leiss, W., Kline, S. and Jhally, S. (1986) *Social Communication in Advertising: Persons, Products and Images of Well-being*. London: Methuen.

Neuendorf, K.A. (2002) *The Content Analysis Guidebook*. Thousand Oaks, CA: Sage.

Riffe, D., Lacy, S. and Fico, F.G. (1998) *Analyzing Media Messages: Using Quantitative Content Analysis in Research*. Mahwah, NJ: Lawrence Erlbaum.

Rosengren, K.E. (ed.) (1981) *Advances in Content Analysis*. Beverly Hills, CA: Sage.

West, M.D. (ed.) (2001) *Applications of Computer Content Analysis*. Westport, CT: Ablex.

Discourse analysis

Cazden, C.B. (1988) *Classroom Discourse: The Language of Teaching and Learning*. Portsmouth, NH: Heinemann.

Edwards, D. and Potter, J. (1992) *Discourse in Psychology*. London: Sage.

Faircloth, N. (1992) *Discourse and Social Change*. Cambridge: Polity Press.

Foucault, M. (1977) *Discipline and Punish: The Birth of the Prison*. Harmondsworth: Penguin.

Gill, R. (1996) 'Discourse analysis: practical implementation'. In Richardson, J. (ed.), *Handbook of Qualitative Research Methods for Psychology and the Social Sciences*. Leicester: British Psychological Society.

Gumperz, J.J. (1982) *Discourse Strategies*. Cambridge: Polity Press.

Potter, J. (1996) *Representing Reality: Discourse, Rhetoric and Social Construction*. London: Sage.

Rhetorical analysis

Cole, T. (1991) *The Origins of Rhetoric in Ancient Greece*. Baltimore, MD: Johns Hopkins University Press.

Gross, A. and Keith, B. (eds) (1997) *Rhetorical Hermeneutics: Invention and Interpretation in the Age of Science*. Albany, NY: SUNY.

McCloskey, D.N. (1994) 'How to do a rhetorical analysis, and why'. In Blackhouse, R.E. (ed.), *New Directions in Economic Methodology*. London: Routledge.

Meyer, M. (1994) *Rhetoric, Language, and Reason*. University Park, PA: Pennsylvania State University Press.

Nelson, J., Megill, A. and McCloskey, D. (1987) *The Rhetoric of the Human Sciences: Language and Argument in Scholarship and Public Affairs*. Madison, WI: University of Wisconsin Press.

Toulmin, S. (1958) *The Uses of Argument*. Cambridge: Cambridge University Press.

Semiological analysis

Barthes, R. (1977) *Elements of Semiology*. New York: Hill and Wang.

Barthes, R. (1986) *Mythologies*. London: Paladin.

Gottdiener, M.P. (1995) *Postmodern Semiotics: Material Culture and the Forms of Postmodern Life*. Oxford: Blackwell.

Hawkes, T. (1992) *Structuralism and Semiotics*. London: Routledge.

Saussure, F. de (1974) *Course in General Linguistics*. London: Fontana.

Williamson, J. (1978) *Decoding Advertisements: Ideology and Meaning in Advertising*. London: Marion Boyars.

Narrative/life history

Cortazzi, M. (1993) 'Narrative analysis'. Vol. 12. *Social Research and Education Studies*, ed. by R.G. Burgess. London: Falmer.

International Conference on Narrative. http://www.uky.edu/~jknuff/narrative_conference.

Lee, D.J. (ed.) (1994) *Life and Story: Autobiographies for a Narrative Psychology*. Westport, CT: Praeger.

Lieblich, A. and Josselson, R. (eds) (1994) *Exploring Identity and Gender: The Narrative Study of Lives*. Thousand Oaks, CA: Sage.

Narrative resources, Hevern, V.W., LeMoyne College, Syracuse, NY. http://maple.lemoyne. edu/~hevern/narpsych.html.

Oral History Society: http://www.oralhistory.org.uk/.

Oral history: techniques and procedures http://www.army.mil/cmh-pg/books/oral.htm.

Reinharz, S. (1992) 'Introduction'. *Feminist Methods in Social Research*. New York: Oxford University Press.

Riessman, C.K. (1993) *Narrative Analysis*. Vol. 30, Qualitative Research Methods, ed. by P.K. Manning, J. van Maanen and M.L. Miller. Newbury Park, CA: Sage.

Rubin, H.J. and Rubin, I.S. (1995) *Qualitative Interviewing: The Art of Hearing Data*. Thousand Oaks, CA: Sage.

Spradley, J.P. (1979) *The Ethnographic Interview*. New York: Holt, Rinehart and Winston.

Weiss, R.S. (1994) *Learning from Strangers: The Art and Method of Qualitative Interview Studies*. New York: Free Press.

Werner, O. and Schoepfle, G.M. (1987) *Systematic Fieldwork*. Vol. 1. Foundations of Ethnography and Interviewing. Beverly Hills, CA: Sage.

Yow, V.R. (1994) *Recording Oral History: A Practical Guide for Social Scientists*. Thousand Oaks, California: Sage Publications Inc.

References

Abbott, A. (1983) 'Professional ethics'. *American Journal of Sociology*, 88(5): 855–85.

Alasuutari, P. (1995) *Researching Culture: Qualitative Method and Cultural Studies*. London: Sage.

Alvesson, M. and Sköldberg, K. (2000) *Reflexive Methodology: New Vistas for Qualitative Research*. London: Sage.

Anderson, R.J., Hughes, J.A. and Sharrock, W.W. (1985) *The Sociology Game: An Introduction to Sociological Reasoning*. London: Longman.

Arendell, T. (2003) *Co-Parenting: A Review of the Literature*. National Center on Fathers and Families. http://www.ncoff.gse.upenn.edu/litrev/cplr.htm (accessed 1 December 2003).

Armstrong, C.J. and Large, A. (eds) (2001) *Manual of On-line Search Strategies*. 3rd edn. Vol. 3: Humanities and Social Sciences. London: Gower.

Atkinson, J.M. (1978) *Discovering Suicide: Studies in the Social Organization of Sudden Death*. London: Macmillan.

Barker, E. (1988) *The Making of a Moonie: Choice or Brainwashing?* Oxford: Blackwell.

Bauer, M.W. and Gaskell, G. (eds) (2000) *Qualitative Researching with Text, Image and Sound: A Practical Handbook*. London: Sage.

Becker, H. (1967) 'Whose side are we on?' *Social Problems*, 14: 239–48.

Becker, H.S. (1953) 'Becoming a marihuana user'. *American Journal of Sociology*, 59: 235–42.

Bell, C. and Newby, H. (1977) *Doing Sociological Research*. London: Allen and Unwin.

Beloff, H. (ed.) (1980) 'A balance sheet on Burt'. *Supplement to the Bulletin of The British Psychological Society*, Volume 33.

Bentz, V.M. and Shapiro, J.J. (1998) *Mindful Inquiry in Social Research*. Thousand Oaks, CA: Sage.

Bettelheim, B. (1976) *The Uses of Enchantment: On the Meaning and Importance of Fairy Tales*. Harmondsworth: Penguin.

Bingham, N. (2003) 'Writing reflexively'. In Pryke, M., Rose, G. and Whatmore, S. (eds), *Using Social Theory: Thinking Through Research*. London: Sage and Open University Press: 145–62.

Black, T.R. (1993) *Evaluating Social Science Research: An Introduction*. London: Sage.

Blaikie, N. (1991) 'A critique of the use of triangulation in social research'. *Quality and Quantity*, 25: 115–36.

Booth, C. (1902–3 [1889]) *Life and Labour of the People in London*. 17 vols. London: Macmillan.

Booth, W. (1970 [1890]) *In Darkest England and the Way Out*. London: Charles Knight.

Bourdieu, P. (1990 [1980]) *The Logic of Practice*. (Trans. R. Nice). Cambridge: Polity Press.

British Sociological Association Code of Ethics (1996) See www.britsoc.co.uk.

Bryant, P.E., Bradley, L., Maclean, M. and Crossland, J. (1989) 'Rhyme and alliteration, phoneme detection, and learning to read'. *Developmental Psychology*, 26: 429–38.

Bryman, A. (1988) *Quantity and Quality in Social Research*. London: Unwin Hyman.

Bulmer, M. (1984) *The Chicago School of Sociology*. Chicago: University of Chicago Press.

Burt, C. (1966) 'The genetic determination of intelligence: a study of monozygotic twins reared together and apart'. *British Journal of Psychology*, 57: 137–53.

Buzan, T. and Buzan, B. (1993) *The Mind Map Book*. London: BBC Books.

Cadwell, B. (1994) *Beyond Positivism: Economic Methodology in the Twentieth Century*. 2nd edn. London: Routledge.

Cameron, S. (1997) *The MBA Handbook*. Edinburgh: Pearson Educational.

Campbell, D.T. and Fiske, D.W. (1962) 'Convergent and discriminant validation by multitrait-multimethod matrix'. In Jackson, D.N. and Messick, S. (eds), *Problems in Human Assessment*. New York: McGraw Hill. pp. 124–31.

Caplan, P.J. (1994) *Lifting a Ton of Feathers: A Woman's Guide to Surviving in the Academic World*. Toronto: University of Toronto Press.

Cicourel, A. (1964) *Method and Measurement in Sociology*. New York: Free Press.

Clough, P. and Nutbrown, C. (2002) *A Student's Guide to Methodology*. London: Sage.

Cochrane, A.L. (1972) *Effectiveness and Efficiency: Random Reflections on Health Services*. London: Nuffield Provincial Hospitals Trust. (Reprinted in 1989 in association with the British Medical Council.)

Cochrane, A.L. (1989) 'Forward'. In Chalmers, I., Enkin, M.K. and Keirse, M.J.N.C. (eds), *Effective Care in Pregnancy and Childbirth*. Oxford: Oxford University Press.

Cohen, S. (1980) *Folk Devils and Moral Panics: The Creation of Mods and Rockers*. Oxford: Robertson.

Cohen, S. and Young, J. (1973) *The Manufacture of News: Social Problems, Deviance and the Mass Media*. London: Constable.

Cone, J.D. and Foster, S.L. (1999) *Dissertations and Theses from Start to Finish: Psychology and Related Fields*. Washington, DC: American Psychology Association.

Cooke, A. (2001) *A Guide to Finding Quality Information on the Internet: Selection and Evaluation*. 2nd edn. London: Library Association.

Cooper, H. (1998) *Synthesizing Research*. (3rd edn). Thousand Oaks, CA: Sage.

Cooper, H. and Hedges, L.V. (1994) *The Handbook of Research Synthesis*. New York: Russell Sage Foundation.

Coutler, J. (1989) *Mind in Action*. Cambridge: Polity Press.

Cox, S. (2002) 'Approaches to assist the formulation of project ideas'. Occasional paper. School of Computing, University of Central England, Birmingham.

Cronbach, L. and Meehl, P. (1955) 'Construct validity in psychological tests'. *Psychological Bulletin*, 52(4): 281–302.

Crotty, M. (1998) *The Foundations of Social Research: Meaning and Perspective in the Research Process*. London: Sage.

Cuff, E.C., Sharrock, W.W. and Francis, D.W. (1998) *Perspectives in Sociology*. 4th edn. London: Routledge.

Darwin, C. (1859) *The Origin of Species by Means of Natural Selection, or The Preservation of Favoured Races in the Struggle for Life*. London: John Murray.

Deaconescu, A. (2000) 'Change in Romanian academic libraries'. Unpublished MSc dissertation, School of Information Studies, University of Central England, Birmingham.

Denscombe, M. (2002) *Ground Rules for Good Research: A 10-point Guide for Social Researchers*. Buckingham: Open University Press.

Denzin, N. (1970) 'Strategies of multiple triangulation'. In Denzin, N. (ed.), *The Research Act in Sociology: A Theoretical Introduction to Sociological Method*. New York: McGraw-Hill.

Denzin, N.K. (1991) 'Harold and Agnes: a Feminist narrative undoing'. *Sociological Theory*, 18(2): 198–216.

Derrida, J. (1987 [1980]) *The Post Card*. Chicago, IL: University of Chicago Press.

Douglas, J. (1967) *The Social Meanings of Suicide*. Princeton: Princeton University Press.

Durkheim, E. (1952 [1897]) *Suicide: A Study in Sociology*. (Trans. J.A. Spaulding and G. Simpson). London: Routledge and Kegan Paul.

Durkheim, E. (1982 [1895]) *The Rules of Sociological Method*. London: Macmillan.

Duster, T., Matza, D. and Wellman, D. (1979) 'Field work and the protection of human subjects'. *American Sociologist*, 14(3): 136–42.

Dwyer, J. and Jackson, J. (2001) *Literature Review: Integrated Bed and Patient Management*. Commissioned by the Patient Management Task Force, Victoria La Trobe University/Monash University.

Eckhardt, K.W. and Ermann, M.D. (1977) *Social Research Methods: Perspective, Theory and Analysis*. New York: Random House.

Evans, C. (2000) 'The cultural role of public libraries'. Unpublished MA dissertation. School of Information Studies, University of Central England, Birmingham.

Evans-Pritchard, E.E. (1965) *Witchcraft, Oracles and Magic among the Azande*. Oxford: Clarendon Press.

Ferrero, G.L. (1912 [1896–7]) *Criminal Man According to the Classification of Cesare Lombroso, Briefly Summarised by his Daughter Gina Lombroso Ferrero*. New York: Putnam.

Fetterman, D.M. (1989) *Ethnography Step by Step*. Newbury Park, CA: Sage.

Feyerabend, P. (1993) *Killing Time*. Chicago, IL: University of Chicago Press.

Field, A. and Hole, G. (2002) *How to Design and Report Experiments*. London: Sage.

Fielding, N.G. and Fielding, J.L. (1986) *Linking Data*. Qualitative Research Methods Series No. 4. London: Sage.

Fink, A. (1998) *Conducting Research Literature Reviews: From Paper to Internet*. Thousand Oaks, CA: Sage.

Fish, S. (1989) *Doing What Comes Naturally: Change, Rhetoric, and the Practice of Theory in Literary and Legal Studies*. Oxford: Clarendon.

Fletcher, R. (1971) *The Making of Sociology: Beginnings and Foundation*. Vol 1. London: Nelson.

Fowler, C. (1996) 'Library and information service provision to NHS community-based staff in the South and West region'. Unpublished MA dissertation. School of Information Studies, University of Central England, Birmingham.

Fowler, R. (1991) *Language in the News*. London: Routledge.

Gans, H. (1963) *The Urban Villages: Group and Class in the Life of Italian-Americans*. Glencoe: Free Press.

Garfinkel, H. (1967a) 'Passing and the managed achievement of sex in an intersexed person'. In Garfinkel, H., *Studies in Ethnomethodology*. Englewood Cliffs, NJ: Prentice-Hall. pp. 116–85, 285–8.

Garfinkel, H. (1967b) *Studies in Ethnomethodology*. Englewood Cliffs, NJ: Prentice-Hall.

Garfinkel, H. (1981) *Forms of Explanation*. Yale, CT: Yale University Press.

Garfinkel, H. (2002) *Ethnomethodology's Program: Working out Durkheim's Aphorism*. New York: Rowman and Littlefield.

Garner, W.R. (1954) 'Context effects and the validity of loudness scales'. *Journal of Experimental Psychology*, 48: 218–24.

Garner, W.R., Hake, H.W. and Eriksen, C.W. (1956) 'Operationism and the concept of perception'. *Psychological Review*, 63: 149–59.

Garrett, H.E. and Bonner, H. (1961) *General Psychology*. 2nd edn. New York: American Book Company.

Geertz, C. (1973) *The Interpretation of Cultures*. New York: Basic Books.

Gerth, H. and Mills, C.W. (1948) *Essays from Max Weber*. London: Routledge and Kegan Paul.

Gerth W. and Smith M.E. (1991) 'The Delphi Technique. Background for use in probability estimation'. *Human Health Economics MHHD*. Merck and Co., September.

Giddens, A. (1976) *The New Rules of Sociological Method*. London: Hutchinson.

Gilbert, N. and Mulkay, M. (1983) 'In search of the action'. In Gilbert, N. and Abell, P. (eds), *Accounts and Action*. Aldershot: Gower.

Gill, R. (1996) 'Discourse analysis: practical implementation'. In Richardson, J. (ed.), *Handbook of Qualitative Research Methods for Psychology and the Social Sciences*. Leicester: British Psychological Society.

Gillie, O. (1976) 'Crucial data was faked by eminent psychologist'. London: *Sunday Times*, 24 October: 1–2.

Glaser, B.G. and Strauss, A.L. (1967) *The Discovery of Grounded Theory: Strategies for Qualitative Research*. Chicago, IL: Aldine.

Glucksmann, M. (1974) *Structuralist Analysis in Contemporary Social Thought: A Comparison to the Theories of Claude Lévi-Strauss and Louis Althusser*. London and Boston: Routledge and Kegan Paul.

Goddard, H.H. (1912) *The Kallikak Family: A Study in the Heredity of Feeble-mindedness*. New York: Macmillan. Available from: 'Classics in the history of psychology', an Internet resource by Christopher D. Green at www.yoku.ca/dept/psych/classics/Goddard/ (accessed 20 December 2003).

Goddard, H.H. (1914) *Feeble-mindedness: Its Causes and Consequences*. New York: Macmillan.

Goddard, H.H. (1917) 'Mental tests and the immigrant'. *Journal of Delinquency*, 2: 243–77.

Goddard, H.H. (1927) 'Who is a moron?' *Scientific Monthly*, 24: 41–6.

Goffman, E. (1959) *The Presentation of the Self in Everyday Life*. Garden City, NY: Doubleday Anchor.

Goffman, E. (1961) *Encounters: Two Studies in the Sociology of Interaction*. Indianapolis, IN: Bobbs-Merrill.

Goffman, E. (1963a) *Stigma: Notes on the Management of Spoiled Identity*. Englewood Cliffs, NJ: Prentice-Hall.

Goffman, E. (1963b) *Behaviour in Public Places: Notes on the Social Organization of Gatherings*. Glencoe: Free Press.

Goffman, E. (1968) *Asylums: Essays on the Social Situation of Mental Patients and Other Inmates*. Harmondsworth: Penguin. Original 1961. Garden City, NY: Doubleday.

Goffman, E. (1969) *Interaction Ritual: Essays on Face-to-face Behavior*. Garden City, NY: Doubleday Anchor.

Goffman, E. (1971) *Relations in Public: Micro-studies of the Public Order*. New York: Basic Books.

Goffman, E. (1974) *Frame Analysis: Essays on the Social Organization of Experience*. Pennsylvania, PA: University of Pennsylvania Press.

Goldthorpe, J.H., Lockwood, D., Bechhofer, F. and Platt, J. (1968–9) *The Affluent Worker Studies*. Cambridge: Cambridge University Press.

Goodwin, C. (1984) 'Notes on story structure and the organization of participation'. In Atkinson, J.M. and Heritage, J. (eds), *Structures of Social Action: Studies in Conversation Analysis*. Cambridge: Cambridge University Press.

Gouldner, A.W. (1975) *The Dark Side of the Dialectic*. Amsterdam: Sociology Institute, University of Amsterdam.

Grathoff, R. (ed.) (1978) *The Theory of Social Action: The Correspondence of Alfred Schutz and Talcott Parsons*. Bloomington, IN: Indiana University Press.

Gray, M.J.A. (2001) *Evidence-based Health Care: How to Make Health Policy and Management Decisions*. London: Churchill Livingstone.

Kolb, D.A., Rubin, I.M. and MacIntyre, J.M. (1984) *Organizational Psychology*. 4th edn. London: Prentice-Hall.

Koluchova, J. (1972) 'Severe deprivation in twins: a case study'. *Journal of Child Psychology and Psychiatry*, 13: 107–14.

Kuhn, T. (1970) *The Structure of Scientific Revolutions*. (Revised edn.) Chicago, IL: University of Chicago Press.

Kuhn, T. (1977) *The Essential Tension*. Chicago, IL: University of Chicago Press.

Kuper, A. and Kuper, J. (eds) (1999) *The Social Science Encyclopaedia*. London: Routledge.

Latour, B. (1987) *Science in Action*. Milton Keynes: Open University Press.

Latour, B. (1999) *Pandora's Hope: Essays on the Reality of Science Studies*. Cambridge, MA: Harvard University Press.

Latour, B. (2002) 'Promises of constructivism'. http://ensmp.fr/~latour/articles/087.html. (Accessed November 2003). In Ihde, D. (ed.), *Chasing Technoscience: Matrix of Materiality*. Bloomington, IN: Indiana University Press.

Leach, E. (1970) *Lévi-Strauss*. Bungay, Suffolk: Fontana/Collins.

Leach, E.R. (1970) *Claude Lévi-Strauss*. New York: Viking Press.

Lévi-Strauss, C. (1958) *Anthropologie Structurale*. Paris: Plon.

Lévi-Strauss, C. (1961) *Tristes Tropiques*. (Trans. J. Russell.) New York: Criterion Books.

Lévi-Strauss, C. (1963) *Structural Anthropology 1*. (Tr. from the French by Claire Jacobson and Brooke Grundfest Schoepf.) Harmondsworth: Penguin.

Lévi-Strauss, C. (1966 [1962]) *The Savage Mind* (Nature and Human Society Series). Chicago: Chicago University Press.

Lévi-Strauss, C. (1967) *The Structural Study of Myth and Totemism*. London: Travistock Publications.

Lévi-Strauss, C. (1969 [1949]) *The Elementary Structures of Kinship*. London: Eyre and Spottiswoode.

Lévi-Strauss, C. (1990 [1964]) *The Raw and the Cooked: Mythologies*. Chicago: University of Chicago Press. (Originally published in French as *Mythologiques 1964–1968*).

Lévi-Strauss, C. (1992 [1955]) *Tristes Tropiques*. (Trans. J. Weightman and D. Weightman.) New York: Penguin.

Lombroso, C. (1912 [1896–7]) *L'uomo delinquente*. 5th edn., 3rd vol. Tr. as *Criminal Man According to the Classification of Cesare Lombroso, Briefly Summarised by his Daughter Gina Lombroso Ferrero*. New York: Putnam.

MacKintosh, N.J. (1995) *Cyril Burt: Fraud or Framed*. New York: Oxford University Press.

Mason, J. (1996) *Qualitative Researching*. London: Sage.

Massey, A.S. and Walford, G. (1998) 'Children learning: ethnographers learning'. In Walford, G. and Massey A.S. (eds), *Children Learning in Context*. London: JAI.

Mathison, S. (1988) 'Why triangulate?' *Educational Researcher*, 17(2): 13–17.

May, T. (2001) *Social Research: Issues, Methods and Process*. 3rd edn. Buckingham: Open University Press.

Mayhew, H. (1985 [1851]) *London Labour and the London Poor*. London: Penguin.

McRobbie, A. and Thornton, S. (1995) 'Rethinking "Moral Panic" for multi-mediated social worlds'. *British Journal of Sociology*, 46: 559–74.

Mertens, D.M. (1998) *Research Methods in Education and Psychology: Integrating Diversity with Quantitative and Qualitative Approaches*. Thousand Oaks, CA: Sage.

Michels, R. (1949) *Political Parties*. (Trans. E. Paul and C. Paul). New York: Free Press. (Originally published in German in 1911.)

Milgram, S. (1974) *Obedience and Authority*. London: Harper Row.

Mitchell, E.S. (1986) 'Multiple triangulation: a methodology for nursing science'. *Advances in Nursing Science*, 8(3): 18–26.

Moustakas, C. (1994) *Phenomenological Research Methods*. Thousand Oaks, CA: Sage.

Mulkay, M. (1979) *Science and the Sociology of Knowledge*. London: Allen and Unwin.

Murrey, J.P. (2003) *The Impact of Television Violence*. http://www.ksu.edu/humec/impact.html (accessed 17 July 03).

Noblit, G.W. and Hare, R.D. (1998) *Meta-Ethnography: Synthesizing Qualitative Studies*. Thousand Oaks, CA: Sage.

The Nuremberg Code (1947) In Mitscherlich, A. and Mielke, F. *Doctors of Infamy: The Story of the Nazi Medical Crimes*. New York: Schuman, 1947: xxiii–xxv.

Oakley, A. (1974) *The Sociology of Housework*. Oxford: Robertson.

Oliver, J. (1998) 'Health information in women's magazines'. Unpublished MSc dissertation. School of Information Studies, University of Central England in Birmingham.

Orna, E. and Stevens, G. (1995) *Managing Information for Research*. Buckingham: Open University Press.

Outherwaite, W. and Bottomore, T. (eds) (1993) *The Blackwell Dictionary of Twentieth Century Social Thought*. Oxford: Blackwell.

Packer, M.J. and R.B. Addison (eds) (1989) *Entering the Circle: Hermeneutic Investigation in Psychology*. Albany, NY: State University of New York Press.

Parkin, F. (2003) *Max Weber*. Rev. edn. London: Routledge.

Patton, M.Q. (1990) *Qualitative Evaluation and Research Methods*. 2nd edn. Newbury Park, CA: Sage.

Piantanida, M. and Garman, B.N. (1999) *The Qualitative Dissertation: A Guide for Students and Faculty*. Thousand Oaks, CA: Corwin.

Pike, K. (1967) *Language in Relation to a Unified Theory of the Structure of Human Behaviour*. The Hague: Mouton.

Popper, K. (1959) *The Logic of Scientific Discovery*. New York: Basic Books.

Popper, K.R. (1972) *Objective Knowledge: An Evolutionary Approach*. Rev. edn. Oxford: Clarendon Press.

Potter, J. (1996) *Representing Reality: Discourse, Rhetoric and Social Construction*. London: Sage.

Psathas, G. (1995) *Conversation Analysis: The Study of Talk-in-interaction*. Qualitative Research Methods Series 35. London: Sage.

Putnam, H. (1975) *Mathematics, Matter and Method*. Cambridge: Cambridge University Press.

Putnam, H. (1978) *Realism and Reason*. Cambridge: Cambridge University Press.

Putnam, H. (1981) *Reason, Truth and History*. Cambridge: Cambridge University Press.

Ragin, C.C. (1994) *Constructing Social Research: The Unity and Diversity of Method*. Thousand Oaks, CA: Pine Forge Press.

Raine, A., Buchsbaum, M. and LaCasse, L. (1997) 'Brain abnormalities in murderers indicated by positron emission tomography'. *Biological Psychiatry*, 42: 495–508.

Reinharz, S. (1992) *Feminist Methods in Social Research*. New York: Oxford University Press.

Ricoeur, P. (1981) *Hermeneutics and the Human Sciences*. Cambridge, MA: Cambridge University Press.

Robson, C. (2002) *Real World Research: A Resource for Social Scientists and Practitioners*. 2nd edn. Oxford: Blackwell.

Rock, P. (1979) *The Making of Symbolic Interactionism*. London: Macmillan.

Rosaldo, R. (1989) *Culture and Truth: The Remaking of Social Analysis*. London: Routledge.

Rosenthal, R. and Jacobson, L. (1966) 'Teachers' expectancies: determinants of pupil's IQ gains'. *Psychological Reports*, 19: 115–18.

Rowntree, B.S. (2000 [1901]) *Poverty: A Study of Town Life*. Bristol: Polity Press.

Ryle, G. (1949) *The Concept of Mind*. Harmondsworth: Penguin.

Sacks, H. (1963) 'Sociological description'. *Berkeley Journal of Sociology*, 8: 1–16; reprinted in Coutler, J. (ed.) (1990) *Ethnomethodological Sociology*. London: Edward Elgar.

Sacks, H. (1992) *Harvey Sacks: Lectures on Conversation*. In Jefferson, G. (ed.), 2 vols. Oxford: Basil Blackwell.

Said, E. (1982) 'Opponents, audiences, constituencies, and community'. *Critical Inquiry*, 9(1): 1–26.

Savan, B. (1988) *Science Under Siege: The Myth of Objectivity in Scientific Research*. Montreal: CBC Enterprises.

Sawbridge, J. (2001) 'Information needs of probation staff using lotus notes'. Unpublished MSc dissertation. School of Information Studies, University of Central England, Birmingham.

Sawyer, F.S. (ed.) (1972) *The Heritage of Modern Criminology*. Cambridge, MA: Schenkman.

Schegloff, E.A. (1992) 'Introduction'. In Jefferson, G. (ed.), *Harvey Sacks: Lectures on Conversation*. Oxford: Basil Blackwell.

Sharrock, W. and Watson, R. (1988) 'Autonomy in social theories: the incarnation of social structures'. In Fielding, N. (ed.), *Actions and Structure*. London: Sage.

Shoolbred, M. (2003) 'MSc research methods module: Teaching notes'. MSc Library and Information Management, University of Central England, Birmingham. (Unpublished.)

Silverman, D. (1989) 'Telling convincing stories: a plea for cautious positivism in case-studies'. In Glassner, B. and Moreno, J. (eds), *The Qualitative–Quantitative Distinction in the Social Sciences*. Dordrecht: Kluwer.

Silverman, D. (1997) *Interpreting Qualitative Data: Methods for Analysing Talk, Text and Interaction*. London: Sage.

Silverman, D. (2000) *Doing Qualitative Research: A Practical Handbook*. London: Sage.

Smith, H.W. (1975) 'Triangulation: the necessity for multi-method approaches'. In Smith, H.W. (ed.), *Strategies of Social Research: The Methodological Imagination*. Englewood Cliffs, NJ: Prentice-Hall.

Smith, M. (1998) *Social Science in Question*. London: Open University/Sage.

Smith, M.L. and Glass, G.V. (1977) 'Meta-analysis of psychotherapy outcome studies'. *American Psychologists*, 32: 752–60.

Smullen, E. (1999) 'Survey of librarians' attitudes to popular romance books'. Unpublished MSc dissertation. School of Information Studies, University of Central England, Birmingham.

Snow, K. (2002) 'Structural analysis of sources on Arthurian legend'. Unpublished MA dissertation. School of Information Studies, University of Central England, Birmingham.

Stanley, L. and Wise, S. (1993) *Breaking out Again: Feminist Ontology and Epistemology*. London: Routledge.

Teare, R. (1999) 'Supporting managerial learning in the workplace'. *Management Literature in Review*, 1.

ten Have, P. (1999) *Doing Conversation Analysis: A Practical Guide*. London: Sage.

Times, The (1908) 'Child murders in France'. London, 13 May.

Thompson, K. (1998) *Moral Panics*. London: Routledge.

Trochim, B. (2002) 'Measurement validity types'. *Research Knowledge Base*. http://trochim.human. cornell.edu/kb/considea.html (accessed 19 November 2003).

Tucker, W.H. (1997) 'Re-considering Burt: beyond reasonable doubt'. *Journal of the History of the Behavioural Sciences*, 33(2): 145–62.

van Dalen, D.B. (1979) *Understanding Educational Research: An Introduction*. New York: McGraw-Hill.

Vartuli, S. (ed.) (1982) *The PhD Experience: A Woman's Point of View*. New York: Praeger.

Watson, R. (1994) 'Harvey Sacks' sociology of mind in action'. Review article, *Theory, Culture and Society*, 11: 169–86.

Weber, W. (1948) 'Objectivity in social science'. In Shils, E.A. and Finch, H.A. (eds), *The Methodology of the Social Sciences*. New York: Free Press.

Weightman, A. (1998) 'Evidence into practice: a study of professional attitudes to the *Health Bulletins* in Wales'. Unpublished MA dissertation. School of Information Studies, University of Central England, Birmingham.

Winch, P. (1990 [1958]) *The Idea of a Social Science*. London: Routledge.

Wittgenstein, L. (1958) *Philosophical Investigations*. (Trans. and ed. G.E.M. Anscombe and G. von Wright). Oxford: Blackwell.

Wolcott, H. (1990) *Writing up Qualitative Data*. Sage: London.

Woolgar, S. (1988) *Knowledge and Reflexivity: New Frontiers in the Sociology of Science*. London: Sage.

Wright-Mills, C.W. (1978 [1959]) *The Sociological Imagination*. Oxford: Oxford University Press.

Yale University (1975) *The Yale University Catalog, 1975–76*. New Haven, CT: Yale University.

Young, J. (1971) *The Drugtakers: The Social Meaning of Drug Use*. London: Paladin.

Young, M. and Willmott, P. (1973) *The Symmetrical Family*. Harmondsworth: Penguin.

Yow, V.R. (1994) *Recording Oral History: A Practical Guide for Social Scientists*. Thousand Oaks, CA: Sage.

Zenderland, L. (1998) *Measuring Minds: Henry Herbert Goddard and the Origins of American Intelligence Testing*. Cambridge, MA: Cambridge University Press.

Index

Page numbers in *italics* refer to figures and tables; *a* indicates appendix.